READING AND STUDY SKILLS

FORM A

READING AND STUDY SKILLS is also available in an alternate edition known as Form B. Form B has essentially the same text as Form A but different reading selections and activities. An instructor can therefore use alternate versions of the text from one semester to the next.

READING AND STUDY SKILLS

FIFTH EDITION FORM A

JOHN LANGAN
Atlantic Community College

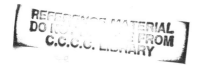

LEARNING ENHANCEMENT
CENTER

McGRAW-HILL, INC.

*New York   St. Louis   San Francisco   Auckland   Bogotá   Caracas
Lisbon   London   Madrid   Mexico   Milan   Montreal   New Delhi
Paris   San Juan   Singapore   Sydney   Tokyo   Toronto*

READING AND STUDY SKILLS, FORM A

3 4 5 6 7 8 9 0   DOC   DOC   9 0 9 8 7 6 5 4 3 2

ISBN 0-07-036383-8

Acknowledgments appear on pages 543–545, and on this page by reference.

This book was set in Times Roman by Monotype Composition Company.
The editors were Lesley Denton and Susan Gamer;
the production supervisor was Janelle S. Travers.
The cover was designed by Rafael Hernandez.
R. R. Donnelley & Sons Company was printer and binder.

Library of Congress Cataloging-in-Publication Data

Langan, John, (date).
    Reading and study skills / John Langan. — 5th ed., form A.
      p.   cm.
    Includes index.
    ISBN 0-07-036383-8
    1. Study, Method of.   2. Reading (Higher education)—United
States.   I. Title.
LB2395.L346   1992
378.1'70281—dc20   91-23763

ABOUT
THE
AUTHOR

John Langan has taught reading and writing at Atlantic Community College near Atlantic City, New Jersey, for over twenty years. The author of a popular series of college textbooks on both subjects, he enjoys the challenge of developing materials that teach skills in an especially clear and lively way. Before teaching, he earned advanced degrees in writing at Rutgers University and in reading at Glassboro State College. He also spent a year writing fiction that, he says, ''is now at the back of a drawer waiting to be discovered and acclaimed posthumously.'' While in school, he supported himself by working as a truck driver, machinist, battery assembler, hospital attendant, and apple packer. He presently lives with his wife, Judith Nadell, near Philadelphia. Among his everyday pleasures are running, working on his Macintosh computer, and watching Philadelphia sports teams or *L.A. Law* on TV. He also loves to read: newspapers at breakfast, magazines at lunch, and a chapter or two of a recent book (''preferably an autobiography'') at night.

CONTENTS

PART SEVEN
MASTERY TESTS 447

PART EIGHT
ADDITIONAL LEARNING SKILLS 503

TO
THE
INSTRUCTOR

Reading and Study Skills will help students learn and apply the essential reading and study skills needed for success in college work. The book also provides a brief review of important word skills that students must have. And it will help students examine their attitudes about college and about studying, set goals for themselves, and take responsibility for their own learning.

The book covers a good number of skills because, quite simply, students often need to learn or review that many. In the best of academic worlds, students would have an unlimited amount of time to spend on study skills, word skills, motivation for achievement, and so on. In such an ideal scheme of things, they could use a series of books over several semesters to strengthen their learning ability. But in reality, students usually have only one or two semesters for improving their reading and study skills, and all too often they are asked to handle regular academic subjects at the same time as their developmental course. They should, then, have a book that presents all the central skills they need to become more effective learners. The book should also be organized in self-contained units, so that students can turn quickly and easily to the skills needed in a given situation.

With *Reading and Study Skills,* an instructor can cover a wide range of skills and activities that might otherwise require several books or one limited book and a bundle of handouts and supplementary exercises. In addition to its comprehensiveness, *Reading and Study Skills* has a number of other important features:

- The book is highly *versatile.* Its eight parts, and many sections within these parts, are self-contained units that deal with distinct skills areas. An instructor can present in class those areas most suited to the general needs of students and then assign other sections for independent study. Also, because the book is so flexible, an instructor can more easily sustain students' attention by covering several skills in one session. For example, in a three-hour class period, work could be done on a study skill such as time control, a motivational skill such as setting goals, and a reading skill such as locating main ideas in short selections.

- The book is *practical.* It contains a large number and wide range of activities so that students can practice skills enough to make them habits. There are, for instance, over sixty separate exercises in the section on study skills, over fifty activities in the section on reading comprehension skills, and twenty-five mastery tests that cover most of the skills in the book. No instructor is likely to cover all the exercises in the book, but the chances are good that an instructor will be able to select the combination of skills best suited to the needs of a reading class or individual students.

- The book is *easily used.* It has a simple conversational style and explanations that are friendly and nonpatronizing. It presents skills as processes that can be mastered in a step-by-step sequence. Besides its many activities, the book uses a question-answer format to help students learn the material. After a set of ideas is presented, one or more questions may follow so that students can check their understanding of those ideas. Such questions are signaled in the text with a bullet (■). Finally, the book features high-interest materials. For instance, selections on how people react to conflict, on the influence of television, on fatigue in everyday life, and on the dynamics of the family are used to practice reading skills.

- The book is *realistic.* It uses material taken from a variety of college textbooks (in one instance, an entire textbook chapter) and gives practice in common study situations. Wherever possible, students are asked to transfer skills to actual study and classroom activities. A particular value of *Reading and Study Skills* for teachers should be its emphasis on activities that help students practice and apply study skills; the lack of such activities is a drawback in many currently available texts. In the past, too much attention has been given to increasing students' skill in reading selections rapidly and answering questions about the selections. Such drill has some value, but it does not prepare students to cope with an essay, control their study time, memorize material effectively (on those still-too-frequent occasions when memory work is emphasized), take useful classroom notes, or carry out the study assignments in a textbook chapter. *Reading and Study Skills* treats all the study skills that students need to survive in their courses at the same time they are working in other parts of the book to improve their reading skills.

- The book includes *learning aids.* There is a set of thirty *ditto masters,* free to instructors adopting the book, which provide extra activities and tests for many skills. A "user-friendly" *software disk* will help students review and practice many of the skills in the text. And an *Instructor's Manual and Test Bank* is made up of suggestions for using the book, a model syllabus, a full answer key, a guide to the computer disk, and additional activities and tests. All three learning aids are available from the local McGraw-Hill representative or by writing to the College English Editor, McGraw-Hill, Inc., 1221 Avenue of the Americas, New York, New York 10020.

CHANGES IN THE FIFTH EDITION

There are some substantial changes in this new edition.

- A *new opening chapter,* "Introduction," helps students determine right away what motivational skills, reading skills, and study skills they need to learn or strengthen.
- The presentation of *textbook study* (which appeared as three chapters in previous editions) has now been reduced to one chapter—"Textbook Study I: The PRWR Study Method"—enabling students to see at once the whole process of studying a textbook.

    As part of this change, a study method known as *PRWR (preview-read-write-recite)* has replaced the familiar SQ3R. I have not made this change lightly. But any teacher who has taught SQ3R knows as well as I do that there is a flaw in the formula: it does not specifically ask students to make writing a part of the study process. The direction that students take written notes should be explicit, because without note-taking a student cannot expect to master a chapter. Writing notes is as central to the learning process as reading the chapter and reciting the notes to oneself. And while the command "Question" in SQ3R is helpful, it should be presented equally with other important advice: to look for definitions, examples, and basic enumerations. All three of these guidelines appear as substeps of PRWR.

    For those teachers who still are more comfortable with SQ3R, I suggest telling students that "Recite" in the SQ3R formula should be *written* recitation. With that step taken, it is easy enough to ask students to apply the SQ3R formula to all the practice materials in this new edition of *Reading and Study Skills.*

■ Following "Textbook Study I"—the overview of the textbook study process—are two chapters of *practice materials for studying textbooks.* "Textbook Study II" offers practice in a variety of textbook passages of intermediate and longer length. "Textbook Study III" gives students guided, hands-on experience in taking notes on an entire textbook chapter. (The chapter is from a popular introductory sociology text published in a fourth edition in 1991.) Students are shown specifically how to take a thirty-six page chapter full of material and pull out the most important ideas, reducing the chapter to only five pages of written notes.

■ One part of the book, "A Brief Guide to Important Word Skills," has been moved. It now follows "Study Skills" and precedes "Reading Skills." Thus "Study Skills" comes immediately after "Motivational Skills," encouraging students to begin work right away on study skills they will need if they are taking content courses at the same time as their reading course.

■ The chapter on the *library* has been revised and updated; it now explains the computerized search facilities that are increasingly a part of today's libraries.

■ Part Eight, "Additional Learning Skills," is a reorganized and significantly expanded version of the former appendixes. In addition to its coverage of reading graphs and tables, studying mathematics and science, and understanding important connections between reading and writing, it now has three new chapters—"Reading Literature and Making Inferences," "Reading for Pleasure: A List of Interesting Books," and "Writing a Research Paper."

■ Throughout the book, much of the material has been added to or freshened. For example, students are given more how-to advice in "Setting Goals for Yourself" in Part One. Some of the hints in "Taking Classroom Notes" in Part Two have been expanded. New tests have been developed for "Signal Words" in Part Four. Two new selections, both from textbooks, have been added to "Skim Reading" in Part Five, and a new reading has been added to "Rapid Reading" in Part Six.

■ A newly designed *Instructor's Manual* includes separate answer sheets for each skill; teachers can easily copy the sheets and pass them out to students for self-teaching.

■ A revised and expanded set of *ditto masters,* free to instructors adopting the book, provides more tests and activities than were available previously.

ACKNOWLEDGMENTS

I owe thanks to the reviewers and class testers of the book, who provided helpful suggestions and comments as I worked on this major revision: Ann L. Engle, Iowa Western Community College; Sharon A. Green, D'Youville College; Ida W. Holmes, Florida A&M University; Dave Hopkins, Rio Hondo College; Jim Roth, Spokane Community College; Cindy Thompson, Northeast Louisiana University; and Joanne Vaughn, Southwest Baptist University. Special thanks go to Pat Gregory of Philadelphia Community College, who provided a fourteen-page, single-spaced review, as insightful as it was lively, based on ten years of classroom experience using the book.

I appreciate as well the help of my two editors at McGraw-Hill: Lesley Denton, who secured the detailed reviews and saw to it that I had dozens of representative college textbooks to examine; and Sue Gamer, who shepherded a challenging project through the many steps needed to bring it to publication. Finally, I remain grateful for the inspiration of my many students over the years who have had the desire to learn and sought only to find an effective means.

John Langan

READING AND STUDY SKILLS

FORM A

INTRODUCTION

While working my way through school, I had all kinds of summer and part-time jobs. One of my first summer jobs was as a drill-press operator in a machine shop. When I reported to begin work, the supervisor said to me, "Langan, I want you to spend the first couple of nights going around and observing the operators and picking up everything you can. Then I'll put you on a machine." So for three nights, I walked around and watched people, was bored stiff, and learned very little. I didn't learn the skill of operating a drill press until I was actually put on a machine with a person who could teach me how to run it and I began practicing the skill. I have found that my experience in the machine shop holds true for skill mastery in general. One picks up a skill and becomes good at it when a clear explanation of the skill is followed by plenty of practice. This book, then, tries to present clearly the reading and study skills that you will need to succeed in your school or career work. And it provides abundant activities so that you can practice the skills enough to make them habits.

The skills in this book should help make you an independent learner—a person able to take on and master almost any learning challenge. However, the book cannot help you at all unless you have a personal determination to learn the skills. Back in the machine shop, I quickly learned how to run the drill press because I had plenty of motivation to learn. The job was piecework, and the more skilled I became, the more money I could make. In your case, the more reading and study skills you master, the more likely you are not only to survive but also to do well in your college courses.

OVERVIEW OF THE BOOK

Here are the eight parts into which this book is divided.

- *Part One: Motivational Skills*   This part describes important steps you must take to get off to a strong start with your college career.
- *Part Two: Study Skills*   Part Two explains and gives practice in all the key study skills you need to do well in your courses.
- *Part Three: A Brief Guide to Important Word Skills*   The information here will help you quickly brush up on important word skills.
- *Part Four: Reading Comprehension Skills*   Part Four explains and offers practice in comprehension skills that will help you read and take notes on your textbooks and other college materials.
- *Part Five: Skim Reading and Comprehension*   Here you will learn how to do skimming, or selective reading.
- *Part Six: Rapid Reading and Comprehension*   This part of the book will suggest a method for increasing your reading speed.
- *Part Seven: Mastery Tests*   Part Seven consists of a series of mastery tests for many of the skills in the book.
- *Part Eight: Additional Learning Skills*   This last part of the book presents other learning skills that can help you with your college work.

WHAT SKILLS DO YOU NEED TO MASTER?

Which learning skills do you need most? To help yourself answer this question, respond to the groups of statements that follow. The statements will tell you important things about yourself as a student.

The statements will make you aware, first, of your attitude toward study. By recognizing negative feelings you may have about yourself or about student life, you can begin to deal with those feelings. The statements will also make you aware of important reading and study skills you have—or do not have—right now. You can then use the book to master the skills you need.

Read and consider each statement carefully. Check the space for *True* if a statement applies to you most of the time. Check the space for *False* if a statement does not apply to you most of the time. Remember that your answers will be of value only if they are honest and accurate.

True   False   Attitude about Studying

——   ——   1. I feel there are personal problems that I have to straighten out before I can be a good student.

___ ___	2. I seem to be so busy all the time that I don't have the chance to do my schoolwork regularly.
___ ___	3. If a subject is boring to me, I don't make the full effort needed to pass the course.
___ ___	4. I often get discouraged about how much I have to learn and how long it's going to take me.
___ ___	5. I will let myself be distracted by almost anything rather than study.
___ ___	6. I want to be a successful student, but I hate studying so much that I often don't bother.
___ ___	7. I often get moody or depressed, and then I am not able to study.
___ ___	8. I keep trying to do well in school, but I don't seem to be making any progress.
___ ___	9. I am still trying to develop the willpower needed to study consistently.
___ ___	10. I am not completely sure that I want to be in school at this time.

Evaluating Your Responses: If you answered *true* more than twice in questions 1 to 10, you should read and work through all of Part One in this book. Part One will encourage you to think about the commitment you must make to become an independent learner. It will also help you set goals for yourself and will show you a series of five important survival strategies.

It may also be important for you to discuss your situation with a counselor, a friend, a teacher, or some person whose opinion you respect. All too often, people try to keep problems closed up inside themselves. As a result, they may limit their potential unnecessarily and waste valuable time in their lives. Talking with another person can help you get a perspective on your own situation and so help you deal better with that situation. If you care about making yourself a strong and successful person, you should take the risk of sharing your feelings and concerns with someone else.

True   False   ## Taking and Studying Classroom Notes

When I must take classroom notes,

___ ___	11. I have trouble deciding what to write down.
___ ___	12. I sometimes miss a point the teacher is making while I am writing down an earlier point.
___ ___	13. I often get sleepy or begin to daydream when the teacher talks for long periods.
___ ___	14. I don't know how to organize my notes, and so they are often hard to understand later.

____ ____ 15. I write down what the teacher puts on the board but usually don't take notes on anything else.

____ ____ 16. I seldom go over my notes after a class to make them easy to understand or to fill in missing points.

____ ____ 17. I don't have an effective way of studying my notes for a test.

Evaluating Your Responses: If you answered *true* more than twice in questions 11 to 17, you should read and work through the first chapter on study skills, "Taking Classroom Notes" (pages 39–66). The chapter will show you how to take effective notes in class and how to study those notes. If you are taking any content course such as business, psychology, sociology, or a science at the same time as your course in reading and study skills, you should *read this chapter first.*

True   False   *Time Control and Concentration*

____ ____ 18. I never seem to have enough time to study.

____ ____ 19. I don't have a schedule of regular study hours.

____ ____ 20. I never make up a list of what I need to study in a given day or week.

____ ____ 21. I don't write down test dates and paper deadlines in a place where I will see them every day.

____ ____ 22. When I sit down to study, I have trouble concentrating.

____ ____ 23. I often end up having to cram for a test.

Evaluating Your Responses: If you answered *true* more than twice in questions 18 to 23, you should read and work through "Time Control and Concentration" (pages 67–85) early in the semester. You'll learn how to use your time effectively—a key to success in college as well as career—and to develop consistent study habits.

True   False   *Textbook Study*

____ ____ 24. I'm not sure how to preview a textbook chapter.

____ ____ 25. It takes me a very long time to read and understand a textbook chapter.

____ ____ 26. When I have a lot of reading to do, my mind wanders or I get sleepy.

____ ____ 27. I'm never sure what is important when I read a textbook.

____ ____ 28. I don't have a method for marking important passages while reading a textbook chapter.

____ ____ 29. I don't have a really good way of taking notes on a textbook chapter.

____ ____ 30. I don't have a really good way of studying my notes on a textbook chapter.

Evaluating Your Responses: If you answered *true* more than twice in questions 24 to 30, you should read and work through the entire chapter "Textbook Study I" on pages 86–102. This chapter will provide immediate help to you as you begin getting textbook assignments in other courses. Then go on to "Textbook Study II" and "Textbook Study III."

As time permits, you will then want to work through Part Four of the book, which explains and offers practice in seven key reading comprehension skills. Students often ask, "What can I do to understand and remember more of what I read?" The first five skills (pages 313–359) will help you locate and understand important points in articles and textbook chapters. The sixth and seventh skills (pages 360–390) will enable you to take down and remember those key points in the form of clear and concise study notes.

True   False   *Memory Training*

____   ____   31. I have trouble concentrating and often "read words" when I try to study.

____   ____   32. I don't know any "memory techniques" to help me remember material.

____   ____   33. I often forget something almost as soon as I have studied it.

____   ____   34. I usually don't organize material in any special way before I try to study it.

____   ____   35. I don't know how to study and remember a large amount of material for a test.

Evaluating Your Responses: If you answered *true* more than twice in questions 31 to 35, you should read and work through "Building a Powerful Memory" on pages 190–204. That chapter presents techniques to help you remember both classroom and textbook notes.

True   False   *Taking Tests*

____   ____   36. When I take a test, I often panic and forget what I have learned.

____   ____   37. Before a test, I never make a careful and organized review.

____   ____   38. When I prepare for a test, I am never sure what is important enough to study.

____   ____   39. I don't know how to go about preparing for an essay test.

____   ____   40. When I write an essay answer, I have trouble organizing my thoughts.

____   ____   41. I sometimes misread test questions and give an answer other than the one called for.

____   ____   42. I don't know any hints to keep in mind when taking a true-false or multiple-choice test.

____   ____   43. I sometimes spend too much time with some questions on a test and don't have enough time for others.

Evaluating Your Responses: If you answered *true* more than twice in questions 36 to 43, you should read and work through "Taking Objective Exams" (205–219) and "Taking Essay Exams" (220–229). These chapters show you how to prepare for both kinds of exams and explain test-taking techniques. Use them whenever exams are approaching.

True	False	## Using the Library
____	____	44. I'm not sure how to look up or find a book in my library.
____	____	45. I don't know how to use the *Readers' Guide, Magazine Index,* or other files for looking up magazine, newspaper, and journal articles.
____	____	46. I don't know how to look up information about books or articles by using the computer terminals in my library.
____	____	47. I don't know how to get a copy in the library of a magazine or journal article I want to read.
____	____	48. I don't know how to use subject headings to get ideas for a report or a research paper.

Evaluating Your Responses: If you answered *true* more than once in questions 44 to 48, you should read and work through "Using the Library" on pages 230–246. You'll learn all the basics you need to know in order to use the library for researching a topic and preparing a research paper.

True	False	## Word Skills
____	____	49. I'm not sure how to use prefixes, suffixes, and roots to improve my pronunciation and spelling of words.
____	____	50. I have trouble pronouncing unfamiliar words.
____	____	51. I'm not sure how to use the dictionary for pronouncing words.
____	____	52. I feel that I should be a better speller.
____	____	53. If I see an unfamiliar word, I'm not able to guess its meaning by looking at the rest of the sentence.
____	____	54. I feel that my vocabulary is limited and that this keeps me from understanding my textbooks.
____	____	55. Very seldom, if ever, do I read a book for pleasure.

Evaluating Your Responses: If you answered *true* more than twice in questions 49 to 55, you should read and work through all of Part Three of the book. Part Three will help you improve your spelling and show you how to pronounce unfamiliar words, including specialized terms in your various subjects. You'll also learn ways to develop your vocabulary—a vital matter, because a small word base will limit your understanding of what you read. The concise information about word skills in Part Three can be supplemented with practice materials that are probably available in your college learning center.

True	False	*Other Reading Skills*
___	___	56. I have trouble locating definitions when I read.
___	___	57. I have trouble locating examples of ideas when I read.
___	___	58. I have trouble locating enumerations (lists of items) when I read.
___	___	59. I don't know how to use headings or subheadings when I read.
___	___	60. I don't know what kinds of words are used to signal important facts or ideas.
___	___	61. I have trouble locating main ideas in what I read.
___	___	62. I would benefit from practice in outlining and summarizing.
___	___	63. I don't know how to skim-read a textbook chapter effectively.
___	___	64. I think it would help me to learn how to speed-read.
___	___	65. I feel my lips moving as I read silently.
___	___	66. My eyes go back a lot to reread earlier lines on a page.

Evaluating Your Responses: If you answered *true* more than twice in questions 56 to 66, you should read and work through Parts Four, Five, and Six of the book. The chapters on textbook study in Part Two offer a quick course in becoming a better reader and note-taker; the chapters in Part Four provide a more detailed step-by-step process to strengthen your textbook reading and note-taking skills.

Part Five gives you practice in skim reading—going through a selection quickly and selectively to find important ideas. Skimming is a valuable technique when it is not necessary to read every word of a passage.

Part Six introduces you to rapid reading—processing words at a faster rate than is your normal habit. You will learn that rapid reading is not a cure-all for reading problems but simply one technique used by effective readers.

The overall purpose of Parts Four, Five, and Six is to make *you* an effective, flexible reader—able to apply ''study reading,'' skim reading, or speed reading (or all three), depending on your purpose for reading and on the nature of the material. You will improve your comprehension, slowly but surely, if you isolate and work on important reading skills in a systematic way.

True	False	*Other Reading and Study Skills*
___	___	67. I have trouble making sense of charts and graphs.
___	___	68. I find it especially hard to deal with a math or science textbook.
___	___	69. I would like tips on reading short stories, poems, and other literary works.
___	___	70. I need to know just how to go about doing a research paper.
___	___	71. The connections between reading and writing are not clear to me.
___	___	72. I'd like to start reading some good books but have no idea what to read.

Evaluating Your Response: If you answered *true* to any of questions 67 to 72, read and work through the appropriate chapter in Part Eight of the book.

ACHIEVING YOUR GOAL

You should now have a good sense of just what skills you most need to work on. Many students, I find, say that they want to improve in almost *all* the areas listed above. Whatever your specific needs, the material in this book should help.

Your goal as you begin your work is to become an independent learner—a person who can take on the challenge of any college course. Achieving the goal depends upon your personal determination to do the work it takes to become a successful student. If you decide—something that only you can decide—that you want to make your college time productive and worthwhile, this book will help you reach that goal. I wish you a successful journey.

PART ONE

MOTIVATIONAL SKILLS

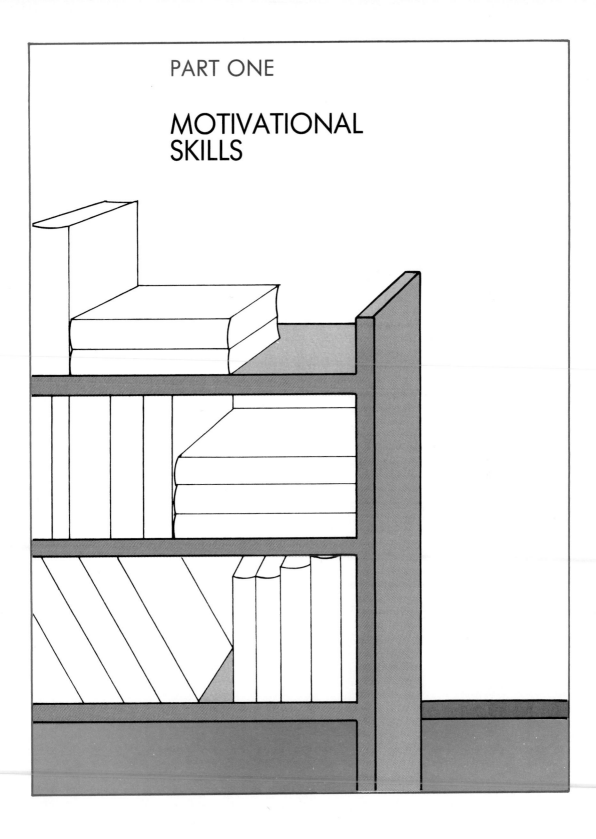

PREVIEW

Part One is about important steps you must take to get off to a
strong start in your college career. The point stressed throughout
the first chapter, "Your Attitude: The Heart of the Matter," is
that you must make a personal decision and commitment to do
the diligent work that learning requires. The chapter describes
several students who made or failed to make this a commitment,
and also asks a series of questions that will help you measure
your own willingness to make it. The second chapter, "Setting
Goals for Yourself," will encourage you to think actively about
your eventual career goal and the practical steps you should take
to start working toward that goal. In the third chapter, "Learning
Survival Strategies," a successful student talks about the
importance of planning for a realistic career, of getting
organized, of learning how to persist, of being positive, and of
remaining open to growth.

YOUR ATTITUDE: THE HEART OF THE MATTER

This book is chiefly about the reading and study skills you need to do well in your college work. But your *attitude* toward college work is even more crucial than any reading or study skill. Without the proper frame of mind, you might as well throw this book in the trash. And without the proper frame of mind, you may be wasting your time in school.

DOING THE WORK

Your attitude must say, "I will do the work." I have found that among the two hundred or so students I meet each year, there is almost no way of telling at first which students have this attitude and which ones do not. Some time must pass for people to reveal their attitude by what they do or do not do. What happens is that as the semester unfolds and classes must be attended and work must be done, some people take on the work and persist even if they hit all kinds of snags and problems; others don't take on the work or don't persist when things get rough. It becomes clear which students have determined inside themselves, "I will do the work," and which have not.

The crucial matter is seldom the *speed* at which a person learns; the crucial matter is his or her determination—"I *will* learn." I have seen people who had this quality of determination or persistence do poorly in a course, come back and repeat it, and eventually succeed. And two years or so later, in June, I have heard their names being called out and have seen them walking up to the commencement stage to get their degrees.

For example, I have seen the woman who wrote the following piece as her first assignment in a reading and writing class go up to receive her associate of arts degree:

> Well its 10:48 and the kids are all in bed. I don't know yet what Im going to write about but I hope I think of something befor this ten minutes are up. boy I don't even like to write that much. I never send my letters or cards because I dislike writing, may be because I never took the time to sit down and really write, I've always wishes I could, put thing on paper that were in my mind. but my spelling isn't at all good, so when I had to take the time to look up a word or ask one of my children how to spell it, I said to heck with it, but, I can't do that with this any way I don't believ I can write for ten mintes straght, but Im trying I refus to stop until Ive made It. Ive always given my self credit for not being a quiter, so I guess I have to keep fighting at this and every thing else in the future, If I wish to reach my gols wich is to pass my GED and go in to nursing. I know it will take me a little longer then some one who hasen't been out of school as long as I have but no matter how long it takes I'm shure I will be well worth It and I'll be glad that I keep fighting. And Im shur my children will be very prowd of ther mother some day.

Through knowing such determined people as this woman, I have come to feel that the single most important factor for college survival and success is *an inner commitment to doing the work*. When the crunch comes—and the crunch is the plain hard work that college requires—the person with the commitment meets it head-on; the person without the commitment avoids it in a hundred different ways.

Doing the Work Despite Difficulties

The person who is committed to the work needed to succeed in college is not necessarily one without confusions and difficulties in his or her life. A joke that is sometimes made about freshman orientation—the day or so preceding the start of the first semester, when the student is introduced to college life—is that for some people freshman orientation takes a year or more. The joke is all too often true. I can remember my own confusing first year at La Salle College in Philadelphia. I entered as a chemistry major but soon discovered that I could not deal with the mathematics course required. As hard as I tried, I couldn't pass one of the weekly quizzes given in the class. I felt the teacher was poor and the text unclear, but since other people were passing the tests, I felt the problem was in me, too. It was a terribly confusing time. Because I doubted my ability to do the work, I began questioning my own self-worth.

At the same time that I doubted whether I *could* do the work in mathematics, I began to know that I did not *want* to do the work. Even if I eventually passed the course and the other mathematics courses I would have to take, I realized I did not want to spend my life working with numbers. Very quickly my career plans disintegrated. I was not going to be a chemist, and I was left in the confused and anxious vacuum of wondering what I *was* going to be.

My career identity was not my only problem. My social identity was precarious as well. The one male friend that I had from high school had gone into the Army and was in Germany. And because I was shy, I found no one immediately at the college to share experiences with. My one female friend—or supposed friend—from high school had gone off to a school in Chicago, and we did not bother to write to each other. I realized dismally that we didn't write because we didn't really know each other anyway. We had gone together in high school for the sake of form and convenience—so we would each have a partner for social events. There had never been real communication and sharing between two people. I had no one to help me shape my fragile social and sexual identities, and I felt very alone. To make matters worse, in the midst of all this, my blood was burning. I yearned desperately for someone to burst into flame with—and felt lost that I had no one. In sum, my first college year was a very worried, confused, and anxious time.

I responded to my general unhappiness partly by trying to escape. One way I did this was by resorting to games. In some respects my real major that first year at La Salle was the game room located in the student center. Before and after classes I went there to play endless games of chess and Ping-Pong. I played, I now realize, not only to find relief from my worries but also as an indirect way of trying to meet other people. For a while I had a roommate who was in college only because his parents wanted him to be; he too was desperately unhappy. We seldom talked because we had very little in common, but we would spend entire evenings playing chess together. One day soon after midsemester grades were sent out, I came back to the dorm to find that my roommate, his clothes, chessboard—everything—had disappeared.

The games were not enough escape for me, and so I decided to get a job. I did not absolutely need a job, but I told myself I did. Not only did I need an excuse to get away from my dismal days at the college; I also wanted to shore up my unsure self-image. If I could not be a successful student or friend or lover, I could at least be a successful wage earner. Fortunately, I did not get a full-time job but instead began working as a graphotype operator two nights a week in downtown Philadelphia. The job made me feel a little older and closer to being independent, so it helped lift my spirits.

Had I gotten a full-time job, it might have provided enough excuse for me to drop out of school, and I might have done so. As it was, I stayed, and—despite general unhappiness and partial escape through games and my part-time job—I did the work. Mathematics was hopeless, especially because there was no tutoring program or mathematics lab at the college, so I dropped the course. But I knew I would need the chemistry course that I was taking as a basic science requirement for graduation. The course meant a massive amount of work for me, and I studied and studied and went into a test hoping to get a grade that would reflect all the studying I had done. Instead, I always came out with D's. The grades were the more discouraging because I felt so generally displeased with myself anyway. They seemed to be saying to me, "You are a 'D' person." However, I kept studying. I read and underlined the text, took lots of notes, and studied the material as best I could. I was determined to get the course behind me and, with a final grade of low C, I did.

I have known students who experienced far rougher personal times at college than I did in my first year. And those people *who were determined to do the work,* despite all their difficulties, were the ones who succeeded. To overcome the worries, fears, and demands that may seem overwhelming during a semester, you must make a firm decision to do the work. Running from the work, you may lose precious time and opportunities in your life.

It is true that in a given situation you may decide it is better to drop a course or drop out for a semester rather than to try to do the work. You may be right, *but* it is important that you first talk to someone about your decision. One of the things that helped me stay in school during the hard first year was talking to a teacher I liked and felt I could trust. At your school you will find there are people—counselors, teachers, and others—who will care about listening to your special situation. Talking with someone about your concerns will enable you to do something you cannot possibly do alone—get a perspective on yourself. We all need from time to time the insights into ourselves that can come from such perspectives. So if you are having trouble making yourself do the work that college requires, it is in your best interest to talk to someone about it.

Discovering the Commitment to Do the Work

I have often seen people come to college almost accidentally. Perhaps they are in doubt about what to do after high school, or are discontented with their limited job opportunities, or are looking for other interests to fill the time they once spent with their children. So they come to college uncommitted, vaguely looking for a change of pace in their lives. Without a commitment, they often drift along for a couple of weeks or months or semesters and then fade away—silent, shadowy figures in both their coming and going.

But in some instances a spark ignites. These people discover possibilities within themselves or realize the potential meaning that college can have in their lives. As a result, they make the commitment to do the work that is absolutely essential to success in college. Here is one student's account of such a discovery:

> My present feeling about college is that it will improve my life. My first attitude about college was that I didn't need it. I had been bored by high school where it seemed we spent grades 9 to 12 just reviewing everything we had learned up through grade 8. I had a job as a bottle inspector at Wheaton's and was taking home over $125 a week. Then I was laid off and spent whole days hanging around with nothing to do. My roommate was going to Atlantic Community College and talked me into going, and now I hope I'll be thanking her one day for saving my life.
>
> When I entered college in January I thought it was fun but that's all. I met a lot of people and walked around with college textbooks in my hand playing the game of being a college student. Some weeks I went to class and other weeks I didn't go at all and went off on trips instead. I didn't do much studying. I really wasn't into it but was just going along with the ball game.
>
> Then two things happened. My sociology class was taught by a really cool person who asked us questions constantly, and they began getting to me. I started asking *myself* questions and looking at myself and thinking, "What am I about anyway? What do I want and what am I doing?" Also I discovered I could write. I wrote my own version of the Red Riding Hood story and it was read in class and everyone, including the teacher, roared. Now I'm really putting time into my writing and my other courses as well.
>
> In my first version of this paper, the teacher asked me, "What is the point at which you changed? When was the switch thrown to 'On' in your head?" I don't know the exact moment but it was just there, and now it seems so real I can almost touch it. I know this is my life and I want to be somebody and college is going to help me do it. I'm here to improve myself and I'm going to give it my best shot.
>
> Earlier in the semester things seemed so bad to me. I was busted for drugs, I got an eviction notice, and I was having man-trouble too. I was going to quit school and get a job and try to get a new start. But then I realized this is my start and this is where I will begin. I can tell you with a strong mind that nothing will discourage me, and that I will make it.

Running from the Commitment to Do the Work

I said earlier that as a semester unfolds and the crunch of work comes, people are put up against the wall. Like it or not, they must define their role in college. There are only two roads to take. One road is to do the work: to leave the game table, click off the stereo or television, turn down the invitation to go out, get off the telephone, stop everything and anything else, and go off by oneself to do the essentially lonely work that study is. The other road is to avoid the work, and there are countless ways of doing this.

Here is one student's moving account of the avoidance pattern in his life and his discovery of it:

Somewhere, a little piece of me is lost and crying. Someplace, deep in the shadows of my subconscious, a piece of my soul has sat down and anchored itself in defeat and is trying to pull me down into the darkness with it. This might sound strange to someone who is not familiar with the inner conflicts of a person that can tear and pull at his soul until he begins to stop and sink in his own deep-hollow depths. But sinking doesn't take much. It takes only one little flaw which left unattended will grow and grow . . . until like cancer it consumes the soul.

My flaw, the part of me that has given up, is best seen when it is winning. Then I am lost like a rudderless ship after the storm has abated, motor gone, drifting . . . pushed about by the eddying currents in little circles of lassitude and self-doubt, just waiting . . . just waiting . . . peering at the ominous dark clouds in the sky, waiting for help to arrive.

I know now, and I have always known, that help comes first from within. I know that if one doesn't somehow come to one's own rescue, then all is lost. I know it is time for me to look at myself, which I would rather avoid. But in order to break free of my own chains, I must look at myself.

I could relate the incidents of my youth. I could tell of the many past failures and what I think caused them. But I won't, for one example will show where I'm at. At the beginning of this summer I set my goals. These goals consisted of the college courses I wanted to complete and where I wanted to be physically and mentally when the summer was over. Listed among the goals to be accomplished were courses I needed in writing and accounting. To help me become at ease with my writing, I took English Composition 101, and to clear up my accounting deficiency, I took the course a second time. But now here, at the end of July, I am so far behind in both courses it looks as if I will fail them both. I ask myself, "Why?" I know that if I work enough I can handle the courses. So, why have I been so lazy? Why is it that the things I seem to want most, I either give up or in some way do not strive for? These are the questions I must try to answer.

I remember when I was about five or six—a little, dreamy boy living in the country—the much-older neighbor's boy told me one rainy afternoon, just when the rain had stopped and the sun peered with glistening rays of gold through gray and white fluffy clouds, that "there is a pot of gold at the end of the rainbow." And right then a pulsating, glowing rainbow of violets, blues, and golds raced from the clouds and down past the hill. It sent me scampering across the wet, weedy field and up the hill and down the other side, where fields with rows of wet corn stood. There my rainbow had moved a little farther on. I should have known then, but I kept walking through the puddles in the muddy fields watching my rainbow fade farther and farther away with each step. I started home when the rainbow faded, but in the puddles of water I saw little rainbows and dreamed that the next time I would get the pot of gold under the big rainbow.

I think it's time for me to stop chasing rainbows in the sky. It's time to stop looking into the sky waiting for help to arrive. It's time for me to start bailing the rot out of my mind, to stop dreaming and not acting, before I have nothing left to hope for. I can see now that I've never given it the total effort, that I've always been afraid I would fail or not measure up. So I've quit early. Instead of acting on my dreams I've laid back and just floated along. I've lived too much time in this world unfulfilled. I've got to make my dreams work. I've suffered enough in this world. I must do this now and all it takes is the doing. Somehow I must learn to succeed at success rather than at failure, and the time to start is now.

AVOIDANCE TACTICS

Described below are some of the tactics that people may use in avoiding doing the hard work that college requires. If you see yourself in any of these situations, you should do some serious thinking about whether now is the right time for you to be in college. If you are unsure of your commitment, don't coast along, trying to ignore the situation. Instead, make an appointment with a counselor, your academic adviser, or some other interested person. That way you will confront your problem and begin to deal with it.

"I Can't Do It"

The only way people will really know that they cannot do something is by first trying—giving it their best shot. The temptation is to use a defeatist attitude as an excuse for not making a real effort. Remember that many colleges can give you help if you decide to try. There may be a tutoring program and writing, reading, and mathematics labs. And you can often go to your teacher as well. If you think you "can't do it," the reason may be that you are not trying.

"I'm Too Busy"

Some people *make* themselves too busy, taking on a job that is not absolutely necessary or working more hours on a job than they need to. Others get overly involved in social activities on and off campus. Others allow personal or family problems to become so tangled and pressing that they cannot concentrate on their work. There are real cases where people are so busy or troubled that they cannot do their work. But there are many cases where people unconsciously create conflicts in order to have an excuse for not doing what they know they should.

"I'm Too Tired"

People with this excuse usually become tired as soon as it's time to write a paper or study a book or go to class. Their weariness clears up when the work period ends. The "sleepiness syndrome" also expresses itself in the imagined need for naps during the day and then ten hours or more of sleep at night. Such students are, often literally, closing their eyes to the hard work that college demands.

"I'll Do It Later"

Everyone tends at times to procrastinate—to put things off. Some students, however, constantly postpone doing assignments and setting aside regular study hours. Time and time again they put off what needs to be done so they can watch TV, talk to a friend, go to the movies, play cards, or do any one of a hundred other things. These students typically wind up cramming for tests and writing last-minute papers, yet they often seem surprised and angry at their low grades.

"I'm Bored with the Subject"

Students sometimes explain that they are doing poorly in a course because the instructor or the subject matter is boring. These students want education to be entertainment—an unrealistic expectation. On the whole, college courses and instructors balance out: Some are boring, some are exciting, many are in between. If a course is not interesting, students should be all the more motivated to do the work so that they can leave the course behind once and for all.

"I'm Here, and That's What Counts"

Some people spend their first weeks in school lost in a dangerous kind of fantasy. They feel, "All will be well, for I am now here in college. I have a student identification card in my pocket, a parking sticker on the bumper of my car, and textbooks under my arm. All this proves I am a college student. I have it made." Such students have succumbed to a fantasy we all at times succumb to: the belief that we will get something for nothing. But everyone knows from experience that such a hope is a false one. Life seldom gives us something for nothing—and college won't either. College, like life, is demanding. And because this is so, to get somewhere and to become someone we must be prepared and able to make a solid effort. We must accept the fact that little can be won or achieved or cherished in life without hard work. The decision that each of us must make is the commitment to do the hard work required for success in college—and ultimately in life. By making such a decision, and acting on it, we assume control of our lives.

■ Questions to Consider

Your instructor may put you into small groups of three or four and ask you to take turns reading aloud to each other the discussion about attitude on pages 11–18. The instructor may then ask you to discuss with each other the questions that follow. Every person in the group should try to contribute to the sharing of experiences. The more honest and real you can be in exchanging individual experiences, the more meaningful and valuable the discussion can be.

1. Tell the group about some skill you have learned and how you went about learning it. Do you think the basic principles involved in learning that skill could hold true with reading and study skills as well?

2. "A person who does not go to class faithfully is showing that he or she is not committed to doing the work that college requires." Give your reasons for agreeing or disagreeing with this statement.

3. Have you or has anyone you've known had a "time of decision" like the one described by the person who wrote the paper on page 15?

4. Have you or has anyone you've known ever run from the commitment to do the work like the person who wrote the paper on pages 16–17?

5. Have you or has anyone you've known experienced the "sleepiness syndrome" described on page 18?

6. Have you or has anyone you've known ever experienced the "dangerous kind of fantasy" described on page 18?

7. Everyone uses avoidance tactics from time to time. Share with the group the ones that you may sometimes use. (You've already discussed two; four more are described on pages 17–18—and there may be other kinds of escape you can think of.) Also discuss whether you think avoidance tactics have ever been harmful to you in meeting goals in life.

8. What is your purpose, or what are your purposes, in taking college courses? Take a few minutes to write down on a separate sheet of paper your specific goals for four months from now, one year from now, and two years from now. Then share these goals with the other members of the group.

9. Do you think your chances of reaching your goals are 100 percent? 70 percent? 30 percent? Specifically, what odds would you give on yourself—and why? Share these odds with the group, and then give your reasons for setting the odds as you do. (Tell what you see as your strengths and weaknesses.)

Your instructor may ask you to write a paper that responds *in detail* to one of the preceding questions. He or she may stress that honesty—the expression of your real thoughts and feelings and experiences—is more important than sentence skills in the paper that you write.

SETTING GOALS FOR YOURSELF

If you asked a cross section of students why they are in college, you would probably get a wide range of responses. Following are some reasons people give for going to college. Check the reasons that you feel apply to you. Be honest; think a bit about each reason before you go on to the next one.

Reasons Students Go to College	Apply in My Case
■ To have some fun before getting a job	_____
■ To prepare for a specific career	_____
■ To please their families	_____
■ To educate and enrich themselves	_____
■ To be with friends who are going to college	_____
■ To fill in time until they figure out what they want to do	_____
■ To take advantage of an opportunity they didn't have before in their lives	_____
■ To find a husband or wife	_____
■ To see if college has anything to offer them	_____
■ To do more with their lives than they've done so far	_____
■ To take advantage of VA benefits or other special funding	_____
■ To earn the status that they feel comes with a college degree	_____
■ To get a new start in life	_____

Get together with one or more other students to compare and discuss your responses to this list. Talk about what you feel are the "bottom-line" reasons you are in college. Make a genuine effort to be as honest about yourself as possible.

Now write in the spaces that follow the basic reason or reasons you have for being in college.

_____

_____

_____

_____

If you do not have one or more solid reasons for being in college, you may have trouble motivating yourself to do the hard work that will be required. When difficult moments occur, your concentration and effort will lag unless you can remember that you have good reasons for persisting.

LONG-TERM GOALS

For many students, a main reason for being in college is to prepare themselves for a career goal—the specific kind of work they intend to do in life. If you have not been thinking actively about this long-range goal, you should begin doing so during your first college year. Here are four specific steps you can take to start formulating a career goal.

1 If you are not sure of a major, visit the college's counseling center. The center probably administers an *interest inventory* and a *vocational preference test*. The first identifies what you like and can do well; the second points to careers that match your interests and abilities. With this information, the counseling staff at the center can help you decide on a possible major. You should begin taking courses in this prospective major as soon as you can in order to learn for sure that it is right for you.

2 Some time early in college, make an appointment to talk with a faculty member in the department of your intended major. Most department advisers set aside a certain period of time to meet with students and discuss their course of study. Ask such advisers the following questions:

What courses are required in the major?

What courses are recommended?

What courses, if any, offer practical work experiences?

3   Also, plan to go to the placement office some time during your first year to get specific information on careers. Many students have the mistaken notion that placement offices provide career information only to students who are about to graduate. Such is not the case. *It is very important for beginning students to speak to the placement staff to obtain updated information about the future of specific fields.* For example, it would make little sense for you to plan to become a history teacher if that particular job market is expected to have few openings at the time you graduate.

4   See if your counseling center has the latest copy of the *Occupational Outlook Handbook,* which is an invaluable source of information about the many kinds of jobs currently available and the best job prospects in the future. In fact, it makes sense to order the book for your personal reference early in your school career. Write to the Superintendent of Documents, U.S. Government Printing Office, Washington, DC 20402, and ask for the latest paperback edition of the *Occupational Outlook Handbook.* The book will probably cost you about $20.

Activity

Answer the following questions.

1. What is a vocational preference test? _____

    _____

2. Does your counseling center or library have a current copy of the *Occupational Outlook Handbook?* _____ What are three promising career fields identified in the *Handbook?*

    a. _____

    b. _____

    c. _____

3. Have you asked a counselor for his or her professional opinion on the best job opportunities in your area of the country? _____

4. Describe your long-range career goal (or what you think will be your goal):

    _____

    _____

5. Mark with a check the expected job prospects in your major at the time you graduate. (You can answer this only after you have visited the placement center or spoken to a knowledgeable person in the field.)

    _____ Excellent   _____ Good   _____ Fair   _____ Poor

SETTING GOALS FOR YOURSELF **23**

SHORT-TERM GOALS

There is a familiar saying that a long journey begins with a single step. To achieve your long-term career goal, you must set and work toward a continuing series of short-term goals. These can be as simple as a list of specific objectives that you have for your present semester in college. In Activity 1 is an example—the short-term goals that one student, Barbara, set for herself.

Personal and Study Goals

Activity 1

Specific goals can consist of both *personal* goals and *study* goals. In the spaces beside the items on Barbara's list, indicate whether the goal listed is a personal or a study goal.

Barbara's Short-Term Goals

1. *To get to know at least two people in each of my classes*
   (_____)
2. *To earn a B in my Basic Math class* (_____)
3. *To earn a B or better in my reading class* (_____)
4. *To earn a B in my Introduction to Business class*
   (_____)
5. *To start exercising regularly* (_____)
6. *To miss not more than three classes in any subject*
   (_____)
7. *To limit my television watching to no more than five hours a week* (_____)
8. *To spend at least ten study hours on my courses every week*
   (_____)

You can help yourself succeed in your present semester of college by setting a series of personal and study goals. The goals must be honest ones that you choose yourself—goals that you truly intend to work on and that you have the time to achieve during the semester. If necessary, you can change or add to your goals as needed. What matters is that you have a series of definite targets that will give you direction and motivation during the semester. A list of specific goals will help you do the *consistent* work that is needed for success.

Activity 2

Use the following space to set a series of short-term goals for yourself. Indicate in parentheses whether each goal is a personal or a study goal. Set real targets for yourself. At the same time, be realistic about how much you can achieve in one semester.

Goals for the _____ Semester, 19_____

1. _____
2. _____
3. _____
4. _____
5. _____
6. _____
7. _____
8. _____
9. _____
10. _____

_____

_____

_____

_____

_____

_____

_____

_____

Use the extra space provided if you decide to change or add to your goals. Refer frequently to your goals as the semester progresses. When a goal is completed, cross it out and put initials beside it.

Steps for Achieving Short-Term Goals

At the same time that you set short-term goals, you should decide on *specific steps* you must take to achieve those goals. By looking closely at what you must do to reach your goals, you can determine whether they are realistic and practical. You can also get a good sense of just how you will reach them.

Look at some of the specific steps that Barbara decided she must take to reach her goals:

Goal: *To take and earn Bs in three courses this semester.*

Specific steps for achieving this goal:

I must get my mother to agree to watch my seven-year-old son three evenings a week.

I must get my ex-husband to agree to take my son one day every weekend.

My boss must agree to limit my work hours to no more than twenty a week.

I am going to have to do my food shopping and all my cleaning on Friday evenings, so that I can have more of the weekend free to study.

I need the phone numbers of at least two people in each class, so if I ever have to miss a class, I can find out right away what happened.

I must limit my television watching to no more than five shows a week.

Activity 3

Now choose three of your most important goals and list specific steps you must take to achieve each of them.

Goal 1: _____

Specific steps for achieving goal 1:

_____

_____

_____

_____

_____

_____

Goal 2: _____

Specific steps for achieving goal 2:

_____

_____

_____

_____

_____

Goal 3: _____

Specific steps for achieving goal 3:

_____

_____

_____

_____

_____

Activity 4

Your instructor may now put you in a group with one or two other students so that you can compare your goals and discuss the steps you plan to take to achieve them. You should try to give each other feedback on what seems realistic about your goals—and what does not. *Or,* your instructor may sit down with you individually to review your goals.

Activity 5

Answer the following questions as honestly as you can.

■ How important do you think it is that you set specific goals for yourself and consciously work toward those goals?

Very important _____

Fairly important _____

Somewhat important _____

Unimportant _____

■ How important do you think it is to work out the specific steps that you must take to achieve your goals?

Very important _____

Fairly important _____

Somewhat important _____

Unimportant _____

■ Are you already a disciplined person? Or will you have to make a special effort to work consistently toward your goals during the semester?

_____

■ On the basis of your present situation in life and what you know about yourself, what do you think will be your greatest obstacles in reaching your short-term goals?

_____

_____

_____

■ How would you rate your chances for success in achieving your short-term goals?

Excellent _____

Good _____

Fair _____

Uncertain _____

LEARNING
SURVIVAL
STRATEGIES

Note: *Over the years I have spoken with a number of successful students who started college with a reading and study skills course and then went on to earn their college degrees. Essentially, what I asked them was, "What would you want to say to students who are just starting out in college? What advice would you give? What experiences would it help to share?" The comments of one student, Jean Coleman, were especially helpful. In several conversations I had with Jean, she identified several strategies for surviving in college that other students often spoke of as well. Jean's comments are presented mostly in her own words on the pages that follow.*

THE ADVICE AND EXPERIENCE
OF A SUCCESSFUL STUDENT

"Be Realistic"

The first advice that I'd give to beginning students is: "Be realistic about how college will help you get a job." Some students believe that once they have college degrees, the world will be waiting on their doorsteps, ready to give them wonderful jobs. But the chances are that unless they've planned, there will be *nobody* on their doorsteps.

I remember the way you dramatized this point in our first class, John. You played a student who had just been handed a college degree. You opened up an imaginary door, stepped through, and peered around in both directions outside. There was nobody to be seen. I understood the point you were making immediately. A college degree in itself isn't enough. We've got to prepare while we're in college to make sure our degree is a marketable one.

At that time I began to think seriously about (1) what I wanted to do in life and (2) whether there were jobs out there for what I wanted to do. I went to the counseling center and said, ''I want to learn where the best job opportunities will be in the next ten years.'' The counselor referred me to a copy of the *Occupational Outlook Handbook* published by the United States government. The *Handbook* has good information on what kinds of jobs are available now and which career fields will need workers in the future. In the front of the book is a helpful section on job hunting. The counselor also gave me a vocational interest test to see where my skills and interests lay.

The result of my personal career planning was that I graduated from Atlantic Community College with a degree in accounting. I then got a job almost immediately, for I had chosen an excellent employment area. The firm that I worked for paid my tuition as I went on to get my bachelor's degree. They're now paying for my work toward certification as a CPA, and my salary increases regularly.

By way of contrast, I know a woman named Sheila who majored in French. She earned a bachelor's degree with honors in French. After graduation, she spent several unsuccessful months trying to find a job using her French degree. Sheila eventually wound up going to a specialized school where she trained for six months as a paralegal assistant. She then got a job on the strength of that training—but her years of studying French were of no practical value in her career at all.

I'm not saying that college should serve only as a training ground for a job. People should take some courses just for the sake of learning and for expanding their minds in different directions. At the same time, unless they have an infinite amount of money (and few of us are so lucky), they must be ready at some point to take career-oriented courses so that they can survive in the harsh world outside of college.

In my own case, I started college at the age of twenty-seven. I was divorced, had a six-year-old son to care for, and was working full time as a hotel night clerk. If I had had my preference, I would have taken a straight liberal arts curriculum. As it was, I did take some general-interest courses—in art, for example. But mainly I was getting ready for the solid job I desperately needed. What I am saying, then, is that students must be realistic. If they will need a job soon after graduation, they should be sure to study in an area where jobs are available.

"Get Organized"

One of the problems that can start a student off in the wrong direction is failing to get organized right at the beginning of the semester. It's funny, but even a disorganized first day—just one day—can set a negative tone for the semester that just seems to snowball. For instance, I have seen students come to the first day of class as if the first class were some kind of unimportant rehearsal. They don't bother to bring pens or notebooks, and they let the important information they're receiving just float by. You get the feeling that they believe they'll catch up later, but they usually don't.

I think students who are disorganized like this have never learned to take responsibility for their own behavior. They have had parents, teachers, and bosses telling them what to do, so they can't cope when they're placed in an atmosphere that says, "Nobody here is going to protect you from the consequences if you don't take care of things yourself." Students like this miss classes, fail to get the notes they missed, or don't know the most basic information, such as where their teachers' offices are. Then they act surprised when their grades take a nose dive—they feel as if they've been cheated because no one "rescued" them with warnings, reminders, or prodding.

I would tell all students to get organized right at the start of school. To help them do this, I would pass out the following checklist of important items:

_____ ■ Remember that the first meeting of any class is crucial. Bring two pens and a notebook with you, for many teachers not only distribute basic information about assigned textbooks and requirements—they also start lecturing the first day.

_____ ■ Don't put off getting your books, even if you have to wait in a long, boring line at the bookstore. You will need your books right away if you don't want to fall behind, so make the sacrifice.

_____ ■ Find out, early in the semester, the names and phone numbers of some students in the class. Students who feel "funny" about this or are too shy to do it are really hurting themselves. If you miss class, it's your responsibility to go *prepared* to the next class. At the college level, you can't get away with saying to a professor, "I don't have the assignment because I was absent" or "Could you tell me what I missed?" If you have some of your classmates' numbers, you can find out what happened in class and get the notes or assignments you missed. Of course, if you start missing too many classes or showing up late for your classes, just getting the notes won't help you keep up.

_____ ■ Have a specific place at home for all your school materials. In other words, have some kind of headquarters. You just can't study when you sit down to work and discover that your biology book is in the trunk of your brother's car, your lab notes are in a locker at school, and you can't find the handout the teacher gave you. All school-related materials should be kept somewhere convenient for you—a desk, a worktable, a closet, or a corner. This kind of very basic organization makes a big difference.

_____ ■ Decide, right from the start, how much work you can handle. If you are taking five courses, working at a full-time job, and caring for two children, for example, you're asking for a nervous breakdown—no matter how organized you are. I heard a good rule of thumb for this, and it seems accurate: For every ten hours per week you work, deduct one course from a full-time college course load. For example, if you don't work, you can do a good job on five courses; if you work ten hours, you should attempt only four courses; if you work twenty hours, take three courses maximum, and so on. You might have to bend this rule, however, depending on your family responsibilities and the level of difficulty of the courses you are taking.

I think what all this comes down to is that there seem to be two kinds of students—the ones who have a mature, professional attitude toward being a student and the ones who act like children who have to be taken care of. It's important to realize that college teachers aren't baby-sitters or disciplinarians. They want to teach, but they want to teach adults who meet them halfway and take responsibility for themselves. When I have seen students who have the attitude "I'm sitting in class, so I've done my job—now you make me learn something," I have wanted to ask them, "What are you doing here?" They just never accept, or choose to ignore, the fact that *they*—not the teachers—are the ones who determine whether they will succeed or fail.

"Persist"

The older I get, the more I see that life visits some hard experiences on us. There are times for each of us when simple survival becomes a deadly serious matter. We must then learn to persist—to struggle through each day and wait for better times to come—as they inevitably do.

I think of one of my closest friends, Neil. After graduating from high school with me, Neil spent two years working as a stock boy at a local department store in order to save money for college tuition. He then went to the guidance office at the small college in our town. Incredibly, the counselor there told him, "Your IQ is not high enough to do college work." Neil decided to go anyway and earned his degree in five years—with a year out to care for his father, who had had a stroke one day at work.

Neil then got a job as a manager of a regional beauty supply firm. He met a woman who owned a salon, got married, and soon had two children. Three years later he found out that his wife was having an affair. I'll never forget the day Neil came over and sat at my kitchen table and told me what he had learned. He always seemed so much in control, but that morning he lowered his head into his hands and cried. "What's the point?" he kept saying in a low voice over and over to himself.

But Neil has endured. He divorced his wife, won custody of his children, and learned how to be a single parent. Recently, Neil and I got letters informing us of the tenth reunion of our high school graduating class. Included was a short questionnaire for us to fill out that ended with this item, "What has been your outstanding accomplishment since graduation?" Neil wrote, "My outstanding accomplishment is that I have survived." I have a feeling that most of our high school classmates, ten years out in the world, would have no trouble understanding the sad truth of his statement.

I can think of people who started college with me who had not yet learned, like Neil, the basic skill of endurance. Life hit some of them with unexpected low punches and knocked them to the floor. Stunned and dismayed, they didn't fight back and eventually dropped out of school. I remember Yvonne, still a teenager, whose parents involved her in their ugly divorce battle. Yvonne started missing classes and gave up at midsemester. There was Alan, whose girlfriend broke off their relationship. Alan stopped coming to class, and by the end of the semester he was failing most of his courses. I also recall Nelson, whose old car kept breaking down. After Nelson put his last $200 into it, the brakes failed and needed to be replaced. Overwhelmed by his continuing car troubles, Nelson dropped out of school. And there was Rita, discouraged by her luck of the draw with teachers and courses. In sociology, she had a teacher who wasn't able to express ideas clearly. She also had a mathematics teacher who talked too fast and seemed not to care at all about whether his students learned. To top it off, Rita's adviser had enrolled her in an economics course that put her to sleep. Rita told me she had expected college to be an exciting place, but instead she was getting busywork assignments and trying to cope with hostile or boring teachers. Rita decided to drop her mathematics course, and that must have set something in motion in her head, for she soon dropped her other courses as well.

In my experience, younger students seem more prone to dropping out than do older students. I think some younger students are still in the process of learning that life slams people around without warning. I'm sure they feel that being knocked about is especially unfair because the work of college is hard enough without having to cope with some of life's special hardships.

In some situations, withdrawing from college may be the best response. But there are going to be times in college when students—young or old—must simply determine, "I am going to persist." They should remember that no matter how hard their lives may be, there are many other people out there who are quietly having great difficulties also. I think of Dennis, a boy in my introductory psychology class who lived mostly on peanut butter and discount store loaves of white bread for almost a semester in his freshman year. And I remember Estelle, who came to school because she needed a job to support her sons when her husband, who was dying of leukemia, would no longer be present. These are especially dramatic examples of the faith and hope that are sometimes necessary for us to persist.

"Be Positive"

A lot of people are their own worst enemies. They regard themselves as unlikely to succeed in college and often feel that there have been no accomplishments in their lives. In my first year of college, especially, I saw people get down on themselves all too quickly. There were two students in my developmental mathematics class who failed the first quiz and seemed to give up immediately. From that day on, they walked into the classroom carrying defeat on their shoulders the way other students carried textbooks under their arms. I'd look at them slouching in their seats, not even taking notes, and think, "What terrible things have gone on in their lives that they have quit already? They have so little faith in their ability to learn that they're not even trying." Both students hung on until about midsemester. When they disappeared for good, no one took much notice, for they had already disappeared in spirit after that first test.

They are not the only people in whom I have seen the poison of self-doubt do its ugly work. I have seen others with resignation in their eyes and have wanted to shake them by the shoulders and say, "You are not dead. Be proud and pleased that you have brought yourself here to college. Many people would not have gotten so far. Be someone. Breathe. Hope. Act." Such people should refuse to use self-doubts as an excuse for not trying. They should roll up their sleeves and get to work. They should start taking notes in class and trying to learn. They should get a tutor, go to the learning center, see a counselor. If they honestly and fully try and still can't handle a course, only then should they drop it. Above all, they should not lapse into being "zombie students"—ones who have given up in their heads but persist in hanging on for months, going through hollow motions of trying.

Nothing but a little time is lost through being positive and giving school your best shot. On the other hand, people who let self-doubts limit their efforts may lose the opportunity to test their abilities to the fullest.

"Grow"

I don't think that people really have much choice about whether to grow in their lives. To not be open to growth is to die a little each day. Grow or die—it's as simple as that.

I have a friend, Jackie, who, when she's not working, can almost always be found at home or at her mother's. Jackie eats too much and watches TV too much. I sometimes think that when she swings open her apartment door in response to my knock, I'll be greeted by her familiar chubby body with an eight-inch-screen television set occupying the place where her head used to be.

Jackie seems quietly desperate. There is no growth or plan for growth in her life. I've said to her, "Go to school and study for a job you'll be excited about." She says, "It'll take me forever." Once Jackie said to me, "The favorite time of my life was when I was a teenager. I would lie on my bed listening to music and I would dream. I felt I had enormous power, and there seemed no way that life would stop me from realizing my biggest dreams. Now that power doesn't seem possible to me anymore."

I feel that Jackie must open some new windows in her life. If she does not, her spirit is going to die. There are many ways to open new windows, and college is one of them. For this reason, I think people who are already in school should stay long enough to give it a chance. No one should turn down lightly such an opportunity for growth.

In Conclusion

Maybe I can put all I've said into perspective by describing briefly what my life is like now. I have inner resources that I did not have when I was newly divorced. I have a secure future with the accounting firm where I work. My son is doing OK in school. I have friends. I am successful and proud and happy. I have my fears and my loneliness and my problems and my pains, to say the least, but essentially I know that I have made it. I have survived and done more than survive. I am tough, not fragile, and I can rebound if hard blows land. I feel passionately that all of us can control our own destinies. I urge every beginning student to use well the chances that college affords. Students should plan for a realistic career, get themselves organized, learn to persist, be positive, and open themselves to growth. In such ways, they can help themselves find happiness and success in this perilous and wonderful world of ours.

■ **Questions to Consider**

In groups of three or four, discuss the questions that follow. Every person in the group should try to contribute. The more honest you can be in sharing experiences, the more meaningful and valuable the discussion will be.

1. Do you know yet what kind of work you want to do after college?
   a. If your answer is *no,* have you visited the counseling center to take a vocational interest test?
   b. Are you thinking actively about possible careers and getting information on those careers?
   c. If your answer is *yes,* have you checked with the counseling center or teachers in the field or through your own reading about whether there will be good job opportunities available at the time you graduate?

2. Do you know any people with a recent two- or four-year college degree? How successful have they been in getting jobs? Based on their experiences, what areas seem to offer good job opportunities?

3. People often limit themselves by taking only career-oriented courses in college. Are there any courses you plan to take just for the sake of learning?

4. Were you aware of all the tips Jean Coleman discusses in her section on getting organized? Which of her suggestions do you practice, and which ones have you ignored? Describe how well or poorly your actions compare with the organized-student habits that Coleman recommends.

5. Have there been difficult times in life when you or one of your friends has simply had to persist, as did Jean Coleman's friend Neil on pages 31–32?

6. Are any people you know like the four Jean Coleman describes on page 32 who dropped out of school when their lives became very hard? What do you think might have helped them decide to stay in school?

7. Are there any students you know who continued in school despite tough luck? What kinds of struggles did they have?

8. Do you know any students whose feelings of inferiority are keeping them from making an honest effort to learn in college? What do you think students with self-doubts could do to become more positive?

9. Do you know any "zombie students" like the ones the writer describes on page 33—students who are going through the motions of being college students but are not really committed to study? What are some of the ways they are deluding themselves?

10. Describe one person you know well who is open to growth in life and one person who is not open to such growth. How do they show their willingness or reluctance to grow in their everyday lives?

Your instructor may ask you to write a paper that responds *in detail* to one of the preceding questions.

PART TWO

STUDY SKILLS

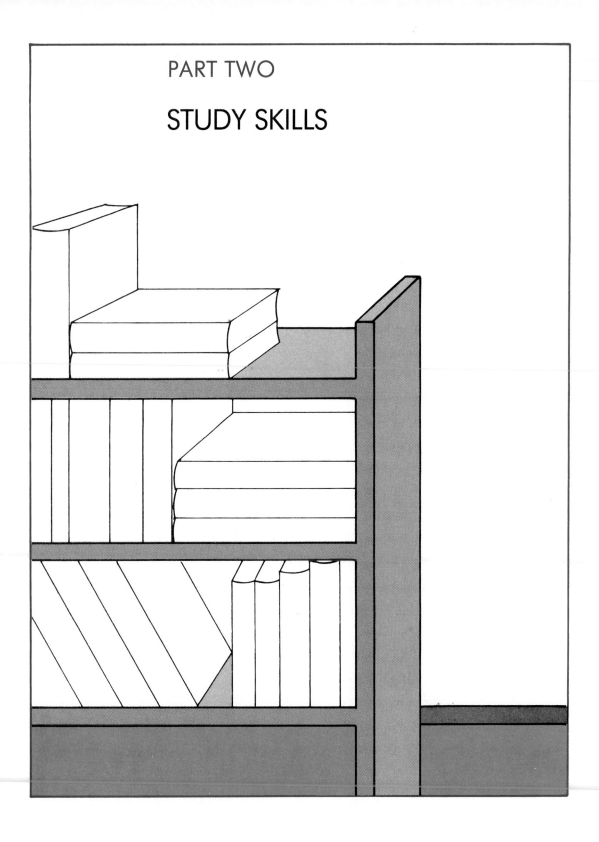

PREVIEW

Part Two presents study skills that you need if you are to do well in your courses. Each skill is explained and illustrated, and a number of activities are given to help you practice and master it. "Taking Classroom Notes" lists a number of hints for note-taking, explains how to study your class notes, and discusses handwriting and listening efficiency. In "Time Control and Concentration," you will learn several ways to make better use of your time and to develop the persistence in your work that is vital to success in school. "Textbook Study I" describes a four-step method you can use to read and study chapters in your textbooks. "Textbook Study II" gives you practice in that method with short and medium-length textbook passages. "Textbook Study III" shows you how to apply the method to an entire textbook chapter. In "Building a Powerful Memory," you will learn seven steps you can take to improve your memory. "Taking Objective Exams" and "Taking Essay Exams" show you how to prepare for both kinds of exams and explain test-taking techniques. Finally, the section on "Using the Library" prepares you for projects that require library research by explaining just how you can use the library to look up information about a subject.

TAKING CLASSROOM NOTES

This chapter will show you how to:

- Take effective classroom notes
- Study and remember your notes
- Improve your handwriting and listening efficiency

Introductory Projects

1. Consider this common study situation:

> Howard has trouble taking notes in all his classes. He is seldom sure about what is important enough to write down. Also, he has trouble organizing material when he does write it down. Often the only points he records are the ones the teacher puts on the board. The connections between these points are usually clear to him in class, for he spends most of his time listening carefully to the teacher rather than taking notes. However, several weeks later, when he is studying for a test, he has trouble remembering many of the relationships among points. His notes do not provide a complete, unified understanding of the subject but seem instead to consist of many isolated bits of information.
>
> One course that gives Howard special problems is sociology. In class the teacher asks students questions and uses their comments as takeoff points for discussing course ideas. Sometimes she is five minutes into an important idea before Howard realizes it is important—and he hasn't taken a single note on that point. He often winds up with such a frustrating shortage of notes that he decides not to go to class at all. In another course, biology, the teacher talks so fast that Howard cannot keep up. Also, he misspells so many words that it is often impossible for him to understand his notes when he tries to read them over weeks later, before an exam.

This chapter will provide answers to Howard's study problem. But take a few minutes first to examine your own ideas. What do you think are three specific steps that Howard could take to become a better note-taker?

2. Within a small group, read aloud to each other the thirteen hints for taking effective classroom notes described on the following pages. Someone should read the first hint to the group, someone else the second, and so on. Pay careful attention to each hint as it is being read. Think to yourself, "Do I practice this hint? If not, should I?"

Then, as a group, decide which five hints seem most important. Argue about the five choices among yourselves; the final decision of the group should be based on your agreement about which five hints seem most necessary and useful. Write your final decisions in the spaces that follow.

3. If you are working on this section individually, read through the hints carefully. Then decide on the five most important ideas and list them here:

a. _____

b. _____

c. _____

d. _____

e. _____

THE IMPORTANCE OF ATTENDING CLASS

If you really want to do well in a course, you must promise yourself that you will go to class faithfully and take good notes. This chapter will offer a series of tips on how to take effective classroom notes. However, the hints will be of no value if you do not attend class. The importance of *regular class attendance* cannot be emphasized enough. Students who cut class rarely do well in college.

The alternatives to class attendance—reading the text or using someone else's notes—can seldom substitute for the experience of being in class and hearing the instructor talk about key ideas in the course. These ideas are often the ones you will be expected to know on exams.

If you do not attend classes regularly, you may be making an unconscious decision that you do not want to attend college at this time. If you think this may be how you feel, talk to a counselor, teacher, or friend. Another person can often help you clarify your own thoughts and feelings so that you can achieve a perspective on your situation.

■ Have you made a personal decision (be honest!) to attend all your classes

regularly? _____

■ If not, are you willing to think about why you are reluctant to make the

commitment to college work? _____

THIRTEEN HINTS FOR TAKING
EFFECTIVE CLASSROOM NOTES

Hint 1: Keep a Written Record

Get down a written record for each class. It's important that you write down the material covered because forgetting begins almost immediately. Studies have shown that within two weeks you probably will forget 80 percent or more of what you have heard. And in four weeks you are lucky if 5 percent remains! The significance of these facts is so crucial that the point bears repeating: To guard against the relentlessness of forgetting, you must write down much of the information presented in class. Later, you will study your notes so that you understand and remember the ideas presented in class. And the more complete your notes are when you review them, the more likely you are to master the material.

How many notes should you take? If you pay attention in class, you will soon develop an instinct for what is meaningful and what is not. If you are unsure whether certain terms, facts, and ideas are significant, here is a good rule to follow: *When in doubt, write it down.* This doesn't mean you should (or could) get down every word, but you should be prepared to do a good deal of writing in class. Also, do not worry if you don't understand everything you record in your notes. Sometimes a teacher will phrase an idea several different ways, and it may turn out that it is the third version of the idea that you clearly understand. It is easy to cross out later the material that you don't need but impossible to recover material you never recorded in the first place. Keep in mind that writing too much, rather than too little, may mean the difference between passing and failing a course or between a higher grade and a lower one.

■ Explain briefly why you should get down a written record of each class.

Hint 2: Sit Where You'll Be Seen

Sit where the teacher will always see you, and where you can see the blackboard clearly and easily. Your position near or at the front will help you stay tuned in to what the instructor does in class. If you sit behind someone, are hidden in a corner, or are otherwise out of the instructor's line of vision, it may be a reflection of your attitude—either you are worried that you may be noticed and called on (a common anxiety) or you don't really want to be in the classroom at all (something worth thinking about).

Analyze your attitude. If you're hiding, know that you're hiding and try to understand why. It is all right not to want to be in a class; teachers can be boring and subjects uninteresting. However, the danger in such cases is that you may slide into a passive state where you won't listen or take notes. Don't fool yourself. If a class is deadly, there is all the more reason to make yourself take good notes—that way you will pass the course and get out of the class once and for all.

■ Explain briefly two reasons why you should sit near the front.

_____

_____

Hint 3: Do Some Advance Reading

Ideally, read in advance about the topic to be discussed in class. All too often, students don't read assigned textbook material on a topic until after class is over. Lacking the necessary background, they have trouble understanding the new ideas discussed in class. However, if they have made an initial breakthrough on a topic by doing some advance reading, they will be able to listen and take notes more easily and with greater understanding. And they should be able to write more organized and effective notes because they will have a general sense of the topic.

If you don't know what the topic is going to be, check with your instructor at the end of the preceding class. Simply ask, "Is there a chapter in the textbook that I can read in advance of your next class? I'd like to get a head start on what you're going to cover." At the least, you are going to make a good impression on the instructor, who will appreciate your seriousness and interest.

In particular, try to read the textbook in advance when the subject is very difficult. Reading in advance is also a good idea if you have spelling problems that hinder note-taking. As you read through the text, write down key terms and recurring words that may come up in the lecture and that you might have trouble spelling.

■ Explain briefly why you should read your textbook in advance of a lecture.

_____

_____

Hint 4: Record Notes Systematically

1   Use full-sized 8½- by 11-inch paper. Do *not* use a small note tablet. As explained below, you will need the margin space provided by full-sized paper. Also, on a single page of full-sized paper you can often see groups of related ideas that might not be apparent spread over several small pages.

2   Use a ballpoint pen. You will often need to write quickly—something that you cannot do as well with a pencil or a felt-tip pen. (Don't worry about making mistakes with a pen that makes marks you can't erase. Just cross out the mistakes!)

3   Keep all the notes from each course together in a separate section of a notebook. Use a loose-leaf binder with sections indicated by dividers and index tabs, or use a large spiral notebook that has several sections. A spiral notebook is simpler. But a loose-leaf binder has the advantage of letting you insert handout sheets and supplementary notes at appropriate points. If you use a binder, you may want to leave previous notes safe at home and just bring to each class the last day or so of notes and some blank paper.

4   Date each day's notes.

5   Take notes on one side of the page only and leave space at the top of the page and at the left-hand margin. (You might use notebook paper that has a light red line down the left side.) Using only one side of the paper eliminates the bother, when studying, of having to flip pages over and then flip them back to follow the development of an idea.

   Leaving wide margins gives you space to add to your notes if desired. You may, for example, write in ideas taken from your textbook or other sources. Also, the margins can be used to prepare study notes (see pages 50–51) that will help you learn the material.

6   Write legibly. When you prepare for a test, you want to spend your time studying—not deciphering your handwriting.

7   To save time, abbreviate recurring terms. Put a key to abbreviated words in the top margin of your notes. For example, in a biology class *ch* could stand for *chromosome;* in a psychology class *o c* could stand for *operant conditioning.* (When a lecture is over, you may want to go back and fill in the words you have abbreviated.)

   Also abbreviate the following common words, using the symbols shown:

$+$ = and	*def* = definition
w/ = with	$\therefore$ = therefore
eg = for example	*info* = information
ex = example	*1, 2, 3* = one, two, three, etc.

Note, too, that you can often omit words like *a, and,* and *the.*

8 Note prominently exams or quizzes that are announced as well as assignments that the teacher gives. It's a good idea to circle exam dates and put a large *A* for *assignment* in the margin. (Be sure you have a definite system for keeping track of assignments. Some students record them on a separate small note pad; others record them at the back of the notebook devoted to a given course.)

■ What do you consider the three most helpful suggestions for recording notes?

_____

_____

_____

Hint 5: Use an Outline for Notes

Try to write down your notes in the following outline form. Start main points at the margin. Indent secondary ideas and supporting details. Further indent material subordinate to secondary points.

Main points are listed at the margin.
Secondary points and supporting details are indented.
Material subordinate to secondary points is indented further.

Definitions, for instance, should always start at the margin. When a list of terms is presented, the heading should also start at the margin, but each item in the series should be set in slightly from the margin. Examples, too, should be indented under the point they illustrate.

Here is another organizational aid: When the speaker moves from one idea or aspect of a topic to another, show this shift by skipping a line or two, leaving a clearly visible white space.

In the rapid pace of a lecture, you won't always be able to tell what is a main point and what is secondary material. Be ready, though, to use the outline techniques of indentation and extra space whenever you can. They are the first steps toward organizing class material.

■ Explain briefly what is meant by *indentation*.

_____

_____

Hint 6: Be Alert for Signals

Watch for signals of importance:

1   Write down whatever your teacher puts on the board. Ideally, *print* such material in capital letters. If you don't have time to print, write as you usually do and put the letters *OB* in the margin to indicate that the material was written on the board. Later, when you review your notes, you will know which ideas the teacher emphasized. The chances are good that they will come up on exams.

2   Always write down definitions and enumerations. Most people instinctively write down definitions—explanations of key terms in the subject they are learning. But they often ignore enumerations, which are often equally important. An *enumeration* is simply a list of items (marked 1, 2, 3, etc., or with other symbols) that fit under a particular heading. (See also page 320.)

   Teachers use enumerations, or lists, to show the relationship among a group of ideas. Being aware of enumerations will help you organize material as you take notes. Enumerations are signaled in such ways as: "The four steps in the process are . . ."; "There were three reasons for . . ."; "Five characteristics of . . ."; "The two effects were . . ."; and so on. When you write a list, always mark the items with 1, 2, 3, or other appropriate symbols. Also, always be sure to include a clear heading that explains what a list is about. For example, if you list and number six kinds of defense mechanisms, make sure you write at the top of the list the heading "Kinds of Defense Mechanisms."

3   Your instructor may say, "This is an important reason . . ."; or "A point that will keep coming up later . . ."; or "The chief cause was . . ."; or "The basic idea here is . . ."; or "Don't forget that . . ."; or "Pay special attention to . . ."; and so on. Be sure to write down the important statements announced by these and other emphasis words, and write in the margin *imp* or some other mark (such as * or ‡ or →) to show their importance.

4   If your teacher repeats a point, you can usually assume it is important. You might write *R* for *repeated* in the margin so that you will know later that your instructor stressed that idea.

5   A teacher's voice may slow down, become louder, or otherwise signal that you are expected to write down exactly what is being said, word for word. Needless to say, do so!

■   Which two signals of importance do you think will be most helpful for you to remember? _____

_____

Hint 7: Write Down Examples

Write down any examples the teacher provides and mark them with *ex.* The examples help you understand complex and abstract points. If you don't mark them with *ex,* you are likely to forget their purpose when you later review them for study. You may not have to write down every example that illustrates an idea, but you should record at least one example that makes a point clear.

Hint 8: Write Down Details That Connect or Explain

Be sure to write down the details that connect or explain main points. Too many students copy only the major points the teacher puts on the board. They do not realize that as time passes, they may forget the specifics that serve as connecting bridges between key ideas. Be sure, then, to record the connecting details the instructor provides. That way you are more apt to remember the relationships among the major points in your notes.

In science and mathematics classes especially, students often fail to record the explanations that make formulas or numerical problems meaningful. Their notes may consist only of the letters and numbers the instructor chalked on the board. But to understand how the letters and numbers are related, they should also write down accompanying explanations and details.

Always take advantage of the connections teachers often make at the beginning or end of a class. They may review material already covered and preview what is to come. Write down such overviews when they are presented and label them *review* or *preview,* as the case may be. An instructor's summaries or projections will help the course come together for you.

■ How often do you forget to write down connections between ideas?

_____ Frequently   _____ Sometimes   _____ Almost never

Hint 9: Leave Some Blank Spaces

Leave blank spaces for items or ideas you miss. Right after class, ask another student to help you fill in the gaps. Ideally, you should find a person in each course who will agree to be your note-taking partner—someone with whom you can compare and fill in notes after a class. If another person is not available, you might want to tape each class and play back the tape right away to get any missing material. (Don't ever, though, fall into the trap of relying upon a tape recorder to take most of your notes. In no time at all, you'll have hours and hours of tape to go through—time you probably cannot afford to take. Use a tape only to help you fill in occasional missing spots.)

When you do fall behind in note-taking during class, don't give up and just stop writing. Try to get down what seem to be the main ideas rather than supporting facts and details. You may be able to fill in the supporting material later.

Hint 10: Ask Questions

Don't hesitate to ask the instructor questions if certain points are confusing to you. Probably, other students have the same questions but are reluctant to ask to have the material clarified. Remember that teachers look favorably upon students who show interest and curiosity.

- How often do you ask questions in class?

    _____ Frequently

    _____ Sometimes

    _____ Almost never

Hint 11: Take Notes during Discussions

Do not stop taking notes during discussion periods. Many valuable ideas may come up during informal discussions, ideas that your instructor may not present formally later on. If your instructor puts notes on the board during a class discussion, it's a good sign that the material is important. If he or she pursues or draws out a discussion in a given direction, it's a clue that you should be taking notes. And don't forget the advice in hint 1 on page 41: When in doubt, write it down.

Hint 12: Take Notes Right Up to the End of Class

Do not stop taking notes toward the end of a class. Because of time spent on discussions, teachers may have to cram important points they want to cover into the last minutes of a class. Be ready to write as rapidly as you can to get down this final rush of ideas.

Be prepared, also, to resist the fatigue that may settle in during class. As a lecture proceeds, the possibility of losing attention increases. You do not want to snap out of a daydream only to realize that an instructor is halfway into an important idea and you haven't even begun writing.

- Are you one of the many students whose note-taking slows down at the end of a class? _____

Hint 13: Review Your Notes Soon

Go over your notes soon after class. While the material is still clear in your mind, make your notes as clear as possible. A day later may be too late because forgetting sets in almost at once.

As far as possible, make sure that your punctuation is clear, that unfinished ideas are completed, and that all words are readable and correctly spelled. You may also want to write out completely words that you abbreviated during the lecture. Wherever appropriate, add connecting statements and other comments to clarify the material. Make sure important items—material on the board, definitions, enumerations, and so on—are clearly marked. Improve the organization, if necessary, so that you can see at a glance the differences between main points and supporting material as well as any relationships among the main points.

This review does more than make your notes clear: it is also a vital step in the process of mastering the material. During class, you have almost certainly been too busy taking notes to absorb all the ideas. Now, as you review the notes, you can roll up your sleeves and wrestle with the ideas presented and think about the relationships among them. You can, in short, do the work needed to reach the point where you can smile and say, "Yes, I understand—and everything I understand is down clearly in my notes."

■ Explain briefly why you should go over your notes soon after class.

    _____

    _____

HOW TO STUDY CLASS NOTES

The best time to start studying your notes is within a day after taking them. Because of the mind's tendency to forget material rapidly, a few minutes of study soon after a class will give you more learning for less time and effort than almost any other technique you can practice.

One Effective Method for Studying Class Notes

Here is one effective way to study your notes:

1 Use the margin space at the side (or top) of each page. Jot down in the margin a series of key words or phrases from your notes. These key words or phrases, known as *recall words,* will help you pull together and remember the important ideas on the page.

On page 50 are notes from a business course. Take the time now to look them over carefully. You will notice in the side margin the recall words that the student, Janet, used for studying this page of notes.

2 To test yourself on the material, turn the recall words in the margin into questions. For instance, Janet asked herself, "What is the origin of economics?" After she could recite the answer without looking at it, she asked herself, "What is the definition of economics?" Janet then went back and retested herself on the first question. When she could recite the answers to both the first and second questions, she went on to the third one.

Shown below are most of the questions that Janet asked herself. Fill in the missing questions.

What is the origin of economics?
What is the definition of economics?

_____

What is the definition of economic resources?

_____

What are the two kinds of property resources and their definitions?
What are the three kinds of human resources and their definitions?

Janet tested herself on each of the seven questions and retested herself on those from earlier lectures, until she could recite all of them from memory. (For more information on repeated self-testing, see page 194.)

This approach, if it is pursued regularly, will help you remember the material covered in your classes. With such a study method, you will not be left with a great deal of material to organize and learn right before an exam. Instead, you will be able to devote preexam time to a final intensive review of the subject.

Another Good Method for Studying Class Notes

Some students prefer to write out on separate sheets of paper the material they want to learn. They prepare study sheets that often use a question-and-answer format. The very act of writing out study notes is itself a step toward remembering the material. Shown on page 51 is a study sheet that Janet could have prepared.

At the left are the recall words Janet placed in the margin.

	Business 101 11-7-91 ec = economic(s) res = resource
	Economics—from Greek words meaning "HOUSE" and
Origin of ec	"TO MANAGE." Meaning gradually extended to cover not
	only management of household but of business and governments.
Def of ec	Ec (definition)—STUDY OF HOW SCARCE RESOURCES
	ARE ALLOCATED IN A SOCIETY OF UNLIMITED WANTS.
	Every society provides goods + services; these are available
	in limited quantities and so have value.
Imp	One of the most imp. assumptions of ec: Though res of
assumption	world are limited, wants of people are not. This means an ec system
	can never produce enough to satisfy everyone completely.
Def of ec res	Ec res—all factors that go into production of goods + services.
2 types of	Two types:
ec res	1. PROPERTY RES—2 kinds:
2 kinds of	a. LAND—all natural res (land, timber, water, oil, minerals)
property	b. CAPITAL—all the machinery, tools, equipment, + building
res + defs	needed to produce goods + distribute them to consumers.
3 kinds of	2. HUMAN RES—3 kinds
human	a. LABOR—all physical and mental talents needed to produce
res + defs	goods + services
	b. MANAGEMENT ABILITY—talent needed to bring together
	land, capital, + labor to produce goods and services.
	c. TECHNOLOGY—accumulated fund of knowledge which
	helps in production of goods + services.

Sample Study Sheet

What is the origin of economics?

From Greek words "house" and "manage." Word gradually extended to include business and government.

What is economics?

Study of how scarce resources are allocated in a society of unlimited wants.

What is an important assumption of economics?

Resources are limited but people's wants are not.

What are economic resources?

All the factors that go into production of goods + services.

What are the two types of economic resources?

Property + human resources.

What are the two kinds of property resources?

a. Land—all natural resources (land, timber, water, oil, minerals).

b. Capital—all the machinery, tools, equipment, and building needed to produce goods + distribute them to consumers.

What are the three kinds of human resources?

a. Labor—all physical and mental talents needed to produce goods + services.

b. Management ability—talent needed to bring together land, capital, + labor to produce goods + services.

c. Technology—accumulated fund of knowledge which helps in production of goods + services.

TWO SPECIAL SKILLS THAT HELP NOTE-TAKING

Two special skills that will help you take effective classroom notes are handwriting efficiency and listening efficiency. The following pages explain and offer practice in these skills.

Increasing Handwriting Efficiency

Activity 1

To check your handwriting efficiency, write as fast as you can for ten minutes. Don't stop for anything. Don't worry about spelling, punctuation, erasing mistakes, or finding exact words. If you get stuck for words, write ''I am looking for something to say'' or repeat words until something comes. You have two objectives in this rapid-writing activity: to write as many words as you can in the ten minutes (you will be asked to count the words later) and to write words legibly enough so that you can still understand them several weeks from now.

Count the number of words you have written in the ten minutes and record the number here: _____.

Handwriting Speed and Legibility: In Activity 1, you should have been able to write at least 250 legible words in ten minutes—and ideally a hundred or so more than that. Handwriting speed is important because it is basic to effective note-taking in fast-moving lectures. If you cannot write quickly enough, you are likely to miss valuable ideas presented in such classes. Also, you may have trouble writing out full answers on essay exams. And in either situation, if your handwriting is not legible, there is hardly any point in writing at all.

Improving Speed: There are several steps you can take to improve your handwriting speed.

One step is to practice *rapid writing*—writing nonstop for ten or fifteen minutes at a time about whatever comes into your head. Try to increase the number of pages you fill with words in the limited time period. With several practice sessions, you should be able to increase your handwriting speed significantly.

Another way to increase speed is to use abbreviations. Abbreviate words that occur repeatedly in a lecture class, and put a key for such words in the top margin of your notes. For example, if the name *Linnaeus* keeps recurring in a botany class, at the top of the page write *L = Linnaeus,* and from then on in your notes that day simply use *L.*

■ What keys could you make for a psychology class on Skinner and behaviorism? _____ _____

Following is a list of other symbols that can be made part of a general "shorthand" for your writing. (Note that you can often omit *a, and, the,* and other connecting words.)

$$+ = \text{and}$$
$$\text{w/} = \text{with}$$
$$\text{eg} = \text{for example}$$
$$\text{ex} = \text{example}$$
$$\text{def} = \text{definition}$$
$$\text{imp} = \text{important}$$
$$\text{ind} = \text{individual}$$
$$\text{info} = \text{information}$$
$$\text{sc} = \text{science}$$
$$\text{soc} = \text{sociology}$$
$$\text{psy} = \text{psychology}$$
$$1, 2, 3, = \text{one, two, three, etc.}$$

Finally, you can write faster if you streamline your handwriting by eliminating unnecessary high and low loops in letters. For example,

Instead of	Write	Instead of	Write
b	b	k	K
d	d	l	l
f	f	p	p
g	g	t	t
h	h	y	y

You will find that this streamlined, print-style writing is learned easily and will help you write faster.

■ Go back and put the numbers 1, 2, and 3 in front of the three methods described for increasing handwriting speed.

Improving Legibility: To improve and maintain legibility, check a sample of your writing for the four common types of faulty handwriting illustrated here. Or give your writing sample to someone else to analyze for handwriting faults.

1 Overlapping letters from one line to the next. For example:

One of the main types of faulty handwriting is the overlapping of letters from one line to the next.

Note the improvement in legibility when this fault is eliminated:

One of the main types of faulty handwriting is the overlapping of letters from one line to the next.

2 Slanting letters in more than one direction. For example:

Another kind of faulty handwriting is to slant letters in all directions instead of just one.

Note how legibility improves when slants are consistent:

Another type of faulty handwriting is to slant letters in all directions instead of just one.

3 Making decorative capitals and loops. For example:

The use of decorative capitals and loops may result in a script that

You can greatly improve legibility by *printing* capital letters and restraining your loop letters.

4 Miswriting the letters *a, e, r, n,* and *t.* Common errors include writing the letter *e* like *i* (closing the loop) and putting a loop in nonloop letters like *i* and *t.* Check your handwriting to be sure you form these letters clearly. Also, look for other letters that you may miswrite consistently.

To help legibility, follow two other tips as well. First, always use a ball point pen rather than a pencil. A dull-edged pencil will slow down your writing speed and hinder legibility. You can get a Bic pen for 45 cents. Second, be sure to hold your pen between the thumb and index finger, resting it against the middle finger. Don't grip the pen tightly, but just firmly enough to keep it from slipping. And don't hold it, as some people do, too close to the tip—you won't be able to see what you're writing. Hold it about ³/₄ inch from the point.

If you follow these suggestions, you should become a more efficient handwriter. Clear and rapid handwriting is a mechanical technique; once you decide to learn it and begin to practice, mastery is almost bound to follow. People should not allow their failure to write skillfully to limit their note-taking performance, whether in school or on the job.

Activity 2

Write again for ten minutes without stopping. Try to write more words than you did in Activity 1. At the same time, be sure to keep your words legible.

Number of words in Activity 1: _____   In Activity 2: _____

Increasing Listening Efficiency

Activity 1

To take effective classroom notes, you must be able to listen attentively. This activity will test your ability to listen carefully and to follow spoken directions. The instructor will give you a series of thirteen directions. Listen closely to each one and then do exactly what it calls for. Each direction will be spoken only once.

If you are working on this book independently, get a friend to read the directions to you, or read each direction aloud once to yourself and then try to follow it. Do the same for other activities in this section as well.

Direction 1: Do not say a word at any point during this exercise. Do not raise your hand or look at your neighbor. There will be thirteen directions in the exercise. Follow every one of them except for the last direction, which you should disregard.

Direction 2: Get out a sheet of paper and write your full name in the upper-left-hand corner of the paper.

Direction 3: Write the numbers 1 to 8 down the left-hand side of the page.

Direction 4: Write beside space 2 the word *quiet,* which is spelled *q-u-i-e-t.*

Direction 5: Write down the name of the street where you live beside space 3. Do not write down the street number.

Direction 6: Think of the name of the high school that you went to. Do not write it down beside space 1.

Direction 7: Think of the name of the toothpaste that you use. Write it down on the back of your sheet of paper.

Direction 8: Listen to the following set of numbers and then put them down beside space 4. The numbers are 8, 12, 20, 31, 45.

Direction 9: Think of the name of a television show that you like, turn your paper upside down, and write the name of the show beside space 5.

Direction 10: Turn your paper back to the original position. Then count the number of people in the room, including yourself. Write out the number beside space 6.

Direction 11: Print in capital letters your first name or nickname beside space 7.

Direction 12: Write the word *banana*—spelled *b-a-n-a-n-a*—beside space 8. Then draw a picture of a pear on one side of the word *banana* and a picture of an apple under the word *banana*.

Direction 13: This is the last direction. Crumple your paper into a ball and throw it to the front of the room.

If you followed all directions correctly, you have done an effective job of attending closely. It is a skill that will help you be a good listener and note-taker.

Skills in Good Listening: Effective listening and note-taking require not only the ability to attend but other skills as well. At the same time you are writing down what the teacher has said, you must be able to listen to what the teacher is now saying and to decide whether it is important enough to write down as well. Also, in a rapid lecture you must be able at times to store one or more ideas in your memory so that you will be able to write them down as soon as you complete a present one. If you can "listen ahead" and process and remember what you hear at the same time that you are writing rapidly, you will be listening efficiently. Your brain will be able to work along with and ahead of your pen.

Activity 2
This activity will give you practice in developing your listening efficiency.

Group A: Your instructor will read each sentence in group A once, at a normal speaking speed. Listen carefully and, after the instructor has read the sentence, see if you can write down what has been said. The instructor will give you time to finish writing before starting the second sentence. Do not worry about getting down every little word; do try to get down the basic idea. (If there are words you cannot spell, try to spell them the way they sound. In actual note-taking situations, you can later look up correct spellings in your textbook or dictionary.) There are three practice sentences in group A.

1. Almost one in every seven Americans is affected by hypertension—that is, by high blood pressure.
2. A half hour of TV nightly news, if printed, would not fill one page of *The New York Times*.
3. In 1900 about one in thirteen marriages ended in divorce; today one in three ends in divorce.

Group B: The three examples in group B are almost twice as long as those in group A. They require, then, an increased listening efficiency. Your instructor will read the two sentences in each example at a normal speaking rate. You can begin writing as soon as the instructor starts the first sentence. You will have to listen to and remember the second sentence in each example at the same time you are writing the first sentence.

1. The popular idea that you can tell the age of a rattlesnake by the number of rattles on its tail is false. A healthy snake can grow several new rattles in a single year.
2. The usual age of retirement in America is sixty-five. Many experts are now questioning the fairness of a system that removes people from their jobs no matter how qualified they are.
3. People have a great advantage over computers, for we can understand visual images drawn from our environment. Computers can process only facts that are put into numerical form.

Group C: The three examples in group C are about three times as long as those in group A. They create, then, an even more realistic note-taking situation, and they require a further increase in listening efficiency. Again your instructor will read the sentences in each example at a normal rate of speed. You will have to "listen ahead" and remember what you hear at the same time that you are writing rapidly.

1. When trapped in quicksand, do not struggle, or you will be sucked in deeper. The body floats on quicksand, so you should fall on your back, stretching out your arms at right angles, as if floating on water. Then, after working your legs free from the sand, begin rolling your entire body toward safe ground.
2. Ralph Nader has suggested that voting be required in this country, as it is in several other countries. In Australia, students learn that if they don't vote at age eighteen, they may have to pay a fine equal to about $15 in American money. The result is that about 90 percent of qualified voters go to the polls.
3. Babies seldom cry for no reason at all. They cry because of some discomfort that they feel. In the first year of life in particular, it is important that parents respond to a baby's cries rather than ignore them. A prompt response helps build a sense of security and trust in the baby.

You will receive additional practice in listening when you take notes on the short lectures that appear on pages 61–66.

PRACTICE IN TAKING CLASSROOM NOTES

Activity 1

Taking Notes: Evaluate your present note-taking skills by putting a check mark beside each of the thirteen note-taking hints that you already practice. Then put a check mark beside those steps that you plan to practice. Leave a space blank if you do not plan to follow a particular strategy.

Now Do   **Plan to Do**

____ ____   1. Take notes on classroom work.

____ ____   2. Sit near the front of the class.

____ ____   3. Read in advance textbook material about the topic to be presented in class.

4. Record notes as follows:

____ ____   a. Use full-sized 8½- by 11-inch paper.

____ ____   b. Use a ballpoint pen.

____ ____   c. Use a notebook divided into parts.

____ ____   d. Date each day's notes.

____ ____   e. Take notes on one side of the page only.

____ ____   f. Write legibly.

____ ____   g. Abbreviate common words and recurring terms.

____ ____   h. Indicate assignments and exams.

5. Write notes in outline form as follows:

____ ____   a. Start main points at the margin; indent secondary points.

____ ____   b. Use white space to show shift in thought.

6. Watch for signals of importance:

____ ____   a. Write whatever the teacher puts on the board.

____ ____   b. Write definitions and enumerations.

____ ____   c. Write down points marked by emphasis words.

____ ____   d. Record repeated points.

____ ____   e. Note the hints given by the teacher's tone of voice.

____ ____   7. Write down examples.

____ ____   8. Write down connecting details and explanations.

9. Do as follows when material is missed:

____ ____   a. Leave space for notes missed.

____ ____   b. Try to get the broad sweep of ideas when you fall behind.

____ ____   10. Question the instructor when an idea isn't clear.

____ ____   11. Do not stop taking notes during discussion periods.

____ ____   12. Do not stop taking notes toward the end of a class.

____ ____   13. Go over your notes soon after class.

Studying Notes: Now, evaluate your skills in studying class notes.

—— ——   ■   Jot in the margin key words to recall ideas.
—— ——   ■   Turn recall words into questions.
—— ——   ■   Use repeated self-testing to learn the material.
—— ——   ■   Apply this study method regularly.

Activity 2

Write a one-page (or longer) essay in which you respond in detail to the study situation described on page 39. Apply what you have learned in this chapter to explain all the steps that Howard should take to become an effective note-taker.

Alternatively, your instructor may ask you to prepare an oral answer to this question. In this case, you should jot down brief notes (below) that you can refer to when presenting your answer to other people in your class.

Notes for Oral Answer

_____

_____

_____

_____

_____

_____

_____

_____

_____

_____

_____

_____

_____

_____

_____

Sociology 101   11-27-91

In the million years or so of life on earth, human beings have sought truth in many places. FIVE SOURCES OF TRUTH in particular are important to note: (1) intuition, (2) authority, (3) tradition, (4) common sense, and (5) science.

1. INTUITION—any flash of insight (true or mistaken) whose source the receiver cannot fully identify or explain.

    Ex.—Galen in second century made chart of human body showing exactly where it might be pierced without fatal injury. Knew which zones were fatal through intuition.

2. AUTHORITY—persons who are experts in a specific field.

Two kinds of authority:

a. SACRED—rests upon faith that a certain tradition or document—eg., the Bible—is of supernatural origin.

b. SECULAR—arises from human perception + is of two kinds:

    (1) secular scientific—rests upon empirical observation.

    (2) secular humanistic—rests upon belief that certain "great people" have had special insight.

Activity 3

On the opposite page is an excerpt from notes taken during an introductory lecture in a sociology class. In the margin of the notes, jot down key words or phrases that could be used to pull together and so recall the main ideas on the page.

Activity 4

Turn in to your instructor a copy of one day's notes that you have taken in one of your classes. These notes should fill at least one side of a sheet of paper. If you have never taken a full page of notes in class, add a second or third day's notes until you complete at least one sheet. In the top or left-hand margin of your notes, write down key words or phrases you could use to master the material in the notes.

Activity 5

The activity that follows will give you practice in taking lecture notes. The activity is based on a short lecture on listening given in a speech class. Take notes on the lecture as your instructor or a friend reads it aloud. Items that the original lecturer put on the board are shown at the top of the lecture. As you take your notes, apply the hints you have learned in this chapter. Then answer the questions that follow the selection by referring to your notes but not to the selection itself. Write your answers on separate sheets of paper.

LECTURE ABOUT LISTENING

On Board

Problem of losing attention	Spare time
125 wpm = talking speed	Three techniques for concentration
500 wpm = listening speed	Intend to listen

I'm going to describe to you a listening problem that many people have. I'll also explain why many people have the problem, and I'll tell you what can be done about the problem. The listening problem that many people have is that they lose attention while listening to a speaker. They get bored, their minds wander, their thoughts go elsewhere.

Everyone has had this experience of losing attention, but probably few people understand one of the main reasons why we have this trouble keeping our attention on the speaker. The reason is this: There is a great deal of difference between talking speed and listening speed. The average speaker talks at the rate of 125 words a minute. On the other hand, we can listen and think at the rate of about 500 words a minute. Picture it: The speaker is going along at 125 wpm and we are sitting there ready to move at four times that speed. The speaker is like a tortoise plodding along slowly; we, the listeners, are like the rabbit ready to dash along at a much faster speed. The result of this gap is that we have a lot of spare time to use while listening to a speech.

Unfortunately, many of us use this time to go off on side excursions of our own. We may begin thinking about a date, a sports event, a new shirt we want to buy, balancing our budget, how to start saving money, what we must do later in the day, and a thousand other things. The result of the side excursions may be that when our attention returns to the speaker, we find that we have been left far behind. The speaker has gotten into some new idea, and we, having missed some connection, have little sense of what is being talked about. We may have to listen very closely for five minutes to get back on track. The temptation at this point is to go back to our own special world of thoughts and forget about the speaker. Then we're wasting both our time and the speaker's time. What we must do instead is work hard to keep our attention on the speaker and to concentrate on what is being said.

Here are three mental techniques you can use to keep your concentration on the speaker. First of all, summarize what the speaker has said. Do this after each new point is developed. This constant summarizing will help you pay attention. Second, try to guess where the speaker is going next. Try to anticipate what direction the speaker is going to take, based on what has already been said. This game you play with yourself arouses your curiosity and helps maintain your attention. Third, question the truth, the validity, of the speaker's words. Compare the points made with your own knowledge and experience. Keep trying to decide whether you agree or disagree with the speaker on the basis of what you know. Don't simply take as gospel whatever the speaker tells you; question it—ask yourself whether you think it is true. Remember, then, to summarize what the speaker has said, try to guess where the speaker is going next, and question the truth of what is stated.

All three techniques can make you a better listener. But even better than these techniques, I think, is making a conscious effort to listen more closely. You must intend to concentrate, intend to listen carefully. For example, you should go into your classes every day determined to pay close attention. It should be easier for you to make this important mental decision if you remember how easily attention can wander when someone else is speaking.

Questions on the Lecture

1. What is a listening problem that many people have?
2. What are common talking and listening speeds?
3. What are three techniques to help you pay attention when someone is talking?
4. What is the most important step you can take to become a better listener?

Activity 6

Follow the directions given for Activity 5.

LECTURE ABOUT PROPAGANDA TECHNIQUES

On Board

Propaganda   Testimonial   Bandwagon   Plain folks   Transfer

We all know that advertising sells products. How many times have you bought a particular item because you saw it advertised on TV? We all have, of course, and that is the power of advertising. One thing that makes ads work is propaganda. Propaganda may be defined as *messages intended to persuade audiences to adopt a certain opinion.* We know that Communist governments use propaganda to win people to their side. But propaganda is also used by our own politicians, editorial writers, and advertisers. Today, we will discuss four propaganda techniques often used by advertisers.

The first of these techniques is called the *testimonial.* This means that celebrities are used to pitch an idea or sell a product. For example, you may have seen ads that used celebrities like Joe Montana, Michael J. Fox, and Ray Charles to sell Coke and Pepsi. Other well-known personalities like James Earl Jones and Candice Bergen have sold telephone services. The testimonial is a propaganda method because the audience associates the star qualities of the celebrity with the product—whether or not the celebrity knows anything at all about beer or cameras. Our good feelings about the person, in other words, spill over to the product. You can all think of famous people who have appeared in TV or magazine or billboard ads to sell products.

Another propaganda technique used by advertisers is the *bandwagon.* This method encourages people to do or buy something because "everyone else is doing it." Advertisers, for example, tell us that "Nobody doesn't like Sara Lee" or that we should "make the switch to Burger King" because everyone else (in the ads, at least) is doing just that. Countless ads have begun with the statement "All over America, people are switching to . . . using . . . buying." You are expected to do the same if you don't want to feel "out of it." The bandwagon, then, tells us that by buying a certain product we can get "on board."

Plain folks is a third propaganda method, one in which the product being sold is associated with "ordinary" people—people we can identify with. They're not glamorous types; they're just folks like you and me. When you see "regular" people, the kind that don't seem to be actors, explaining how Anacin helped their headaches, or how Bounce made their wash softer, or how much better Pepsi tasted than Coke, you are seeing the plain folks method. Advertisers know that consumers will believe people who seem down-to-earth, honest, and just like the folks next door.

A final propaganda technique is called *transfer*. In this method, the product is associated with something else that is attractive, respectable, or admirable. For example, countless advertisements for cars show gorgeous models leaning over the hood or sliding into a plush interior. The audience will transfer its feeling about the model ("I want her" or "She is beautiful") to the car ("I want it" or "It is beautiful"). Advertisers use transfer, too, when they associate their products with patriotic symbols, such as the bald eagle or the Liberty Bell. When we see an eagle flying over the land while a narrator tells us about the Westinghouse Corporation's philosophy of quality, we transfer our patriotic feelings to the company.

This, then, has been an introduction to some of the propaganda methods that advertisers use to sell their products.

Questions on the Lecture

1. What is propaganda?
2. What are four propaganda techniques used by advertisers?
3. Explain the bandwagon technique.
4. Explain the technique of transfer.

Activity 7

Follow the directions given for Activity 5.

LECTURE ON EFFECTIVE WRITING

On Board

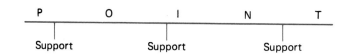

1: Make a point.
2: Support the point (BS).
3: Organize the support.
4: Write clear sentences.

Many people think that writing a good paragraph or paper is a kind of magical skill—one that some people have and others don't. When such people find that they have to do a great deal of writing themselves, either in college or on their jobs, they become angry and frustrated. Why should they have to write? After all, people aren't asked to play the piano or draw a picture if they have no training or talent. Isn't it just as unfair to be asked to write?

Probably the best-kept secret about writing is that it is a skill that can be mastered. That's right—you can learn to write a decent paper, learn to do well in writing assignments in school or on the job, no matter how much trouble you may have had with writing before. Writing consists of a series of steps that you can follow. When you finish, you should have an organized, effective paper.

The first step in writing an effective paper is to *make a point of some kind*. A point is an assertion, a statement that goes beyond a mere fact—a point has your opinion injected into it. We all make points all day long. If we could gather several points from the conversations around us, we might hear things like: "That movie was a waste of money"; "Our sociology professor is the best teacher I have ever had"; "I don't vote, because politicians are crooks"; "Going out for an evening is getting to be really expensive." Starting to write means deciding to focus on a point similar to any of these. For example, let's take a subject we all know something about: high school proms. When we were in high school, we all went to proms, or talked about people who went to proms, or stayed home from proms. We could make many points about proms; each of you would have some opinion about them. Let's take one point in particular, though. My point is that proms should be banned. If I said this to you as we were talking, I might go on to give you my reasons, or I might refuse to talk about it any more, or I might change the subject. In writing, however, once I made this point, I would have to support it.

That's the second step in writing—*supporting your point*. You saw that the first step wasn't too hard; this one isn't either. When I say support your point, I mean back it up. In other words, give reasons, details, examples, anything you can think of to make your point a convincing one. In addition, you should BS a lot. Yes, I said, BS. You must remember to BS in your writing if you want to be effective. Of course, you all know what BS stands for—"Be specific." The details that support your point should be exact, precise, particular—not vague and general. In other words, they should be specific.

Let's try to come up with some specific details to support my point about proms. Perhaps I feel proms should be banned, first of all, because they cost too much money. Now I have to develop this reason with specific details. If I write "All the things a person has to buy to go to the prom are too expensive," I have failed my readers. "Too expensive" is not specific. Instead, I might write, "Attending the prom means buying a gown for $150, a bouquet of flowers for $35, a pair of tickets at $50 apiece, and a set of photographs that can cost $100 and up." Now I'm communicating better, for I have given my readers a clear idea of exactly how much money I'm talking about. Now there's a much better chance that they will eventually agree with my opening point—or at least respect my opinion. You can see, too, that specific details are a lot more interesting and lively than general ones. If you don't want your reader to fall asleep, then remember to BS.

The third step in writing a good paper is *organizing your supporting details*. Without some method of organization, your paper will sound confused and illogical, no matter how good your details are. How do you organize the details? Basically, there are two methods: *time order* and *emphatic order*. Time order means that the details are arranged as they occur in time. For example, if you were writing about a day in your life, you might start with getting up in the morning and end with watching Jay Leno through bleary eyes. My prom paper could be organized this way; I might begin with the preparations for the prom and end with prom night itself. Of course, I would weave in my reasons for banning proms along the way. I might begin with before-prom expenses and end with after-prom drinking.

The other method of organization is, again, emphatic order. Emphatic order means saving the best, most dramatic, or most important detail for last. In other words, you build up to the best. I could decide to use emphatic order for my prom paper. I would make a scratch outline of my reasons for wanting proms banned. Then I would save for last my most important reason for wanting proms banned. For me, that reason would be the drunken driving that often seems to go along with prom night. Drunken driving is more important than prom expenses or anything else.

Finally, after you have made a point, supported it, and organized your supporting details, you have one last step. You must be sure you have written *clear, correct sentences.* This means checking for spelling, grammar, and punctuation mistakes. The importance of this step should be obvious; it won't matter how good your ideas are if no one can understand them. I can't go into detail about individual grammar skills in the time I have left. Let me just say, then, that a dictionary and English handbook are essential for this step.

Let's end with a summary. To write an effective paper, you must take the four steps you see on the board:

1: Make a point.
2: Support the point (BS).
3: Organize the support.
4: Write clear sentences.

You can definitely learn how to follow these four steps. It's a matter of practice and a matter of thinking, planning, checking, and rewriting. If you work hard, you will produce clear and effective pieces of writing. And writing is a skill that will help you immeasurably both in school and later in your career.

Questions on the Lecture

1. What are the four steps in effective writing?
2. What does BS in writing refer to?
3. What are two methods of organizing details in writing?
4. What is meant by emphatic order?

TIME CONTROL AND CONCENTRATION

This chapter will show you how to manage your time through the use of:

- A large monthly calendar
- A weekly study schedule
- A "to do" list
- A series of hints on concentration

Introductory Project

Consider this common study situation:

> Cheryl has trouble managing her study time. She claims that the only time she can make herself study is right before a test. "If I'm not in a crisis situation with a test just around the corner," she says, "I usually won't study. When I'm in the right mood, I do try to study a bit to keep things from piling up. But most of the time I'm just not in the mood. Some mornings I get up and say to myself, 'Tonight you will do at least two hours of schoolwork.' Then, 95 percent of the time, I let something distract me." Cheryl recently had to face the shortcomings of her cram study method. She found herself with only one night to prepare for two exams and a report; the result was several disastrous grades.

This chapter will provide answers to Cheryl's study problem. But take a few minutes first to examine your own ideas. What do you think are three specific steps that Cheryl could take to prevent such a situation from happening again?

All of us need free time, hours without demands and obligations, so we can just relax and do what we please. But it is easy to lose track of time and discover suddenly that there aren't enough hours to do what needs to be done. No skill is more basic to survival in college than time control. If you do not use your time well, your college career—and the life goals that depend on how well you do in college—will slip like sand through your fingers. This chapter describes three methods to help you gain control of your time: You will learn how to use a large monthly calendar, a weekly study schedule, and a daily or weekly ''to do'' list. There is also a series of hints on concentration—how to use your study time more effectively.

A LARGE MONTHLY CALENDAR

You should buy or make a large monthly calendar. Such a calendar is your first method of time control because it allows you, in one quick glance, to get a clear picture of what you need to do in the weeks to come. Be sure your monthly calendar has a good-sized block of white space for each date. Then, as soon as you learn about exam dates and paper deadlines, enter them clearly in the appropriate spots on the calendar. Hang the calendar in a place where you will see it every day, perhaps on your kitchen or bedroom wall. The monthly calendar made up by one student is shown on the following page.

Activity

In the following spaces, write the names of the courses you are taking. Also, record the dates on which papers or other assignments are due and the dates on which exams are scheduled. Due dates are often listed in a course syllabus as well as announced by a course instructor.

Courses	Paper Due Dates	Exam Dates
_____	_____	_____
_____	_____	_____
_____	_____	_____
_____	_____	_____
_____	_____	_____

October

Sun	Mon	Tues	Wed	Thurs	Fri	Sat
				1	2	3
4	5 *Soc test*	6	7	8	9 *English essay due*	10
11	12	13 *Bio field trip*	14	15 *Psych quiz*	16	17
18	19 *Speech*	20	21	22	23 *English essay due*	24
25	26 *Bio test*	27	28	29 *Business report due*	30	31

Transfer all this information to a monthly calendar.

■ Write here what you think would be the best place for you to post a monthly calendar:

_____

■ *Complete the following statement:*
A monthly calendar will keep you constantly aware of exam and paper

target days, so that you can _____

well in advance.

A WEEKLY STUDY SCHEDULE

Evaluating Your Use of Time

A weekly study schedule will make you aware of how much time you actually have each week and will help you use that time effectively. Before you prepare a weekly study schedule, however, you need to get a sense of how you spend your time *each day*. The activity that follows will help you do that.

Activity

The daily schedule of one student, Rich, follows. Rich has three classes. Assuming that every hour of class time should receive at least one hour of study time, how could Rich revise his schedule so that he would have at least three full study hours in addition to time for "rest and relaxation"? Make your suggested changes by crossing out items and adding study time to his schedule. Your instructor may then have you compare answers with those of others in the class.

Rich's Daily Schedule	
Time	Activity
6:30–7:30	Get up, wash, eat
7:30–8	Travel to school
8–9	Class (English)
9–10	Read newspaper in the library
10–11	Class (General Psychology)
11–1	Cafeteria for lunch
1–2	Class (biology)
2–2:30	Video games in game room
2:30–3	Drive to work
3–6	Work at A & P
6–7:30	Travel home, eat supper, read paper
7:30–9	Nap, telephone, English homework
9–11:30	TV
11:30	Bed

Next, use the chart that follows to record a *typical* school day in your life. Be honest: You want to see clearly what you are doing so that you will be able to plan ways to use your time more effectively.

Time	Activity

Now, honestly evaluate your use of time. Write in the number of hours you *actually* used for study in your typical day: _____ hours. Next, go back to your chart and block off time in the day that you *could* have used for study. (Remember to still allow for "rest and relaxation" time, which is also needed.) Write in the number of hours you could have used for study in the day: _____ hours.

Note: People sometimes learn from their schedules that they are victims of a time overload, for they have taken too much work on themselves with too little time to do it. If you think this is your case, you should talk with your instructor or a counselor about possibly dropping one or more courses.

Rich's Weekly Schedule

	Mon.	Tues.	Wed.	Thurs.	Fri.	Sat.	Sun.	
6:00 A.M.								6:00 A.M.
7:00	B		B		B			7:00
8:00	Eng	B	Eng		Eng	B		8:00
9:00				B			B	9:00
10:00	Psych	Phys Ed	Psych		Psych	Job		10:00
11:00		↓						11:00
12:00	L	L		L	L			12:00
1:00 P.M.	Bio	Lab	Bio		Bio		L	1:00 P.M.
2:00		↓						2:00
3:00		↓	Job		Job			3:00
4:00			↓		↓			4:00
5:00	S	S	↓	S		↓	S	5:00
6:00			S			S		6:00
7:00	Speech			Soc	↓			7:00
8:00	↓			↓	S			8:00
9:00	↓			↓				9:00
10:00								10:00
11:00								11:00
12:00	Bed	Bed	Bed	Bed			Bed	12:00
1:00 A.M.								1:00 A.M.
2:00	④	④	③	⑤	②	⓪	⑤	2:00

B = Breakfast   ■ = Study blocks   Psych = Psychology   Eng = English
L = Lunch   ○ = Study hours per day   Soc = Sociology   Phys Ed = Physical Education
S = Supper   Blanks = Free time   Bio = Biology

Important Points about a Weekly Study Schedule

You are now ready to look over the master weekly schedule, shown on the opposite page, that Rich prepared to gain control of his time. You should then read carefully the points that follow; all are important in planning an effective weekly schedule. Note that you will be asked to refer to Rich's schedule to answer questions that accompany some of the points.

Point 1: Plan, at first, at least one hour of study time for each hour of class time.   Depending on the course, the grade you want, and your own study efficiency, you may have to schedule more time later. A difficult course, for example, may require three hours or more of study time for each course hour. Remember that learning is what counts, not the time it takes you to learn. Be prepared to schedule as much time as you need to gain control of a course.

■   How many class hours, excluding lab and phys ed, does Rich have? _____

■   How many study hours has he scheduled? _____

Point 2: Schedule regular study time.   To succeed in your college work, you need to establish definite study hours. If you do not set aside and stick to such hours on a daily or almost daily basis, you are probably going to fail at time control. Jot down in the following spaces the free hours each day that you would use as regular study time. The first column shows Rich's free hours on Monday.

For Rich	*Your Possible Study Hours*						
Mon.	Mon.	Tues.	Wed.	Thurs.	Fri.	Sat.	Sun.
9–10	_____	_____	_____	_____	_____	_____	_____
11–12	_____	_____	_____	_____	_____	_____	_____
2–4	_____	_____	_____	_____	_____	_____	_____

There are many benefits to setting aside regular study hours. First of all, they help make studying a habit. Study times will be as automatically programmed into your daily schedule as, say, watching a favorite television program. You will not have to remind yourself to study, nor will you waste large amounts of time and energy trying to avoid studying; you will simply do it. Another value of regular study time is that you will be better able to stay up to date on work in your courses. You are not likely to find yourself several days before a test with three textbook chapters to read or five weeks of classroom notes to organize and study. Finally, regular study takes advantage of the proven fact that a series of study sessions is more effective than a single long ''cram'' session.

- How many separate blocks of study time has Rich built into his weekly schedule? _____

- How many benefits of regular study hours are described in the preceding paragraph? (*Hint:* Word signals such as "First of all" are clues to each separate value.) _____

Point 3: Plan at least one-hour blocks of study time.   If you schedule less than one hour, your study period may be over just when you are fully warmed up and working hard.

- What is the largest single block of study time that Rich has during the week? (Write down the day and the number of hours.)

  _____

- What is the largest single block of study time available to you each week?

  _____

Point 4: Reward yourself for using study time effectively.   Research shows that people work better if they get an immediate reward for their efforts. So if your schedule permits, try to set up a reward system. Allow yourself to telephone a friend or watch a television show or eat a snack after a period of efficient study. On Rich's schedule, for example, nine to ten o'clock on Tuesday night is free for watching television as a reward for working well in the two-hour study slot before. When you are studying over a several-hour period, you can also give yourself "mini-rewards" of five to ten minutes of free time for every hour or so of study time.

Your reward system won't work if you "cheat," so deprive yourself of such pleasures as television shows when you have not studied honestly.

- Locate the other spots where Rich has built reward time into his schedule after study periods and indicate the hours here: _____

  _____

- Do you think it is a good idea for Rich to reward himself with one day in the week (Saturday) free from study? Why or why not? _____

  _____

Point 5: Try to schedule study periods before and after classes. Ideally, you should read a textbook chapter before a teacher covers it; what you hear in class will then be a "second exposure," so the ideas are likely to be a good deal more meaningful to you. You should also look over your notes from the preceding class in case the teacher discusses the material further. Similarly, if you take a few minutes to review your notes as soon after class as possible, you will be able to organize and clarify the material while it is still fresh in your mind.

■ If a new textbook chapter is to be covered in Rich's sociology class on

Thursday, where in his schedule should he plan to read it? _____

Point 6: Work on your most difficult subjects when you are most alert. Save routine work for times you are most likely to be tired. You might, for example, study a new and difficult mathematics chapter at 8 P.M. if you are naturally alert then and review vocabulary words for a Spanish class at 11 P.M., when you may be a little tired.

■ Assuming that Rich is most naturally alert early in the day and that biology is his most difficult subject, in what time slots should he schedule his work

on that subject? _____

■ At what time of day do you consider yourself most alert? _____

Point 7: Balance your activities. Allow free time for family, friends, sports, television, and so on in your schedule. Note that there is a good deal of free time (empty space) in Rich's schedule, even with his classes, work, and study hours.

■ Where is the biggest block of free time in Rich's schedule? _____

■ Where do *you* plan to have a substantial block of free time? _____

Point 8: Keep your schedule flexible. When unexpected events occur, trade times on your weekly timetable. Do not simply do away with study hours. If you find that your schedule requires constant adjustment, revise it. (Your instructor may be able to give you extra copies of the following schedule.) After two or three revisions, you will have a realistic, practical weekly schedule that you can follow honestly.

■ If Rich went to a family reunion on Sunday at 1 P.M. and didn't get back until eight o'clock that evening, where in his schedule could he make up the

missed hour of study time? _____

Your Weekly Schedule

	Mon.	Tues.	Wed.	Thurs.	Fri.	Sat.	Sun.	
6:00 A.M.								6:00 A.M.
7:00								7:00
8:00								8:00
9:00								9:00
10:00								10:00
11:00								11:00
12:00								12:00
1:00 P.M.								1:00 P.M.
2:00								2:00
3:00								3:00
4:00								4:00
5:00								5:00
6:00								6:00
7:00								7:00
8:00								8:00
9:00								9:00
10:00								10:00
11:00								11:00
12:00								12:00
1:00 A.M.								1:00 A.M.
2:00								2:00

Activity

Keeping the preceding points in mind, use the form on the opposite page to make up your own realistic weekly study schedule. Write in your class and lab periods first; next, add in your hours for job and meals; and then fill in the study hours that you need to do well in your courses. At the bottom of your schedule, make up a key that explains the symbols you have used in the schedule. Also, add up and circle the total number of study hours you realistically plan to set aside each day.

A DAILY OR WEEKLY "TO DO" LIST

How to Make a "To Do" List

A "to do" list is simply a list of things a person wants to accomplish within a limited period. Many successful people make the "to do" list a habit, considering it an essential step in making the most efficient use of their time each day. A "to do" list, made up daily or weekly, may be one of the most important single study habits you will ever acquire.

Rich's "To Do" List

To Do   *Monday*

1. Proofread English paper before class
2. Read Chap. 4 of psychology text
3. Memorize study notes for bio. test on Wednesday
4. Coordinate class bio. notes with Chap. 3 of the text
5. Buy jeans during sale at K-Mart
6. Rehearse 2-minute speech for tonight's class
7. Fix slipcovers on car
8. Wash car
9. Borrow Billy Joel albums from Al
10. Call Sue sometime
11. Borrow + copy notes from psych. class missed last week
12. Monday night football!
13. Review bio. notes 1/2 hour before bed

Important Notes about the "To Do" List

Point 1: Carry the list with you throughout the day. A small notebook can be kept in a purse, and a four- by six-inch slip of paper in a pocket or wallet.

Point 2: Decide on priorities. Making the best use of your time means focusing on top-priority items rather than spending hours on low-priority activities. When in doubt about what to do at any time in the day, ask yourself, "How can I best use my time at this point?" and choose a high-priority item on your list.

■ Look at Rich's list and label each of the items *A, B,* or *C* to indicate what you think is a reasonable priority level for it.

Point 3: Cross out items as you finish them. Don't worry unnecessarily about completing your list; what is not done can usually be moved to the next day's list. What is important is that you make the best possible use of your time each day. Focus on top-priority activities!

Activity

Use this space to make up your own "to do" list for tomorrow. If you cannot think of at least seven items, then put down as well things that you want to do over the rest of the week. Label each item as *A, B,* or *C* in priority.

Your "To Do" List

To Do

CONCENTRATION

A monthly calendar, a weekly study schedule, and a "to do" list are essential methods of organizing your study time. Unfortunately, all your effort in creating them is useless if you waste the study time you have set aside. Unless you master the art of *concentrating* on your work, you will learn very little.

Is concentrating difficult? The answer is both *yes* and *no*. The skill of concentration somewhat resembles a beating heart: When it works, we take it for granted and are hardly aware of it; any malfunction, however, is painfully obvious. For example, you probably find it very easy to concentrate on something you are extremely interested in—a television show, a certain magazine, an elaborate meal you are preparing for friends. But concentration may seem impossible when you are studying a biology chapter or mathematics problems.

- Name an activity on which you can easily concentrate: _____
- Name an activity on which you can concentrate only with great difficulty:

  _____

Why People Can't Concentrate

Why is it often so difficult to concentrate on studying? There are several reasons; one or more of them may apply to you.

You equate studying with punishment.   If you have a history of doing poorly in school, or if you have often received poor grades even though you tried to study, you will naturally have a negative reaction every time you sit down with your books. After all, you may think, the work is hard and probably not worthwhile. You are conditioned to see studying as torture. All your negative experiences have created a study block that hinders your ability to concentrate.

- Do you think you have a block about studying because of past school experiences? _____
- If so, are you ready to break through your block by applying the study skills in this book? _____

You put everything off until the last minute.   The Procrastinators Club holds its Christmas party in February. However, putting off your studies until the last minute is not as harmless and amusing as the Procrastinators' social schedule. Trying to study ten hours for an exam tomorrow or starting at nine o'clock in the morning to write a paper that is due by three o'clock in the afternoon is like trying to work with a gun at your head: concentration is difficult at best.

- Are you a procrastinator? _____

- If so, what do you do to avoid studying? _____

- Does procrastination make you feel anxious and guilty, as it does for most people? _____

You don't feel comfortable or settled.   You're dying of thirst. The chair you're sitting in is sending shooting pains up your spine. Your head is pounding or your eyes are drooping. Your body feels so exhausted that it seems impossible to remain upright any longer. At the same time, dozens of other thoughts may crowd into your mind: next weekend's trip, the argument you had with your mother, the dirty laundry piling up in your closet. Such physical and mental distractions will soon overwhelm any amount of concentration you may have been able to achieve.

- Of the three reasons for not concentrating just listed, which one applies most in your case? _____

Ways to Concentrate

When you can't concentrate, you can take either of two courses. You can give in to defeat by rationalizing your failures. You can tell yourself, for example, that ''nobody could understand this textbook'' or ''I hate this course anyway and I don't care if I fail'' or ''I don't know why I'm in school'' or ''I'll really concentrate next time.'' The better route to take is to decide that you will do everything you can to aid concentration. Here are practical hints that will help you fix your attention on the studying you have to do.

Hint 1: Work on having a positive attitude.   It is a rare student who has a deep interest in every one of his or her college courses. Most students find that at least some of the studying they have to do involves uninteresting material. In such cases, it is essential to examine your priorities and goals. Don't let some less-than-stimulating courses block your route to the college degree you want. Decide that you will do the studying because, someday, the course will be forgotten, but your college education and degree will be benefiting your life.

- What are the most unpleasant study tasks you will have this semester?

  _____

- Is your college degree important enough for you to do these unpleasant tasks? _____

Hint 2: Prepare to work by setting specific study goals. Don't stare at a foot-high pile of thick textbooks and wonder how you'll ever make it through the semester. Instead, go over your assignments and jot down a list of practical goals for the period of study time you have available. These will be the study items on your day's "to do" list. This technique helps you get organized; it also breaks your large study task into manageable units that you can accomplish one at a time. Here are typical study items from a student's daily "to do" list:

> *Answer review questions in Chapter 3 of business text.*
> *Do twenty minutes of freewriting for English class.*
> *Read Chapter 4 in psychology text.*
> *Complete ten mathematics problems.*

You may want to work first on the assignments that seem easiest, or least painful, to you. It's a good feeling to cross something off your list; knowing you've finished at least *one* thing can often give you the confidence you need to continue.

■   Jot down four specific assignments you must complete in the next school week.

_____

_____

_____

Hint 3: Keep track of your lapses of concentration. When you start studying, jot down the time (for example, "7:15") at the bottom of your "to do" list of study items. When you find yourself losing interest or thinking about something else, put the time (for example, "7:35") on that same piece of paper. Catching yourself like this can help train your mind to concentrate for longer and longer periods. You should soon find that you can study for a longer span of time before the first notation appears. The notations, too, should become fewer and fewer.

■   Record the time here whenever you have a lapse in concentration while reading the rest of this chapter.

_____

Hint 4: Create a good study environment. Choose a room that is, first of all, quiet and well lighted. To avoid glare, make sure that light comes from above or over your shoulder, not from in front of you. Also, you should have more than one light source in the room. For example, you might use a ceiling light in addition to a pole lamp behind your chair.

- Do you think that the place where you study is well lighted? _____
- If not, what might you do to improve the lighting? _____
  _____

Second, you should have a comfortable place to sit. Do not try to study in a completely relaxed position. A light muscular tension promotes the concentration needed for study. So sit on an upright chair or sit in a cross-legged position on your bed with a pillow behind you. Keep in mind, also, that you do not have to study while sitting down. Many students stay alert and focused by walking back and forth across the room as they test themselves on material they must learn.

- What is your usual position when you study? _____
  _____

- Are your muscles slightly tense in this position, or are they completely relaxed? _____

Make sure you have all the materials you will need: ballpoint pens, highlighter pens, pencils, loose-leaf or typing paper, and a small memo pad. Ideally (though not essentially), you should have a typewriter and a calculator as well.

Finally, to avoid interruptions in your study place, ask your family and friends to please keep away during study hours. Tell them that you will return telephone calls after you finish studying. Preparing a good environment in advance ensures that when you do achieve concentration, nothing will interrupt you.

If you do not have a room where you can study, use a secluded spot in the library or student center, or find some other quiet spot. If you have one particular place where you usually do most of your studying, you will almost automatically shift into gear and begin studying when you go to that place.

Hint 5: Stay in good physical condition. You do not want to tire easily or have frequent illnesses. Eat nourishing meals, starting with breakfast—your most important meal of the day. For some students, breakfast is simply coffee and doughnuts or a soda and cookies from a vending machine. But a solid breakfast is not merely a combination of caffeine and sugar. It is, instead, protein, as in milk, yogurt, or a whole-grain cereal. Protein will supply the steady flow of blood sugar needed to keep you mentally alert through the entire day.

Try to get an average of eight hours of sleep a night unless your system can manage with less. Also, try to exercise on a regular basis. A short workout in the morning (if only five minutes of running in place) will help sustain your energy flow during the day. Finally, do not hesitate to take a fifteen- to thirty-minute nap at some point during the day. Research findings show that such a nap can provide a helpful energy boost.

- What is your typical breakfast? How could you realistically improve it?

  _____

- What other steps do you take—or should you take—to stay in good physical condition? _____

Hint 6: Vary your study activities. Study sessions need not be four-hour marathons devoted to one subject. When you cannot concentrate anymore, don't waste time staring unproductively at, say, a mathematics problem. Switch over to your English paper or biology report. The change in subject matter and type of assignment can ease mental strain by stimulating a different part of your brain—verbal ability, for instance—while the other part (mathematical ability) rests. By varying your activities, you will stay fresh and alert longer than you would if you hammered away at one subject for hours.

Hint 7: Practice the study skills in this book. Many students can't concentrate on their studies because they don't know _how_ to study. They look at the brief notes they took during a class lecture and wonder what to do with them. They start reading a textbook as casually as if they were reading the sports page of the newspaper, and then they wonder why they get so little out of it. They have perhaps been told that taking good notes and then reciting those notes are keys to effective study, but they are not sure how to apply these skills. Learning and practicing study skills will help you become deeply involved in your assignments. Before you know it, you are concentrating.

Of all the study skills in this book, which are the three most important for

you to practice? _____   _____   _____

Hint 8: Use outside help when needed. Some people find that studying with a friend or friends helps concentration. Others, however, find it more of a distraction than an aid because they spend more time chatting than studying cooperatively. Use the technique of team study only if you think it will be of real value to you. Also, find out if your school has a tutoring service. If so, do not hesitate to use the service to get help in a particular subject or subjects. Having a good tutor could make a significant difference in your grade for a course. And determine if your school, like many, has a learning center where you may work on developing writing, reading, study, and mathematics skills. Finally, learn the office hours of your professors and find out whether you can see them if you need additional help.

- Does your school have a tutoring service? _____
- Does your school have a learning center? _____
- If so, where is each located? _____

SOME FINAL THOUGHTS

You now have several practical means of gaining control of your time: a monthly calendar, a master study schedule, and a "to do" list. In addition, you have learned useful hints for aiding concentration. Use whatever combination of the techniques is best for you. These tools, combined with your own determination to apply them, can reduce the disorder of everyday life, where time slips quickly and silently away. Through time planning, you can achieve the consistency in your work that is absolutely vital for success in school. And through time control and steady concentration, you can take command of your life and accomplish more work than you have ever done before.

PRACTICE IN TIME CONTROL AND CONCENTRATION

Activity 1

Several time control skills and study and concentration habits are listed below. Evaluate yourself by putting a check mark beside each of the skills or habits that you already practice. Then put a check mark beside those steps that you plan to practice. Leave a space blank if you do not plan to follow a particular strategy.

Now Plan
Do to Do

____ ____ ■ Use a large monthly calendar.

____ ____ ■ Use a weekly study schedule.

____ ____ ■ Use a daily or weekly "to do" list.

____ ____ ■ Have regular study hours.

____ ____ ■ Schedule as many hours as needed for a particular course.

____ ____ ■ Have rewards for using study time effectively.

____ ____ ■ Work on difficult subjects at times when you are most alert.

____ ____ ■ Balance activities.

____ ____ ■ Try to have a positive attitude about all courses.

____ ____ ■ Set goals before starting work.

____ ____ ■ Create a good study environment (comfortable but nondistracting).

____ ____ ■ Stay in good physical condition.

____ ____ ■ Vary your study activities.

____ ____ ■ Use outside help when needed.

Activity 2

Several weeks into the semester, your instructor will ask you to hand in copies of the following:

- One month from your monthly calendar
- Your weekly study schedule
- Your most recent daily or weekly ''to do'' list

Do not simply pass in copies of the materials you have prepared while doing this chapter; instead, pass in recent and updated materials. And be honest: If you are not using one or more of these methods of time control, don't pretend you are. Instead, write a short essay explaining why you have decided not to use one or more of the time-control methods in this chapter.

Activity 3

Write a short paper about some aspect of concentration skills. Here are some suggestions.

- Write a paragraph describing the reasons you may not have concentrated effectively in the past. For example, you might have had a poor attitude; you might have procrastinated a great deal; you might have lacked certain study skills; you might have had a poor study environment. Use specific details to give a clear picture of your previous study habits.
- Write a narrative paragraph about your last study session. Be specific about how well *or* how poorly you concentrated and why.
- Write a paragraph detailing three specific changes you are planning to make in the place where you study.
- Write a paragraph on the mistakes the students you see around you make when they study. Note, for example, where you see students studying; the conditions under which they are trying to study; how they are going about studying; and so on.

THE PRWR
STUDY METHOD

This chapter will show you how to study a textbook chapter by:

- Previewing the chapter
- Reading the chapter
- Taking notes on the chapter
- Studying your notes

Introductory Project

Consider this common study situation:

> For tomorrow's test in his Introduction to Business course, Gary has to know three chapters from the textbook. At 1:30 P.M. yesterday, he sat down with a yellow marking pen and started reading the first chapter. At 3 P.M. he wasn't even halfway through the first chapter, and he felt bored and worn out. The sentences were long and heavy and loaded with details. Gary's head became so packed with information that as soon as he read a new fact, it seemed to automatically push out the one before it. When he looked back at what he had covered, he realized he had set off most of the text in yellow. Gary decided then to stop marking and just read. But the more he read, the sleepier he got, and the more his mind kept wandering. He kept thinking about all the things he wanted to do once the test was over. At 5:15 P.M. he had finished reading the first chapter, but he felt completely defeated. He still had to study the chapter, and he had no idea exactly what to study. On top of that, he had to plow through two more chapters and study them as well. He felt desperate and stupid—because he had waited so long to start with the text and because he was having such a hard time reading it.

This and the following two chapters will provide solutions for Gary's study problem. But take a few minutes first to examine your own ideas. What do you think are three specific steps Gary could take to read and study his textbook effectively?

USING YOUR TEXTBOOK: A CAUTION

To begin this chapter on textbook study, let me share an experience with you. When I first began teaching, I was still studying for my advanced degree in reading at a nearby state college. I remember especially a class in statistics I had every Monday night. I would travel to the college after a long day of teaching. I'd be exhausted, and I'd have to sit through a class that was hardly my favorite subject. There was a textbook, but I didn't understand much of it. I remember looking through it when I bought it and thinking, "Good grief! How in the world am I going to survive this?"

As it turned out, the teacher didn't require us to do anything with the textbook. I wasn't too surprised at that, because in many of my undergraduate courses, although we had to buy a textbook, most of the learning actually took place in the classroom. The teachers' attitude seemed to be, "Here is the textbook as a resource. But I'm going to present to you in class the most important ideas."

My statistics teacher did a lot of presenting in class. I remember sitting next to another student whose name was John also. We were a study in contrasts: he was very active in class, constantly asking questions and volunteering answers. In fact, he was so active that he didn't take many notes except to write down what the teacher put on the board. I said very little because I was so tired and neither my heart nor head was in the subject. I did little but sit there and take lots of notes. I wrote down not just everything the teacher put on the board but also the connections between those ideas. As the teacher explained things, I didn't just listen; I wrote it all down. My attitude was, "I can't understand any of this stuff now, but later—when I don't feel turned off and brain dead—I'll be able to go through it and try to make sense of it."

When I began to prepare for my mid-semester exam, I was surprised to see that I had written some ideas down three or even four times. The teacher had repeated them, and I, getting everything down on paper, had repeated them as well. I had so many notes that I was able to make sense of the material. The teacher had done his job: he had used class time to help us understand a difficult subject. His explanations were very clear, and I had gotten them all down on paper. All I needed to study for that exam was right there in my notes. I didn't even open the textbook.

Do you want to guess who got the higher score in the mid-semester exam—the other John or me? I got an 86; the other John got a 74. He saw my paper and felt, I think, a little chagrined. If he had asked me my secret, I would have said, "Take lots of notes."

The point of my story is this: *Don't underestimate the importance of taking class notes in doing well in a course.* If the truth be told, in a number of courses, good class notes will be enough to earn you a decent grade. In many courses, the textbook is only a secondary source of information for the ideas you need to know on exams.

Some students fail to take many notes in class because they think, "I'll get what else I need by reading the textbook." Whatever you do, don't make that mistake. An idea you can get down in five minutes in class might take you two hours to get out of a textbook—if it's there at all! Learn how to use the textbook, but don't *ever* make the mistake of trying to use it as a substitute for classroom note-taking.

- In a chapter on textbook study, do you think so much space should be devoted to a story about classroom note-taking? _____

PRWR: A TEXTBOOK STUDY METHOD

To become a better reader—of textbook or any other material—you should systematically develop a whole series of important reading skills, presented in Part Four. This chapter will give you a plan of attack for dealing with a textbook assignment. It explains four steps needed for studying a chapter. The two chapters that follow give you practice in applying these four steps.

The four-step study method is known as PRWR, and variations of it (the most familiar is known as SQ3R) are taught by many reading instructors. The letters stand for the four steps in the process: (1) Preview, (2) Read, (3) Write, and (4) Recite.

Step 1: Preview

A *preview* is a rapid survey that gives you a bird's-eye view of what you are reading. It involves taking several minutes to look through an entire chapter before you begin reading it closely.

Here is how to preview a selection:

- Study the *title*. The title gives you in a few words the shortest possible summary of the whole chapter. Without reading a line of text, you can learn in a general way what the material is about. For example, if the assigned chapter in a psychology text is titled "Stress and Coping with Stress," you know that everything in the chapter is going to concern stress and how to deal with it.
- Quickly read over the *first and last several paragraphs*. These paragraphs may introduce and summarize some of the main ideas covered in the chapter.
- Then page through the chapter and look at the different levels of *headings*. Are there two levels of headings? Three levels? More? Are any relationships obvious among these headings? (For more detail on this, see "Recognizing Headings and Subheadings" in Part Four of this book.)

- Look briefly at words marked in **boldface** and *italics* and in color; such words may be set off because they are important terms. (For more on this, see "Recognizing Definitions and Examples" in Part Four.)
- Glance at *pictures, charts, and boxed material* in the chapter.

Many students have never been taught to preview. They plunge right into a chapter rather than taking a minute or two to do a survey. But remember that it can help to get the "lay of the land" before beginning to read.

Activity 1

Answer the following questions.

1. Were you taught to preview as part of your reading instruction in school? _____
2. Do you think that previewing seems like a good idea? _____
3. What part of the preview do you think might be most helpful for you?

_____

Activity 2

Take about two minutes to preview the following textbook selection; then answer the questions that follow it.

ALTERNATIVES TO CONFLICT

The conflict process may operate at so great a cost that people often seek to avoid it. Conflict is often avoided through some form of three other processes: *accommodation, assimilation,* and *amalgamation.*

Accommodation

It threw me when my folks got a divorce right after I graduated. I guess I took them for granted. Our home always seemed to me about like most others. At graduation, Dad took me aside and said that he and Mom were calling it quits. He said that they had bugged each other for years, but now that I would be on my own, they were going to separate.

The above story, adapted from a student's life history, is an example of accommodation, a process of developing temporary working agreements between conflicting individuals or groups. It develops when persons or groups find it necessary to work together despite their hostilities and differences. In accommodations, no real settlement of issues is reached; each group retains its own goals and viewpoints but arrives at an "agreement to disagree" without fighting. Two forms of accommodation are described below.

Displacement: Displacement is the process of suspending one conflict by replacing it with another. A classic example is the threat of war to end internal conflicts and bring national unity.

Finding a scapegoat is a favorite displacement technique. The term refers to an ancient Hebrew ceremony in which the sins of the people were symbolically heaped upon a goat which was driven into the wilderness. Unpopular minorities often become scapegoats. For example, in newly independent countries, all problems may be blamed upon the remaining "colonial influences."

Toleration: In some conflicts, victory is impossible and compromise undesirable. Toleration is an agreement to disagree peaceably. Religious conflict is a classic example of this situation. In Europe at the time of the Reformation, both Protestants and Catholics were positive that they had the "true" version of the Christian faith. Neither group was willing to compromise, and in spite of severe conflict, neither group could destroy the other. Adjustment was made on the basis of toleration; each church ceased to persecute other churches while continuing to hold that these other churches were in error.

Assimilation

Whenever groups meet, some mutual interchange or diffusion of culture takes place. This two-way process by which persons and groups come to share a common culture is called assimilation. Assimilation reduces group conflicts by blending different groups into larger, culturally homogeneous groups. The bitter riots against the Irish and the discrimination against the Scandinavians in the United States disappeared as assimilation erased the group differences and blurred the sense of separate group identity.

Amalgamation

Amalgamation is the biological interbreeding of two groups until they become one. For instance, wholesale amalgamation ended the conflicts of the Anglo-Saxons with the Norman invaders of England. An incomplete amalgamation, however, generally creates a status- and conflict-filled system where status is measured by blood "purity" as in Central America and parts of South America.

1. What is the selection about? (This question can be answered by studying the title.) _____

2. What are the three alternatives to conflict? (This question can be answered by looking at the relationship between the title and the main headings.)

   a. _____ b. _____ c. _____

3. What are the two forms of accommodation? (This question can be answered by looking at the relationship between the heading "Accommodation" and the two subheadings under it.)

   a. _____ b. _____

The purpose of this activity is probably clear to you: Often a preview alone can help you key in on important ideas in a selection.

Step 2: Read

Read the chapter straight through. In this first reading, don't worry about understanding everything. There will be so much new information that it will be impossible to really comprehend it all right away. You just want to get a good initial sense of the chapter. If you hit snags—parts that you don't understand at all—just keep reading. After you have gotten an overall impression of the chapter by reading everything once, you can go back to reread parts that you did not at first understand.

Read the chapter with a pen in hand. Look for and mark off what seem to be important ideas and details. In particular, mark off the following:

- *Definitions* of terms—underline definitions
- *Examples* of those definitions—put an *Ex* in the margin
- Items in major *lists* (also called *enumerations*)—number the items *1, 2, 3,* and so on.
- What seems to be other *important ideas*—use a star or *Imp* in the margin.

(For more detail, see the chapters in Part Four on recognizing definitions and examples, enumerations, and main ideas.)

Notes about Marking: The purpose of marking is to set off points so that you can easily return to them later when you take study notes. Material can be marked with a pen or pencil, or it can be highlighted with a felt-tip pen.

Here is a list of useful marking symbols:

Symbol	Explanation
_____	Set off a definition by underlining it.
Ex	Set off helpful examples by writing *Ex* in the margin. Do not underline examples.
1, 2, 3	Use numbers to mark enumerations (items in a list).
☆ *Imp*	Use a star or *Imp* to set off important ideas.
│	Put a vertical line in the margin to set off important material that is several lines in length. Do not underline these longer sections because the page will end up being so cluttered that you'll find it difficult to make any sense of the markings.
√	Use a check to mark off any item that *may* be important.
?	Use a question mark to show material you do not understand and may need to reread later.

Marking should be a *selective* process. Some students make the mistake of marking almost everything. You have probably seen textbooks, for example, in which almost every line has been highlighted. But setting off too much material is no better than setting off too little.

Activity 1

Answer the following questions.

1. Why should you mark off definitions, examples, and enumerations when reading? _____

   _____

2. Why do you think you should *not* underline examples? _____

   _____

Activity 2

Go back and read and mark the textbook selection you previewed in Activity 2 on page 89. Remember to be selective. Mark only the most important points: definitions, key examples, enumerations, and what seem to be other important ideas.

Step 3: Write

I can still remember the time when I really learned how to study. I was taking an introductory history course. For our first test, we were responsible for three chapters in the textbook plus an abundance of classroom notes. I spent about two hours reading the first chapter—about thirty pages—and then I started to "study." My "studying" consisted of rereading a page and then looking away and reciting it to myself. After a half hour or so, I was still on the first page! "This is not going to work," I muttered. "I need a faster way to do this."

Here's what I did. I went through the first chapter, rereading and thinking about the material and making decisions about what were the most important points. I then wrote those points down on separate sheets of paper. In a nutshell, I went through a large amount of information and reduced it to the most important points. The very act of deciding what was most important and writing that material down was a valuable step in understanding the material. It took me a couple of hours to prepare my study sheets. Then I was able to close the book and just concentrate on studying those sheets.

I used that study technique successfully through college and graduate school. And when I began my own professional work in reading and study skills, I discovered that almost all successful students use some variation of the same basic strategy.

The third step, then, is to *write*. On the opposite page are specific directions for taking good notes:

What to Write

1 Write the *title* of the chapter at the top of your first sheet of paper. Then write down each *heading* in the chapter. Under each heading, take notes on what seem to be the important points.

2 Rewrite headings as *basic questions* to help you locate important points. For example, if a heading is "One-Parent Families," you might convert it to the question, "How many one-parent families are there?" Then write down the answer to that question if it appears in the text. If a heading is "Choosing a Mate," you could ask "How do we choose a mate?" and write down the answer to that question.

3 Look for *definitions of key terms,* usually set off in color, or **boldface,** or *italics.* Write down each term and its definition.

4 Look for *examples* of definitions. The examples will help make those definitions clear and understandable. Write down one good, clear example for each definition.

5 Look for *major items in a list* (enumerations). Write them down and number them *1, 2, 3,* and so on. For example, suppose the heading "Agents of Socialization" in a textbook is followed by four subheads, "The Family," "Peers," "School," and "The Mass Media." Write down the heading. Then write the four subheads under it and number them *1, 2, 3,* and *4.*

6 Remember that your goal is to take a large amount of information in a chapter and reduce it down to the most important points. Try not to take too many notes. Instead, use headings, definitions, examples, and enumerations in the chapter to help you focus on what is most important.

How to Write

1 Write your notes on letter-sized sheets of paper (8½ by 11 inches). By using such paper (rather than smaller note cards), you will be able to see *relationships* among ideas more easily, because more ideas will fit on a single page.

2 Make sure your handwriting is clear and easy to read. Later, when you study your notes, you don't want to have to spend time trying to decipher them.

3 Leave space in the left-hand and top margin of your study sheet so that you can write down key words to help you study the material. Key words will be described on page 96 of this chapter.

4 Don't overuse outlining symbols when you take notes. To show enumerations, use a simple sequence of numbers (1, 2, 3, and so on) or letters (a, b, c, and so on). Often, indenting a line or skipping a space is enough to help show relationships among parts of the material. Notice, for example, that very few outlining symbols are used in the sample study sheet on page 95, yet the organization is very clear.

5   Summarize material whenever possible. In other words, reduce it to the fewest words possible while still keeping the ideas complete and clear. For instance, in the sample study sheet, the example for "accommodation" has been summarized so that it reads simply, "Parents agree to wait until child graduates before separating."

Activity 1

Answer the following questions.

1.   When you are taking notes on a chapter, how many of the headings in the chapter should you write down? _____

    _____

2.   What are enumerations? _____

    _____

    _____

3.   In "What to Write" on page 93, what do you consider the three most helpful guidelines?

    a. _____

        _____

    b. _____

        _____

    c. _____

        _____

4.   In "How to Write" on page 93, what do you consider the three most helpful tips?

    a. _____

        _____

    b. _____

        _____

    c. _____

        _____

Activity 2

A sample study sheet for the selection "Alternatives to Conflict" appears on the opposite page. Refer to the selection (on pages 89–90) to fill in the notes that are missing.

Sociology, Chapter 14: "Social Processes"

Three Alternatives to Conflict
1. Accommodation—a process of developing temporary
   working agreements between conflicting individuals
   or groups.
       Ex.—Parents agree to wait until child graduates
       before separating

   Two forms of accommodation:
   a. Displacement—process of suspending one conflict by
      replacing it with another.
      Ex.—

   Favorite displacement technique: find a scapegoat.
       Ex.—blame problems of new nation on "colonial
       influences."

   b. Toleration—agreement to disagree peaceably.
       Ex.—Protestants and Catholics during
       Reformation came to tolerate rather than
       persecute each other.
2. Assimilation—

       Ex.—riots against Irish in the United States ceased
       as they were assimilated.

3. Amalgamation—

       Ex.—Anglo-Saxon and Norman invaders of
       England became one, ending conflicts.

Step 4: Recite

Let's review what you need to do to study a textbook chapter. First you *preview* the chapter. Then you *read* it through once, marking off what appear to be important ideas. Third, you reread it, decide on the important ideas, and *write* study notes. Fourth, you need to learn your notes. How can you do this?

To learn your notes, you *recite* the material to yourself. Using key words and phrases—also known as *recall words*—will help you do this. Write the recall words in the margins of your notes. For example, look at the recall words in the margin of the following notes:

3 alternatives to conflict	*Three Alternatives to Conflict*
	1. Accommodation—a process of developing
Def + ex of accommodation	*temporary working agreements between conflicting*
	individuals or groups.
	Ex.—Parents agree to wait until child graduates
	before separating.
2 forms of accommodation	*Two forms of accommodation:*

After you have written the recall words, use them to study your notes. To do so, turn each recall word into a question and go over the material until you can answer the question without looking at the page. For example, look at the recall words "3 alternatives to conflict" and see if you can recite those three alternatives to yourself without looking at the material. You'll find out immediately whether or not you know the material. Go back and reread the items if necessary. Then look away again and try once more to recite the material. Next, look at "Def + ex of accommodation" and see if you can say the definition and give an example of accommodation without looking at the page.

After you finish a section, go back and review previous sections. For instance, after you can recite to yourself the definition and example of accommodation, go back and make sure you can also recite the three alternatives to conflict. Continue like this—studying, reciting, and reviewing—as you move through all the material.

You will discover that recitation helps you pay attention. There is simply no way you can sleepwalk your way through it. Either you do it or you don't. Recitation is, in fact, a surefire way of mastering the material you need to learn. More information about recitation is given in the chapter "Building a Powerful Memory" (page 190).

Activity

Answer the following questions.

1. In the past, have you studied material mainly by reading and rereading it or mainly by reading and reciting? _____

2. A number of experiments have found that students who spend 25 percent of their time reading and 75 percent reciting remember much more than students who spend all their time reading. Will this fact make you spend more of your study time reciting? _____

3. Suppose you learn a group of four definitions until you can say them without looking at them. Then you go on and learn a group of several more definitions. What should you do after learning the second group of definitions?

    _____

4. What are recall words? _____

5. Where should you write recall words? _____

LEARNING TO USE PRWR

The following activities will give you practice in the four steps of PRWR: previewing, reading, writing notes, and reciting.

Activity 1: A Short Passage from a Speech Text

Preview: Take about thirty seconds to preview the following short textbook passage. The title tells you that the passage is about _____.
How many words are set off in *italics* within the passage? _____

NOISE

A person's ability to interpret, understand, or respond to symbols is often hurt by noise. *Noise* is any stimulus that gets in the way of sharing meaning. Much of your success as a communicator depends on how you cope with external, internal, and semantic noises.

External noises are the sights, sounds, and other stimuli that draw people's attention away from intended meaning. For instance, during a student's explanation of how a food processor works, your attention may be drawn to the sound of an airplane overhead. The airplane sound is external noise. External noise does not have to be a sound. Perhaps during the explanation, a particularly attractive classmate glances toward you, and for a moment your attention turns to that person. Such visual distraction to your attention is also external noise.

Internal noises are the thoughts and feelings that interfere with meaning. Have you ever found yourself daydreaming when a person was trying to tell you something? Perhaps you let your mind wander to thoughts of the good time you had at a disco last night or to the argument you had with someone this morning. If you have tuned out the words of your friend and tuned in a daydream or a past conversation, then you have created internal noise.

Semantic noises are those alternative meanings aroused by certain symbols that inhibit meaning. Suppose that a student mentioned that the salesman who sells food processors at the department store seemed like a "gay fellow." If you think of "gay" as a word for *homosexual,* you would miss the student's meaning entirely. Since meaning depends on your own experience, others may at times decode a word or phrase differently from the way you intended. When this happens, you have semantic noise.

Read (and Mark): Read the passage straight through, underlining the four definitions you will find. Also, number the three kinds of noises as 1, 2, and 3 respectively. Put an *Ex* in the margin beside each example of a definition.

Write: Complete the following notes about the passage ''Noise'':

Noise—_____

Kinds of noises:

1. External—_____

    Ex.—_____

2. Internal—_____

    Ex.—_____

3. Semantic—_____

    Ex.—_____

Note that the keys to the main idea here are an enumeration and definitions.

Recite: What recall words could you write in the margin to help you study this passage? _____

After you can recite to yourself the definition of *noise,* you should study until you can say to yourself the definition and an example of *external noises.* What should you then do? _____

Activity 2: A Short Passage from a Sociology Text

Preview: Take about thirty seconds to preview the following short textbook passage. The title tells you that the passage is about _____. How many words are set off in **boldface** within the passage? _____

THE CROWD

The crowd is one of the most familiar and at times spectacular forms of collective behavior. It is a temporary, relatively unorganized gathering of people who are in close physical proximity. Since a wide range of behavior is encompassed by the concept, the sociologist Herbert Blumer distinguishes among four basic types of crowd behavior. The first, a **casual crowd,** is a collection of people who have little in common except that they may be participating in a common event, such as looking through a department-store window. The second, a **conventional crowd,** is a number of people who have assembled for some specific purpose and who typically act in accordance with established norms, such as people attending a baseball game or concert. The third, an **expressive crowd,** is an aggregation of people who have gotten together for self-stimulation and personal gratification, such as at a religious revival or a rock festival. And fourth, an **acting crowd** is an excited, volatile collection of people who are engaged in rioting, looting, or other forms of aggressive behavior in which established norms carry little weight.

Read (and Mark):   Read the passage straight through, underlining the five definitions you will find. Number the types of crowd behavior 1, 2, 3, and 4.

Write: Complete the following notes about the passage ''The Crowd'':

Crowd—_____

Types of crowd behavior:

1. Casual crowd—_____   _____
2. Conventional crowd—_____
3. Expressive crowd—_____
4. Acting crowd—_____

Recite: To help you study this passage, you could write ''crowd'' in the margin as one recall word and _____ as the other recall words.

Activity 3: A Short Passage from a Psychology Text

Preview: Take about thirty seconds to preview the following short textbook passage. The title tells you that the passage is about _____.
How many words are set off in *italics* within the passage? _____

FOUR TYPES OF ESP

Parapsychologists (psychologists who study claims of more-than-normal happenings) have proposed four types of extrasensory perception, or ESP, each of which is said to occur without using the physical senses. *Telepathy* is one person's sending thoughts to another. For example, in an experiment, one person may look at a picture and try to "send" this picture to a "receiver" in another room. *Clairvoyance* is perceiving distant events, such as sensing that one's child has just been in a car accident. *Precognition* is "preknowing" (foretelling) future events, such as the assassination of a political leader. *Psychokinesis* is "mind over matter"—for example, levitating a table or, in an experiment, influencing the roll of a die by concentrating on a particular number.

Read (and Mark): Read the passage straight through, underlining the four definitions you will find. Number them 1, 2, 3, and 4 respectively. Put an *Ex* in the margin beside each example of a definition.

Write: Complete the following notes about the passage "Four Types of ESP":

1. Telepathy—_____

     Ex.—_____

2. Clairvoyance—_____

     Ex.—_____

3. _____

     Ex.—_____

4. _____

     Ex.—_____

Recite: What recall words could you write in the margin to help you study this passage? _____
After you can recite to yourself the definition and an example of *telepathy*, you should then study until you can say to yourself the definition and an example of *clairvoyance*. What should you then do? _____

Activity 4: A Short Passage from a Social Psychology Text

Preview: Take about thirty seconds to preview the following short textbook passage. The title tells you that the passage is about _____.
What words are set off in *italics* within the passage? _____

SEEING OURSELVES FAVORABLY

It is widely believed that most of us suffer from low self-esteem: the "I'm not OK—you're OK" problem. For example, the counseling psychologist Carl Rogers concluded that most people he has known "despise themselves, regard themselves as worthless and unlovable." As the comedian Groucho Marx put it, "I'd never join any club that would accept a person like me." The evidence, however, indicates that the writer William Saroyan was closer to the truth: "Every man is a good man in a bad world—as he himself knows." Although social psychologists are debating the reason for this *"self-serving bias"*—that is, the tendency to perceive oneself favorably—there is general agreement regarding its reality, its prevalence, and its potency.

Experiments have found that people readily accept credit when told they have succeeded (attributing the success to their ability and effort), yet often attribute failure to such external factors as bad luck or the problem's inherent "impossibility." Similarly, in explaining their victories, athletes commonly credit themselves; but they are more likely to attribute losses to something else: bad breaks, bad officiating, the other team's super effort.

And how much responsibility do you suppose car drivers tend to accept for their accidents? On insurance forms, drivers have described their accidents in words like these: "An invisible car came out of nowhere, struck my car and vanished." "As I reached an intersection, a hedge sprang up, obscuring my vision, and I did not see the other car." "A pedestrian hit me and went under my car." Situations that combine skill and chance (for example, games, exams, job applications) are especially prone to the phenomenon: Winners can easily attribute their successes to their skill, while losers can attribute their losses to chance. When I win at Scrabble, it's because of my verbal dexterity; when I lose, it's because "Who could get anywhere with a Q but no U?"

Read (and Mark): Read the passage through, underlining the one definition you will find. Put *Ex* in the margin beside an example of the definition.

Write: Complete these notes about "Seeing Ourselves Favorably" by filling in the definition and then *summarizing* one example in your own words. Summarizing the example will help you understand it and reduce it in size.

Self-serving bias—_____

Ex.—_____

Recite: After you can say the definition without looking at it, make sure that you can say the _____ without looking at it.

Activity 5: A Short Passage from a Business Text

Preview: Take about thirty seconds to preview the following short textbook passage. The title tells you that the passage is about _____.
How many words are set off in *italics* within the passage? _____

FACTORS OF PRODUCTION

A society's resources are referred to by economists as the **factors of production.** One factor of production, *land,* includes not only the real estate on the earth's surface but also the minerals, timber, and water below. The second, *labor,* consists of the human resources used to produce goods and services. The third factor of production is *capital,* the machines, tools, and buildings used to produce goods and services, as well as the money that buys other resources. A fourth factor of production is embodied in people called *entrepreneurs.* They are the ones who develop new ways to use the other economic resources more efficiently. They acquire materials, employ workers, invest in capital goods, and engage in marketing activities. In some societies, entrepreneurs risk losing only their reputations or their positions if they fail. In our society, they also risk losing their own personal resources. On the other hand, our entrepreneurs reap the benefits if they succeed; this possibility is what motivates them to take the risk of trying something new.

Read (and Mark): Read the passage straight through. As you do, underline the five definitions you will find. Also, number as 1, 2, 3, and 4 the four definitions that fit into a group with each other.

Write: Complete the following notes about the passage "Factors of Production":

Factors of production—_____

1. Land—_____

2. Labor—_____

3. Capital—_____

4. Entrepreneurs—_____

Recite: Simply putting the three recall words _____
in the margin would be enough to help you study your notes. Seeing those recall words, you would try to recite to yourself the definition of *factors of production* as well as the "four factors of production" and their definitions.

USING PRWR

This chapter will help improve your textbook study by

- Explaining two helpful memory techniques
- Providing note-taking practice on a series of textbook passages
- Presenting hints and comments on good note-taking

This chapter will provide further practice in the PRWR study system explained in "Textbook Study I." You'll use PRWR with ten readings, longer than the readings in "Textbook Study I" and with more varied activities. Readings 1 to 5 will give you guided practice: each of these passages appears on a left-hand page, with activities and comments on the opposite right-hand page. Readings 6 to 10 will give you more independent practice: these are still longer passages with introductory hints, for which you'll do note-taking on your own.

Before you start on the readings, you should master two valuable memory techniques that will help you recite and learn your notes after you have read and taken notes on a passage. *Catchwords* and *catchphrases* will therefore be explained briefly here. (They are also described in detail on pages 196–198, in the chapter "Building a Powerful Memory.")

TWO MEMORY AIDS FOR PRWR

Catchwords

In "Textbook Study I," you took notes on four kinds of crowds (page 99): (1) casual, (2) conventional, (3) expressive, (4) acting. Chances are that you might forget at least one of these four types. To help ensure that you remember all four types, you could create a catchword.

A *catchword* is a word that is made up of the first letters of several words you want to remember. For example, the first letters of the terms for the four kinds of crowds are:

C (casual)
C (conventional)
E (expressive)
A (acting)

Use these letters to form an easily recalled catchword, rearranging them if necessary. The catchword can be a real word, or it can be a made-up word. For example, you might remember the letters C, C, E, A with the made-up word CACE.

After you create a catchword, test yourself until you are sure that each letter stands for a key word in your mind. For these types of words, you'd make sure that C stands for *casual,* A for *acting,* C for *conventional,* and E for *expressive.* In each case, the first letter serves as a "hook" to help you pull an entire idea into your memory.

This memory device is a proven method for remembering a group of items. Learn to use and apply it!

- "In Textbook Study I," you also took notes on the four factors of production (page 102). The first letter of these four factors are L (land), L (labor), C (capital), and E (entrepreneurs). Make up a catchword that would help you remember these four factors.

  Catchword: _____

Catchphrases

Sometimes you can't easily make up a catchword. In such cases, create a catchphrase instead. A *catchphrase* is a series of words, each beginning with the first letter of a word you want to remember.

Look at the passage on noise in "Textbook Study I" (page 97). The first letters of the three kinds of noise are:

E (external)
I (internal)
S (semantic)

You might not be able to make a good catchword out of E, I, and S, but you could create an easily remembered catchphrase.

For example, I have a friend named Ed, and I quickly came up with the catchphrase, "I shot Ed." This is an outrageous sentence, since I do not expect to shoot Ed or anyone, or even put a gun in my hand. The point is that because I created the sentence and because it is outrageous, I would automatically remember it. That's what you want to do: create a sentence you'll be sure to remember. The catchphrase does not have to be a model of grammar or make perfect sense. It can be so outrageous that you would not want anyone else to know what it is. All that matters is creating a line that will stick in your memory.

The purpose of the catchphrase is to give you the first letters of the words you want to remember. After you create a phrase, test yourself until you are sure each letter stands for the right word in your mind. If you were studying the kinds of noise and used the catchphrase "I shot Ed," you'd make sure that *I* helped you recall *internal, S* helped you recall *semantic,* and *E* helped you recall *external.*

If you were then given a test question asking you to list and describe the three kinds of noise, you would think immediately, "I shot Ed." You would have the first letters *I, S,* and *E.* The letter *I* would be a memory hook to help you remember that one kind of noise is *internal,* the *S* would help you remember that another kind of noise is *semantic,* and the *E* would help you remember that the third kind of noise is *external.*

- In "Textbook Study I," you took notes on the four kinds of ESP (page 100). The first letters of these four types are T (telepathy), C (clairvoyance), P (precognition), and P (psychokinesis). Make up a catchphrase that would help you remember the letters T-C-P-P. (Note that you can put the letters in any order when creating your sentence.)

Catchphrase: _____

GUIDED PRACTICE IN PRWR

Reading 1: A Passage from a Business Text

THE FRANCHISE ALTERNATIVE

One way to avoid some of the management headaches associated with starting a business is to invest in a **franchise,** an approach that enables you to use a larger company's trade name and sell its products or services in a specific territory. In exchange for this right, the **franchisee** (you, the small-business owner) pays an initial fee and often monthly royalties as well to the **franchiser** (the corporation).

There are three basic types of franchises. In a *product franchise,* the franchisee pays the franchising company for the right to sell trademarked goods, which are purchased from the franchiser and resold by the franchisee. Car dealers and gasoline stations fall into this category. In a *manufacturing franchise,* like a soft-drink bottling plant, the franchisee is licensed by the parent company to produce and distribute its products, using supplies purchased from the franchiser. In a *business-format franchise,* the franchisee buys the right to open a business using the franchiser's name and format for doing business. The fast-food chains typify this form of franchising.

If you are an average American, you already know something about franchises. In our economy, they are a factor of rising importance. We buy our houses from franchised real-estate brokers, get our hair cut in franchised beauty salons, and drive cars purchased from franchised dealers. The soda pop we drink is bottled by franchisers, and the food we eat is sold by such franchises as McDonald's, Wendy's, Pizza Hut, and Kentucky Fried Chicken. Franchises account for about one-third of all retail sales in the United States and employ seven million people. With sales growing at four times the rate of the GNP, franchises will be responsible for half of all retail sales within twenty years.

Franchising is not a new phenomenon. It has been around since the nineteenth century, when such companies as Singer and International Harvester established dealerships throughout the world. Early in this century, Coca-Cola, General Motors, and Metropolitan Life Insurance Company, among others, used franchises to distribute or sell their products. But the real boom in franchising began in the late 1950s, with the proliferation of hotels and motels like Holiday Inn and fast-food establishments like Baskin-Robbins and Dunkin' Donuts.

The latest trend in franchising has been diversification in the variety of products and services offered. Today, over two thousand companies offer franchises, ranging from day-care centers and health clubs to dental clinics, video-tape rental outlets, and funeral parlors. By and large, most are service operations.

Source: *Business Today,* Sixth Edition, by David J. Rachman, Michael H. Mescon, Courtland L. Bovee, and John V. Thill. McGraw-Hill, 1990.

Activity for Reading 1

Preview: Take about thirty seconds to preview Reading 1 on the opposite page. The title tells you that the passage is about _____. How many other headings are in the passage? _____ How many words are set off in **boldface** in the passage? _____ How many words are set off in *italics*? _____

Read and Mark: Read the passage straight through. As you do, underline the definitions you find. Mark with an *Ex* in the margin an example that makes each definition clear for you. Also, number the items in an enumeration that you'll find in the passage.

Write: On separate paper, take notes on "The Franchise Alternative":

1. Write down the definitions of *franchise, franchisee,* and *franchiser.*
2. Write down the definitions and examples of the three types of franchise.
3. Also, add details of note by answering these questions.
   a. How widespread are franchises?
   b. Is franchising a new idea?
   c. What is the trend in franchising?

Recite: To remember the three kinds of franchises, create a *catchphrase*: a short sentence made up of the first letters of the three kinds of franchises: P for *product,* M for *manufacturing,* and B for *business*:

   Your sentence: *P* _____ *M* _____ *B* _____

Comments on Reading 1: After you can say the definitions of *franchise, franchisee,* and *franchiser* to yourself without looking at them, go on and see if you can say to yourself the three types of franchises. Doing this should be easy because you will have created a catchphrase that will automatically give you the first letters (P, M, B) of those three types of franchises. You can then use the first letters as "hooks" to help you pull into memory the words themselves. Test yourself, then, to make sure that P stands in your head for *product,* M stands in your head for *manufacturing,* and B stands in your head for *business.*

Reading 2: A Passage from a Psychology Text

ANGER

Anger is indeed an unpleasant emotion. Think of the last time you felt angry with yourself or someone else. Anger usually is aroused by *frustration*, a feeling that results whenever you cannot reach a desired goal. For example, assume you had a long, hard day at work and are anxious to get home at a reasonable hour. Your car engine will not turn over. You have no idea what is wrong, and there is nothing you can do about it. You feel frustrated, and your frustration leads to anger. Frustration occurs whenever you cannot reach a desired goal. Psychologists have found that frustration often results in some form of anger or resentment. If you become irritated and kick the car, your behavior is fairly normal.

There are many possible reasons why you cannot reach a desired goal. Sometimes you simply lack the ability. For example, in the case of your car's failing to start, you were unable to diagnose the problem and correct it. In addition to feeling irritation toward the car, you may have been annoyed with yourself for not learning ways to troubleshoot engine problems. Often people aspire to goals far beyond their abilities. A shy man may wish to be a super-salesman, or a woman with limited finances and intelligence may wish to become a nuclear physicist.

Frustration can also result from confusion about goals. Sometimes people feel pulls in more than one direction. Kurt Lewin specified three types of goal confusion or conflict that people experience. Each of these three types of conflicts leads to a feeling of frustration.

Approach-Approach Conflicts Of the three types of conflicts, these are the least frustrating. An *approach-approach* conflict is one that results from having to choose between two desirable goals. You cannot possibly reach both of them at the same time. Maybe there are two good parties in different parts of town at the exact same time on the same night. You must miss one, but which one? Or assume a rich aunt hands you $50,000 to buy yourself a new car. Both a Mercedes and a Porsche look appealing. You must make a choice, but indeed it is a pleasant dilemma. In an approach-approach conflict, you always win, even if you must lose another appealing alternative. As a result, approach-approach conflicts are only mildly frustrating.

Avoidance-Avoidance Conflicts These are the most frustrating of the three types of conflicts. Here the conflict results from being forced to choose between two undesirable goals. Did your mother ever tell you to clean your messy closet or go to bed? Assuming you disliked cleaning closets and were not tired, you experienced an *avoidance-avoidance conflict*. The thought of wasting hours cleaning a cluttered closet was dreadful, but the notion of suffering hours of boredom was also unappealing. The usual reaction to an avoidance-avoidance conflict is to attempt to escape. Perhaps you threatened to run away from home. When no escape is possible, facing the conflict is inevitable. The result is being forced to make an unpleasant choice. The choice is accompanied by intense frustration and anger.

Approach-Avoidance Conflicts These are the most common of the three types of conflicts. The conflict results from weighing the positive and negative aspects of a single goal. Eating a piece of chocolate fudge will provide a delicious taste. But it will also cause tooth decay and, perhaps, unwanted pounds. Studying for an exam will result in a better grade, but it will require an evening away from friends.

Source: *Applying Psychology*, Second Edition, by Virginia Nichols Quinn. McGraw-Hill, 1990.

Activity for Reading 2

Preview: Take about thirty seconds to preview Reading 2 on the opposite page. The title tells you that the passage is about _____. How many other headings are in the passage? _____ How many words are set off in *italics*? _____

Read and Mark: Read the passage straight through. As you do, underline the definitions you find. Mark with an *Ex* in the margin an example that makes each definition clear for you. Also, number the items in an enumeration that you'll find. And note what seem to be important details.

Write: On separate paper, take notes on "Anger":

1. Write down the definition of *frustration.*
2. Write down the definitions and examples of the three types of conflict.
3. Also, note which is the *least frustrating* conflict, the *most frustrating* conflict, and the *most common* conflict.

Recite: To remember the three kinds of conflict, you might want to create a line like the following: "At least approach Lola since it is most frustrating to avoid her."

This line will help you remember that the first kind of conflict is *approach-approach,* and that it is the least frustrating of conflicts. And it will help you remember that the second kind of conflict is *avoidance-avoidance,* and it is the most frustrating of conflicts. All that's left, then, is for the last conflict to be *approach-avoidance,* and for it to be the most common conflict.

See if you can come up with a line of your own that will help you remember the same information: _____

Comments on Reading 2:   After you have a line you automatically remember to "anchor" your study, test yourself until you can recite from memory the definition of *frustration* as well as the kinds of conflict and definitions, examples, and an important detail about each.

Reading 3: A Passage from a Sociology Text

WHITE-COLLAR AND CORPORATE CRIME

One man robs a gas station of $250 and is sent to prison for six months; another man makes $2.5 million on illegal stock trades and is required only to return the money (plus "interest" in the form of fines). As this example suggests, the social response to white-collar and corporate crime is quite different from the treatment of "common criminals."

The term **white-collar crime** was first used by the sociologist Edwin Sutherland to refer to "a crime committed by a person of respectability and high status in the course of his occupation." Embezzlement, padding expense accounts, stealing from an employer, and personal income tax evasion all fall into this category. So does the misuse of public funds by government officials (accepting bribes, padding payrolls, and the like). One difference between white-collar and "common" crime is that the former more often relies on the sophisticated manipulation of records and concealment than on physical force. A second difference is the magnitude of the crime: In general, white-collar crimes are more costly. For example, bank embezzlers steal an average of $23,000 apiece, whereas bank robbers steal only one-eighth as much ($3,000 or less). A third difference is the treatment of offenders. Ninety percent of bank robbers go to prison, but only about 17 percent of embezzlers are put behind bars.

White-collar crimes are committed for personal gain; **corporate crimes** are illegal acts committed on behalf of a formal organization. As in the Ford Pinto case, many individuals may be involved in a corporate crime, directly or indirectly, knowingly or unknowingly. The primary goal of such crimes is to boost company profits (or avoid losses). Unlike other criminals, corporations are not persons and cannot be jailed. Charges against them are usually filed in the civil courts (in the form of individual or class-action lawsuits), rather than in the criminal courts. Indeed, corporate crimes are often handled outside the court system by government regulatory agencies (the SEC, Federal Trade Commission, Environmental Protection Agency, and the like). In most cases, sanctions against the lawbreakers take the form of relatively small fines in relation to earnings.

David Ermann and Michael Lundman identify four types of corporate crime. The Ford Pinto case was an example of a *crime against customers*. This category includes not only the sale of unsafe products but also false advertising and price fixing. A second type is *crime against employees*. In the previously mentioned Johns-Manville case, workers were knowingly exposed to harmful levels of asbestos dust. Unfair hiring and promotion policies and mismanagement of pension funds are also crimes against employees. The third type of corporate deviance is *crime against the public at large*. The case of Love Canal is one example of a corporation's blatant disregard of public welfare. In 1947 the Hooker Chemical and Plastics Corporation purchased Love Canal to use as a dump for toxic wastes. When the site had outlived its usefulness, Hooker donated it to the local school board for $1. Innocent of the potential danger, the board built a school on part of the site and sold the rest to a housing developer. Over the years, complaints from residents of Love Canal about chemical burns, high cancer rates, and other health problems mounted, but Hooker did nothing. Finally, in 1978, the New York health commissioner took action, declaring that residents of Love Canal were in "great and immediate peril," ordering the evacuation of pregnant women and children under age two, and closing the school. Extensive press coverage of Love Canal was in part responsible for public awareness of the dangers of chemical dumps: Hooker was not alone. The fourth type of corporate deviance rarely makes newspaper headlines. If *crimes against owners* are reported at all, it is on the business page. What does this phrase mean? Most major corporations are "owned" by large numbers of small independent stockholders. In most cases, stockholders have no more information about how a company is being run than does the general public, and few of them attend the annual stockholders' meetings that are required by law. When corporate officers act in their own best interests at the expense of stockholders, they are committing crimes against the corporation's owners.

Source: *Sociology*, Fifth Edition, by Donald Light, Suzanne Keller, and Craig Calhoun. Knopf, 1989.

Activity for Reading 3

Preview: Take about thirty seconds to preview Reading 3 on the opposite page. The title tells you that the passage is about _____. How many terms are set off in **boldface** in the passage? _____ How many terms are set off in *italics*? _____

Read and Mark: Read the passage straight through, underlining the definitions you find. When appropriate, mark with an *Ex* in the margin an example of each definition. Also, number the items in the enumerations that you find.

Write: On separate paper, take notes on ''White-Collar and Corporate Crime'':

1. Write down the definition of *white-collar* and an example.
2. List the three differences between white-collar and common crimes.
3. Write the definition of *corporate crime* and an example.
4. Write down descriptions and examples of the four types of corporate crime.

Recite: The differences between white-collar and common crimes may not be important enough to memorize. But you should study until you can recite from memory the definitions of *white-collar crime* and *corporate crime,* and you should use a catchword to remember the four types of corporate crime.

To create the catchword, first circle a key word in each type of crime:

Crime against (customers)
Crime against (employees)
Crime against (public at large)
Crimes against (owners)

To remember the key words, pick out the first letters of the words: C, E, P, O. You may be able to remember the nonsense word *cepo,* or you may want to create a real word. If you can make a real word out of these letters, or a nonsense word that you prefer to *cepo,* write it here: _____

Comments on Reading 3: While there are no headings here except at the start of the passage, you can use definitions, examples, and enumerations to help focus on the important ideas in the passage.

It also helps to be aware that the authors have used a very common pattern of organization—*contrast*—to present their information. They contrast white-collar and common crimes. Then they contrast white-collar and corporate crimes.

Reading 4: A Passage from a Health Text

ILLNESSES ASSOCIATED WITH LONG-TERM ALCOHOL USE

Alcohol is linked with many serious illnesses that can destroy the body's most important organs and sometimes result in death.

Gastrointestinal Disorders Alcohol stimulates secretion of digestive acid throughout the gastrointestinal system, irritating the lining of the drinker's stomach and the linings of the esophagus and intestines. It is not unusual for alcoholics to develop bleeding ulcers in the stomach and intestines, and sometimes lesions in the esophagus. Alcohol can give "binge drinkers" diarrhea. It may inhibit the pancreas's production of enzymes that are crucial for the digestion of food. When heavily abused, it can also lead to **pancreatitis** (inflammation of the pancreas).

Malnutrition A common myth holds that alcohol, being made from fruit or grain, is food. It is not. Worse, alcohol actually starves the body of essential nutrients. It does consist of calories, so it produces energy, but it does not contain any of the chemical substances the body needs to build and repair tissue. Alcohol abuse has been reported as the most common cause of vitamin deficiency in this country. An alcoholic may undereat; or, because the digestive system is disrupted, he or she may be unable to process properly the nutrients that are eaten. Alcoholics may also suffer nutritional imbalances because of diarrhea, loss of appetite, and vomiting. In short, alcoholism can be a form of slow starvation.

Liver Damage The liver is one of the organs most vulnerable to alcohol abuse. Alcohol changes the way the liver processes important substances; it can also contribute to infections and other disorders. If the liver is disturbed or infected, the body's immune system and ability to flush out poisons are affected. Damage to the liver can also harm other organs, because the liver is essential to the production and modification of many substances the body needs.

Many alcoholics suffer **cirrhosis of the liver,** a chronic inflammatory disease of this organ in which healthy liver cells are replaced by scar tissue. Cirrhosis of the liver caused more than 27,000 deaths in 1983; it was the ninth leading cause of death that year. Drinking can also cause **alcoholic hepatitis,** in which the liver becomes swollen and inflamed. It may also lead to a "fatty liver" condition by changing the way the liver processes fats.

Glandular (Endocrine) Disorders Excessive drinking can damage the body's glandular system, which regulates such important functions as moods and sexuality. Men who drink too much may suffer impotence and reduced levels of the hormone testosterone; in one study, researchers found that the second most frequent reason for impotence among men was excessive drinking. Women may also throw their hormonal system out of balance through heavy drinking; recent studies indicate that alcohol abuse can lead to early menopause.

Source: *Essentials of Health*, Fifth Edition, by Marvin R. Levy, Mark Dignan, and Janet H. Shirreffs. Random House, 1988.

Activity for Reading 4

Preview: Take about thirty seconds to preview Reading 4 on the opposite page. The title tells you that the passage is about _____. How many other headings are in the passage? _____ How many words are set off in **boldface** in the passage? _____

Read and Mark: Read the passage straight through. As you do, underline the definitions you find. Notice that each of the headings under the title is part of an enumeration, so number those headings. Also, place a check beside details that seem important under each heading.

    To decide what is important, turn each heading into a basic question and read to find details that answer it. For example, turn the heading "Gastrointestinal disorders" into the question, "What are examples of gastrointestinal disorders?" Turn the heading "Malnutrition" into the question, "How does alcohol cause malnutrition?" Turn the heading "Liver Damage" into the questions, "How is the liver damaged?" and "What are the kinds of liver damage?"

    The technique of turning headings into basic questions starting with words like *What, How, When,* and *In what ways* is a good way to locate and focus on important details within a section.

Write: On separate paper, take notes on "Illnesses Associated with Long-Term Alcohol Use":

1. Write down the four illnesses associated with long-term alcohol use, along with important details about each illness.
2. Be sure to include the definitions of *pancreatitis, cirrhosis of the liver,* and *alcoholic hepatitis.*

Recite: To remember the four kinds of long-term alcohol-related illness, create a *catchphrase*: a short sentence made up of the first letters of the four kinds of illness: G for *gastrointestinal,* M for *malnutrition,* L for *liver,* and G for *glandular (endocrine) disorders.*

    Your four-word sentence with the letters G, M, L, and G (in any order):

_____

Comments on Reading 4: In a passage such as this one, there are an enumeration and some definitions. At the same time, you must turn headings section. Asking questions that are based on headings can be an excellent way to get inside a block of material. The questions help you understand the material and pick out what might be most important.

Reading 5: A Passage from a Biology Text

BUILDING BLOCKS OF ALL MATTER

Two basic principles of chemistry emerged from the work of French chemist Antoine Lavoisier, English chemist John Dalton, and others in the late 1700s and early 1800s.

■ All matter, living and nonliving, is made up of **elements**, substances that cannot be decomposed by chemical processes into simpler substances. There are ninety-two chemical elements in nature, and thirteen more have been created in the laboratory. Some examples of elements are hydrogen (symbolized H), oxygen (O), sulfur (S), gold (Au), iron (Fe), and carbon (C).

■ Each element is composed of identical particles called **atoms**, the smallest units of matter that still display the characteristic properties of the element. All the atoms in a brick of pure gold, for example, are identical to one another but different from all the atoms in a lump of carbon, an ingot of iron, or a sample of other elements. The properties of an element, such as the dense, shiny, metallic nature of gold or the dull black quality of carbon, are based on the structure of its individual atoms, as we shall see.

The Elements of Life   A natural question arose from the pioneering work of Lavoisier and Dalton: Are living things made up of the same elements as rocks, planets, and stars, or is our chemical makeup different? Living things, it turns out, display a special subset of the ninety-two naturally occurring elements in the earth's crust, but the elements occur in very different proportions. Fully 98 percent of the atoms in the earth's crust are the elements oxygen, silicon (Si), aluminum (Al), iron, calcium (Ca), sodium (Na), potassium (K), and magnesium (Mg), with the first three predominating. In a typical organism, however, 99 percent of the atoms are the markedly different subset carbon, hydrogen, nitrogen (N), and oxygen, with sodium, calcium, phosphorus (P), and sulfur making up most of the remaining 1 percent, plus a few other elements present in trace amounts.

Biologists are not certain why the chemical subsets of living and nonliving things are so different, but they do know that atomic architecture determines the physical properties of elements and, in turn, the properties of living organisms.

Atomic Structure   Atoms are extremely small: about three million atoms sitting side by side would probably cover the period at the end of this sentence. Physicist Gerald Feinberg once calculated that there are more atoms in the human body than there are stars in the known universe. Although minuscule in size, each atom is made up of three types of subatomic particles: protons, neutrons, and electrons. **Protons** have a positive (+) charge; **neutrons** have no electrical charge (they are neutral); and **electrons** have a negative (−) charge. Since these subatomic particles are only parts of atoms, none of them displays properties of elements. The protons and neutrons are clustered in a small dense body at the center of the atom called the *nucleus* (the diameter of an atom is about 100,000 times larger than that of nucleus). The outer limits of the atom are defined by the paths of its electrons, which continuously race about the nucleus in cloudlike orbits. Electrons, protons, and neutrons are themselves made up of a dozen or more smaller subatomic particles held together by special forces.

Source: *Essentials of Biology*, by Janet L. Hopson and Norman K. Wessells. McGraw-Hill, 1990.

Activity for Reading 5

Preview: Take about thirty seconds to preview Reading 5 on the opposite page. The title tells you that the passage is about _____. How many other headings are in the passage? _____ How many words are set off in **boldface** in the passage? _____ What word is set off in *italics*? _____

Read and Mark: Read the passage straight through. As you do, underline the definitions you find. Where appropriate, set off an example of a definition with an *Ex* in the margin. Also, number the items in the two enumerations. Finally, jot down what seem to be important details within the passage.

Write: On separate paper, take notes on ''Building Blocks of All Matter'':
1. Write down the two basic principles of chemistry.
2. Write down examples of elements and atoms.
3. Note whether living things are made up of the same elements as nonliving things.
4. Note the size of atoms.
5. Note the definitions of the three types of subatomic particles and of the nucleus.

Recite: Write here key words that you might put in the margin of your notes to help you study the material:

_____

_____

After you can recite the first scientific principle (involving elements) without looking at it, study until you can say to yourself the second scientific principle (involving atoms) without looking at it. Then go back and review the first principle. Remember that constant review is a key to effective study.

Comments on Reading 5: Remember that a good way of taking notes is to write down all the headings and then place notes under those headings. Textbook authors carefully organize their information through a series of major and minor headings. By writing those headings down, you help organize your own notes.

Like most scientific materials, this passage is densely packed with information. But once again, you have seen how a combination of headings, definitions, and enumerations can help you get down the important information in a textbook selection.

INDEPENDENT PRACTICE IN PRWR

Following are several longer textbook passages. Apply the PRWR—preview, read, write, recite—method to study the material in each passage. Use your own paper to take study notes. Hints for note-taking are provided at the start of each selection.

Reading 6: A Passage from a Psychology Text

Hints: Definitions, examples, and answers to questions provided by the authors are the keys to important ideas in this selection.

Remember that a good way of taking notes is to write down all the headings and then place notes under those headings. Textbook authors carefully organize their information through a series of major and minor headings. By writing those headings down, you help organize your own notes.

DEVELOPMENT OF SOCIAL ATTACHMENTS

"I don't believe you. I know that a baby can't do much more than cry, eat, and sleep. You're saying that your baby recognizes your face. A baby's brain isn't big enough to do that." The neighbor had finished talking and stood there with her arms crossed, looking down at the ten-week-old infant. The mother smiled, "OK, I'll show you. You stand on the left side of the crib and I'll stand on the right. Then we'll play peek-a-boo. If the baby spends more time looking at me, it means that she recognizes my face. If she spends more time looking at you, it means that she doesn't." The mother took her place on the right and the neighbor walked over and stood on the left side of the crib. The neighbor and the mother alternately played peek-a-boo. There was little doubt about the results. The baby spent more time looking at her mother's face. The neighbor was shaking her head from side to side. "Could be a coincidence. I still don't believe that tiny Kim really recognizes your face."

Whom would you believe, the mother or the neighbor? In a study similar to the peek-a-boo game played by the mother and the neighbor, Tiffany Field and her associates reported that four-day-old infants initially spent more time looking at their mother's face than a stranger's. Field concluded that even newborns can learn some distinctive features of their mother's face.

Lewis Lipsitt says that until recently, parents were told that their infants were mostly blind at birth and could not taste, smell, feel pain, learn, or remember. Now we know that newborns can see, taste, feel pain, detect their mother's odor, and show taste and flavor preferences. Even more remarkable, Lipsitt has shown that infants can learn and remember. The first time Kim hears a new sound, her heart accelerates briefly. But after the sound is present a number of times, her heart no longer accelerates. This indicates that she "remembers" or recognizes the sound, a process called *habituation*. Lipsitt has also shown that newborn Kim can learn to turn her head at the sound of a tone but not a buzzer to get a taste of sugar water. This is an example of *associative learning*. All these studies indicate that newborn Kim's senses and brain are functioning to a remarkable degree. One way that researchers could assess normal brain development is by analyzing Kim's crying to see whether it fits a normal or abnormal pattern. If her brain development is normal, within months she will develop further sensory and cognitive functions and form attachments to her parents.

Forming Attachments

Between four and six weeks, rhythmically moving stimuli, such as the nodding head of a puppet or a rotating mobile, will cause Kim to smile. Then gradually, between the ages of two and three months, a human face becomes the most effective stimulus for eliciting a smile. Because this smile is directed toward another person, it is called **social smiling.** Psychologists believe that Kim's social smiling may be increased by parental reinforcement. But her social smiling also serves a very important social function, that of communication. The emergence of social smiling is thought to mark the beginning of a period during which the infant forms social attachments with caretakers.

By six months, Kim will recognize her parents' faces. Soon she will begin to give them happy greetings when they reappear after a short absence. When Kim's father comes home from work, she may smile and gurgle, bounce up and down in her highchair, and hold out her arms to him. In a few more months, when Kim is able to crawl, she will begin to follow her parents wherever they go. At the same time, Kim will begin to show distress whenever her mother and father temporarily leave her in the care of someone else. This reaction, called **separation anxiety,** may include loud protests, crying, and agitation, as well as despair and depression when the separation is very long. Both separation anxiety and joyous greetings on reunion are signs that Kim is developing strong affectional bonds toward her parents, bonds called **social attachments.** A social attachment will form toward whoever is a child's primary caretaker—whether mother, father, grandparent, or any other caring adult.

By studying the reactions of infants to being separated from and reunited with their mothers, Mary Ainsworth found that infant-mother attachments vary greatly in quality. When placed in an unfamiliar room containing many interesting toys, a **securely attached** infant tends to explore freely as long as the mother looks on. If the mother leaves, most of these babies cry and become upset. But when mother returns, they greet her happily and are very easily soothed. In contrast, an **anxiously attached** infant does not respond positively when the mother comes back to the room. Some show great ambivalence toward her, one minute clinging and wanting to be held, and the next minute squirming and pushing away. Other anxiously attached infants simply avoid the mother upon her return; they turn their heads in another direction or move away from her.

There is some relationship between the security of the infant-caretaker attachment and the child's later behaviors. For example, the more secure the infant-caretaker attachment, the less dependence the child later shows and the better he or she copes with the stress of attending kindergarten. The development of the infant-caretaker attachment is important because it establishes an initial pattern of trust and understanding in the infant's life.

Why does the quality of infant-caretaker attachments vary so greatly? The answer lies in a complex interaction between traits of the parent, traits of the baby, and the kind of environment in which they both live. For instance, researchers have found that mothers of securely attached infants tend to be more sensitive to their baby's needs than mothers of anxiously attached infants. When the child is crying and upset, these mothers usually respond quickly and offer comfort until the baby is soothed. This style of mothering is called *sensitive care*. Mothers of anxiously attached infants, in contrast, are less likely to respond right away when their baby is distressed and are more apt to let the infant "cry it out." These women may also have more negative feelings toward motherhood and are more tense and irritable toward their child.

At the same time, many infants who become insecurely attached start life with certain characteristics that make them harder for an adult to respond to. For example, anxiously attached infants in general have been found to be less active, less alert, and less socially engaging as newborns. Outside conditions may also enter into the development of an insecure attachment. When a woman with a difficult baby has many additional stresses in her life and little emotional support from others, the relationship between mother and child may get off to a bad start. The development of attachments is a very complex process that involves many interacting factors.

Although psychologists have long studied the infant-mother attachment, they have only recently studied the infant-father attachment. Researchers found that mothers were more likely to interact with their infants during routine caretaking, such as feeding or bathing, and to pick up their infants at these times. In contrast, fathers were more likely to interact with their infants for the sole purpose of play. The researchers concluded that infants become attached to their fathers as well as to their mothers, and that fathers provide different kinds of stimulation and activities than do mothers.

As you can see, the kind of attachment a child develops with a mother, father, or other adult depends on a complex interaction among a host of factors. When this interaction goes very badly, the result can be tragic, as in the development of child abuse.

Source: *Introduction to Psychology*, Second Edition, by Rod Plotnik. Random House, 1989.

Reading 7: A Passage from a Speech Text

Hints: Enumerations, headings, and subheadings are the keys to important ideas here. Notice that each heading under ''How to Become a Better Listener'' is part of an enumeration. When you take notes, number these headings. You will also find another enumeration in this passage that is formed from *subheadings* (headings that fit under a heading); be sure to number these subheadings.

HOW TO BECOME A BETTER LISTENER

Take Listening Seriously

The first step to improvement is always self-awareness. Analyze your shortcomings as a listener and commit yourself to overcoming them. Good listening does not go hand in hand with intelligence, education, or social standing. Like any other skill, it comes from practice and self-discipline.

You should begin to think of listening as an *active* process. Many aspects of modern life encourage us to listen passively. We "listen" to the radio while studying or "listen" to television while moving about from room to room. This type of passive listening is a habit—but so is active listening. We can learn to identify situations in which active listening is important. If you work seriously at becoming a more efficient listener, you will reap the rewards in your schoolwork, in your personal and family relations, and in your career.

Resist Distractions

In an ideal world, we could eliminate all physical and mental distractions. In the real world, however, this is not possible. Because we think so much faster than a speaker can talk, it's easy to let our attention wander while we listen. Sometimes it's very easy—when the room is too hot, when construction machinery is operating right outside the window, when the speaker is tedious. But our attention can stray even in the best of circumstances—if for no other reason than a failure to stay alert and make ourselves concentrate.

Whenever you find this happening, make a conscious effort to pull your mind back to what the speaker is saying. Then force it to stay there. One way to do this is to think a little ahead of the speaker—try to anticipate what will come next. This is not the same as jumping to conclusions. When you jump to conclusions, you put words into the speaker's mouth and don't actually listen to what is said. In this case you *will* listen—and measure what the speaker says against what you had anticipated.

Another way to keep your mind on a speech is to review mentally what the speaker has already said and make sure you understand it. Yet another is to listen between the lines and assess what a speaker implies verbally or says nonverbally with body language. Suppose a politician is running for reelection. During a campaign speech to his constituents he makes this statement: "Just last week I had lunch with the President, and he assured me that he has a special concern for the people of our state." The careful listener would hear this implied message: "If you vote for me, there's a good chance more tax money will flow into the state."

To take another example, suppose a speaker is introducing someone to an audience. The speaker says, "It gives me great pleasure to present to you my very dear friend, Mrs. Smith." But the speaker doesn't shake hands with Mrs. Smith. He doesn't even look at her—just turns his back and leaves the podium. Is Mrs. Smith really his "very dear friend"? Certainly not.

Attentive listeners can pick up all kinds of clues to a speaker's real message. At first you may find it difficult to listen so intently. If you work at it, however, your concentration is bound to improve.

Don't Be Diverted by Appearance or Delivery

If you had attended Abraham Lincoln's momentous Cooper Union speech of 1860, this is what you would have seen:

> The long, ungainly figure upon which hung clothes that, while new for this trip, were evidently the work of an unskilled tailor; the large feet and clumsy hands, of which, at the outset, at least, the orator seemed to be unduly conscious; the long, gaunt head, capped by a shock of hair that seemed not to have been thoroughly brushed out, made a picture which did not fit in with New York's conception of a finished statesman.

But although he seemed awkward and uncultivated, Lincoln had a powerful message about the moral evils of slavery. Fortunately, the audience at Cooper Union did not let his appearance stand in the way of his words.

Similarly, you must be willing to set aside preconceived judgments based on a person's looks or manner of speech. Einstein had frizzy, uncombed hair and wore sloppy clothes; Gandhi was a very unimpressive-looking man who often spoke dressed in a loincloth or wrapped in a blanket; Helen Keller—deaf and blind from earliest childhood—always had trouble articulating words distinctly. Yet imagine if no one had listened to them. Even though it may tax your tolerance, patience, and concentration, don't let negative feelings about a speaker's appearance or delivery keep you from listening to the message.

On the other hand, try not to be misled if the speaker has an attractive appearance. It is easy to assume that because someone is good-looking and has a polished delivery, he or she is speaking eloquently. Some of the most unscrupulous speakers in history have been handsome people with hypnotic delivery skills. Be sure you respond to the message, not to the package.

Suspend Judgment

Unless we listen only to people who think exactly as we do, we are going to hear things with which we disagree. When this happens, our natural inclination is to argue mentally with the speaker or to dismiss everything he or she says. But neither response is fair—to the speaker or to ourselves. In both cases we blot out any chance of learning or being persuaded.

Does this mean you must agree with everything you hear? Not at all. It means you should hear people out *before* reaching a final judgment. Try to understand their point of view. Listen to their ideas, examine their evidence, assess their reasoning. *Then* make up your mind. If you're sure of your beliefs, you need not fear listening to opposing views. If you're not sure, you have every reason to listen carefully. A closed mind is an empty mind.

Focus Your Listening

As we have seen, skilled listeners do not try to absorb a speaker's every word. Rather, they focus on specific things in a speech. Here are three suggestions to help you focus your listening.

Listen for Main Points   Most speeches contain from two to four main points. Here, for example, are the main points of a recent speech by John J. Coury, President of the American Medical Association:

(1) Astronomical malpractice awards and the spiraling cost of malpractice insurance are jeopardizing the quality of health care in America.
(2) A nationwide initiative is needed to meet the growing health crisis among teenagers and adolescents.
(3) If a cure or immunization for AIDS is not found in the near future, it will become the most deadly medical scourge in American history.

These main points are the heart of Dr. Coury's message. As with any speech, they are the most important things to listen for.

Unless a speaker is terribly scatterbrained, you should be able to detect his or her main points with little difficulty. Often a speaker will give some idea at the outset of the main points to be developed in the speech. For example, in his introduction Dr. Coury said, "What I want to talk to you about are three major problems that society and medicine are facing today and that apparently are going to get worse." Noticing this, a sharp listener would have been prepared for a speech with three main points, each dealing with one of the major problems facing society and medicine. Dr. Coury also gave a brief preview statement identifying each of the problems before he started the body of his speech. After this, only the most inattentive of listeners could have been in the dark about Coury's main points.

Listen for Evidence   Identifying a speaker's main points, however, is not enough. You must also listen for supporting evidence. By themselves, Dr. Coury's main points are only assertions. You may be inclined to believe them just because they come from the president of the American Medical Association. Yet a careful listener will be concerned about evidence no matter who is speaking. Had you been listening to Coury's speech, you would have heard him support his claim about the health crisis among teenagers and adolescents with a mass of verifiable evidence. Here is an excerpt:

> We've thought that those years from age eleven or twelve to eighteen, nineteen, or twenty were the healthy young days. . . . But we did a study recently and came up with some very terrible, horrifying figures. Since 1965 the incidence of gonorrhea in teenagers—particularly teenage girls—has gone up 400 percent. . . . We also found out that there are a million teenage pregnancies a year; 400,000 abortions a year; and 40,000 pregnancies a year in children under the age of fifteen. . . .
> I'll bet you didn't know that there are 900,000 teenagers involved in prostitution throughout this country: 600,000 of them are females and about 300,000 are males. They're the runaways, the ignored, those on drugs.
> You probably don't know that alcohol kills about 8,000 teenagers a year in auto accidents, and injures another 40,000 seriously.

There are four basic questions to ask about a speaker's evidence:

Is it *accurate*?
Is it taken from *objective* sources?
Is it *relevant* to the speaker's claim?
Is it *sufficient* to support the speaker's point?

In Dr. Coury's case the answer to each question is yes. His figures about teenage pregnancies, venereal disease, prostitution, and alcohol-related deaths come from AMA-sponsored research and can be verified by independent government and medical sources. They are clearly relevant to Dr. Coury's claim about the teenage health crisis, and they are sufficient to support that claim. If Coury's evidence were inaccurate, biased, irrelevant, or insufficient, you should be wary of accepting his claim.

You should be on guard against unfounded assertions and sweeping generalizations. Keep an ear out for the speaker's evidence and for its accuracy, objectivity, relevance, and sufficiency.

Listen for Technique   We said earlier that you should not let a speaker's delivery distract you from the message, and this is true. However, if you want to become an effective speaker, you should study the methods other people use to speak effectively. When you listen to speeches—in class and out—focus above all on the content of a speaker's message; but also pay attention to the techniques the speaker uses to get the message across.

Analyze the introduction: What methods does the speaker use to gain attention, to relate to the audience, to establish credibility and goodwill? Assess the organization of the speech: Is it clear and easy to follow? Can you pick out the speaker's main points? Can you follow when the speaker moves from one point to another?

Study the speaker's language: Is it accurate, clear, vivid, appropriate? Does the speaker adapt well to the audience and occasion? Finally, diagnose the speaker's delivery: Is it fluent, dynamic, convincing? Does it strengthen or weaken the impact of the speaker's ideas? How well does the speaker use eye contact, gestures, and visual aids?

As you listen, focus on both the speaker's strengths and his or her weaknesses. If the speaker is not effective, try to determine why. If he or she *is* effective, try to pick out techniques you can use in your own speeches. If you listen in this way, you will be surprised how much you can learn about successful speaking.

Source: *The Art of Public Speaking*, Third Edition, by Stephen E. Lucas. Random House, 1989.

Reading 8: A Passage from a Communications Text

Hints: Definitions, examples, enumerations, and headings and subheadings are all keys to important ideas in this selection.

Remember that a good way of taking notes is to write down all the headings and then to place notes under those headings. Textbook authors carefully organize their information through a series of major and minor headings. By writing those headings down, you help organize your own notes.

MANAGING CONFLICTS IN RELATIONSHIPS

One of the primary causes leading to the deterioration of relationships is failure to manage conflict successfully. **Conflict** is the clash of opposing attitudes, ideas, behaviors, goals, and needs. Although many people view conflict as bad (and, to be sure, conflict situations are likely to make us anxious and uneasy), conflict is sometimes useful in that it forces people to make choices and to test the relative merits of their attitudes, behaviors, needs, and goals.

Conflicts include clashes over ideas ("Charley was the first one to talk." "No, it was Mark" or "Your mother is a battle-ax." "What do you mean, a 'battle-ax'?"); over values ("Bringing home pencils and pens from work is not stealing." "Of course it is" or "The idea that you have to be married to have sex is completely outdated." "No, it isn't"); and, perhaps the most difficult to deal with, over ego involvement ("Listen, I've been a football fan for thirty years, I ought to know what good defense is." "Well, you may be a fan, but that doesn't make you an expert").

Methods of Dealing with Conflict

People engage in many behaviors to cope with or manage their conflicts. Some are positive and some are negative. These various behaviors can be broken down into five major patterns: withdrawal, surrender, aggression, persuasion, and discussion. Let's consider each in turn.

Withdrawal   One of the most common—and certainly one of the easiest— ways to deal with conflict is to withdraw. **Withdrawal** entails physical or psychological removal from the situation.

Physical withdrawal is, of course, easiest to identify. Suppose Dorie and Tom are in conflict over Tom's smoking. When Dorie says, "Tom, I thought you told me that whether you stopped smoking completely or not, you weren't going to smoke around the house. Now here you are lighting up!" Tom may withdraw physically, saying, "I don't want to talk about it" as he goes to his basement workshop.

Psychological withdrawal may be more difficult to detect, but it is every bit as common. Using the same example, when Dorie speaks to Tom about his smoking, Tom sits quietly in his chair looking at Dorie, but while she is speaking, he is thinking about the poker game he will be going to the next evening.

Both of these common withdrawal behaviors are negative. Why? Because they neither eliminate nor attempt to manage the nature of the conflict. For instance, when Tom withdraws physically, Dorie may follow him to the basement, where the conflict will be resumed; if not, the conflict will undoubtedly surface later—probably in an intensified manner—when Dorie and Tom try to cope with another issue. When Tom ignores Dorie's comments, Dorie may force Tom to cope with the smoking issue or she may go along with Tom's ignoring her but harbor a resentment that will adversely affect the relationship at some later point.

Nevertheless, conflicts occasionally do go away if left alone. There appear to be two types of situations where withdrawal may work. The first is when the withdrawal represents temporary disengagement used for the purpose of letting the heated emotions brought on by the conflict cool down. For example, when Bill and Margaret begin to argue about having Bill's mother over for Thanksgiving dinner, Margaret feels herself getting angry about what her mother-in-law had said to her recently about the way she and Bill were raising their daughter. Margaret says, "Hold it a minute, let me make a pot of coffee. We can both relax a bit and then we'll talk about this some more." A few minutes later she returns, ready to approach the conflict more objectively. Margaret's action is not true withdrawal; it is not meant as a means of avoiding confrontation. Rather, it provides a cooling-off period that will probably benefit both of them. The second case where withdrawal may work is when a conflict occurs between people who communicate infrequently. Suppose Jack and Mark work in the same office. At two office gatherings they have gotten into arguments about whether the company really cares about its employees, so at the next office gathering Mark avoids sitting near Jack. Withdrawal is a negative behavior pattern only when it is a person's major way of managing conflict.

Surrender   Surrender means giving in immediately to avoid conflict. Some people are so afraid of being in conflict that they will do anything to avoid it. For instance, Jeff and Marian are discussing their vacation plans. Jeff would like just the two of them to go somewhere together, but Marian has talked with two of their friends who are vacationing the same week about going together. After Jeff mentions that he'd like the two of them to go alone, Marian says, "But I think it would be fun to go with another couple, don't you?" Jeff replies, "OK, whatever you want." Even though Jeff really wants the two of them to go alone, rather than describe his feelings or give reasons for his position, he gives in to avoid conflict.

Surrender represents negative behavior for at least two reasons. (1) Decisions should be made on merits and not to avoid conflict. If one person gives in, no evaluation of the decision takes place, so no one knows what would really be best. (2) Surrender can infuriate the other person. When Marian tells Jeff her thoughts, she would probably like Jeff to see her way as the best. But if Jeff just surrenders, Marian will perceive Jeff as a martyr. His unwillingness to present his reasons for not liking her plan thus could cause even more conflict.

Aggression   The use of physical or psychological coercion to get one's way is **aggression**. Through aggression people attempt to force others to accept their ideas. A person using aggression may "win" a conflict, but such "victories" seldom contribute anything positive to a relationship. Aggression is an emotional reaction to conflict by which the aggressor ceases thinking and instead lashes out physically or verbally. Aggression never deals with the merits of the issue—only with who is bigger, can talk louder, or is nastier.

Persuasion   **Persuasion** comprises an attempt to change either the attitude or the behavior of another person. At times during a conflict one person might try to persuade the other that a particular action is the right one. For instance, Doris and Jack are considering buying a new car. Doris says, "Don't we need more room?" Jack might reply, "Enough to get us into the car together, but I don't see why we need any more than that." At this point, Doris and Jack's conflict comes into focus. Now Doris might say, "Jack, remember the other day when you were cussing out our car because it doesn't have much backseat room? We carry a lot of stuff. I do food shopping, you're always carrying equipment for men at the lodge, and there are lots of times when we invite another couple to go somewhere with us." Statements like this one are attempts at resolving the conflict through persuasion.

When persuasion is open and reasonable, it can be a positive means of resolving conflict. But persuasion can also degenerate into manipulation. Although persuasive efforts may fuel a conflict, if that persuasion has a solid logical base, it is at least possible that the persuasion will resolve the conflict.

Discussion   **Discussion**, or verbal problem solving, involves weighing and considering the pros and cons of the issues in conflict. Discussion is the most desirable means of dealing with conflict in a relationship; nevertheless, it is often difficult to accomplish.

Problem solving might follow the formal method of defining the problem, analyzing the problem, suggesting possible solutions, selecting the solution that best fits the analysis, and working to implement the decision. For instance, if Jeff and Marian were discussing how they should spend their vacation, they would first seek to identify the goals they hoped to meet. Then they would suggest places to go and the possibilities of going there with or without others. They would consider how each possibility would meet their goals. Finally, they would select the place and decide whether to go with their friends.

Source: *Communicate!* Sixth Edition, by Rudolph F. Verderber. Wadsworth, 1990.

Reading 9: A Passage from a Business Text

Hints: Definitions, examples, enumerations, and headings and subheadings are all keys to important ideas in this selection.

Remember that a good way of taking notes is to write down all the headings and then to place notes under those headings. Textbook authors carefully organize their information through a series of major and minor headings. By writing those headings down, you help organize your own notes.

CONSUMER PRODUCTS

Consumer products can be subdivided into four groups on the basis of how people buy them: (1) convenience products, (2) shopping products, (3) specialty products, and (4) unsought products.

Convenience Products

Convenience products are items that consumers want to buy with the least possible shopping effort. There are three types of convenience products: staples, impulse items, and emergency products.

Staple items are convenience products for which consumers usually do some planning. Food items are good examples. For instance, though consumers don't seek much information about milk, they do buy it often, and they plan to buy it when preparing to go to the grocery store.

Impulse items are purchased not because of planning but because of a strongly felt immediate need. Thus, distribution is an important factor in marketing impulse products. If they are not located conveniently, exchange will not take place. Shoppers tend to react by impulse in deciding to buy, say, *People* magazine.

Emergency products are items that are needed to solve an immediate crisis. Price and quality are not of primary importance, although the product obviously has to be of sufficient quality to meet the emergency. Thus, while the price of an adhesive bandage means little when one is needed, it *does* have to stick.

Shopping Products

Consumers visit several stores to compare prices and quality before buying *shopping products.* Even before going into the store to examine such products, consumers may study magazines like *Consumer Reports,* or ask friends for their opinions about certain products, or study advertisements. In other words, before buying shopping products, consumers seek information that will allow them to compare two or more brands or substitute products.

Shopping products can be divided into **groups,** depending on how consumers perceive them. *Homogeneous products* are perceived as being essentially similar (canned food items and home insurance policies are examples), whereas *heterogeneous products* are seen as essentially different (furniture, draperies, automobiles, and repair services are examples). With heterogeneous products the different styles and aesthetic features are important, while price is less important. But homogeneous products pose problems for marketers, because they are similar and must be differentiated in consumers' minds.

For instance, there are many smoke detectors on the market, and they all serve the same essential function; all are warning devices. From the marketing viewpoint, however, the similarity ends there. Each brand of smoke detector is technically different, performs somewhat differently, and sells for a different price. It is up to the marketers of a particular smoke detector to differentiate their product in the marketplace. Generally, they will try through advertising to show their product is different from competing brands, and sometimes price will be used to distinguish one product from another. Homogeneous shopping products put demands on consumers because information is needed in order to sort the similar products and make a buying decision. For the same reason, such products require much attention from marketers.

Specialty Products

Specialty products are items for which there are no acceptable substitutes in the consumer's mind. Consumers are willing to search long and hard until they find them. Usually, the buyers of specialty products have investigated the products available and have decided which one they want to buy. And they are willing to search for an outlet for that particular product.

With specialty products, the brand name is extremely important. In fact, that may be most of what consumers are buying. Designer fashions are a good example. People go out of their way to find a store that carries clothes designed by Halston, or Anne Klein, or Bill Blass. Such designers attempt to generate demand for their clothing so that people will search for their products and buy nothing else. A similar situation exists with specialty services like dental and medical care. People do not want to accept substitute goods and services.

Unsought Products

Unsought products are items that consumers do not readily realize they want or need. Most new products fall into this category, until marketers promote their benefits and the needs they satisfy. Not so long ago the trash compacter was an unsought product, because people didn't know they had a need for one. But as the compacter was developed and promoted, the need for it came to be recognized.

Hospitals, convalescent homes, and cemetery plots are other examples of unsought products. Consumers do not shop for such things until a need arises. But when the need is recognized, the products are sought.

Source: *Marketing*, by Charles D. Schewe and Reuben M. Smith. McGraw-Hill, 1980.

Reading 10: A Passage from a Chemistry Text

Hints: Definitions, examples, enumerations, and headings are all keys to important ideas in this densely packed passage from a science text.

Remember that a good way of taking notes is to write down all the headings and then to place notes under those headings. Textbook authors carefully organize their information through a series of major and minor headings. By writing those headings down, you help organize your own notes.

STATES OF MATTER

All matter on earth exists in three physical states: **solid, liquid,** and **gaseous.** Various physical properties distinguish the three states of matter. The properties most often considered are shape, volume, average density, structure, viscosity, and compressibility. Shape, volume, and density have been discussed previously; the last two properties require some explanation.

Viscosity is a measure of the resistance to flow. Substances with high viscosities do not flow readily, whereas substances with low viscosities flow more readily. If we are told that water is more fluid than motor oil, we know that the viscosity of water is less than that of motor oil. **Compressibility** is the measure of the decrease in volume of a substance with an applied pressure. A substance is deemed compressible if a force exerted on its surface (a pressure) results in a compacting of the substance.

Let's consider each physical state individually, starting with the solid state and proceeding to the liquid and gaseous states. The physical state of a substance depends on its temperature and pressure. Unless otherwise noted, room conditions of 25°C (298 K) and normal atmospheric pressure are assumed. Atmospheric pressure is measured in atmospheres, the atmosphere being a unit of gas pressure. Normal atmospheric pressure is equivalent to one atmosphere.

Solids

Solids have fixed shapes that are independent of their container. The volume of a solid is also fixed, and does not change when a pressure is exerted. Solids are almost completely incompressible. Those that seem to be compressible, such as foams or corrugated paper, actually are solids that contain holes, or empty regions, throughout their volume. When these are "compressed," the solid structure fills into the empty regions: the solid itself is not compressed.

Of the three states of matter, solids have the highest average density. Densities in excess of 1 g/cm^3 are the norm for solids. Such is not the case for most liquids and gases. A high average density reflects the fact that the particles within solids are usually packed closer than those in liquids or gases.

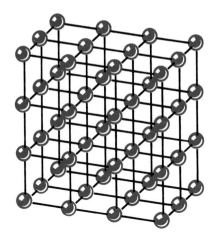

Most solids are composed of a regular array of closely packed particles. Particles within solids are usually more organized and packed more tightly than are the particles within liquids and gases.

The tightly packed particles of solids are also highly organized (see the figure above). The regular patterns of particles found in solids are not detected in either liquids or gases.

Solids have practically no ability to flow because the particles that compose a solid are very tightly bonded. Stated in another way: Solids have very high viscosities.

Liquids

Liquids are quite different from solids in many respects, but the two share some characteristics. Like solids, liquids are essentially incompressible; pressure exerted on liquids generally produces little, if any, change in their volumes. When placed in a container, liquids assume the shape of the container to the level they fill (see the figure below).

A liquid completely fills and takes the shape of the bottom of its container.

As previously mentioned, the average density of liquids is less than that of solids but greater than that of gases. Liquid particles are not bonded as strongly as those in solids, and they are less orderly—more randomly distributed. Both of these factors tend to increase the average volume of liquids relative to that of solids. Thus, for equal masses of an average solid and liquid, the volume of the liquid is usually larger than that of the solid, which results in a lower density.

Viscosities of liquids vary over a broad range. Liquids have much lower viscosities than solids; i.e., they are significantly more fluid than solids. However, the viscosities of liquids are greater than those of gases. The gaseous state is the most fluid state of matter.

Gases

Gases bear little resemblance to the more-condensed states of matter, solids and liquids. To a degree, the properties of gases are the opposite of those of solids. Gases completely fill the volume of their containers, are compressible, have a completely disorganized structure, possess the lowest average density of the three states, and have the lowest viscosities.

Matter can change from one physical state to another. For example, solids, when heated, change to liquids. The characteristic temperature at which a particular solid changes to a liquid is called its **melting point.** At the melting point, the solid and liquid states of the substance coexist. Liquids, in turn, change to solids as they are cooled. The temperature at which a liquid becomes a solid is called the **freezing point.** Freezing and melting occur at the same temperature. In one case, the solid changes into a liquid—it melts. Moving in the other direction, a liquid changes into a solid—it freezes.

$$\text{Solid} \underset{\text{freezing}}{\overset{\text{melting}}{\rightleftharpoons}} \text{liquid}$$

For example, water freezes or melts at 0.0°C.

$$\text{Liquid} \underset{\text{condensation}}{\overset{\text{boiling}}{\rightleftharpoons}} \text{liquid}$$

Numerous solids change directly to their vapors without going through the liquid state. This state change is called **sublimation.** At the temperature and pressure at which a substance sublimes, the solid and vapor states coexist.

$$\text{Solid} \overset{\text{sublimation}}{\longrightarrow} \text{vapor}$$

A good example of a solid that sublimes is "dry ice," or solid carbon dioxide. At −78°C (195 K), solid carbon dioxide and gaseous carbon dioxide coexist.

Source: *Introduction to College Chemistry*, Second Edition, by Drew H. Wolfe. McGraw-Hill, 1988.

CHECKING YOUR MASTERY OF PRWR: QUIZZES

After you study each of the readings in this chapter, you can use the following quizzes to test your understanding of the material. It may take you too much time to study each passage as fully as you would if you were taking a test in a course. However, the very act of reading the material, making decisions on what is important, taking notes, and applying some memory techniques should give you a good basic sense of the material. That is what will be tested in the quizzes that follow.

■ Quiz on Reading 1

1. An example of a manufacturing franchise would be a
   a. fast-food chain.
   b. gasoline station.
   c. car dealer.
   d. soft-drink bottling plant.
2. *True or false?* _____ The *franchiser* is the small-business owner.
3. How many basic types of franchises are there?
   a. One.
   b. Two.
   c. Three.
   d. Four.
4. *True or false?* _____ Franchising is a new phenomenon that began in the late 1950s in American business.

■ Quiz on Reading 2

1. Frustration is caused by
   a. not being able to reach a desired goal.
   b. confusion about goals.
   c. both of the above.
   d. neither of the above.

2. The most frustrating type of conflict is the
   a. approach-approach conflict.
   b. avoidance-avoidance conflict.
   c. approach-avoidance conflict.
   d. anger-frustration conflict.

3. The most common type of conflict is the
   a. approach-approach conflict.
   b. avoidance-avoidance conflict.
   c. approach-avoidance conflict.
   d. anger-frustration conflict.

4. An example of an approach-approach conflict is
   a. having to choose between a Mercedes and a Porsche.
   b. having to choose between cleaning a closet and going to bed.
   c. weighing the advantages and disadvantages of eating chocolate fudge.
   d. kicking your car when the engine will not turn over.

■ Quiz on Reading 3

1. White-collar crimes are committed by people of high status in the course of their
   a. home life.
   b. work.
   c. shopping.
   d. meetings.

2. *True or false?* _____ ''Common criminals'' are more likely to go to prison than white-collar criminals because they tend to steal more money.

3. *True or false?* _____ Corporate crimes are committed for personal gain.

4. One type of corporate crime identified by Ermann and Lundman is the crime against
   a. banks.
   b. profits.
   c. employees.
   d. women and children.

■ **Quiz on Reading 4**

1. The four types of illnesses resulting from long-term alcohol use are: gastrointestinal disorders, malnutrition, glandular disorders, and
   a. infections.
   b. cirrhosis of the liver.
   c. liver damage.
   d. chronic inflammatory diseases.

2. *True or false?* _____ Because alcohol provides calories, it can be considered a food.

3. In alcoholic hepatitis,
   a. the pancreas is inflamed.
   b. bleeding ulcers occur.
   c. hormones are disturbed.
   d. the liver becomes swollen and inflamed.

4. Excessive drinking can cause impotence because of damage to the
   a. liver.
   b. pancreas.
   c. glandular system.
   d. digestive system.

■ **Quiz on Reading 5**

1. *True or false?* _____ Chemical processes cannot break elements down into simpler substances.

2. The smallest units of matter that are still characteristic of an element are
   a. atoms.
   b. protons.
   c. neutrons.
   d. orbits.

3. One of the three subatomic particles is called a(n)
   a. element.
   b. atom.
   c. electron.
   d. orbit.

4. The small dense body at the center of an atom is called a(n)
   a. proton.
   b. element.
   c. neutron.
   d. nucleus.

■ Quiz on Reading 6

1. An infant's getting used to a sound that at first made his or her heart beat rapidly is an example of
   a. habituation.
   b. associative learning.
   c. social attachment.
   d. sensitive care.

2. In social smiling, a baby's smile is always directed toward
   a. a neighbor.
   b. a nodding puppet head.
   c. a mobile.
   d. another person.

3. Separation anxiety is seen when a baby shows distress or great discomfort at
   a. loud buzzing noises.
   b. being left in the care of someone other than the mother or father.
   c. being in an unfamiliar room.
   d. the return of the mother to an unfamiliar room.

4. *True or false?* _____ The more secure the infant-caretaker attachment, the better the child's adjustment in kindergarten.

■ Quiz on Reading 7

1. The author has divided his advice on how to become a better listener into how many main suggestions?
   a. Three.
   b. Four.
   c. Five.
   d. Six.

2. According to the author, listening between the lines is a way to
   a. review mentally what the speaker has already said.
   b. resist distractions.
   c. agree with what you hear.
   d. listen for main points.

3. To focus your listening, pay attention to main points, evidence, and
   a. technique.
   b. conclusions.
   c. problems raised by the speaker.
   d. anecdotes.

4. To judge a speaker's evidence, pay attention to its accuracy, objectivity, relevance, and
   a. main points.
   b. technique.
   c. efficiency.
   d. sufficiency.

■ Quiz on Reading 8

1. *True or false?* _____ Perhaps the most difficult conflict to deal with is over ego involvement.

2. The five major patterns of dealing with conflict are withdrawal, surrender, aggression, persuasion, and
   a. ego involvement.
   b. discussion.
   c. removal.
   d. force.

3. Jeff's giving in to Marian's wish to vacation with friends without explaining his opposition is an example of
   a. withdrawal.
   b. surrender.
   c. aggression.
   d. persuasion.

4. The author defines *discussion* as
   a. a clash of opposing ideas.
   b. an attempt to change another person's attitude or behavior.
   c. verbal problem solving.
   d. defining a problem.

■ **Quiz on Reading 9**

1. The author classifies consumer products according to
   a. cost.
   b. need.
   c. how they are bought.
   d. how important they are.

2. The four groups of consumer products are convenience products, specialty products, unsought products, and
   a. staple items.
   b. impulse items.
   c. shopping products.
   d. brand-name products.

3. *People* magazine is an example of products that tend to be
   a. staple items.
   b. impulse items.
   c. homogeneous products.
   d. unsought products.

4. *True or false?* _____ According to the author, emergency products are a type of specialty product.

■ **Quiz on Reading 10**

1. How many states of matter are there?
   a. Two.
   b. Three.
   c. Four.
   d. Five.

2. Particles are usually most tightly packed in
   a. solids.
   b. liquids.
   c. gases.
   d. oils.

3. A melting point is the characteristic temperature at which a
   a. gas becomes liquid.
   b. liquid becomes solid.
   c. liquid changes to a gas.
   d. solid changes to a liquid.
4. Dry ice is an example of substances that
   a. are easily compressed.
   b. never change their physical state.
   c. have a melting point.
   d. undergo sublimation.

APPLYING PRWR TO A TEXTBOOK CHAPTER

This chapter will help improve your textbook study by:

- Reviewing the PRWR study method
- Providing note-taking practice on an entire textbook chapter
- Presenting hints and comments on good note-taking

To make your practice at textbook study as realistic as possible, you are now going to apply the PRWR method to an entire chapter from a college textbook. The book, *Sociology: An Introduction,* by Michael S. Bassis, Richard J. Gelles, and Ann Levine, was published in a fourth edition in 1991. This Random House book is widely used in colleges throughout the country.

You will read and take notes on the entire chapter by completing the ''activities and comments'' pages placed at five different spots within the chapter. The work you do will help show you just how the enormous amount of information presented within a chapter can be reduced to a limited number of notes. You will also become aware of the techniques that authors use to help communicate their ideas in an organized way.

Ideally, before studying this chapter, you should work through all of the reading skills in Part Four of this book. If you have practiced such individual skills as locating definitions, enumerations, and main ideas, you will be better able to take on an entire textbook chapter. On the other hand, if you need practical guidance right away in how to ready and study a textbook, you may want to proceed now with the sample chapter.

A REVIEW OF PRWR

To read and study this or any textbook chapter, apply the four steps in the PRWR study method. Following is a summary of those steps.

Step 1: Previewing the Chapter

Note the title and reflect for a moment on the fact that this entire chapter is going to be about "The Family." Then skim the chapter (which goes to page 185) to answer the following questions:

- How many major heads are in the chapter? (You'll note that major heads are set off in boldface capital letters.) _____

- Look at the major head on page 174: Divorce. How many subheads (which are set off in boldface capital and lowercase letters) appear under this main head?

- What is the first term that is set off in **boldface** print in the text? _____

- What is the first idea that is set off in *italicized* print in the text? _____

- How many tables, figures, and photographs are in the chapter? _____

- How many boxes with related added material are in the chapter? _____

- Does the chapter have an introduction? _____

- Does the chapter have a summary? _____

- Is there a list of key terms that are central to understanding the chapter? _____

Step 2: The First Reading

Read the chapter all the way through once. As you do so, mark off as a minimum the following: *definitions* (underline them), *examples* (put an *Ex* in the margin), *major enumerations* (number them 1, 2, 3, and so on), and what seem to be *important ideas* (put a check in the margin).

Remember that while you mark, you should not worry about understanding everything completely. Understanding is a process that will come gradually while you continue to work with the text. Bit by bit, as you reread the text, take notes on it, and study the notes, you will increase your understanding of the material.

Step 3: Writing Notes on the Chapter

As you proceed, write down all the major and minor headings in the chapter. The authors have used these headings to organize their material, and you can use the same headings to help organize your notes. Under the headings, write down definitions, examples, enumerations, and main ideas. (You will be shown just how to take such notes.)

Use common sense when taking textbook notes for your actual courses. Write down only what adds to ideas you have learned in class. Have your class notes in front of you while taking textbook notes. If a good definition of a term has been given to you by the teacher, there may be no need to write down a definition that appears in the textbook.

Step 4: Reciting Your Notes

Use the key words you have placed in the margin of your notes to go over the material repeatedly until you have mastered it.

STUDYING THE SAMPLE CHAPTER

How to Proceed

Preview, read, and take notes on the textbook chapter that follows. While previewing, you will see that five sets of "activities and comments" appear within the chapter. All the notes you need for the chapter will go on those "activities and comments" pages. Doing the activities will give you a solid, realistic grounding in the skills needed to read and study textbook material.

The Family

No social institution is as talked about, as idealized, as criticized, and as poorly understood as the family. Many of our fondest memories of childhood and deepest hopes for the future center on the family. "Motherhood and apple pie"—symbols of home—are sacred in American culture. At the same time, we blame the family for all kinds of problems—for failures in our educational system; for the perpetuation of poverty; for mental illness. The idea that the family is dying—an idea that is revived generation after generation—draws cheers from some, who rejoice that "Liberation is coming at last," but appalls others, who fear that "We are on the verge of anarchy."

One reason for these extreme points of view is that American families are as secret as they are sacred (Skolnick, 1987). The family is a backstage area, where people can take off the masks they wear in public and be themselves. Nonfamily are rarely admitted behind the scenes. Hence our knowledge of other people's families is based on their public, onstage performances. Often we are ignorant even about our own families. How many people know how old their parents were when they met? How much their father or mother earns? Much of what we think we know about the family is based on limited knowledge of our own families, superficial knowledge of other people's families, and impressions gathered from the mass media (TV talk shows, soap operas, advice columns in newspapers, and magazines).

The goal of this chapter is to shed light on some of the mysteries—and myths—that surround the family. The first two sections look at family structure and function, and put today's family in historical and cross-cultural perspective. Has the family changed as rapidly and as drastically as the mass media sometimes suggest? The next section explores courtship, marriage, and children. Is marriage simply a matter of meeting and falling in love with Ms. or Mr. Right? Is having children a natural and inevitable sequel to marriage? What impact does women working have on families? The following section considers the dark side of home life:

family violence. Did you know that a person is far more likely to be murdered or injured by a family member than by anyone else? The next section examines divorce. Today, the chances are better than one in three that a first marriage will end in divorce. Taking these "hard facts" into account, the final section considers the future of the family.

[Section 1 begins.]

CROSS-CULTURAL SIMILARITIES AND DIFFERENCES

Every known society has families. But the form the family takes and the functions it performs vary widely over time and among societies. These different arrangements seem as natural to the people who practice them as our family system does to us. Indeed, many would consider American ideas about the family somewhat strange. By the same token, Americans might view the family customs of other cultures as highly unusual. For example, in traditional Navajo society, a wife and husband never live under the same roof. Rather, she lives with her mother, sisters, and their children; he lives in a communal men's house. Their "conjugal relations" are limited to discreet visits. A woman of the Trobriand Islands in the South Pacific expects her brother, not her husband, to provide for her, discipline her sons, and guide them into adulthood. In all but the strictest biological sense, the maternal uncle plays the role of father as we know it in the United States. The Masai of East Africa consider it normal and proper for a man to ask permission to sleep with a good friend's wife. To refuse sexual hospitality is considered rude. There are even societies where parents do not have authority over their children. In Samoa, youngsters wander from one relative's house to another, deciding for themselves where to live.

Family Structure

To most Americans, the word "marriage" is synonymous with **monogamy**—marriage involving only one woman and one man. Yet even in this most basic respect family structure varies widely throughout the world. We consider monogamy the ideal and think of it as the most widespread form of marriage. But this is not the case. In only 25 percent of the world's societies is monogamy the preferred form of marriage.* Some monogamous societies are modern, technological societies like our own. But others are hunting and gathering societies whose populations live off the land, using only the simplest technology (examples are the !Kung of Africa and the Eskimos).

In the other 75 percent of human societies, the preferred arrangement is **polygamy**—marriage involving more than one wife or husband at the same time. In almost all societies this takes the form of **polygyny,** marriage of one man to two or more women. Polygyny was practiced in ancient China—hardly a small, primitive society. It is part of Judeo-Christian cultural history: The ancient Hebrews (including Kings David and Solomon) were polygynists. Up until 1890, so were the Mormons of Utah. And Islam, the second largest religion in the world today, allows a man four wives. In contrast, only four societies have been reported in which **polyandry**—marriage of one woman to two or more men—is the norm.

Most of the men in the societies that permit polygyny do not actually practice it, for the simple reason that there aren't enough women to go around. Even if there were an excess of women, most men could not afford the cost of marrying and maintaining several wives. In practice, polygyny is a privilege that accompanies wealth, power, status, and in most societies, old age. It turns out, then, that monogamy *is* the most commonly practiced form of marriage in the world.

Ironically, it may be more common for a person to have more than one spouse in the United States and other "monogamous" societies than

*The data here are from George P. Murdock's "World Ethnographic Survey" (1957, p. 686), a survey of all societies known to social scientists through history, exploration, and anthropology—a total of 565 societies.

in societies that permit polygamy. The only difference—and one we Americans consider crucial—is that a person must divorce (or outlive) one spouse before acquiring another. According to current projections, almost half of first marriages in America end in divorce. Most divorced people remarry within four years. When second marriages end in divorce, most of these people try marriage a third time (Glick, 1988). Thus, a number of Americans practice **serial monogamy**: one exclusive, legally sanctioned, but relatively short-lived marriage after another (Mead, 1970).

Family Functions

Family functions, like family structures, vary widely. In most traditional, preindustrial societies, the family performs four central functions (Murdock, 1949). The first is the *regulation of sexual activity*. No society leaves people free to engage in sexual behavior whenever they want, with whomever they want. Some societies place a strict ban on sex before marriage; others require a woman to demonstrate that she is fertile by becoming pregnant before she marries. All societies place a taboo on incest, though which family members are included in this taboo varies. The second function of the family (which follows from the first) is *reproduction*. The family bears primary responsibility for replacing members of society who have died or emigrated, and thus keeping society "alive" from generation to generation. The third function is the *socialization of children*. It is not enough simply to produce children; they must be given physical care and trained for adult roles. The family bears primary responsibility for teaching children the language, values, norms, beliefs, technology, and skills of their culture. The fourth function of the family is economic. The family bears primary responsibility for *providing for the physical needs* of both young and old members.

In modern, industrial societies, some of these traditional functions have either changed or been taken over in part by other institutions. With modern birth control devices and safe, legal abortions, the regulation of sexual activity has lost some of its urgency. The socialization function has changed significantly. In traditional societies, family members teach young people all they need to know for a life that will resemble their parents'. The emphasis is on well-defined social roles and skills. The distinction between learning and play is blurred; education is continuous and largely informal. In modern societies like our own, a child's future is unpredictable (as a rule, children do not enter their parents' occupations). Furthermore, skills are complex and often become quickly obsolete. Instruction in everything from mathematics to sex to driving a car has been turned over to other institutions—particularly the schools and the mass media. Day-care centers now expose children to "professional socialization" at a younger age than ever before. Government also has taken over some of the family's former economic functions—for example, the care and financial support of the elderly. The overall trend is for functions that were previously matters of personal care within the family to be taken over by (a) professional experts, (b) large-scale markets, and/or (c) bureaucratic organizations. Health care is an obvious example (Lasch, 1977).

While many of the family's functions have diminished, one that has become increasingly important is *emotional gratification*. Although the schools teach children skills, the family still provides "nurturant socialization" or emotional support and caring (Reiss, 1965). And children are not the only ones to receive emotional gratification from the family. For most of us, the family is the group we count on to satisfy emotional needs on a continuing basis. We expect—or feel we have a right to expect—to find understanding, companionship, and affection at home. The more depersonalized our work and school lives become, the more we come to depend on the family. The modern family has been described as an "intimate environment" (Skolnick, 1987), distinguished from other social groups by the

erotic attachment between husband and wife and the affectionate attachment of parents and children. Ideally, the family is a safe, secure, nurturant "haven in a heartless world"—the world of capitalism, careers, and competition (Lasch, 1977).

Changes in the structure and functions of the family provoke mixed responses. Some observers view serial monogamy as evidence that the family is a highly flexible, adaptable institution. They point out that second marriages are more enduring than first (Bane, 1976). Others see it as a symptom of decay: "[Have we begun] to treat relationships the way we treat cars and clothing, to be used for a short time and then replaced by other models?" (Skolnick, 1987, p. 5). One source of controversy is our differing perceptions of the true nature of the American family.

[Section 1 ends.
Section 2 begins.]

THE AMERICAN FAMILY IN PERSPECTIVE

In times of apparent change and crisis, people tend to idealize the past, to reminisce about "the good old days." Thus today, when the family seems threatened by challenges and problems, many of us look back nostalgically at the rural family of pioneer days. We long for the times when the family represented the permanence, security, and warmth of several generations. (See "Sociology and the Media.")

The Extended Family

Many of us imagine that in days gone by, families stayed together. A couple, their children, and their grandchildren all lived together in a big, rambling house on a farm of their own. This is what sociologists call an **extended family**: members of three or more generations, related by blood or marriage, who live together or near one another. This is also the "classical family of Western nostalgia" (Goode, 1963, p. 6). There were always plenty of children down on Grandma's farm, and plenty of adults to look after them. No one was lonely or idle. The fam-

Many of us imagine the typical nineteenth-century American family as a large, self-sufficient unit. In reality, although some families included grandparents, many others were as nuclear in character as their present-day counterparts.

ily produced and preserved its own food; repaired its own equipment; educated its young in vocational skills (namely, being a farmer or a farmer's wife); settled its own disputes; and cared for its own sick, disturbed, and elderly members. Family pride rested on self-sufficiency. The head of the household was stern but fair. Everyone in the family knew his or her place. Young people married early, to someone of whom their parents approved, and settled on or near the farm. Divorce was rare. But if individuals were abandoned or widowed, they had plenty of kinfolks to rely on. Life may sometimes have been hard, but it was secure.

The problem with this image of the extended family is that it seldom existed in reality. It is a romantic, stereotyped image. True, the average family today is somewhat smaller than it was a century ago: about three members, compared with about five in 1890 (Laslett, 1973; *Statistical Abstract, 1989*, p. 50). But this is due primarily to a drop in the birthrate and to the aging of our population, not to a breakdown of the extended family. Indeed, records from sixteenth-century England indicate that fewer than one family in twenty had a grandparent living in the household (Laslett, 1973). In 1875, 82 percent of families in Rhode Island were nuclear (as opposed to extended; see the following section); in 1960, 85 percent—hardly a huge increase (Pryor, 1972).

Furthermore, most people a century ago lived in one-room cottages, not in big houses.

Studying Section 1

Activities for Section 1

Notice that the title page of the chapter lists all of the main heads and subheads within the chapter. You'll see that the family is examined in six different ways, starting with ''Cross-Cultural Similarities and Differences'' and ending with ''The Family in the Future.''

Now read the first text page of the chapter (page 142) and answer the following question:

■ Which paragraph explains the purpose of the chapter and also previews what will be covered in each section of the chapter?

_____ First paragraph   _____ Second paragraph

_____ Third paragraph   _____ Fourth paragraph

By giving you a quick overview of the entire chapter, the authors help prepare you to read and understand it.

The notes here begin with the first heading. Next there is a main idea presented under that heading, as well as an example of the idea. Complete the following notes on the first page and a half of the text (page 142 and a little over half of page 143). You will have to add a series of definitions, two examples, and four items in an enumeration.

(Chapter 12: The Family)
CROSS-CULTURAL SIMILARITIES AND DIFFERENCES

Americans might view the family customs of other cultures as highly unusual.

Ex.—_____

_____

Family Structure:

1. Monogamy—_____

2. Polygamy—_____

Polygamy is the preferred arrangement in 75% of human societies!

Kinds of polygamy:

a. Polygyny—_____

Ex.—_____

b. Polyandry—_____

Ex.—_____

3. Serial monogamy (in the U.S.)—_____

    Family Functions:

    1. _____

    2. _____

    3. _____

    4. _____

Comments on Section 1

■   The idea that ''Americans might view the family customs of other cultures as highly unusual'' is included in the notes because the authors feel it is important enough to present four different examples supporting it. In your notes, all you need generally include is one example.

■   As a general rule, take notes on a chapter by first writing down all the main headings and subheadings. Then write down whatever seem to be the most important ideas under those headings. This is an extremely important guideline to keep in mind when taking notes on a chapter. In a nutshell, write down headings, definitions, examples, enumerations, and what seem to be other important ideas.

■   Complete the following: Almost all the notes above consist of headings, definitions, _____, and enumerations. This kind of note-taking is typical with introductory textbooks, where you are often learning the special vocabulary of a subject.

■   Add details that seem noteworthy. The above notes include the surprising detail that polygamy is the preferred arrangement in _____ of human societies. Such a startling detail is almost a sure bet to be included in a multiple-choice exam.

■   When taking notes, don't use any more symbols than you need to. When you do use symbols, make sure they really mean something. In the notes above, the symbols ''1'' and ''2'' show the two kinds of family structure. The ''a'' and ''b'' show that polygyny and polyandry are the two kinds of polygamy. Also, the symbols ''1,'' ''2,'' ''3,'' and ''4'' make clear the four functions of the family.

Many students overuse and misuse note-taking symbols. Keep your notes simple!

SOCIOLOGY AND THE MEDIA
"Prime-Time Families"

The changing image of the family on television provides insights into changing attitudes toward the family in society. This is not to say that portrayals of the family on TV mirror reality; they do not. But the dialogue between the television audience and television producers and advertisers, mediated by ratings, does tell us something about how the nation feels about families. As media analyst Ella Taylor (1989) suggests, television speaks to our collective desires, our shared worries and concerns, our wish to improve or repair our own lives, and our need to know what is going on "out there," beyond the borders of our personal family experiences.

The 1950s and 1960s were decade of the happy TV family. The family that viewers saw on prime-time TV was an intact, white, comfortable (though not conspicuously wealthy), middle-class, suburban, nuclear family—as on *Father Knows Best, Ozzie and Harriet*, and *Leave It to Beaver*. Parents on these shows had an endless supply of time, energy, and wisdom, which they devoted to guiding their children toward adult lives that would resemble their own. Blessed with all the modern conveniences, these families also were firmly grounded in traditional values. The outside world of public issues rarely if ever intruded on this contented domestic circle. Programs that dealt with ethnic differences (*Amos 'n' Andy, The Goldbergs*, and *Life with Luigi*) or working-class families (*The Honeymooners, The Life of Riley*) fell by the wayside.

The 1970s was a decade of family discontent. This trend was epitomized by *All in the Family*, the story of a white, middle-aged, working-class couple, living in a soon-to-be-integrated neighborhood in Queens, New York. The show was a battle of the generations, which pitted unrepentant bigot Archie Bunker, with his constant stream of racial and ethnic slurs, against his muddleheaded but kindly wife Edith, his feminist daughter Gloria, and her Polish-American husband Michael, who was studying to become a sociologist. Social problems that had been taboo for the situation com-

[By] far the most popular program about families was (and still is) **The Cosby Show.**

edies of the 1960s were "lined up like ducks in a shooting range and argued back and forth in a contest between tradition and modernity," between the political conservatism of the 1950s and the liberalism of the post-Vietnam years (Taylor, 1989, p. 69). Archie never won an argument; he was always made the fool. But polls showed that about half the TV audience identified *with* him, rather than laughing *at* him as the producers intended (Vidmar and Rokeach, 1974).

With the Bunker household, the family was transformed from a haven of peaceful coexistence into a hotbed of clashing interests and ideologies.

Few farms were large or diversified enough to be self-sufficient. And although divorce may have been rare, there is no evidence that families were any happier than they are now. Indeed, our grandparents were as nostalgic about *their* grandparents' families as we are about theirs (Goode, 1963). Extended families have been the norm in other societies and times, but not in recent Western history.

The Nuclear Family

The 1950s idealized another family type, the **nuclear family** consisting of a husband, wife and

At first by implication, and later in the scripts themselves, family life itself was threatened. The trend toward "relevant" scripts and not-so-happy families continued throughout the 1970s. Two of the only popular shows with happy, "intact" families—*The Waltons* and *Little House on the Prairie*—were set in the past. The 1970s was also the decade when prime-time soap operas in which families divided against themselves (*Dallas, Dynasty*) made their first appearance.

The 1980s was a decade of reorganization for TV families. Alternative family forms were treated as (almost) normal—on *Kate and Allie* (single parents), *The Golden Girls* and *Designing Women* (all-female households), *Dads, My Two Dads,* and *You Again* (all-male households), *Diff'rent Strokes, Gimme a Break* (mixed-race families), and *Who's the Boss?* (role reversals). But by far the most popular program about families was (and still is) *The Cosby Show*. In many ways the Huxtables resemble the happy prime-time families of the 1950s and 60s. Despite high-powered careers (Claire is a lawyer and Cliff, a physician), the Huxtables always have plenty of "quality time" to devote to their children. A typical episode revolves around a lesson in social adjustment for one or another child. "[T]here is no dissent, no real difference of opinion or belief, only vaguely malicious banter that quickly dissolves into sweet agreement—all part of the busy daily manufacture of consensus" (Taylor, 1989, p. 161). Almost all of the action takes place within the Huxtables' brownstone; the outside world does not intrude on this charmed family circle.

The Cosby Show has been widely praised for its revival of the happy family, its reinforcement of traditional family values, and its realism. But it is not without critics (Miller, 1988). One criticism is the show's emphasis on consumption. Everything in the Huxtables' home is new and expensive; characters are defined by their trendy outfits; and whole episodes revolve around possessions (Cliff's new juicer, Theo's expensive sweatshirt, Rudy wearing a dozen wooden necklaces). Bill Cosby himself has admitted that people love him because of his ability to sell everything from Jell-O to E. F. Hutton to a "tough love" style of fatherhood (in Miller, 1988, p. 71). How much work it takes to support this lifestyle of consumption is left to the imagination. A second criticism is the show's lack of attention to race. Anyone can plainly see that the Huxtables are black, but for all intents and purposes the show is "color blind." At no point do the scripts suggest that it might be difficult for a black person to become a physician or a lawyer, or that black professionals might have some responsibility to the black community, or that black children might have to learn to deal with prejudice outside their homes. With his impish grin and affluent lifestyle (on and off camera), Cosby implicitly reassures the audience that the American system is fair. "'Look!' he seems to be saying. 'Even *I* can have it all!' " (Miller, 1988, p. 71). While this message may be comforting to all Americans, white and black, it is hardly realistic. Further, it encourages viewers to forget the large numbers of black Americans who can barely make ends meet and continue to struggle against racism.

Undoubtedly the 1990s will bring new prime time families reflecting changing social concerns.

Source: Unless otherwise noted, this discussion is based on Ella Taylor, *Prime-Time Families: Television Culture in Postwar America.* Berkeley: University of California Press, 1989.

their dependent children living in a home of their own. The defining characteristic of the nuclear family was independence. According to the 1950s stereotype, parents or other relatives might visit or even move in temporarily, but they were expected to act like guests and not "interfere." In times of need the nuclear family turned to professionals (doctors, police, bankers) as well as to relatives. Young people were sent to school and old people to "homes." Typically, the husband was considered responsible for supporting the family, even if the wife worked. He went off each day to work for a corporation or some branch of government, not a

Ideally, the family continues to be a place of security and intimacy in the face of the increasing predominance of markets and bureaucracy.

family-owned enterprise. Typically, the wife was considered responsible for the family's social and emotional well-being, and stayed home at least while the children were small. The couple had sole responsibility for their children. (Grandparents and other relatives took over only as a favor or in emergencies.) But the children were expected to leave home and start families of their own in their twenties. What careers they pursued, where they lived, and whom they married were up to them.

In the 1950s and early 1960s, an independent nuclear family was the ideal toward which all (or nearly all) young people aspired. Champions of the nuclear family praised its freedom from the tyranny of large kin groups; critics bemoaned its isolation. The one point on which they agreed was that "modern" families were on their own. Yet careful research shows that the independence of nuclear families was in part a myth. In a classic study of middle-class urban families, Marvin Sussman (1959) found that over 90 percent received some kind of aid from ex-

tended family members. Direct financial aid (say, the down payment for a house), indirect financial aid (a gift of a major appliance or a savings account for grandchildren), help during illness, and baby-sitting were all cited. In most cases aid flowed from parents to children, but adult children also helped their parents and one another. It didn't seem to matter how far apart members of the family lived; they came to one another's aid when the need arose.

Family ties remain strong today. Most Americans keep in touch with their extended families over their lifetime, look to kin for financial aid and help with daily problems, enjoy their extended family and wish they had more time to spend with them. Today as in the past, women are the glue that holds families together. Of all kinship bonds, the mother-daughter tie is the strongest, spanning generations. Women are also more likely than men are to keep in close touch with other relatives, especially their sisters, aunts, nieces, and grandmothers (*The Gallup Report*, July 1989, Report No. 286). Ac-

TABLE 12-1   Family Ties

HOW OFTEN WE SEE OUR PARENT(S)

Every day	22%
Once a week or more	32
Once a month or more	16
Several times a year	19
Once a year	7
Less than once a year	3
Never	1
	100%

HOW OFTEN WE TALK WITH OUR PARENT(S)

Every day	19%
Once a week or more	49
Once a month or more	18
Several times a year	4
Once a year	*
Less than once a year	*
Never	9
No opinion	1
	100%

THINGS PARENTS DID FOR ADULT CHILDREN

Said they loved you	86%
Gave gifts	83
Gave personal advice	65
Helped with errands, etc.	42
Gave financial help	40
Helped with children	30

THINGS ADULT CHILDREN DID FOR PARENTS

Gave gifts	94%
Said you loved them	89
Helped with errands, etc.	76
Gave personal advice	65
Gave financial help	30

*Less than 1 percent. (Asked of 816 respondents with at least one living parent.)

Source: *The Gallup Report*, July 1989, Report No. 286, pp. 29, 30. Reprinted by permission of The Gallup Organization.

cording to Gallup polls, members of most American families stay in touch and continue to display affection toward one another (see Table 12-1).

The special relationship between grandparents and grandchildren, which leaps a generation, remains intact (Cherlin and Furstenberg, 1986). Indeed, more people are living long enough to become grandparents today than in the past. Moreover, many of today's grandparents have more time and money to devote to their grandchildren, and advances in transportation and communication make it easier for them to keep in touch, even though they probably do not live together.

The Modified Extended Family

The nuclear family, then, is isolated only in terms of residence. A more appropriate term for this arrangement would be **modified extended families**: networks of nuclear families that establish separate residences but maintain ties (Litwak, 1960). With divorce and remarriage, modern kinship networks can be quite extensive. These interlocking families often provide significant aid to one another. But their feeling of being connected does not depend on living near one another, working together, or falling under the authority of a strong parent, as in classical extended families. Participation in the modified extended family is voluntary, not obligatory; some individuals do "drop out." Kinship has become more like friendship. People often "interact with their relatives according to how they feel about them" (Skolnick, 1987, p. 129). Good relationships are considered ends in themselves.

Today's Families

Yet another common assumption is that the vast majority of Americans live in a nuclear family. In fact, less than a third of households in the United States today consist of a husband, a wife, and their children. The numbers of single people living alone, single parents living with children, married couples with no children (or no children living at home), and unmarried, unrelated adults living together have grown steadily (see Figure 12-1). Nuclear families are a statistical minority. Who are the people in other arrangements? And why haven't they "settled down" in the conventional way?

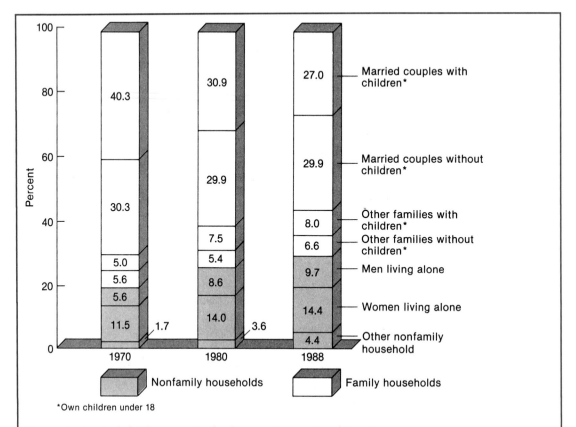

Figure 12-1 Today's Changing Family. *(Source:* Current Population Reports, *series P-20, No. 432 [Sept. 1988], fig. 1, p. 3.)*

Singlehood

One reason for the changing composition of American households is that more people remain single for longer periods of time. In 1960, only 28 percent of American women ages twenty to twenty-four had not yet married; today more than 60 percent of women in this age group are single (*Statistical Abstract, 1989*). The main reason for this increase is that more young adults are postponing marriage, not that a significant number are deciding to never marry. A larger proportion are going to college and to graduate or professional school, which tends to delay marriage. And because of more relaxed attitudes, marriage is no longer a prerequisite for a satisfying sex life, for women or men (Davidson and Darling, 1988).

The stereotype of the "swinging single" conceals a wide range of variations, however (see Figure 12-2). Of the approximately 74 million unmarried adults in this country, about 50 million have never married, 13 million are divorced, and 14 million are widowed [*Current Population Reports*, Series P-20, No. 433 (March 1988), p. 3]. For some people, singlehood is a voluntary but temporary position (Stein, 1981). They have not rejected the possibility of marriage, but for the moment they give higher priority to education, career, politics, or other activities. Many young and recently divorced people fall into this category. For others, singlehood is a voluntary but stable position. They have decided not to marry and are happy with the choice. Many gay men and women fall into

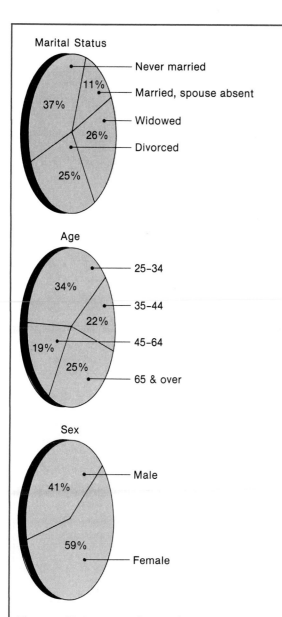

Figure 12-2 America's Singles Population (Over Age 25). *(Data from H. McCubb and B.B. Dahl,* Marriage and the Family. *New York: Wiley, 1985.)*

this category (though other homosexuals establish stable partnerships that are quite similar to heterosexual marriages). For a third group, singlehood is involuntary but temporary. They do

not like being single and are actively seeking marriage partners. For a fourth group, singlehood is involuntary but stable. They would like to marry but have resigned themselves to not being able to find a partner. Many older divorcées, widows, and widowers fall into this category. Singlehood is not always exciting and glamorous.

Singlehood changes over the life cycle (Stein, 1981). The twenties are often a period of trying different lifestyles and making provisional choices. Many young adults are wary of full commitments. Singles have a good deal of company in this stage. The early thirties tend to be a period of reevaluation, when people weigh the possibilities of changing careers and/or living arrangements. People who are married may consider the alternatives; those who are single may feel increased internal and external pressures to marry. The number of singles drops off in this stage. Twenty-three percent of men and 15 percent of women thirty to thirty-four years old have never married (*Statistical Abstract, 1989*, p. 43). And the never-married singles are joined by the newly divorced. The middle years reveal a different pattern. Only 6 percent of men and 5 percent of women age forty-five to fifty-four have never married. Singlehood seems to be more positive for women than for men in this stage. Indeed, there is some evidence that marriage creates obstacles to women's other goals. Never-married women age forty and older tend to have advanced further, in terms of their education, occupation, and income, than either married women or single men. In contrast, there is an increase in mental health problems among older single men.

One-Parent Families

In the last two decades, the number of one-parent families nearly tripled, reaching 9.2 million in 1990 (*Statistical Abstract, 1989*, p. 50). This figure does not include single parents with children over eighteen in their home (3.3 mil-

Two out of three children born in the 1980s will spend at least part of their youth in a single-parent family. Do such children benefit from extra attention or are they disadvantaged?

lion in 1984), single parents who live with their parents (1.5 million in 1984), or single parents who live with other relatives or friends (360,000 in 1984) (Norton and Glick), 1986). Moreover, this figure represents only the number of *current* one-parent families; the number of people who will ever live in this type of family is much larger. Today about 25 percent of children live in one-parent families [*Current Population Reports*, Series P-20, No. 433 (January 1989), p. 62]. But estimates are that 60 percent of all children born in the 1980s will spend a year or more in a single-parent family before reaching age eighteen (Norton and Glick, 1986).

In the past, the major cause of single-parent families was widowhood; today the major cause is divorce, followed by births without marriage. Between 1985 and 1988, the proportion of first children born or conceived before first marriage was 79 percent for black women, 33 percent for white women (Census Bureau, reported in *The New York Times*, June 22, 1989, p. A16).

One-parent families are found in all social categories. However the great majority of full-time single parents are women (*Statistical Abstract, 1989*, p. 50). Single mothers are much more likely than are married parents or single fathers to have less than a full high school education, to be living in poverty, and to be members of a minority group (Norton and Glick, 1986). Often these mothers live at the mercy of welfare agencies. Their children's teachers, health care workers, and local merchants tend to treat them with less respect than they show women with partners, no matter how poor. Their own children may blame them for their circumstances. One seven-year-old declared his mother a "nobody" (Ambert, 1985, p. 23).

For other single mothers, poverty is relative. Whether or not a woman held a job before she was divorced or widowed, whether or not she receives child support payments or her deceased husband's pension, she is likely to experience a drop in her standard of living once she is on her own. The divorced mother who is awarded the house in the suburbs but cannot afford its taxes and upkeep is not unusual (see Chapter 10).

The problems of single fathers are somewhat different. Men are far less likely than women to suffer financial reversals if their spouses die or abandon them.* But single fathers often are as unprepared for housework as women who never worked are for the job market. Divorced fathers may find themselves contributing to the costs of two households. And even if they pay child support, they may be cut off from contact with their children.

Independence and flexibility are luxuries for virtually all single parents. Unlike other single people, they cannot stay out all night dancing, decide on a business trip at the last minute, or spend the weekend reading a novel; they are "on call" all the time. Their full-time responsibilities furnish a strong incentive for single parents to marry and share the load, yet at the same time constitute an obstacle to their meeting eligible mates.

Families without Children
The number of Americans who do *not* have children has also climbed. More than one out of five married women ages eighteen to forty-four has never had a child (*Statistical Abstract, 1989*, p. 68). Some of these women will have children in the future. A survey conducted by the U.S. Census Bureau in 1988 found that 54 percent of married women in their early thirties plan to become parents someday (*The New York Times*, June 22, 1989, p. A16). But 10 percent of adult women say they never plan to have children, and 15 percent are undecided. Rates of childlessness are highest among whites (20 percent of women ages eighteen to forty-four) and lowest among blacks and Hispanics (11 and 12 percent, respectively). This may be a reflection of social class, not racial or cultural differences (Boyd, 1989). Women with college educations and careers are more likely to postpone having

children, or never have children, than are women with a high school education or less and a low-paying job.

Arthur Neal and his colleagues questioned a random sample of 600 recently married couples about their attitudes toward children and toward life in general (Neal, Groat, and Wicks, 1989). They found that modern couples still place a high value on children. Many see having children as necessary for a "real family life" and as an important source of love and affection. But modern couples also value personal freedom, careers, and time alone together. While they rate having children as more important than having extra money to save or invest and more important than having a neat, orderly household, they worry that parenthood will mean a drastic change in lifestyle and, in particular, disrupt the wife's career.

Individuals who hold traditional definitions of gender roles, accept religious teachings, spend a good deal of time visiting relatives, and are optimistic about the future (about 30 percent of those questioned) are the most likely to see children as central to their life plans. But many other young couples see children as an option, not an obligation—as a desirable experience, but one that must be weighed against other goals. As a result, many are ambivalent about becoming parents. They see many advantages, but also many disadvantages. Neal and his colleagues suggest that ambivalent couples may postpone making a decision until the wife becomes pregnant accidentally, or until they reach middle age and it is too late to have children. Instead of making a decision, they drift.

Other studies confirm this pattern. According to one estimate, only 3 to 6 percent of couples actually make a decision not to have children, and this rate has held steady over the past thirty years (Houseknecht, 1987). The main reason for increased childlessness is that more couples postpone parenthood, and rates of infertility and miscarriage increase with age. Voluntarily childless couples usually report that

---

*The courts usually award child custody to the mother in divorce cases, so most full-time single fathers are not divorced, but either widowed or abandoned.

they did not make this decision before they got married or in the early years of their marriage (Gilbert, 1988). Rather they began to reconsider parenthood after they had been married for some years and had developed a lifestyle and vision of their future that they were reluctant to change. The main reasons given for remaining childless are freedom from responsibility, greater opportunity for self-fulfillment and career development, and a happier marital relationship.

A Summary

This survey of family forms and functions shows that the major change in recent decades is an increase in the *variety* of family experiences people encounter over the life cycle. In the past, most Americans could expect to spend their childhood in one family and their adulthood in another much like the first. Today, however, many youngsters spend part of their childhood in a single-parent household or alternating between two households after their parents divorce. Many young adults are postponing marriage or living with someone to whom they are not married. More couples are postponing or forgoing parenthood. Adults who do marry are more likely to become single again in middle or old age, as the result of divorce or the death of a spouse. Many more people have stepparents and/or stepchildren.

[Section 2 ends.]
[Section 3 begins.]

COURTSHIP, MARRIAGE, AND CHILDREN

The variety of family lifestyles in evidence today should not blind us to the fact that the great majority of Americans do get married and become parents. Why do people get married? Who marries whom? What is marriage like today? How do children affect a couple's relationship?

Choosing a Mate

Despite the increase in singlehood, marriage is about as popular in the United States today as

Marriage has not lost its appeal.

it ever was. Americans wait somewhat longer to get married than in the past. But every year millions get married (there were about 2.5 million marriages a year in the mid-1980s). Over 95 percent marry at least once in their lives.

Why do people get married? Most Americans think the overarching reason is—or should be—"for love." This is not a universal view. Nearly all societies do recognize that, on occasion, a man and woman may develop a "violent emotional attachment" to each other—what we call love (Linton, 1936). But few societies consider this attachment desirable, much less a basis for marriage. In most societies marriages are arranged by older relatives. If eventually the two become fond of each other, so much the better. The idea of free choice in marriage partners (as opposed to marriages arranged by families) is spreading to non-Western societies, but marrying for love is still not accepted everywhere (Murstein, 1986). Arranged marriages are still the norm in Saudi Arabia, for example. One woman explained, "When my father told me I had been proposed to, he said 'Do you want to see him, do you want to sit with him?' I said, 'If you sit with him, it is enough for me.' " The woman, who sits on the ten-woman board of directors of a computer training business, added that arranged marriages are an improvement over the past. At the age of eight, her mother had been kidnapped and sold to the man who became her husband (*The Wall Street Journal*, November 9, 1989, p. 10).

Analysis of marriage patterns shows that even in our own society, Cupid's dart is highly selective. We eliminate a large number of prospective mates before we start looking. James Loewen (1979) shows how Suzie (a hypothetical example) plays the mating game. Suzie is a single white Catholic college student of average height who wants to get married. How does Suzie go about selecting a husband from the total United States population of about 250 million?

1 Suzie is a woman and wants to marry a man. This cuts the pool of eligibles in half. (Her pool of eligibles becomes 125 million)

2 If she is like most people, Suzie wants to marry someone who is about her age—say, between eighteen and twenty-five years old. Only about 14 percent of the male population meets this qualification. (Pool: 17.5 million)

3 Most Americans marry someone of the same race. Because 86 percent of the United States population is white, this reduces Suzie's pool of eligibles only slightly. (Pool: 15 million)

4 Most Americans also marry someone of the same religion. Only about 23 percent of the population is Catholic like Suzie, so this reduces her pool of eligibles substantially. (Pool: 3.5 million)

5 In all likelihood, Suzie will want to marry someone who has about the same levels of intelligence and education as she has. In terms of physical characteristics, she prefers men who are taller than she is. She wants to marry some-

one she finds attractive and likeable, someone whose interests and abilities mesh with hers. And she can marry only someone who is marriageable (single, divorced, or widowed) and who wants to get married. All these factors limit her pool of potential mates still further. (Pool: about 96,000.)

6 Finally, Suzie can marry only someone whom she *knows*. An extremely generous estimate of the number of men Suzie has met or will meet in the next year or two would be 2,500, or .0001 percent of the total United States population. Suzie's pool of potential mates is reduced to nine (.0001 percent of 96,000)! In real life, of course, criteria for dating are not this rigid. But Suzie's pool of potential spouses is smaller than one might think.

This exercise is designed to illustrate **homogamy**: the tendency to marry someone who is like ourselves in the social attributes our society considers important. In principle, we are free to marry anyone we like. In practice, however, our choices are limited by social forces. The same social forces influence the neighborhood in which we live, where we go to school, and whom we meet. Moreover, some of Suzie's criteria (intelligence and level of education, age, and college attendance) tend to overlap. If Suzie enrolls in a large university, she is likely to meet dozens of men who meet her criteria. The question becomes, how does she choose among them?

Exchange theory holds that mate selection is the result of a series of conscious or unconscious calculations. Bernard Murstein (1986) reasons that each of us has an image of our value on the dating market, based on cultural standards and previous experience. In deciding whether to approach a member of the opposite sex, we compare the other person's assets to our own. If the other person has a much higher value, the potential risk of being rejected outweighs the possibility that he or she may be interested. We do not ask for a date. (To simplify, a man who considers himself successful

Studying Section 2

Activities for Section 2

Continue your note-taking on the sample chapter by completing the partial notes below. These notes cover page 144 to part of page 156.

THE AMERICAN FAMILY IN PERSPECTIVE

The Extended Family:

_____

_____

This "good-old-days" family seldom existed in reality!

The Nucleur Family:

_____

_____

—Another idealized family type.

The Modified Extended Family:

_____

_____

Today's Families:

1. Nuclear family of husband, wife, and children—less than a third of today's households.

2. Singlehood: More people remain single for longer periods of time.
   —May be (a) voluntary but temporary, (b) voluntary but stable, (c) involuntary but temporary
   —Changes over life span: twenties try out, thirties evaluate, by mid-forties to mid-fifties most have married

3. One-parent families: Have tripled in last _____ years

   —Major cause is _____

   —Most single parents are (men or women?) _____

4. Families without children: More than one of five married women has never had a child; more and more, children seen as an option

Comments on Section 2

- The notes above, which cover almost ten pages in the text, are based on definitions, an enumeration, and key details. The three terms being defined are obvious because the authors set off the terms in (*fill in the missing word*)

  _____ type in the text.

- The key to the enumeration is the series of three subheadings that appears under the heading "Today's Families." These subheadings, starting with "Singlehood" on page 152, all represent "alternative family forms." It would have helped if the authors had used the heading, "Today's Families: Many Forms." Actually, they give a clearer overview in the second paragraph of their summary of the chapter on page 185. (Keep this in mind: sometimes a look at a summary will help you organize and take notes on the material in the chapter.)

  Even if the authors had *not* provided the summary, they do provide the heading "Today's Families" followed by three subheadings, "Singlehood," "One-Parent Families," and "Families without Children." The point to remember here is that when a heading is followed by subheadings, *figure out the relationship between the heading and the subheadings!* Doing so is going to help you understand and take notes on the material.

- Note that under each form of the family, you can add details that seem important. There's no need to number each detail: instead, just set it off with a dash, as shown above. Minor enumerations can be included here, such as the one shown on the three kinds of (*fill in the missing word*)

  _____.

- Taking brief notes on some details will probably help you remember many of the details. You will be learning material even as you make decisions on what to write down.

but not good-looking would approach a woman who is good-looking but not high on the career ladder, but not one who is both beautiful and successful.) Thus self-esteem plays as important a role in courtship as attraction. During the initial dating stage, couples spend much of their time comparing values. He asks what she thought of the party where they met; she asks what he usually does on weekends; the conversation may turn to elections, sports, religion, or food. The couple are most likely to develop strong liking for one another if their values are similar. Values are the goals people hold in life; roles can be seen as the means to those goals. Murstein holds that progress beyond attraction and liking depends on role fit. If both like to play a nurturant role (the one to whom others turn for comfort), they are less likely to get together than if one sees him- or herself as supportive and the other sees him- or herself as needy and dependent. Thus similarity may "heat up" a relationship in the dating stage, but "cool it down" in the decision stage. Moreover, each measures the other against their image of an ideal mate.

Murstein suggests that only those individuals who are high in self-esteem and have numerous assets can truly be said to *choose* a mate. Individuals who are low in self-esteem and/or have as many liabilities as assets often find they must settle for someone who is less than their ideal.

Exchange theory helps to explain gender differences in courtship, and how they might be changing (Howard, Blumstein, and Schwartz, 1987; Schoen and Wooldredge, 1989). Traditionally, marriage has been seen as an exchange of the man's economic resources for the women's social and domestic services. Women once were more concerned about their partner's socioeconomic assets (occupational status, potential income, ambitiousness), and men more concerned about their partner's noneconomic assets (physical attractiveness and popularity or social skills). Moreover, the cost of not getting married has been greater for women than for

men (Murstein, 1986). Unmarried women generally enjoy lower social status than unmarried men, if only because they earn less, on average, than men do. In addition, opportunities to marry decline as women get older but increase for older men. The main reason is that women generally date and marry men who are slightly older than they are. Thus a woman who is a freshman in college (and went directly from high school to college) might go out with any underclassman, while a male freshman is usually limited to women in his class. By their senior year this situation is reversed. Conventionally, a senior woman will date only other seniors, whereas a senior male can choose among women in any year. As a result, men usually have more power over the mating game than women do: To simplify, men often choose and women often settle. However, as women move toward greater equality with men in the job market, and the differences between male and female roles fade, the need for exchange and gender inequality in courtship may diminish.

Living Together: A New Stage in Courtship

The number of unmarried couples who live together nearly tripled in the 1970s, leveling off at about 2.5 million in the mid-1980s. Half of men and women now in their thirties lived with someone before they got married (Woodward, 1989). Most cohabitors are young couples with no children, though the number of parents who live with someone after a divorce has also grown. A number of related factors contributed to the rise of cohabitation, including: postponement of marriage (due in part to increased sexual freedom among young adults and in part to more women going to college and pursuing careers); postponement of childbirth (which delays the need to marry to "legitimize" children); and greater acceptance of alternative lifestyles (which reduces the pressure to get married). Quite simply many young couples are finding cohabitation more attractive and their parents are less critical of the arrangement—as long as the couple are financially independent and do not have children (Glick and Spanier, 1980).

Only a small percentage of couples see cohabitation as a substitute for, or alternative to, marriage (Clayton and Voss, 1977; Macklin, 1978; Risman et al., 1981). For most it has become a stage en route to marriage, somewhat like engagement. Most couples either get married or break up within a few years of moving in together (Blumstein and Schwartz, 1983). One might think that couples who "look before they leap" are more likely to stay together after marriage. In fact, most studies show that they have slightly higher divorce rates than other couples do. This does not necessarily mean that cohabitation is a "mistake." The explanation may be that cohabitors are less conventional than other couples, and more likely to leave a relationship that does not fulfill their expectations (Murstein, 1986).

Marriage and Children

For many couples, getting married is only the first step in creating a family. Having their first baby—making the transition from "young married" to "parent"—is a far more serious commitment than is getting married. As Alice Rossi (1968) has stressed, the experience of becoming a parent is unique in a number of ways.

First, whereas getting married is a matter of choice, becoming a parent *may or may not be voluntary*. Couples have more control over reproduction today than ever before, but accidents happen. Abortion is a difficult decision—especially for married couples. Even if they aren't quite ready, many couples probably decide to have the unplanned child.

Second, parenthood is *irrevocable*. If a marriage doesn't work, the couple can get a divorce. If a job is unsatisfying, a person can always quit and look for a new one. But how does a person undo the commitment to parenthood? "We

can have ex-spouses and ex-jobs but not ex-children" (Rossi, 1968, p. 32).

Third, many people have *little preparation* for their roles as mothers and fathers. In other areas, people learn by doing. A doctor, for example, goes through an internship and residency before starting private practice. But unless they grew up in large families, which are increasingly rare, today's couples have no practical experience in child care.

Fourth, the move from "young married" to "parent" is an unusually *abrupt transition*. With virtually no apprenticeship, a new parent goes on twenty-four-hour duty. The new parents take on full responsibility for a fragile, mysterious, and totally dependent infant. Few other jobs or social roles are thrust upon us so suddenly, and few require so many adjustments. How does parenthood affect a couple's marriage?

Pregnancy

Ralph LaRossa (1986) has surveyed the literature on becoming a parent. Husband and wife experience similar emotions on learning that she is pregnant for the first time. On the one hand they are proud of this clear sign of their fertility, but on the other they worry about how a baby will change their lives. Expectant mothers find that they are the object of constant attention, both wanted and unwanted. Their husbands, friends, and relatives tend to fuss over them; strangers tend to stare and offer unsolicited advice. Many pregnant women worry that their husbands find them fat and unattractive. Expectant fathers sometimes find that they are the butt of jokes—or worse, ignored. Most parents-to-be report that they have sex less often,* but that they feel closer; the pregnancy gives them a common focus. In late pregnancy, the division of labor in the household (who does laundry, dishes, and so forth) may be more

---

*In most cases there is no medical reason not to have sex during pregnancy; rather, pregnancy serves as an "excuse" for less frequent sex.

egalitarian than at any other time, as the husband pitches in (Goldberg, Michaels, and Lamb, 1985). But although the balance of attention may shift to the wife, the balance of power may shift to the husband—because some couples believe a pregnant woman is in a "delicate" condition and/or because the wife might be giving up her job or going on maternity leave and depending on her husband financially.

The First Child

Our culture defines the birth of a child, especially a first child, as a "blessed event." Yet a large number of studies have found that marital satisfaction declines sharply when a couple become parents (see, for example, Glenn and McLanahan, 1982; Miller, 1976; Rollins and Cannon, 1974; Rollins and Feldman, 1970). Some common explanations of the parental blues are that children add to a couple's financial burden; affection for children dilutes the couple's attention to one another; gender roles tend to become more rigid and traditional after the birth of children; and all these changes combine to cause role strain and role conflict (see Chapter 5).

The sociologists Lynn White and Alan Booth (1985) questioned this association of children with marital dissatisfaction. Is our cultural belief that children bring joy into the family a mass delusion? Reviewing the literature, they saw two possible flaws in methodology. Some of the studies were cross-sectional—that is, they compared parents and nonparents at the same time. The reason why nonparents in these studies expressed greater satisfaction with their marriages could be that people who choose to postpone or forego parenthood tend to have more education and higher incomes than "early" parents do. Their greater satisfaction could be due to their socioeconomic advantages, not to the absence of children. Other studies were longitudinal: They followed couples over a period of time but did not include comparison groups. The finding that couples were less satisfied with their marriages after the birth of children could

This woman will soon face the difficult choice between postponing her career to stay home with her child or giving up time with her child to maintain her family's standard of living.

be a function of the duration of their marriage and the fact that the "honeymoon stage" was over, not the presence of children.

To correct for these possible errors, White and Booth questioned a random sample of married individuals about their marriages in 1980, requestioned the same individuals again in 1983, and compared the responses of those who had become parents in the interim to those who had not. The interview included questions about marital happiness (such as how much affection they received from their spouse), marital interaction (what the couple did together), the division of labor in the household (and whether or not the person was satisfied with this), how often and how violently they disagreed, and whether they had problems in their marriage (moodiness, jealousy, drinking, and the like).

Contrary to other researchers, White and Booth found few significant differences between parents and nonparents. New parents were slightly more likely to report declines in marital happiness and marital interaction and increases in marital problems and disagreements. But the differences between the two groups were not statistically significant. The only substantial difference was that 10 percent of the nonparents got divorced or permanently separated during the course of the study, compared to only 1 percent of the parents. White and Booth suggest that children have a "braking effect" on marital dissolution. Either the desire to become parents or the presence of a child seems to cause couples to stay together, even though their marriage is less than perfect. Conversely, childless couples may feel more free to consider divorce.

This is not to say that babies mean bliss. Few new parents honestly enjoy waking up for 2 A.M. feedings. The most common complaint among new parents is that they never have uninterrupted time to themselves (Harriman, 1983). Nearly all new parents worry about whether their baby is healthy (especially during early infancy) and whether he or she is developing normally (especially during late infancy and toddlerhood) (McKim, 1987). Becoming a parent requires countless adjustments, but most parents do adjust.

The experience of becoming a new parent is different for mothers and fathers. Whether or not they return to work, mothers spend more time caring for a baby than fathers do; are more likely to be alone with the baby; devote more time to routine care (feeding, diapering, bathing) and less to play; and assume ultimate responsibility for the child (LaRossa, 1986). Usually it is the mother who knows when it's time to make an appointment with the pediatrician, whether there are enough diapers in the closet, when the baby should be given solid food, and

the like. For most fathers, parenting is something you do; for most mothers, parenting is someone you are (Ehrensaft, 1985). In addition, many mothers resume primary responsibility for housekeeping after the baby is born. No wonder, then, that mothers more often than fathers report difficulties adjusting to changes in their lifestyle after the birth of their first child (Goldberg, Michaels, and Lamb, 1985).

Most industrial, Western nations have experienced a "baby bust" in recent decades (couples having fewer children or no children). In contrast, most Third World nations are experiencing baby booms. China is one nation that has taken concrete steps to reverse that trend (see "Communist Societies in Transition").

Dual-Earner and Dual-Career Families

One seldom hears the expression, "A woman's place is in the home" today. The reason is simple: Women aren't there anymore (Tavris and Wade, 1984). More than two out of three married women work outside the home today, including a majority of mothers with small children or infants. More than 11 million children under age six have mothers in the labor force (*U.S. Children and Their Families*, 1989).

Working women are not a modern phenomenon. On the contrary, in most societies and times women have played a critical role in providing for their families. American families of the 1950s and 1960s, in which most husbands were the sole providers and most wives were full-time homemakers and mothers, were not a "natural" arrangement, but an unusual one. Nevertheless, there are two distinctive features about women's reentry into the labor market in recent times. The first is that work nearly always requires a woman to be away from her home and children; the second, that the sharp distinction between men's and women's work found in most societies has faded.

Arlie Hochschild and her colleagues (1989) conducted intensive interviews with fifty dual-earner families over a six-year period, and ob-

COMMUNIST SOCIETIES IN TRANSITION
China's One-Child Family Policy

During the 1950s and 1960s, China's health care and economy improved dramatically. These are the factors that make populations grow. At the time, Chairman Mao Zedong and other leaders of the Communist Party held that population growth was not a problem. In their view, what others called a "population problem" was in fact a combination of (1) unequal distribution of wealth under capitalism, and (2) insufficient economic production. They believed that their economic policies would remedy both of these failings. Moreover, Mao shared Marx's belief that population growth is always good, because people are the source of labor and hence of wealth. As a result, China experienced a huge baby boom.

By the late 1970s, the children of the Chinese baby boom were reaching childbearing age themselves. The government realized that its own earlier policies had created a massive problem. Although the Chinese economy was growing faster than ever, population growth was keeping *per capita* income low and holding the country back. The government first proposed relatively mild policies: a limit of two children per family, free contracep-

tion, and laws requiring people to postpone marriage until their late twenties. In the early 1980s, the government realized that this was not enough to stop population growth. Even if the birth rate were held to 1.5 children per family (below the replacement level), the Chinese population would continue to grow well into the twenty-first century. The reason was the age structure, and the large number of young people reaching childbearing age. And so the

---
The population growth rate has been cut in half.
---

government of Deng Xiaoping introduced a one-child family policy.

Under this policy, couples must secure permission from their places of work and residence before having a child. Hospitals are allowed to deliver a baby only if the parents have the proper permission documents. A second child is allowed only if the first dies or is born with severe birth defects, or if the parents themselves were only

served a dozen families in their homes. She found three basic orientations toward gender roles in these families. Even though she works, the *traditional* wife bases her identity on her activities around the home (as wife and mother), sees her husband's identity as grounded in his work, and wants him to be the head of their household. The traditional husband holds the same views. The *egalitarian* man or woman believes that a husband and wife should identify with the same spheres and share power within the family equally. Some want the couple to put the home first; some, to put careers first; and

some to achieve a balance between the two. But the egalitarian spouse does not see work or the family as exclusive right or responsibility of one or the other. In between these two types are the *transitional* spouse. The transitional wife wants to be seen as a worker and a wife/mother, but expects her husband to focus on earning a living; the transitional husband applauds his wife working, but also expects her to assume primary responsibility for the home and the children. Most of the couples Hochschild studied were transitional, even though many professed egalitarian ideals.

children. Parents who limit their families to a single child enjoy a number of privileges. Medical, nursery, and educational fees for a single child are waived; the family's housing and private land allocations are the same as that for a two-child family; and the parents' pensions are increased. A couple receives a "one-child certificate" and cash award when their child reaches age four and they have not had another or if they undergo sterilization. Enforcement of the one-child family rule is strict and punishment for "excess children" severe. If a couple has a second child, they forfeit these privileges and must repay cash awards. If they have a third child, that child is denied free education, housing space, and grain allocations, and is otherwise treated as an "illegitimate" child; the parents' monthly earnings are cut by 10 percent. To prevent excess children, the government encourages sterilization after the birth of a first child; provides free abortions as a birth control of last resort; and may enlist neighbors, coworkers, and local officials to persuade the couple to seek an abortion if the wife becomes pregnant again.

The one-child family policy, and the measures used to enforce it, have drawn criticism. The traditional Chinese preference for sons led to a revival of female infanticide, particularly in under developed rural areas. (The Chinese government tried to fight this prejudice with posters pointing out that daughters are cheaper to raise than sons are, and often are more devoted to their elderly parents.) The new policy of allowing families to earn private income, introduced in the 1980s, led to spectacular increase in food production but inadvertently created an incentive to have more children to help in the fields. Moreover there is concern that a whole generation of (mostly) single children will not be able to support elderly Chinese in the future.

However extreme its methods, China's population policy seems to be working, at least somewhat. The main successes are in urban areas; the countryside has been slower to change. Overall, the population growth rate has been cut in half, even though health care and life expectancy have been improved. If this trend continues, China will cease to be the world's most populous nation around the year 2000.

Sources: M. K. Whyte and W. L. Parish, *Urban Life in Contemporary China*. Chicago: University of Chicago Press, 1984, Chaps. 5 and 7; World Bank, 1985; China's One-Child Policy: A Conference, University of North Carolina at Chapel Hill, April 4 and 5, 1985; P. R. Ehrlich and A. H. Ehrlich, "Population, Plenty and Poverty." National Geographic Magazine (December 1988), p. 922.

Housework

A major issue for families in which both the husband and wife work is, who does the housework? The great majority of husbands and wives say that when the wife works, the husband should do more around the house (Ferber, 1982). But the reality falls short of this ideal. In general, women are doing less and men more than was true in the past, but women still do most of the housework (see Table 12-2). Using her own observations and other studies, Hochschild calculated the amount of time men and women devote to their paid jobs, housework, and childcare. She found that on average, women work about fifteen hours more than men do each week. This means that over a year, women work an extra month of twenty-four hour days, and over a dozen years, an extra year of twenty-four-hour days. "Just as there is a wage gap between men and work in the workplace, so there is a 'leisure gap' between them at home. Most women work one shift at the office or factory and a 'second shift' at home" (Hochschild, 1989, p. 4).

The extra time women devote to housework and child care is only part of the story. Whereas

TABLE 12-2   Who's Doing the Housework?

	MEN*			WOMEN*			RATIO DONE BY WOMEN†		
	1965	1975	1985	1965	1975	1985	1965	1975	1985
FEMALE-DOMINATED									
Cooking meals	1.3	1.3	2.0	8.4	7.8	6.9	77	86	87
Meal clean-up	0.3	0.2	0.4	4.1	2.5	1.9	83	91	92
Housecleaning	0.4	0.7	1.4	6.7	6.2	5.1	78	90	95
Laundry, ironing	0.1	0.1	0.3	5.1	3.0	2.2	88	96	98
Subtotal	2.1	2.3	4.1	24.3	19.5	16.1	80	89	92
MALE-DOMINATED AND SHARED									
Outdoor chores	0.5	1.4	1.4	0.2	0.4	0.5	26	22	33
Repairs, etc.	1.0	2.2	1.8	0.2	0.7	0.4	18	24	18
Garden, animal care	0.2	0.3	1.0	0.5	0.6	0.9	47	63	67
Bills, other	0.8	0.8	1.7	1.8	0.5	1.6	48	36	68
Subtotal	2.5	4.7	5.9	2.7	2.2	3.4	37	32	51
Total	4.6	7.0	9.8	27.0	21.7	19.5	67	76	85
Change			+5.2			−7.5			

*Time men and women aged 18 to 65 spent doing household tasks, in hours per week 1965–1985.
†Assuming equal numbers and backgrounds of men and women, percentages, subtotals, and totals may vary due to rounding.
Source: 1985: Americans' Use of Time Project, Survey Research Center, University of Maryland; 1965, 1975: Americans' Use of Time Project, Survey Research Center, University of Michigan; appeared in J.P. Robinson, "Who's Doing the Housework?" *American Demographics* (Dec. 1988), p. 26. [Reprinted with permission. © *American Demographics*, December 1988.

men "pitch in" around the house, women feel responsible for the house and the children. Even when couples do share housework, women are more likely to do jobs that lock them into rigid daily routines (such as cooking and cleaning), and men, the nonroutine jobs that can be performed more or less at their leisure (getting the car greased and oiled or mowing the lawn). Women do more of the least desirable jobs (scrubbing the bathroom versus taking the TV to be repaired). In child care, mothers spend more time on maintenance (feeding and bathing children) and fathers, more on special activities (taking them to the zoo).

Hochschild found that many couples develop a "family myth" that rationalizes and/or covers up the actual division of labor in the home. Thus one middle-class couple who claimed to be egalitarian explained that the wife was responsible for upstairs and the husbands for downstairs. "Upstairs" turned out to mean the first-floor living areas and second-floor bedrooms;

"downstairs" was the basement where the husband kept his tools and an extra TV. The wife took care of the children; the husband cared for the dog. They rationalized this arrangement in terms of personalities: She was "compulsive," they claimed, while he was "lazy." A traditional, working-class couple Hochschild studied also had a myth. Both the husband and wife believed that the man should be the "head of the house" and have the "final say," and that the woman should "stay home and look after the children." But because they could not make ends meet on his $12,000 a year salary, she cared for neighbors' children in her home. Both described this situation as "temporary." To explain away the fact that he did nearly half the work around the house, they invoked the myth of female helplessness. He paid the bills because she was helpless with a calculator; he took her shopping because she couldn't drive a car; and so on. As these examples suggest, middle-class couples are more likely to preach egalitarian ideals than to practice them, while working-class couples are somewhat more likely to practice equal role division while preaching traditional gender ideals (see also Bernardo et al., 1987).

Child Care

Another major issue for couples who both work is child care. The United States is the only industrialized nation that does not have a national policy for parental leave following the birth of a child (with or without pay) or a national day-care program. As a result, parents are on their own.

Who takes care of children while their parents are at work? Most children under the age of five are being cared for in a home environment—either their own or someone else's home. The type of care working parents choose for their child depends on the child's age, the mother's education and income, and how much she works. Infants are most likely to be cared for in a home environment, whereas toddlers are more often cared for in a group environment. Mothers who work full-time are more likely to choose group care, whereas mothers who work part-time are more likely to choose family care. Likewise, mothers with more schooling and higher incomes are more likely to place a child in group care or to use a paid caregiver in their home, whereas mothers with less schooling and low incomes are more likely to rely on relatives or neighbors. About 2.1 million children ages five to thirteen have no adult supervision after school: 1.6 million of this group care for themselves; the others are cared for by a relative or neighbor who is under age fourteen (*U.S. Children and Their Families*, 1989).

In terms of sharing, today's fathers get better reports for child care than for housework. A survey conducted by the Bank Street College of Education in conjunction with *Fortune* magazine found that fathers and mothers generally agree that they share child care equally (see Figure 12-3). Fathers also share some of the worry and guilt about leaving their child in someone else's care (Chapman, 1987).

How much time fathers devote to child care depends on several factors (Barnett and Baruch, 1987). One is their wife's schedule: The more hours the mother works, the more the father pitches in. Another factor is the mother's gender role attitudes: If the mother believes the husband is competent at child care, the father is likely to be more involved (though which is cause and which effect is difficult to say). The father's relationship with his own father is also a factor: Fathers who were dissatisfied with their own fathers are likely to devote more time to their children than are fathers with happier memories. Finally, fathers are more likely to take part in child care if the child is a boy.

Role Conflict and Overload

Does balancing work and family create role conflict and/or role overload? Most studies have focused on working wives and mothers. In general they have found that working women are better off than full-time housewives (Tavris and Wade, 1984). Working wives "pay" for their greater freedom and independent incomes with reduced time for themselves and more hectic, complicated lives. But the "psychological protection" of having two roles seems to compensate for added responsibilities (Crosby, 1982). Working women are slightly more likely than housewives to report that they are "very happy" with their marriages (Wright, 1978). They also tend to be higher in self-esteem—to have more confidence and a higher opinion of their own abilities—than do most housewives. But working mothers are more likely than any other group to experience symptoms of anxiety (Thoits, 1985). They are tired and get sick more often than their husbands do (Hochschild, 1989). And they resent the fact that their husbands are not sharing the burden (Pleck, 1985).

Ironically, the most successful women—those who attempt to combine a high pressure career with family—may experience the most difficulty. In her study of female lawyers, the sociologist Cynthia Epstein (1983) concluded that

	MEN	WOMEN
Report that both spouses share equally in child care responsibility	55.1%	51.9%
Say the job interferes with family life	37.2%	40.9%
Sought less demanding job to get more family time	20.5%	26.5%
Refused a job, promotion, or transfer because it would mean less family time	29.6%	25.7%
Felt nervous or under stress in past three months	49.2%	70.2%
Missed at least one workday in the past three months due to family obligations	37.8%	58.6%
Think children of working parents benefit by having interesting role models for parents	77.5%	86.3%
Think children of working parents suffer by not being given enough time and attention	55.4%	58.2%
Would like their companies to provide a subsidized child care center	38.5%	54.1%
Would like their companies to offer flexible working hours	34.8%	54.1%
Think companies can do more to help manage work/family responsibilities	34.5%	30.9%

Figure 12-3 What Working Parents Say about Child Care. *(From F. Chapman, "Executive Guilt: Who's Taking Care of the Children?"* Fortune, *February 16, 1987, p. 35. © 1987 Time Inc. All rights reserved.)*

women are able to combine career and family successfully—if the most important people in their lives accept their desire to play by "new rules." "The successful women I have studied have in common one crucial element—the goodwill and supportiveness of others in their life on their way of 'having it all'" (p. 103).

The great majority of men (85 percent) approve of their wife working, and recognize the importance of her income to their family lifestyle (Astrachan, 1986). But only a minority (5 to 10 percent) support women's demands for equality. Men may be happy to see their wives step up into positions of power and prestige formerly reserved for men, but they do not want to step down into the kitchen and the nursery. They still like to think of the woman's salary as

"second income." When a wife earns more than her husband, when the traditional balance of power in the family is reversed, most men are not pleased (see "Close Up" in Chapter 10).

A recent study (Voydanoff, 1988) compared men and women in dual-earner families. The study found that both sexes experience stress, but for different reasons. Men are slightly more likely to feel that work problems (pressure and role conflict or ambiguity on the job) intrude on their family life, whereas women are more likely to feel that family demands (the number and age of children, the amount of housework) intrude on their work life.

There is little doubt that dual-earner and dual-career families are here to stay. The question is how soon our society will adapt—for example, with flexible work schedules and high-quality, affordable day care.

[Section 3 ends.
  Section 4 begins.]

BEHIND CLOSED DOORS: VIOLENCE IN THE FAMILY

"And they lived happily ever after." Hundreds of stories about marriages and families end with this line. Loved ones are reunited; obstacles to marriage overcome; problems with children resolved. Indeed, the very idea of living happily ever after is linked, in our minds, with the special warmth of the family. Yet if we look behind the closed doors of many American households, we discover that all is not peace and harmony.*

Myths and Realities

With the exception of the police and the military, the family is the most violent social group in American society. The home is a more dangerous place than a dark alley. A person is more likely to be murdered in his or her home, by a member of the family, than by anyone else, anywhere else, in society.

Fifteen or twenty years ago, few Americans would have believed these statements. Today most people recognize that family violence is a serious social problem. Yet myths abound.

▪ *Myth 1: Family violence is rare or epidemic.* Public attention to family violence has skyrocketed in recent years. The growing number of books, articles, and TV reports on the problem has lead some people to believe we are in the midst of an epidemic. Others have concluded that all this attention is "hype." Both are wrong. Family violence is not a modern phenomenon; it has existed in virtually all societies and times. Experts may disagree about whether family violence is increasing or decreasing. But all agree that it is a serious problem that will not go away by itself.

*Unless otherwise noted, the data and conclusions in this section are from Gelles and Straus, 1988.

▪ *Myth 2: Abusers are mentally ill.* When we read a description of family violence, we would like to believe that only someone who is sick could beat up a pregnant woman or torture a child. Health workers often find that abusers are disturbed. But whether they committed violent acts because they were disturbed or became disturbed after the act is impossible to say. Only about 10 percent of abusers are clinically diagnosed as mentally ill.

▪ *Myth 3: Abuse occurs only in poor, minority families.* Rates of abuse are higher in poor and minority households, but violence occurs in families at all socioeconomic levels. One reason that poor and nonwhites are greatly overrepresented in official statistics is that they are more likely to be labeled as "abusers" or "victims." The sociologists Patrick Turbett and Richard O'Toole (1980) gave groups of physicians and nurses a file describing an injured child and the child's parents. These professionals were more likely to conclude the child was a victim of abuse when they were told the father was a janitor than when they were told he was a teacher, and when they were told the child was black as opposed to white. Except for these social markers, which were varied at random, the files were identical.

▪ *Myth 4: The real causes of family violence are alcohol and drugs.* A news report might highlight the fact that a man who murdered his family was a "crack addict." Victims of family violence often say, "He only did it when he was drunk." Does this mean drugs cause abuse? No. Cross-cultural studies show that the effects of alcohol vary from society to society. In some, people become quiet and withdrawn when they drink; in others, they become loud and aggressive. Our society is one of the latter. We define being drunk as a "time out" from normal rules of behavior, when a person can claim "I didn't know what I was doing." As a result, both abusers and victims often cite alcohol as the excuse for violence. In one study half the men arrested for beating their wives claimed that they had been drunk, but only 20 percent had enough

Studying Section 3

Activities for Section 3

Continue your note-taking on the sample chapter by completing the partial notes below. These notes cover page 156 (starting partway down) through page 168, and the first two lines on page 169.

COURTSHIP, MARRIAGE, AND CHILDREN

Choosing a Mate:

In most societies, marriages are _____

Why do we marry? Because of the principle of homogamy—_____

_____

   Ex. of Suzie: her pool of eligibles cut from 250 million to 9 men!
Factors involved include physical attraction, self-esteem, values, and role fit.

Living Together—A New Stage in Courtship:
Number of unmarried couples who live together nearly tripled in the 1970s.
Cohabitors felt marriage and children could be postponed.

Marriage and Children:
Reasons why becoming a parent is more significant than getting married—

1. _____

2. _____

3. _____

4. _____

Pregnancy (*If no one idea jumps out under a heading, there is no need to take notes.*)

The first child: (*add noteworthy detail*) _____

_____

Dual-Earner and Dual Career Families:
Women aren't home as much; more than (*complete this important detail*)—

_____ work outside the home.

Major Issues for Couples Who Work:

1. Housework: Women do more!

2. Child care: (*add important detail here*) _____

_____

3. Role conflict and overload: Working women are better off than full-time housewives

   because (*complete the idea*) _____

   _____

Comments on Section 3

- Enumerations and important details are the keys to important ideas in this stretch of the text.
- Take a close look at a typical page of paragraphs in the text. Most of the six full paragraphs on page 163 have a clearly stated main idea. Write down the first words in the main-idea sentence for each of the following:

  First full paragraph: _____

  Second full paragraph: _____

  Third full paragraph: _____

- Notice that the last full paragraph on the page (beginning ''Working women are not . . .'') contains two main ideas. What are they?

  First main idea: _____

  Second main idea: _____

- Being aware that paragraphs may center on a main idea (often stated in the first or second sentence) can help you read and understand material. It's to be hoped that the authors of your textbooks, like the authors of this chapter, will write clearly organized paragraphs that center on main ideas.

  It is not realistic to expect, though, that every paragraph will contain a main idea. For example, a paragraph might contain an idea that is implied rather than directly stated, might have more than one idea, might be simply a short transitional paragraph, or might just be poorly written—or there may be some other reason why a main idea is missing.

alcohol in their blood to be considered legally intoxicated (Bard and Zacker, 1974). Frequent drunks (and nondrinkers) are less likely than occasional drinkers to become violent. Much less is known about the effects of illegal drugs on behavior. But the only one that has been conclusively linked with increased aggression (in studies with monkeys) is amphetamine.

- *Myth 5: Children who are abused grow up to be abusers.* Children who are victims of family violence are *more likely* to be abusive as adults than are children who experienced no family violence. But this does not mean that *all* violent adults were abused as children, or that *all* abused children grow up to be violent. Abuse makes children more vulnerable to a host of social and emotional problems, but it does not determine how they will behave as adults.
- *Myth 6: Battered wives like being hurt.* Most people are badly upset by reports of battered children but puzzled by reports of battered wives. After all, the woman is an adult; if her husband beats her, why doesn't she leave him? Abused wives are often assumed to be masochists or, worse, to have provoked their husbands to violence ("She asked for it...."). Anyone who has been through a divorce knows that there is more to ending a marriage than simply walking out the door. In most cases, violence isn't an everyday event. It may be easier to talk oneself into believing it won't happen again than to face the world on one's own, with little money, credit, or experience, and perhaps children to care for as well. Where can the battered wife go? Because our society has mixed feelings about battered wives, we have been slow to build shelters.

If you reread this list of myths you will see a common theme: Only people *other than us* assault their loved ones. Assigning family abusers to deviant categories (mentally disturbed, poor, drunk) allows us to avoid thinking that it could happen to us. These myths also blind us to the structural characteristics of the family that promote or at least allow violence.

Sociological Explanations

The potential for violence is built into the family. Many of the characteristics we cherish most about families also make us most vulnerable within the family. One is *intimacy*. Family members are intensely involved with one another. They know the private details of one another's lives, and what makes the others feel proud or ashamed. When quarrels break out or problems arise, the stakes are higher than in other social groups. For example, a man who is amused by the behavior of a female colleague who is drunk may become enraged if his wife has a little too much to drink. A politician who has been an active supporter of gay rights, at some risk to her career, may be appalled to discover that her own child is homosexual. Why? Because we perceive the behavior of a member of our family as a direct reflection on ourselves. The intensity of family relationships tends to magnify the most trivial things, such as a burned dinner or a whining child. When did you last hear of someone beating up the cook in a restaurant for preparing an unacceptable meal? But minor offenses and small oversights often spark violent family fights.

A second factor contributing to violence in the home is *privacy*: because family affairs are regarded as private, there are few outside restraints on violence. When a family quarrel threatens to become a fight, there are no bystanders to break it up, as there might be on the street or in some other public place. The shift from extended to nuclear families, the move to detached single-family houses in the suburbs, and the trend toward having fewer children have all increased the potential for family violence, simply because there are fewer people around to observe (and try to stop) abuse. Children in isolated single-parent families are at high risk (Gelles, 1989). One reason the rates of family violence in black families are lower than one might expect (given high rates of single parenthood, poverty, and unemployment) is that blacks generally have more extensive social networks, and more frequent contacts with relatives and neighbors, than whites do.

A third factor is *inequality*. Few social groups routinely include members of both sexes and different ages. In school, for example, we are segregated by age; at work we are often segregated by sex—for example, men doing heavy labor, women doing clerical work. Because men are usually bigger and stronger than women, and women bigger and stronger than children, they can get away with violent behavior that would provoke retaliation from someone their own size and strength. Moreover, the costs of leaving an abusive family—becoming a runaway child or a single mother—may seem higher to some family members than to others.

Fourth, and perhaps most disturbing, there is a good deal of *social and cultural support* for the use of physical force in the family. Parents are allowed—indeed, sometimes expected—to spank their children. "Spare the rod and spoil the child," the saying goes. Most people do not think of spanking a child as violence. Indeed, in a recent survey almost three out of four Americans said they saw slapping a twelve-year-old as often necessary, normal, and good. But suppose a teacher slapped the child, or a stranger slapped you for something you did or said in the supermarket? Either would constitute assault and battery in a court of law—but not in the family. In effect, a marriage license in our society is a license to hit. This applies not only to children, but also to spouses. In the same national survey one in four wives and one in three husbands said that slapping a spouse was sometimes necessary, normal, and good.

Finally, in the process of *socialization* we learn to associate violence with the family. Our first experience of force nearly always takes place at home. Most of our parents use physical punishment on occasion—for our own good, of course, and because they love us. (The child is told, "This hurts me more than it hurts you.") From here it is only a small step to the conclusion that the use of violence is legitimate whenever something is really important. And the things that are most important to us are often family matter.

An Update: Good News and Bad

The First National Family Violence Survey, conducted in 1975 to 1976 by the sociologists Murray Straus, Richard Gelles, and Suzanne Steinmetz (1980), found that physical abuse in the home was far more common than anyone suspected:

> Three out of four parents had struck their child at least once, and nearly four in one hundred had used severe violence on a child. In all, 1.4 million children ages 3 to 17—roughly one child in every U.S. classroom—had been the victim of physical abuse.
>
> One out of six wives had been struck by a husband; one in 22 had been victims of violent abuse; and the average battered wife was attacked three times a year.
>
> More than four of every 100 husbands had been victims of spousal violence. (In nearly all cases, however, the husband initiated violence and the wife acted in self-defense.) (Steinmetz, 1978)

A second national survey was conducted in 1985, to determine whether rates of family violence had changed (Straus and Gelles, 1986; Gelles and Straus, 1988). To their surprise the researchers found that the rate of child abuse had declined by 47 percent, and the rate of spouse abuse had declined by 27 percent. This does not mean that the problem of family violence has disappeared; far from it. At today's "lower" rates, more than a million children were abused and 1.6 million wives were battered in 1985. Nevertheless, the change is substantial.

Gelles and Straus (1988) believe that a major reason for this decline is changing public attitudes toward family violence. America seems to be undergoing a "moral passage" (Gusfield, 1963), in which behavior that formerly was considered acceptable is now seen as abuse. An allegedly rare private problem has been redefined as a widespread social problem. As a result, people may be less willing to quietly accept being hurt by their parents or spouse, and more willing to intervene when they believe a friend, neighbor, or relative is being abused. (The redefinition of family violence may also make people less likely to admit to a pollster that they slapped their spouse or punched their child.)

A number of structural changes in the family and society as a whole may also have contributed to the decline in family violence. First, many Americans are delaying the age at which they get married and have their first child. Many more women have entered the labor force. And today's couples have a full range of family planning services at their disposal. Late marriage, egalitarian marriage, and wanted children are all associated with a lower risk of family violence. Second, both child and wife abuse are linked to unemployment and economic stress. By chance, the second survey was conducted in the most prosperous year in a decade, at least for intact families. Third, between 1975 and 1985 policies toward family violence have changed, and the number and variety of programs for treating abusers and victims have increased. All states now have laws that make reporting child abuse or neglect mandatory. Police manuals used to recommend that officers summoned to the scene of domestic violence separate the warring parties and leave; now most require that a man who has beaten his wife be arrested. The number of shelters for battered women and their children increased from a mere four in 1975 to more than 1,000 in 1985. The number of family therapists tripled in the 1980s. Self-help groups for abusive parents and battered spouses have been formed. While these services do not begin to meet the need, they provide some troubled families with alternatives and may embolden victims of family violence to take steps on their own.

In short, there is no one reason why rates of child and wife beating have declined. The bulk of the evidence suggests that the more coverage given a problem in the media and the more resources devoted to correcting that problem, the more likely both attitudes and behavior will change. But we are still a long way from becoming a society that bans the use of physical force and injury in the home. Sweden did outlaw spanking in 1979, and there is no evidence that this led to a whole generation of spoiled children. Most Americans would consider such a law an invasion of family privacy, but that is just the point. There is no penalty for using corporal punishment in Sweden. Rather, the law allows grandparents, neighbors, and strangers to intervene when they see a child being abused. Sweden also provides families with a wide range of social and economic supports. The level of family violence is much lower in Sweden than in the United States.

[Section 4 ends.
Section 5 begins.]

DIVORCE

Then there are men and women who live more or less happily ever after, but not together. Marriages end every day, for all sorts of reasons—of which violence is one, cited in 20 to 40 percent of divorce suits (Levinger, 1966). Indeed, divorce is becoming an accepted part of our way of life, or so it appears. What are the facts?

Understanding Divorce Statistics

Raw data can be deceptive, as statistics on divorce make abundantly clear. In 1985 there were about 2.4 million marriages in America. That same year, 1.19 million marriages ended in divorce (*Statistical Abstract, 1989*, p. 85). This means that half of marriages today end in divorce—right? Not necessarily. Direct comparisons of marriage and divorce rates for a given year are based on a fallacy. The pool of men and women eligible for marriage in a year is relatively small. It consists primarily of single people aged about eighteen to thirty, plus some

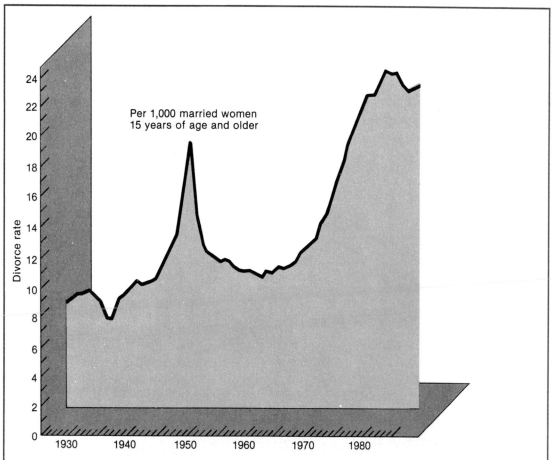

Figure 12-4   Recent Trends in Divorce. *(From S. J. Price and P. C. McHenry,* Divorce. *Newbury Park, CA: Sage, 1988, p. 19. Copyright © 1988 by Sage Publications, Inc. Reprinted by permission.)*

younger and older single people, widows, and divorced people. The pool of men and women "eligible" for divorce, in contrast, includes everyone who is currently married, whether the wedding took place yesterday or fifty years ago. That is, the "divorce pool" includes most of the adult population. Thus, measuring the marriage rate against the divorce rate for a given year is highly misleading. Comparing the number of divorces issued this year with the number issued five or ten years ago is also misleading, for the population is growing and changing.

The **divorce rate** is the number of divorces per 1,000 married women (or men) in a given

year. For example, in 1960 there were 42.6 million married women in the United States; 393,000 got divorced that year. Thus the divorce rate for 1960 was 9.2 divorces per 1,000 married women. By 1979 the rate had tripled, reaching 22.8 divorces per 1,000 married women (Census Bureau, 1981). In the 1980s, the rate stabilized at about 22 divorces per 1,000 married women (see Figure 12-4).

Who Gets Divorced and Why

At current rates, the chances that a thirty-year-old will be divorced (now or in the future) are

Studying Section 4

Activities for Section 4

Continue taking notes. An enumeration will help you take notes and understand this stretch of the material, which covers page 169 to part of page 174.

BEHIND CLOSED DOORS: VIOLENCE IN THE FAMILY
Myths and Realities:

1. Myth 1—Family violence is rare or epidemic.
   Fact—A serious problem that has existed in all families at all times.

2. Myth 2—_____
   Fact—_____

3. Myth 3—_____
   Fact—_____

4. Myth 4—_____
   Fact—_____

5. Myth 5—_____
   Fact—_____

6. Myth 6—_____
   Fact—_____

   Sociological Explanations:
   Five factors contribute to violence in the family—

1. Intimacy—_____
   _____

2. _____
   _____

3. _____
   _____

4. _____
   _____

5. _____
   _____

An Update: Good News and Bad

Bad news—_____

_____

Good news—_____

_____

Comments on Section 4

- Notice how the headings here help you take notes. When you see a head like "Myths and Realities," you should immediately convert it into questions: "What are myths?" "What are realities?" When you see a heading like "An Update: Good News and Bad," you should change it into the question, "What is the good news, and what is the bad?"

    Such headings are good choices as essay questions on course exams. You could easily see a teacher giving you this question: "Write an essay describing myths and realities about violence in the family." Always keep your eye out for likely essay questions and be sure to prepare for them. Very often, an essay question will involve an enumeration.

- While there were no definitions in this part of the chapter, what helped you take notes were the following: headings, questions about the headings, and enumerations.

about one in three (Glick and Norton, 1976). But all marriages do not have an equal chance of success or failure, some segments of our population are more prone to divorce than others.

The likelihood of a marriage lasting depends, first, on *age at first marriage*. Couples who get married before age twenty are two or three times more likely to get divorced than are couples who marry in their twenties (Norton and Moorman, 1987). Not only are young marrieds more emotionally immature, they are more likely to belong to the lower class and they are more likely to have rushed into marriage to escape an unhappy family life or because of a premarital pregnancy (Furstenberg, 1976; Glenn and Suspanic, 1984).

Socioeconomic status is also correlated with divorce. Divorce rates are highest in lower socioeconomic groups, and decline as one moves up the socioeconomic ladder (Price and McKenry, 1988). Presumably this is because poor families experience more stress than do families who are better off. Also, higher-income couples have more to lose (the house, the cars, and so on). But divorce may be a cause of low income, rather than a consequence. Women with children nearly always experience a decline in standard of living after a divorce, and many slip into poverty.

Race is another factor in divorce. Black women are twice as likely as white women to be separated or divorced. The main reason is that black women are more likely to be young and poor when they get married. Divorce rates for whites and blacks at the same socioeconomic level are about the same (Cutright, 1971).

A fourth factor in divorce is *religion*. Historically, religion has been a major barrier to divorce, though this may be weakening (Price and McKenry, 1988). In general, the more often a person attends religious services, the less likely he or she is to be divorced (Teachman, 1983). Divorce rates are higher among Protestants than Catholics. An increase in the number of Catholics who sought divorce in the 1960s and 1970s

was a major ingredient in the rising divorce rates during that period. Even so, Catholics are still more likely to separate but not divorce than are other members of other Christian denominations (Price and McKenry, 1988). One might predict that divorce rates would be lower for Fundamentalists than for mainstream Christians, but in fact the reverse seems to be true. The explanation may be that Fundamentalists tend to be rigid and inflexible in their rules for everyday behavior, that they are more concerned about the next life than about this one, and/or that they generally come from lower socioeconomic groups (Eshleman, 1985).

Geography also influences marital stability. Divorce rates are higher in *urban* than in rural areas. Couples enjoy more anonymity in big cities than in small towns, and so may be less subject to pressures to stay married (Eshleman, 1985). The wider range of occupational opportunities, social services, and lifestyles in the city may encourage individuals to leave unhappy marriages. In the city, social life is not so family-oriented and divorce does not bear as much social stigma. For the same reasons, individuals who are divorced, or are contemplating divorce, may move from small towns to cities, inflating the urban divorce rate (Glenn and Shelton, 1985).

Divorce rates are also higher in the *Sun Belt* than in the Northeast and Midwest. A number of factors may be at work here, including the relative youth of the population and the fact that many residents of the Sun Belt recently moved into the area and have fewer family and community connections. Perhaps people who are willing to cut their roots to their home community are also more likely to end an unsatisfactory marriage (Glenn and Shelton, 1985).

Why did divorce rates rise in the 1960s and 1970s, then level off in the 1980s? There is no simple explanation, but three reasons stand out (Adams, 1986; Price and McKenry, 1988). The first reason is political: the end of the war in Vietnam. During a war, some people rush into marriage after only a brief courtship. Others are separated for a long time and so have more opportunities for extramarital involvements. Fewer people file for divorce while a war is in progress, for practical as well as patriotic reasons, but many do when the war is over. After the postwar "rush," divorce rates usually level off.

The second reason is demographic: an increase in the numbers of people in the high-risk early years of marriage. Most divorces occur either in the first years of marriage or after the children are grown. The large baby boom generation passed through its twenties and married for the first time during 1965 to 1975. By 1980, members of this generation had either separated or settled down, so the divorce rate leveled off.

The third main reason for changes in the divorce rate is cultural: a general shift from faith in institutions to concern with individual fulfillment. Sharon Price and Patrick McKenry (1988) compared interviews with men and women who divorced in the late 1940s (Goode, 1956) to similar interviews of men and women who divorced in the 1980s (Bloom, Niles, and Tatcher, 1985). In the earlier interviews, the main reasons given for divorce were failure to live up to instrumental family roles (nonsupport, lack of interest in the home, excessive drinking and gambling). In the more recent interviews, the main reasons given for divorce were related to personal fulfillment and growth (problems in communication, conflicts over values, boredom, sexual incompatibility). Thus our definitions of a successful marriage have changed from living up to social responsibilities to finding individual happiness. Many couples want both togetherness and individual freedom, a difficult balance to achieve (Birdwhistell, 1970).

The 1965 to 1975 decade also saw the passage of no-fault divorce laws, women's movement into the labor force, growing acceptance of alternatives to traditional marriage, and re-duction of the shame associated with divorce and single parenthood. But whether these were a cause or a consequence of increases in the divorce rate is difficult to say.

It is important to view recent changes in historical perspective (Cherlin, 1981). When you compare divorce rates in the 1960s and 1970s to rates in the 1950s, it looks as if the family is falling apart. When you look further back in history, however, you see that divorce rates have been climbing more or less steadily since the late nineteenth century. The 1950s were an exception to this trend. Perhaps in reaction to the instability of the Great Depression and World II, Americans placed an unusually high value on family life in this decade. In the 1970s the pendulum swung the other way. Comparing these two exceptional decades creates the false impression of a divorce "boom." How divorce rates might change in the future is impossible to predict (Glick, 1988).

Children and Divorce

Each year about a million children—almost 2 percent of all children in the United States—are involved in a divorce (*U.S. Children and Their Families*, 1989) (see Figure 12-5). But this is only a fraction of the number of children who have been or will be directly affected by divorce. Estimates are that 40 percent of all American children will see their parents divorce before they themselves reach their eighteenth birthday (Glick, 1988). Black children are 50 percent more likely to experience marital disruption than white children are, and less likely to acquire a stepparent (Furstenberg et al., 1983).

Generalizations about the impact of divorce on children are difficult at best (Demo and Acock, 1988). Children's adjustment to divorce depends on numerous factors, including: their age at the time of the divorce, whether they have brothers and sisters, their parents' economic resources, whether they have grandparents or

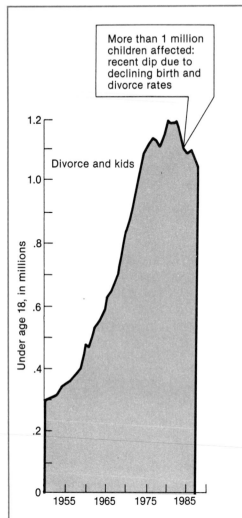

Figure 12-5 Children and Divorce. *(From U.S. Census Bureau, National Center for Health Statistics;* Newsweek *Special Edition: The 21st Century Family, Winter/Spring 1990. © 1990, Newsweek, Inc. All rights reserved. Reprinted by permission.)*

other relatives nearby, whether their parents remarry, the relationship between their divorced parents, and their own relationships to those parents. Nevertheless, some tentative conclusions are possible.

The transition from a two-parent to a single-parent family is stressful for everyone involved

(Price and McKenry, 1988). Divorce means the loss of family members, developing new patterns of interaction, and adjusting to a new lifestyle (often in a smaller home and a poorer neighborhood) all at once. Most children live with their mother after a divorce. Their relationship with their father is usually cut to visits. They may also receive less attention from their mother, as she struggles to combine the roles of homemaker and breadwinner, nurturer and disciplinarian.

Children nearly always are surprised to learn their parents are getting divorced, even if they fought constantly. Most suffer temporary problems in adjustment. Younger children have more difficulty accepting the fact of divorce than older children do, and tend to blame themselves for their parents' problems. Boys tend to cause more problems than girls do (by being less compliant and more aggressive). Most studies find that within a year or two, relations between the custodial parent and child are back on track. There is little evidence that divorce has long-term negative effects on self-esteem (though family conflict does). Indeed, adolescents whose parents are divorced tend to be more self-confident than adolescents in two-parent families, and they tend to show a stronger sense of responsibility. There is some evidence that children of divorced families don't do quite as well in school as other children do. They may also be a little slower to make friends, though as adolescents they may be more active in dating and sexual relations. Finally, adolescents in mother-only homes (and in conflict-ridden homes) are more prone to delinquency. In short, divorce may have some negative (and a few positive) effects on children, at least in the short run (see Demo and Acock, 1988, for review). Long-term negative effects are probably the result of disruption in lifestyle, the downward mobility most children experience after a divorce, and conflict between their parents before and after divorce (Price and McKenry, 1988).

Ultimately, the most important factor in children's adjustment to divorce seems to be stable, loving relationships with *both* parents. Unfortunately, contact with the nonresidential parent (usually the father) tends to diminish over time. In a national survey 50 percent of children said that they had not had any contact whatsoever with their nonresidential parent in the past year, and a third had not heard from their nonresidential parent in five years (Furstenberg et al., 1983).

Many professionals today recommend joint *legal* custody, in which parents share the authority and responsibility for child rearing after a divorce. There is evidence that fathers who are awarded joint custody are more likely to remain involved with their children (Bowman and Ahrms, 1985). However, joint *physical* custody, in which children divide their time between their divorced parents' homes, is controversial (Price and McKenry, 1988). Advocates maintain that this arrangement relieves children of the pressure to "take sides" in their parents' divorce, relieves adults of the stress of being a single parent and the strain of being a visiting parent, and fosters better relations both between parents and child and between ex-spouses. Critics maintain that children who shuttle back and forth between two homes have trouble forming a secure relationship with either parent. The available evidence (Gardner, 1982; Luepmitz, 1982) suggests that joint physical custody works well for some families—if both parents live in the same community and if they are able to cooperate (not compete) with one another in child rearing.

Remarriage and Stepfamilies

For most Americans, divorce and single parenthood are temporary (Ihinger-Tallman and Pasley, 1987). Put another way, divorce is a rejection of a specific, unsuccessful relationship, not a rejection of the idea of marriage and family (Spanier, 1989). Four out of five divorced persons remarry. But Americans are not returning to the alter as quickly as they did in the past (Glick and Lin, 1986). In 1970, the average interval between divorce and marriage was 2½ years; today it is about 3½ years. Even so, divorced people are more likely to get married than people who have never married, in every age group. Although blacks are more likely to separate or divorce than whites, whites are more likely to remarry than are blacks. Despite their tendency to say they aren't interested in marriage, men are more likely to remarry than are women. Social class has different effects on divorced men and women. The more education a man has, the higher his income, the more likely he is to remarry. The reverse is true for women—either because they feel less need to remarry than do women with little education and low-paying jobs, or because they have more trouble finding a mate who is their educational and occupational equal.

About 29 percent of remarriages are between a divorced woman and a single man; 35 percent, between a divorced man and a single woman; and about 35 percent between two divorced persons (Cherlin and McCarthy, 1985). In general, remarried couples report as high levels of marital satisfaction as couples who are in their first marriage (Ihinger-Tallman and Pasley, 1987). Yet about 60 percent of second marriages end in divorce. The reason may be that individuals who have been through one unhappy marriage and divorce are less willing to endure an unsatisfactory marriage and are more willing to break the taboo against divorce a second time (Furstenberg and Spanier, 1984).

About eight in ten remarriages involve children. As a result, nearly 7 million children live with a stepparent today. Estimates are that a third of all children will participate in a stepfamily before they reach age eighteen (Kantrowitz and Wingert, 1989). **Stepfamilies** take different forms: a mother, her children from a previous marriage, and a stepfather; a father, his children from a previous marriage, and a step-

Stepfamilies live in uncharted territory. The rules about how new and part-time parents and children should relate to one another are far from clear. Should a boy call his stepfather "Dad" or "Bill"? Should a stepmother challenge her husband's bedtime rules for his children? These and countless other everyday issues must be renegotiated.

mother; a mother, father, and both their children from a previous marriage; any of the above combinations and a new child from the current marriage. The children of previous marriages may live with the couple full-time or part-time (under joint physical custody), or one spouse's children may live with the couple and the other spouse's children may visit.

Stepfamilies are not simply new families. They differ from other families in a number of ways (Furstenberg and Spanier, 1984; Visher and Visher, 1978). First, some members of the family have recently experienced a disruption in a close relationship (with a parent, a child, and/or a spouse), an experience that shapes their attitudes toward the new family. Second, the relationship between the parent and child predates that between the new husband and wife. The parent and child have a longer history together, and may know one another better than the new spouse does. Third, the children usually belong to more than one household, for they have another parent living elsewhere. The couple may not have exclusive control over the child; comparisons between the two homes are perhaps inevitable. Fourth, there is no legal tie between the stepparent and stepchild. Neither has legal rights and responsibilities toward the other.

These special characteristics create special problems. The couple may have unrealistic expectations of righting past wrongs and solving everyone's problems with the new marriage. A spouse who has never had children may have fantasies of instant parenthood, and see her- or himself as "coming to the rescue." These fantasies soon collide with unanticipated realities. The new spouse may have underestimated the amount of time and attention the parent is accustomed to giving his or her children. The couple may find that they have established very different styles of being a parent with their respective children. For small children, the new marriage may mean giving up a secret dream that their parents will get back together. For older children, the new marriage may mean giving up the position as second-in-command and special friend to their custodial parent. Within a year or two of the remarriage, about half of children living in stepfamilies are faced with a new baby. Although parents may hope the baby will bring the family closer together, it may have the opposite effect of making older children feel like outsiders. All stepfamilies go through a period of adjustment. Many settle down into comfortable patterns after a year or two, but a relatively high proportion fall apart.

[Section 5 ends.
Section 6 begins.]

THE FAMILY IN THE FUTURE

Is the family an endangered institution? Some social scientists have thought so. In the 1920s the pioneer behavioral psychologist John B. Watson predicted that the family would disappear by 1977. Ten years later, the sociologist Pitirim Sorokin predicted that home would become "a mere overnight parking place mainly for the sex relationship." In the 1970s the sociologist Amitai Etzioni warned that, given current trends, not a single family would be left in 1990.

Certainly the American family is changing. Knock on a house or apartment door today and who do you find? About 30 percent of households contain a married couple with no children. A smaller proportion (27 percent) include a married couple with children. Often, however, the couple is remarried and the children are stepchildren. Almost a fourth of households contain a single man or woman. The remainder are unmarried mothers and their children, cohabiting couples, and some other arrangements (such as grandparents caring for grandchildren Spanier, 1989). Women are spending more time at work and less time at home, whether or not they have children. Some children are becoming parents in their teens, while others still live with their parents well into their twenties (see Chapter 4).

The family we once considered the heart of the American way of life—in which the husband was the sole provider, the wife a full-time mother and homemaker, and the marriage lasted for life—has become a statistical minority. But the fact that families are different does not necessarily signal decline.

To some extent, the ideal family has always been fiction. Throughout America's history, changes in the age at which people marry, variations in the sex ratio and pool of eligible partners, migration patterns, war, mortality rates, ethnic variations, economic conditions, out-of-wedlock births, cohabitation, separation and divorce, and widowhood "have conspired in varying combinations…to make variation [in family structure] the norm" (Spanier, 1989, p. 5).

Nevertheless, the ideal of lifelong stable marriages, two-parent families, and family lines extending down the generations exerts a powerful hold on our imagination. Most Americans worry about family life (see Figure 12-6). Some of this concern over the current state of the family results from romanticized images of the past. The family seems to bring out a conservative streak. "In technology, progress is the standard. In social institutions, continuity is the standard, and when change occurs, it is seen as decline rather than advance" (Bane 1976, p. 4).

But much of our concern for today's family is based on real patterns (Spanier, 1989). For most Americans, marriage is occurring later and lasting for a smaller proportion of the adult life cycle (Sweet and Bumpass, 1987). Other adult roles have begun to compete with the roles of spouse and parent for our commitment. The contemporary family is based on voluntary associations (Schwartz, 1987). Parents may or may not get married, spouses are free to leave, children (and older people) can turn to outsiders for nurturance and support, and the costs and benefits of each association are weighed against alternatives.

Family life has become more complicated. The plot used to go: "First comes love, then

Is the American family better off or worse off than it was 10 years ago?

49% Worse   39% Better

Will the American family be better off or worse off 10 years from now?

42% Better   42% Worse

Which do you feel is more important for a family these days?

68% To make some financial sacrifices so that one parent can stay home to raise the children

27% To have both parents working so the family can benefit from the highest possible income

When husbands and wives with young children are not getting along, should they stay together for the sake of the children? Or should they separate rather than raise the children in a hostile atmosphere?

70% Separate   24% Stay together

Which one of these family concerns causes you to worry the most?

21% Finding and paying for good health care

17% Keeping up with housing costs/payment

16% Paying for children's college tuition

12% Financing your retirement

9% Getting good day care for children

9% Taking care of elderly, ailing parents

Should unmarried couples, including homosexual couples, have the same legal rights as married couples?

	Yes	No
Unmarried couples	33%	61%
Homosexual couples	23%	69%

Figure 12-6 For Better or Worse? Americans are worried about the family, and they don't approve of some of the shapes it has taken. Substantial majorities say one parent should stay at home with the children; but, divorce is better than hostility. Only a minority recognize gay marriage as legitimate. *(Source: Newsweek Special Edition: The 21st Century Family, Winter/Spring, 1990. © 1990, Newsweek, Inc. All rights reserved. Reprinted by permission.)*

comes marriage, then comes Mary with the baby carriage." Today John and Mary are likely to live together before marriage, if they get married. And there is a sequel (Kantrowitz and Wingert, 1989). Not long after baby Paul is born, John and Mary split up. John moves in with Sally, who has two sons by her previous marriage. A year later Mary meets Jack, who had three children with his first wife. Mary and Jack get married. Two-year-old Paul now has a mother, a father, a stepmother and a stepfather, five stepbrothers and stepsisters, four sets of grandparents, and dozens of aunts, uncles, and cousins. Soon Mary is pregnant with Paul's first half-sibling. Today's family trees are beginning to look like twisting vines of ivy (Spanier, 1989).

One of the big issues for the twenty-first century will be deciding who counts—and who can be counted on—as kin (Furstenberg, in Kantrowitz and Wingert, 1989). Are stepsiblings really brothers and sisters? Is one's father's ex-second-wife or one's sister's stepson a relative? Can stepparents be counted on to behave as grandparents? Will stepchildren feel responsible for stepparents as they grow older?

Family life has also become more fragile. Many children are growing up knowing only one parent, and some have no family at all. More than 13 million children live in poverty; an estimated 500,000 are homeless (Kozol, 1989). The wonder, says the sociologist Graham Spanier (1989), is that many children experience divorce, abuse, poverty, and neglect, and yet reach adulthood with the belief that family life can be rewarding.

Spanier believes the family survives for two reasons. First, it has always been the most efficient means of meeting our most basic needs. Second, through socialization we come to see the family as "a group who love and care for each other."* Even if our own families do not

---

*The definition of the family chosen by three-quarters of respondents in a recent poll conducted by the Massachusetts Mutual Insurance Co. (*Newsweek Special Issue: The 21st Century Family*, 1989, p. 18).

live up to this ideal, the mass media, the political system, and religious affiliation all strongly promote family life. The challenge is to keep the traditional vision of the family alive in the face of nontraditional realities. Spanier does not believe the family will survive into the future simply because it has always survived in the past. We can no longer afford to take the family for granted. We must learn more, not only about why some families fail, but also about why some succeed against the odds.

[Section 6 ends.]

SUMMARY

Every known society has families. But the structure of the family (the number of spouses a man or woman may have and household composition) varies from culture to culture, and the functions the family performs have changed over time.

The changes in the American family have not been as radical as many assume. Both the **extended family** of the past (several generations in one household) and the isolated **nuclear family** of the 1950s (a husband, wife, and their children, living alone with few ties to kin) were largely myths. Nevertheless, acceptance of alternative family forms is growing. The numbers of singles, single parents, and couples who decide not to have children have increased rapidly in recent years. The nuclear family is a statistical minority today.

Sociological analysis suggests that courtship, marriage, and parenthood are not as romantic as many people would like to believe. Most Americans say they marry for love, but research shows that love is highly selective. Most people marry someone with similar social characteristics (the principle of **homogamy**). Exchange theory portrays courtship as an exchange of assets and liabilities in which people weigh the costs and benefits of a potential partner. Although Americans think of parenthood as a natural process, research indicates that the role of parents requires numerous adjustments. With wives working, the daily routine may become more hectic, but there is little evidence that two careers either harm or improve the quality of family life.

All families do not live happily ever after. Recent surveys have shown that violence in the American family is more common than most people imagine, at all socioeconomic levels. Intimacy, privacy, cultural support for the use of force, and socialization all contribute to this social problem.

The **divorce rate** reached an all-time high in the United States in 1979, and the number of divorces involving children has grown. But the high rate of remarriage after divorce, and the number of **stepfamilies** indicate that people believe as strongly in the institution of marriage as they ever did.

The challenge for the future is reconciling traditional images of the family with nontraditional realities.

KEY TERMS

divorce rate
extended family
homogamy
modified extended family
monogamy
nuclear family
polyandry
polygamy
polygyny
stepfamily
serial monogamy

Studying Sections 5 and 6

Activities for Sections 5 and 6

Continue taking notes. This stretch of material covers page 174 to part of page 185.

DIVORCE

Understanding Divorce Statistics:

Divorce rate—_____

_____

    Ex.—_____

_____

Who Gets Divorced and Why:
Chance that a thirty-year-old in today's world will get divorced is 1 in 3.

Factors in divorce—

1. _____
2. _____
3. _____
4. _____

Divorces rose in 1960s and 1970s and leveled in 1980s for several possible reasons: (a) war, (b) baby boom fell off, (c) general shift from faith in institutions to concern with individual fulfillment.

Children and Divorce:
2% of children involved in divorce every year; 40% of children by age 18.

Most important factor in adjusting to divorce is stable, loving relationships with *both* parents. Therefore, professionals today recommend joint *legal* custody if not joint physical custody.

Remarriage and Stepfamilies:
60% of second marriages end in divorce.
About 8 in 10 remarriages involve children.
Stepfamilies involve different forms.

THE FAMILY IN THE FUTURE
Family life has become more complicated, with all the stepparents, stepsisters, and so on.
Big issue is who counts as kin.

Comments on Sections 5 and 6

- Once again, the keys to important ideas are a definition, an example, and enumerations. In addition, notes include major details under some of the headings.

- Notice that the authors use *emphasis words* to show us directly that a detail is significant. The authors state that the "most important factor" in adjusting to divorce is a solid relationship with parents. They also tell us that one of the "big issues" of the next century is deciding who counts as kin. Always be on the lookout for such emphasis words; they signal important ideas and details.

- The chapter closes with a summary and a list of key terms. Just as the preview has given you an overview of the chapter, so also the summary can provide such an overview. These opening and closing overviews help ensure that you do not lose sight of the forest for the trees. And in the list of key terms, the authors themselves underscore how important *definitions* are in learning the chapter. Always use a summary and list of key terms—or other end-of-chapter study aids—as a check to make sure you have not missed some important ideas.

Closing Comments

In the process of taking notes, you have reduced almost forty pages of material to five pages! These five pages provide an anchor for your understanding of the chapter. Keep in mind that if your teacher intends to test you on just this chapter, you may need to have a very detailed knowledge of the material, and you may want to do more rereading and add even more notes. On the other hand, if your teacher intends to test you on this and two other chapters, plus several weeks of classroom notes, it may well be that the five pages of notes is more than enough. You will quickly develop skill at making a good judgment call about just how much you need to learn.

- Complete the following description of the final stage of textbook study: After taking as many notes as you need, your final step is to study the notes.

  To do so, put _____ words in the margin. For instance, the words "family structure" and "family functions" would help you learn the material on the first page of your notes. Your purpose would be to study

  until you could _____ to yourself the family structures and family functions without looking at them. You could then go on to study the other four pages of notes. After completing each page of notes, you should

  go back and _____ the previous pages. Through this process of repeated self-testing, you will effectively learn the material.

CHECKING YOUR MASTERY:
A QUIZ ON THE SAMPLE CHAPTER

After you have completed taking notes on the sample chapter, you or your teacher may decide that you should spend some time studying the notes. You can then use the following quiz to see how well you have learned the material.

■ Quiz on "The Family"

1. *True or false?* _____ Monogamy is the *preferred* arrangement in most human societies.

2. The term for the marriage of one man to two or more women at the same time is
   a. polygamy.
   b. polygyny.
   c. polyandry.
   d. serial monogamy.

3. A more appropriate term for the nuclear family is
   a. extended family.
   b. modified extended family.
   c. one-parent family.
   d. family without children.

4. *True or false?* _____ The major cause of single-parent families today is divorce.

5. In most societies, marriages are
   a. based on love.
   b. arranged by older relatives.
   c. the result of kidnapping.
   d. becoming outdated.

6. Homogamy is the tendency to marry someone
   a. our own age.
   b. like ourselves in important ways.
   c. we've lived with.
   d. rich.

7. *True or false?* _____ Many couples consider having a first child to be a more serious commitment than getting married.

8. *True or false?* _____ The real causes of family violence are alcohol and drugs.

9. According to the authors, one factor influencing whether a couple gets divorced is
   a. health.
   b. age at high school graduation.
   c. socioeconomic status.
   d. difference in age between spouses.
10. The most important factor in children's healthy adjustment to divorce seems to be
    a. living with the mother.
    b. financial support from the father.
    c. a stable, loving relationship with both parents.
    d. joint physical custody.

BUILDING
A POWERFUL
MEMORY

This chapter will show you how to develop your memory by:

- Organizing the material to be learned
- Intending to remember
- Testing yourself repeatedly
- Using several memory techniques
- Spacing memory work over several sessions
- Overlearning
- Studying before sleep

Introductory Projects

Project 1: Mastering class names.   Your instructor may present this activity on memory skills in one of the first classes of the semester, when you still do not know the names of the other people in the class. The instructor will ask you to learn each other's first names and (so as not to get in your way while you do this) will leave the room for ten or fifteen minutes. On returning, the instructor will call for volunteers to introduce him or her on a first-name basis to all the people in the room.

Afterward, the instructor will ask you to describe *how* you went about mastering the first names of all the people in the class. You will then have a chance to compare ideas with others on the memory processes that were used. You will probably find that in most cases the methods used to learn the names were similar. You may also realize for the first time that there *is* a definite process, or sequence of steps, involved in an act of memorization.

Project 2: A study problem.   Consider this common study situation:

> In two days, Steve will have a biology quiz in which he will have to write the definitions of ten terms that have been discussed in the course. As a study aid, the teacher has passed out a list of thirty terms that students should know thoroughly. Steve has gone through his class notes and textbook and copied down the definitions of the thirty terms. He tries to study the terms by reading them over and over, but he has trouble concentrating and merely keeps "reading words." He decides to write out each definition until he knows it. Hours later, he has written out ten definitions a number of times and is still not sure he will remember them. He begins to panic at spending such an enormous amount of time for such meager results. He decides to play Russian roulette with the terms—to study just some of them and hope they are the ones that will be on the test.

This chapter will provide answers to Steve's study problem. But take a few minutes first to examine your own ideas. What do you think are three specific steps that Steve could take to learn the thirty definitions?

Perhaps you think that memorizing material for a test is a waste of time; you may be convinced that you will forget what you memorize as soon as a test is over. Moreover, because some teachers believe that memorization and learning are incompatible, they may tell you that you shouldn't *memorize* material; rather, you should *understand* it.

Memorization, however, can be an important aid to understanding—and not just in situations where basic, uncomplicated material is involved. Effective memorizing requires that you organize and repeatedly test yourself on the material to be learned. As you do this, you are sure to enlarge your comprehension of the material and notice relationships you had not seen before. In short, memorization and understanding *reinforce* one another. Together, they help you learn—and learning is the goal of education. What you need, then, is a series of strategies, or steps, to help you memorize effectively. The following pages present seven such steps:

1   Organize the material to be learned.
2   Intend to remember.
3   Test yourself repeatedly on the material to be memorized.
4   Use several memory techniques.
5   Space memory work over several sessions.
6   Overlearn the material.
7   Use as a study period the time just before going to bed.

STEP 1: ORGANIZE THE MATERIAL TO BE LEARNED

The first key to effective remembering is that you organize in some meaningful way the material to be learned. For example, in the memorization activity described on page 190, students often begin by introducing themselves in isolated pairs. This is not an effective method for learning all the names, however, and someone usually suggests that the introductions be done in an organized manner. What then happens is that, one by one, people take turns giving their names. Some students even jot down a rough seating chart (a further organizational device) to aid them in learning all the names. The point is that some meaningful kind of *organization* is a vital first step in the memory process. The following two examples should also show how organizing material will aid memory.

Example A: Suppose you had to memorize these numbers in any sequence:

1, 10, 7, 12, 22, 28, 20

You could eventually memorize the numbers by sheer mechanical repetition. However, you could learn them far more quickly, and remember them far longer, by grouping them in a meaningful and logical way:

$$10 + 12 = 22$$
$$1 + 7 + 20 = 28$$

Example B: Suppose before you left for school or work, you were asked to look at a list of the shopping items on the kitchen blackboard and to pick them up later at the store. To save the time of writing down the items, and to exercise your memory, you look over the list:

Vaseline

cheese

Bufferin

graham crackers

Oreo cookies

minute steaks

Crest

pressed ham

M & M's

It would be difficult to memorize the items at random, and so you organize them into meaningful groupings.

Medicine-Chest Items	*Snacks*	*Staples*
Crest	graham crackers	cheese
Bufferin	Oreo cookies	minute steaks
Vaseline	M & M's	pressed ham

The three groups of related items are far easier to study and remember than are the nine random items.

To be an effective student, you must learn how to organize the material in classroom lectures and reading assignments. It is easier to remember ideas and details that are related to one another than ones that are isolated, unorganized, and unrelated. In this book, ''Taking Classroom Notes'' will help you learn how to organize the material in classroom lectures, and the three chapters on textbook study (pages 86–189) will help you tie together ideas and details in reading assignments. You will then be ready to memorize any of the information that it is necessary for you to remember.

■ Material in your class notes and textbooks should be _____ in some meaningful way before you attempt to memorize it.

STEP 2: INTEND TO REMEMBER

An important aid to memory is that you *decide* to remember. This bit of advice appears to be so obvious that many people overlook its value. But if you have made the decision to remember something and you then work at mastering it, you *will* remember. Anyone can have a bear-trap memory by working at it; no one is born with a naturally poor memory.

In the project about memorizing class names, students are often surprised at their ability to learn the names of their peers so quickly and completely. A main reason for their success is that they have *decided* to learn—for it might be embarrassing if they were the only ones not to have mastered the names when the instructor returned. The lesson here is that *your attitude is crucial in effective memorization:* You must begin by saying, ''I am going to master this.''

■ Do you ever have trouble, as many people do, in remembering the names of persons you are introduced to? _____ Yes _____ No

■ If you do, the reason is probably that you did not consciously decide to remember their names. Suppose you were introduced to a person who was going to borrow money from you. Is it safe to say you would make it a point to remember (and so *would* remember) the person's name? _____ Yes _____ No

STEP 3: TEST YOURSELF REPEATEDLY ON THE MATERIAL TO BE LEARNED

After you have organized the material you intend to learn, memorize it through repeated self-testing. Look at the first item in your notes; then look away and try to repeat it to yourself. When you can repeat the first item, look at the next item; look away and try to repeat it. When you can repeat the second item, *go back* without looking at your notes and repeat the first *and* second items. After you can recall the first two items without referring to your notes, go on to the third item, and so on. In short, follow this procedure: *After you learn each new item, go back and test yourself on all the previous items. This constant review is at the heart of self-testing* and is the key to effective memorization.

■ If you were memorizing a list of ten definitions, what would you do after you mastered the second definition? The sixth? The tenth?

STEP 4: USE SEVERAL MEMORY TECHNIQUES

The following techniques will help you in the self-testing process:

1 Use several senses.
2 Use key words.
3 Use catchwords.
4 Use catchphrases.

The last two techniques are sometimes called *mnemonic* (*nĭ mŏn'ĭk*) devices. (The term is derived from the Greek word for *memory*.) Each technique is explained and illustrated on the pages ahead.

Use Several Senses

Use several senses in the self-testing process. Studies have shown that most people understand and retain information more effectively when several senses are involved in learning the material. Do not, then, merely recite the information silently to yourself. Also repeat it out loud so that you *hear* it, and write it down so that you both *see* and, as it were, *touch* it. These steps will help you learn more than you would if you only repeated the information silently to yourself.

■ What senses do you use in studying material? _____
_____

Use Key Words

Key words can be used as "hooks" to help you remember ideas. A *key word* stands for an idea and is so central to the idea that if you remember the word, you are almost sure to remember the entire concept that goes with the word.

Here is an illustration of how key words may function as hooks to help you recall ideas. Assume that your biology instructor has announced that the class will be tested on a textbook chapter dealing with the ecology of urban life. This is one important paragraph taken from that chapter.

> Urban planners who want to replace living plants with plastic ones seem to think that the city does not need to have living plants in it. Actually, plants do many useful things in a city even if they are not producing food for people. Plants improve the quality of the air by giving off oxygen and woodsy-smelling compounds, such as those emitted by pine trees. Smog contains some gases that, in low concentrations, can be used as nutrients by plants. Thus plants can absorb some air pollutants. Evaporation of water from plants cools the air; also, the leaves of plants catch falling dust particles. Trees and shrubs muffle the noise of what otherwise could be the deafening sound of street traffic and construction work. Finally, the roots of plants—even weeds on vacant lots—help to hold earth in place and reduce the number of soil particles blown into the air and washed into sewers.

Since you want to learn this information, you would first prepare study notes that might look something like this:

Uses of Plants in City

1. *Give off oxygen (and pleasant smell)*
2. *Absorb air pollutants (gases used as nutrien...*
3. *Cool the air (evaporation from leaves)*
4. *Catch dust particles*
5. *Muffle noises (traffic, construction)*
6. *Hold earth in place*

It is now necessary for you to memorize the study notes, and to do that you will need a technique.

One way to memorize these study notes is to use key words as hooks. What you do is circle a key word from each of the listed items. The word you select should help you pull into memory the entire idea that it represents. Write each of the words, one after the other, under the study notes. Here is how your notes would look.

Uses of Plants in City

1. *Gives off* oxygen *(and pleasant smell)*
2. *Absorb air* pollutants *(gases used as nutrients)*
3. Cool *the air (evaporation from leaves)*
4. *Catch* dust *particles*
5. Muffle *noises (traffic, construction)*
6. *Hold* earth *in place*

Key words: oxygen, pollutants, cool, dust, muffle, earth

After you pick out key words, the next step would be to test yourself repeatedly until you remember each of the six key words *and* the concepts they stand for.

- Take five minutes to study your six key words for the uses of plants in the city. Test yourself until you can recite from memory all the words and the ideas they stand for. Your instructor may then ask you to write from memory the six words and concepts on a sheet of paper.

Use Catchwords

Sometimes people who use key words to pull central ideas into memory can't remember one of the key words, and so they forget the entire concept the word represents. Using catchwords is one way to ensure that you remember an entire series of key words and so the ideas they stand for. *Catchwords* are words made up of the first letters of other words. (See also page 104.)

Follow these guidelines when you prepare catchwords. First, circle the key words in your study notes. Then write down the first letter of each key word. Here are the first letters for the key words in the paragraph about city plants: O (oxygen), P (pollutants), C (cool), D (dust), M (muffle), and E (earth). Now, if necessary, rearrange the letters to form an easily recalled catchword. It can be a real word or a made-up word. For example, you might remember the letters O-P-C-D-M-E with the made-up word MEDCOP.

What matters is that you create a word that you can automatically remember and that the letters in the word help you recall the key words (and so the ideas the key words represent).

After you create a catchword, test yourself until you are sure each letter stands for a key word in your mind. Here is how you might use the catchword MEDCOP to pull into memory the textbook paragraph about city plants:

MEDCOP
M = muffle
E = earth
D = dust
C = cool
O = oxygen
P = pollutants

Cover the key words (*muffle, earth,* etc.) with a sheet of paper, leaving only the first letter exposed. Look at the letter M and see if you can recall the key word *muffle* and the idea that plants muffle noise. Next, look at the letter E and see if you remember the key word *earth* and the idea that plant roots hold the earth in place. Then do the same for the other four letters. In each case, the letter serves as a hook to pull into memory the key word and then the whole idea.

Here is an illustration of how first letters and key words help you remember ideas. As shown here, the first letter helps you remember the key word, which helps you pull the entire idea into memory.

First Letter		Key Word		Entire Idea
M	⟶	muffle	⟶	muffle noise of traffic and construction
E	⟶	earth	⟶	hold earth in place
D	⟶	dust	⟶	catch dust particles
C	⟶	cool	⟶	cool the air
O	⟶	oxygen	⟶	give off oxygen
P	⟶	pollutants	⟶	absorb air pollutants

■ An instructor in a psychology class described the following four techniques used in behavior therapy: (1) extinction, (2) imitation, (3) reinforcement, and (4) desensitization. Make up a catchword that will help you remember the four techniques and write the word here: _____

Use Catchphrases

Another way to remember key words is to form some easily recalled *catchphrase* (see page 105). Each word in a catchphrase begins with the first letter of a different key word. For example, suppose you had to remember the six uses of city plants in the exact order in which they are presented in the textbook paragraph (*oxygen, pollutants, cool, dust, muffle, earth*). You would write a six-word phrase with the first word beginning with *O*, the second with *P*, the third with *C*, and so on. Here is a catchphrase you might create to help remember the order of the six letters and the key words they stand for:

Our **p**arents **c**ook **d**inner **m**ost **e**venings.

Your catchphrase does not have to be perfect grammatically; it does not even have to make perfect sense. It simply needs to be a phrase which will stick in your memory and which you will automatically remember.

Once you create a catchphrase, follow the testing process already described above in the section on catchwords. Note that the first letter of each word in the catchphrase pulls into memory a key word and the key word recalls an entire idea. For example, the *O* in *Our* recalls the key word *oxygen* and the idea that plants give off oxygen, the *P* in *parents* helps you remember the key word *pollutants* and the idea that plants absorb air pollutants, and so on.

■ Suppose an instructor wants you to learn the following five influences on a child's personality. The influences are listed in order of importance.

Influences on Children
One: Parents
Two: Siblings (brothers and sisters)
Three: Friends
Four: Close relatives
Five: Teachers

Make up a catchphrase that will help you remember in sequence the five influences on children and write the phrase here:

_____

STEP 5: SPACE MEMORY WORK OVER SEVERAL SESSIONS

If you try to do a great deal of self-testing at any one time, you may have trouble absorbing the material. Always try to spread out your memory work. For instance, three two-hour sessions will be more effective than one six-hour session.

Spacing memory work over several time periods gives you a chance to review and lock in material you have studied in an earlier session but have begun to forget. Research shows that we forget a good deal of information right after studying it. However, review within a day reduces much of this memory loss. So try to review new material within twenty-four hours after you first study it. Then, if possible, several days later review again to make a third impression or "imprint" of the material in your memory. If you work consistently to retain ideas and details, they are not likely to escape you when you need them during an exam.

- Do you typically try to study the material for a test ''all at once,'' or do you spread out your study over several sessions?

  _____

- How might you spread out six hours of memory work that you need to do for a biology exam?

  _____

  _____

STEP 6: OVERLEARN THE MATERIAL

If you study a subject beyond the time needed for perfect recall, you will increase the length of time that you will remember it. You can apply the principle of overlearning by going over several times a lesson you have already learned perfectly. The method of repeated self-testing is so effective partly because it forces you to overlearn. After you study each new idea, the method requires that you go back and recite all the previous ideas you have studied.

Another way to apply the principle of overlearning is to devote some time in each session to review. Go back to restudy—and overlearn—important material that you have studied in the past. Doing so will help ensure that you will not ''push out'' of memory old ideas at the time you are learning new ones.

- If you memorize a list of ten definitions using the process of repeated self-testing, how many times, at a minimum, will you have tested yourself on the first definition? _____

STEP 7: STUDY BEFORE GOING TO BED

Study thoroughly the material to be learned. Then go right to sleep without watching a late movie or allowing other activities to interfere with your new learning. Your mind will work through and absorb much of this material during the night. Set your clock a half hour earlier than usual so that you will have time to go over the material as soon as you get up. The morning review will complete the process of solidly fixing the material in your memory.

- Have you ever used this technique and found it to be helpful? _____

  _____

- Do you think you should practice the technique daily or more as a study aid in the review period before an exam? _____

PRACTICE IN BUILDING A POWERFUL MEMORY

Activity 1

1. An instructor in a psychology class describes the following four kinds of defense mechanisms. Make up a catchword that will help you remember all four mechanisms.

   Denial
   Repression
   Projection
   Identification

2. An instructor in a sociology class writes on the board the following five sources of truth. Make up a catchword that will help you remember these five sources.

   Sources of Truth
   Intuition
   Authority
   Tradition
   Common sense
   Science

3. The following six avoidance tactics often used by students were described on pages 17–18 of this book. Circle a key word in each of these tactics and then create a catchword or catchphrase to help remember the six key words. The key words, in turn, will help you remember the six avoidance tactics.

   I can't do it.
   I'm too busy.
   I'm too tired.
   I'll do it later.
   I'm bored with the subject.
   I'm here, and that's what counts.

4. You have memorized three groups of items individually. Now take ten to fifteen minutes to prepare for a quiz in which you will be asked to write from memory the four kinds of defense mechanisms, the five sources of truth, and the six avoidance tactics.

Activity 2

1. A psychology text explains Abraham Maslow's theory of basic human needs. The needs, in order of importance, follow. Use a catchphrase to memorize *in sequence* these five needs.

    Basic Human Needs
    First: Biological needs
    Second: Safety needs
    Third: Need for companionship
    Fourth: Esteem needs
    Fifth: Need for self-actualization

2. Many articles and textbooks refer to Holmes and Rohe's scale of specific life experiences that result in stress. Memorize *in sequence* the first six experiences on that scale as well as the point value assigned to each.

Death of spouse	100
Divorce	73
Marital separation	65
Jail term	63
Death of close family member	63
Personal injury or illness	53

3. A sociology text describes the following seven steps that are taken in scientific research. Use a catchphrase to memorize *in sequence* the seven steps.

    First: Define the problem.
    Second: Review the literature.
    Third: Formulate the hypotheses.
    Fourth: Plan the research design.
    Fifth: Collect the data.
    Sixth: Analyze the data.
    Seventh: Draw conclusions.

4. You have memorized three groups of items individually. Now take ten to fifteen minutes to prepare for a quiz in which you will be asked to write from memory, and *in sequence,* the five human needs, the six sources of stress, and the seven steps in scientific research.

Activity 3

1. Read the following selection taken from a consumer information text. Then look over the study notes on the selection.

HOUSEHOLD BUDGET HINTS

Here are some household tips that may increase your chances of living within your household budget. First, if you have a dishwasher, stop it before the dry cycle. Instead of using this cycle, the one requiring the most electricity, open your dishwasher door and let the dishes air-dry. Another hint is to try to cook entire meals at one time in your oven. Many foods with different cooking temperatures can be cooked together at the same temperature, with little loss in taste or nutritive value. Also, if you have a washer in your home, wash full loads. Save clothes until you are ready to do many at one time. And try to wash all your clothes in cold settings; tests indicate that most fabrics can be thoroughly cleaned with cold-water detergents. Next, when you go to the grocery store, go with a list, and shop only for the items on the list. If you don't resist the urge to put extra items in your shopping cart, you may quickly double your bill. Finally, don't open doors unnecessarily. For example, don't stand with the refrigerator door open trying to decide what you want to eat. Decide before you open the door. Don't constantly peek in the oven door to check on how a roast is doing; use a meat thermometer and a timer instead. Don't keep a door of the house open for any longer than necessary when entering or leaving. You're likely to let too much outside air into the house, and your air conditioner or heater will have to work more as a result.

Study Notes

Household Budget Tips
One: Stop dishwasher before dry cycle
Two: Cook entire meals at one time in oven
Three: Do full clothing loads with cold water in washer
Four: Buy only items on shopping list
Five: Open refrigerator, oven, house doors only when needed

Pick out a key word for each of the five budget hints and then use a catchword or catchphrase to memorize the hints.

2. Read the following selection taken from a psychology textbook. Then look over the study notes on the selection.

PERSONAL SPACE

In addition to what you wear and how you stand, where you stand can communicate your attitude. One researcher, E. Hall, identified four types of personal zones or spaces. The first type of personal space is intimate distance (from body contact to one foot away). This space is reserved for a limited few, including lovers, parents, children, and close friends. In addition, health professionals, such as doctors, nurses, and dentists, are allowed to enter this space. If anyone else got this close, we would feel very uncomfortable. The second zone is personal distance (one to four feet away). This zone is used for personal conversations with close friends. If you are sitting in a half-empty theater or bus, and someone takes the seat next to you, you will probably feel annoyed. A stranger in our personal zone makes us feel ill at ease. If people must be packed together—as on a crowded bus—they often avoid eye contact as a way of protecting their personal space. The third zone is social distance (four to ten feet). This zone is used for social and casual conversations or for business transactions. The final zone is public distance (ten feet and beyond). Communication within a large lecture hall, or the relationship of an audience to a sports event or performance, takes place at public distance. Often, in these situations, we consider private behavior or comments inappropriate.

Study Notes

Personal Zones
One: Intimate distance (body contact to one foot away)
Two: Personal distance (one to four feet)
Three: Social distance (four to ten feet)
Four: Public distance (ten feet and beyond)

Pick out a key word for each of the four personal zones and then use a catchword or catchphrase to memorize the four zones.

3. You have memorized two groups of items individually. Now take ten to fifteen minutes to prepare for a quiz in which you will be asked to write from memory the five budget tips and the four personal zones.

Activity 4

Use catchwords to memorize this outline of a selection on job hunting.

Four Stages in Getting a Job

A. Make contact through:
   1. College placement bureau
   2. Want ads and employment agencies
   3. Telephone calls
   4. Personal connections
B. Prepare essential written materials
   1. Résumé
   2. Cover letter
C. Go out on interview
   1. Interview etiquette
   2. Prepare responses to some typical questions
      a. "Why are you interested in this job?"
      b. "What are your greatest strengths and weaknesses?"
      c. "Tell me about yourself."
      d. "Why should we hire you?"
   3. Come across as a competent person
D. Follow up on interview with thank-you note

Activity 5

This will help you apply memory techniques to different kinds of lecture and textbook notes. Use catchwords or catchphrases to do one or more of the following:

- Learn the four steps in writing a paper (pages 64–66).
- Learn the concentration hints (pages 80–83).
- Learn the six motivations of drug users (page 323).
- Learn the five methods for dealing with conflict (pages 123–125).

Activity 6

From one of your course textbooks or the class notes from one of your courses, select a list of important items that you will need to remember. Then do these three things, and turn in a copy of your work to your instructor.

1. Write the full list on a sheet of paper.
2. Circle key words that will help you remember each item on the list.
3. Make up a catchword or catchphrase for the first letters of the key words.

Activity 7

Select four lists of important items to remember from the sample textbook chapter on pages 141–185. Then do the three things listed in Activity 6.

TAKING OBJECTIVE EXAMS

This chapter will show you how to:

- Prepare for and take tests in general
- Prepare for objective exams
- Take objective exams
- Cram when you have no other choice

Introductory Project

Consider this common study situation:

> Most of the exams Rita takes include both multiple-choice and true-false questions as well as at least one essay question. She has several problems with such tests. She often goes into the test in a state of panic. "As soon as I see a question I can't answer," she says, "big chunks of what I do know just fly out the window. I go into an exam expecting to choke and forget." Another problem is her timing. "Sometimes I spend too much time trying to figure out the answer to tricky multiple-choice or true-false questions. Then I end up with only fifteen minutes to answer two essay questions." Rita's greatest difficulty is writing essay answers. "Essays are where I always lose a lot of points. Sometimes I don't read a question the right way, and I wind up giving the wrong answer to the question. When I do understand a question, I have trouble organizing my answer. I'll be halfway through an answer and then realize that I skipped some material I should have put at the start or that I already wrote down something I should have saved for the end. I have a friend who says that essays are easier to study for because she can usually guess what the questions will be. I don't see how this is possible. Essay tests really scare me since I never know what questions are coming."

This chapter and the following chapter will provide answers to Rita's study problem. But take a few minutes first to examine your own ideas. What do you think are three specific steps that Rita should take to begin dealing more effectively with tests?

AVOIDING EXAM PANIC

A familiar complaint of students is, "I'm always afraid I'll panic during an exam. I'll know a lot of the material, but when I sit down and start looking at the questions, I forget things that I know. I'll never get good grades as long as this happens. How can I avoid it?" The answer is that if you are *well prepared,* you are not likely to block or panic on exams.

"How, then," you might ask, "should a person go about preparing for exams?" The answer is plain: You must go to class consistently, read the textbook and any other assigned material, take class and textbook notes, and study and at times memorize your notes. In short, you must start preparing for exams in the first class of the semester. The pages that follow offer a series of practical suggestions to help you use your study time efficiently.

Note: Many of the suggestions offered in this chapter assume that you know how to take effective classroom and textbook notes and that you know how to memorize such notes. If you have not developed these essential skills, refer to the appropriate chapters.

Complete the following sentence: You are unlikely to forget material during exams if you are _____

WHAT TO STUDY

You will not always know beforehand if a scheduled exam will be an objective or an essay test (or a combination of both). To be prepared for whichever kind is given, you should, throughout the course, pay attention to the following.

Key Terms: Look for key terms, their definitions, and examples that clarify the meaning of the terms (see also page 313). Look for this material in your class and textbook notes. If your textbook notes are not complete, go back to the original reading material to locate key terms. This information is often set off in *italic* or **boldface** type.

■   Which of the courses you are now taking contains a number of new terms you will probably have to know for exams? _____

Enumerations: Look for enumerations (lists of items) in your class and textbook notes (see also page 320). Enumerations are often the basis of essay questions.

Items in a list will probably have a descriptive heading—for example, characteristics of living things, major schools of contemporary psychology, primary consequences of the Industrial Revolution—and the items may be numbered. Be sure to learn the heading that describes the list as well as the items in the list.

Points Emphasized: Look for points emphasized in class or in the text. Often phrases such as *the most significant, of special importance, the chief reason,* and so on (see page 342) are used to call attention to important points in a book or a lecture. When you take notes on such material, mark these significant points with an *imp,* an asterisk (*), or some other mark.

Also, as you go through your class notes, concentrate on areas the instructor spent a good deal of time discussing. For example, if the instructor spent a week talking about present-day changes in the traditional family structure, you can reasonably expect to get a question on the emphasized area. Similarly, review your textbook. If many pages in a chapter deal with one area, you may be sure that subject is important and so you should expect a question about it on an exam.

- Write down here the name of one of your courses and an area that your instructor has spent a good deal of time discussing in the course.

    Course: _____

    Area: _____

Topics Identified by the Instructor: Pay attention to areas your instructors have advised you to study. Some instructors conduct in-class reviews during which they tell students what material to emphasize when they study. Always write down these pointers; your instructors have often made up the test or are making it up at the time of the review and are likely to give valuable hints about the exam. Other instructors indicate the probable emphasis in their exams when they distribute reviews or study guides. You should, of course, consider these aids very carefully.

- One study-skills instructor has said, "I sometimes sit in on classes, and time and again I have heard teachers tell students point-blank that something is to be on an exam. Some students quickly jot down this information; others sit there in a fog." Which group of students do you belong to?

    _____

- What are some specific study aids instructors have given to help you prepare

    for tests? _____

    _____

Questions on Earlier Tests: Pay attention to questions on past quizzes and reviews as well as tests at the end of textbook chapters.

If you follow these suggestions, you will have identified most, if not all, of the key concepts in the course.

The following hints will help you make the most of your time before a test.

Hint 1:   Spend the night before an exam making a final review of your notes. Then go right to bed without watching television or otherwise interfering with the material you have learned. Your mind will tend to work through and absorb the material during the night. To further lock in your learning, get up a half hour earlier than usual the next morning and review your notes.

■   Do you already review material on the morning of an exam? _____

If so, have you found it to be very helpful? _____

Hint 2:   Make sure you take with you any materials (pen, paper, eraser, dictionary, and other aids allowed) you will need during the exam.

Hint 3:   Be on time for the exam. Arriving late sets you up to do poorly.

Hint 4:   Sit in a quiet spot. Some people are very talkative and noisy before an exam. Since you don't want anything to interfere with your learning, you are better off not talking with others during the few minutes before the exam starts. You might want to use those minutes to make one final review of your notes.

■   How do you typically spend the minutes in class right before an exam?

_____

Hint 5:   Read over carefully *all* the directions on the exam before you begin. Many students don't take this important step and end up losing points because they fail to do what is required. Make sure you understand how you are expected to respond to each item, how many points each section is worth, and how many questions you must answer. Also listen carefully to any oral directions or hints the instructor may give. Many students wreck their chances at the start because they do not understand or follow directions. Don't let this happen to you.

■   Do you already have the habit of reading all the directions on an exam carefully before you begin? _____

Hint 6:   Budget your time. Take a few seconds to figure out roughly how much time you can spend on each section of the test. Write the number of minutes in the margin of your exam paper or on a scratch sheet. Then stick to that schedule. Be sure to have a watch or to sit where you can see a clock.

Exactly *how* you budget your time depends on what kinds of questions you are good at answering (and so can do more quickly) and the point value of different sections of the test. Keep in mind that the reason for budgeting your time is to prevent you from ending up with ten minutes left and a fifty-point essay still to write or thirty multiple-choice questions to answer.

Activity 1

This activity will check your skill at following written directions.

A Test in Following Directions: First read all ten directions carefully. Then follow them.

_____   _____

1. Print your full name, last name first, on the line at the right above.
2. Write your full name, first name last, under the line at the left above.
3. Count the number of *e*'s in this sentence and write out the total number in the margin to the right of this line.
4. Fold this page in half, side to side; then open it again.
5. Read the following question carefully and answer it in the space provided. "A plane crashes on the United States–Canadian border. On which side are the survivors buried?" _____
6. Disregard the fourth instruction.
7. If Ted and Ellen each have $100, how much would Ted have to give Ellen for her to have $10 more than he has? _____
8. How many birthdays does the average hippopotamus have? _____
9. Block out the three-letter words, circle the four-letter words, and underline the five-letter words in this sentence. Then indicate in the space that follows the number of words left unmarked. _____
10. If Glug zorted the rochenelle and hochwinded a swattorg, what fortig dorts Glug?

Activity 2

Here is an activity that will check your skill at budgeting time. Suppose that you had two hours for a test made up of the following sections:

Part 1:	10 true-false questions worth 10 points	(_____minutes)
Part 2:	40 multiple-choice questions worth 40 points	(_____minutes)
Part 3:	2 essay questions worth 50 points	(_____minutes)

In the spaces provided, write how much time you would spend on each part.

One possible division of time is to spend an hour on the first two parts (about ten minutes on the true-false questions and fifty minutes on the multiple-choice questions) and a half hour on each essay question. Because the essay questions are worth half the points on the test, you want at least an hour to work on them.

PREPARING FOR AND TAKING OBJECTIVE EXAMS

Objective exams may include multiple-choice, true-false, fill-in, and matching questions. Perhaps you feel that objective tests do not require as much study time as essay exams do. A well-constructed objective test, however, can evaluate your understanding of major concepts and demand just as sophisticated a level of thinking as an essay exam. In short, do not cut short your study time just because you know you will be given an objective test.

To do well on objective tests, you must know how to read test items carefully. The pages that follow describe a number of strategies you can use to deal with the special problems posed by objective tests.

Getting Ready for Objective Exams

Hint 1: Be prepared to memorize material when studying for an objective test. The test may include short-answer questions. For example, the instructor may give several technical terms and ask you to define them. Or the instructor may include headings such as ''Three Values of the Social Security Act'' and expect you to list the values underneath. He or she may include fill-in questions such as ''An important leader of the stimulus-response school of psychology has been _____.''

Even objective tests made up only of multiple-choice and true-false questions can include such fine distinctions that memorization may be necessary. In addition, memorization helps keep your study honest: it forces you to truly *understand* the material you are learning.

There is one difference worth noting between the kind of memorizing needed for essay exams and the kind needed for objective tests. In an essay test, you are expected to actually *recall course material.* For example, an essay test might ask you to list and explain three kinds of defense mechanisms. In an objective test, you are expected to *recognize the correctness of course material.* For instance, an objective test might give you a defense mechanism followed by a definition and ask you whether that definition was true or false. In either kind of test, however, memory is required.

■ Describe the specific kinds of objective exams that your instructors give:

_____

Hint 2: Ask your instructor what kind of items will be on the test. Not all instructors will provide this information. However, finding out beforehand that an exam will include, let's say, fifty multiple-choice and fill-in items relieves you of some anxiety. At least you know what to expect.

Hint 3: Try to find a test that is similar to the one you will be taking. Some instructors distribute past exams to help students review. Also, some departments keep on file exams given in earlier semesters. Looking at these exams closely can familiarize you with the requirements, format, and items you may reasonably expect on your exam.

Hint 4: Be sure to review carefully all the main points presented in the course. These were detailed in "What to Study" on pages 206–207. To sharpen your understanding of the course's key material, apply the techniques of repeated self-testing (page 194) to the recall words written in the margin of your class and textbook notes (pages 48 and 96).

Hint 5: Make up practice test items when you study. That way you will be getting into the rhythm of taking the test, and you may even be able to predict some of the questions the instructor will ask.

Taking Objective Exams

Hint 1: Answer all the easier questions first. Don't lose valuable time stalling over hard questions. You may end up running out of time and not even getting a chance to answer the questions you can do easily. Instead, put a light check mark (√) beside difficult questions and continue working through the entire test, answering all the items you can do right away. You will find that this strategy will help give you the momentum you need to go confidently through the rest of the exam.

Hint 2: Go back and spend the time remaining with the difficult questions you have marked. Often you will find that while you are answering the easier questions, your unconscious mind has been working on questions you at first found very difficult. Or later items may provide just the extra bit of information you need to answer earlier items you found difficult. Once you answer a question, add a mark to the check you have already made (√) to show you have completed that item.

Hint 3: Answer *all* questions unless the instructor has said that points will be deducted for wrong answers. Guess if you must; by doing so, you are bound to pick up at least a few points.

Hint 4: Ask the instructor to explain any item that isn't clear. Not all instructors will provide this explanation but probably many will. Most experienced instructors realize that test questions may seem clear and unambiguous to them as they make up the exam but that students may interpret certain questions in other and equally valid ways. In short, you can't lose anything by asking to have an item clarified.

Hint 5: Put yourself in the instructor's shoes when you try to figure out the meaning of a confusing item. In light of what was covered in the course, which answer do you think the instructor would say is correct? If a test item is worded so ambiguously that no single response seems correct, you may—in special situations—use the margin of your test paper to explain to the instructor what you feel the answer should be. Obviously, use this technique only when absolutely necessary.

Hint 6: Circle or underline the key words in difficult questions. This strategy can help you untangle complicated questions and focus on the central point in the item.

Hint 7: Express difficult questions in your own words. Rephrasing the item in simpler terms and then writing it down or even saying it to yourself can help you cut through the confusion and get to the core of the question. Be sure, however, not to change the original meaning of the item.

Hint 8: Take advantage of the full time given and go over the exam carefully for possible mistakes. People used to say that it is not a good idea to change the first answer you put down. However, as long as you have a good reason, you *should* change your earlier answers if they seem incorrect. At the same time, be on guard against last-minute anxiety that prompts you to change, without good reason, *many* of your original answers. You should control any tendency you may have to make widespread revisions.

Activity

Write here the three most important of the preceding hints for you to remember in taking objective exams.

1. _____

2. _____

3. _____

Specific Hints for Answering Multiple-Choice Questions

1 Remember that a perfect answer to every question may not be provided in multiple-choice exams. You must choose the best answer *available*.

2 Cross out answers you know are incorrect. Eliminating answers is helpful because it focuses your attention on the most reasonable options. If you think all options are incorrect, the correct answer is "none of the above."

3 Be sure to read all the possible answers to a question, especially when the first answer is correct. Remember that the other options could also be correct. In this case, "all of the above" would be the correct response.

4 Minimize the risk of guessing the answer to difficult items by doing either of the following:

    a Read the question and then the first possible answer. Next, read the question again and the second possible answer and so on until you have read the question with each separate answer. Breaking the items down this way will often help you identify the option that most logically answers the question.

    b Try not to look at the answers when you return to difficult items. Instead, read the question, supply your own answer, and then look for the option on the test that is closest to your response.

5 Use the following clues, which may signal correct answers, *only* when you have no idea of the answer and must guess.

    a The longest answer is often correct.

        ■ *Use this clue to answer the following question:* The key reason students who are well prepared still don't do well on exams is that they (a) are late to the test, (b) don't have all their materials, (c) forget to jot down catchphrases, (d) haven't studied enough, (e) don't read all the directions before they begin the test.

        The correct answer is *e,* the longest answer.

    b The most complete and inclusive answer is often correct.

        ■ *Use this clue to answer the following question:* If you have to cram for a test, which of these items should receive most of your attention? (a) The instructor's tests from other years, (b) important ideas in the class and text notes, including such things as key terms, their definitions, and clarifying examples, (c) the textbook, (d) class notes, (e) textbook notes.

        The correct answer is *b,* the most complete and inclusive choice. Note that the most complete answer is often also the longest.

c An answer in the middle, especially if it is longest, is often correct.

■ *Use this clue to answer the following question:* Many students have trouble with objective tests because they (a) guess when they're not sure, (b) run out of time, (c) think objective exams are easier than essay tests and so do not study enough, (d) forget to double-check their answers, (e) leave difficult questions to the end.

The correct answer is *c,* which is in the middle and is longest.

d If two answers have opposite meanings, one of them is probably correct.

■ *Use this clue to answer the following question:* Before an exam starts, you should (a) sit in a quiet spot, (b) join a group of friends and talk about the test, (c) review the textbook one last time, (d) read a book and relax, (e) study any notes you didn't have time for previously.

The correct answer is *a.* Note that *a* and *b* are roughly opposite.

e Answers with qualifiers, such as *generally, probably, most, often, some, sometimes,* and *usually,* are frequently correct.

■ *Use this clue to answer the following question:* In multiple-choice questions, the most complete and inclusive answer is (a) never correct, (b) often correct, (c) always correct, (d) all of the above, (e) none of the above.

The correct answer is *b,* the choice with the qualifying word *often.* Note also that answers with absolute words, such as *all, always, everyone, everybody, never, no one, nobody, none,* and *only,* are usually incorrect.

■ *Use this clue to answer the following question:* In multiple-choice questions, the answer in the middle with the most words is (a) always correct, (b) always incorrect, (c) frequently correct, (d) never wrong, (e) never right.

The correct answer is *c;* all the other answers use absolute words and are incorrect.

Activity

Write here what you think are the three most helpful clues for you to remember when guessing the answer to a multiple-choice question.

1. _____

2. _____

3. _____

Specific Hints for Answering True-False Questions

1   Simplify questions with double negatives by crossing out both negatives and then determining the correct answer.

■   *Use this hint to answer the following question: True or false?* _____ You won't be unprepared for essay exams if you anticipate several questions and prepare your answers for those questions.

The statement is true. It can be reworded to read, ''You will be prepared for essay exams if you anticipate several questions and prepare your answers to those questions.''

2   Remember that answers with qualifiers such as *generally, probably, most, often, some, sometimes,* and *usually* are frequently true.

■   *Use this hint to answer the following question: True or false?* _____ Some instructors will tell students what kinds of items to expect on an exam.

The statement, which contains the qualifier *Some,* is true.

3   Remember that answers with absolute words such as *all, always, everyone, never, no one, nobody, none,* and *only* are usually false.

■   *Use this hint to answer the following question: True or false?* _____ You should never review your notes on the morning of an essay exam.

The statement, which contains the absolute word *never,* is false.

Specific Hints for Answering Fill-In Questions

1   Read the questions to yourself so you can actually hear what is being asked. If more than one response comes to mind, write them both lightly in the margin. Then, when you review your answers later, choose the answer that feels most right to you.

2   Make sure each answer you provide fits logically and grammatically into its slot in the sentence. For example: An _____ lists ideas in a sequence. The correct answer is *enumeration.* Note that the word *an* signals that the correct answer begins with a vowel.

3   Remember that not all fill-in answers require only one word. If you feel that several words are needed to complete an answer, write in all the words unless the instructor or the directions indicate that only single-word responses will be accepted.

Specific Hints for Answering Matching Questions

1 Don't start matching items until you read both columns and get a sense of the choices. Often, there's an extra item or two in one column. This means that not all items can be paired. Some will be left over. For example:

1. Sentence-skills mistakes _____
2. Absolute words _____
3. Connecting words _____
4. Qualifying words _____
5. Direction words in instructions _____

a. compare, explain, analyze
b. often, usually, most
c. from, over, in, with
d. misspelled and omitted words
e. all, never, only
f. first, second, next, also

The correct answers are 1-*d,* 2-*e,* 3-*f,* 4-*b,* and 5-*a.* Item *c* is extra.

2 Start with the easiest items. One by one, focus on each item in one column and look for its match in the other column. Cross out items as you use them.

A FINAL NOTE: HOW TO CRAM WHEN YOU HAVE NO OTHER CHOICE

Students who consistently cram for tests are not likely to be successful; they often have to cram because they have not managed their time well. However, even organized students may sometimes need to cram because they run into problems that disrupt their regular study routine. If you're ever in this situation, the following steps may help you do some quick but effective studying.

1 Accept the fact that, in the limited time you have, you are not going to be able to study everything in your class notes and textbook. You may even have to exclude your textbook if you know that your instructor tends to base most of a test on class material.

2 Read through your class notes (and, if you have them, your textbook notes) and mark off those ideas that are most important. Use as a guide any review or study sheets that your instructor has provided. Your purpose is to try to guess correctly many of the ideas your instructor will put in the test.

   Important ideas often include definitions, enumerations (lists of items), points marked by emphasis words, and answers to basic questions made out of titles and headings. See also "What to Study" on pages 206–207.

3 Write the ideas you have selected on sheets of paper, using one side of a page only. Perhaps you will wind up with three or four "cram sheets" full of important points to study.

4 Prepare catchwords or catchphrases to recall the material and then memorize the points using the method of repeated self-testing described on page 194.

5 Go back, if time remains, and review all your notes. If you do not have textbook notes, you might skim your textbook. Do not use this time to learn new concepts. Instead, try to broaden as much as possible your understanding of the points you have already studied.

PRACTICE IN TEST TAKING

Activity 1

Evaluate your present test-preparation and test-taking skills. Put a check mark beside each of the following steps that you already practice. Then put a check mark beside those steps that you plan to practice. Be honest; leave a blank space if you do not plan to follow a particular point.

Now Plan
Do   to Do   *What to Study*
____ ____   Key terms, definitions, and examples
____ ____   Enumerations (lists of items)
____ ____   Points emphasized in class
____ ____   Reviews and study guides
____ ____   Questions in past quizzes and textbook chapters

General Tips before an Exam
____ ____   1. Study right before sleep.
____ ____   2. Take materials needed to the exam.
____ ____   3. Be on time for the exam.
____ ____   4. Sit in a quiet spot.
____ ____   5. Read all directions carefully.
____ ____   6. Budget your time.

Getting Ready for Objective Exams
____ ____   1. Memorize as necessary.
____ ____   2. Ask instructor about makeup of test.
____ ____   3. Look at similar tests.
____ ____   4. Review carefully all main points of course.
____ ____   5. Make up practice test items.

Taking Objective Exams
____ ____   1. Answer all easier questions first.
____ ____   2. Do difficult questions in time remaining.
____ ____   3. Answer all questions.
____ ____   4. Ask instructor to explain unclear items.
____ ____   5. For difficult questions, think of the instructor's point of view.
____ ____   6. Mark key words in difficult questions.
____ ____   7. State difficult questions in your own words.
____ ____   8. Use all the time given.
____ ____   9. Use the specific hints given for multiple-choice, true-false, fill-in, and matching questions.

Activity 2

All the questions that follow have been taken from actual college tests. Answer the questions by using the specific hints for answering multiple-choice and true-false questions that follow. Also, in the space provided, give the letter of the hint or hints used to determine the correct answer.

Hints for Test Taking

a   The longest multiple-choice answer is often correct.

b   The most complete and inclusive multiple-choice answer is often correct.

c   A multiple-choice answer in the middle, especially one with the most words, is often correct.

d   If two multiple-choice answers have the opposite meaning, one of them is probably correct.

e   Answers with qualifiers, such as *generally, usually, probably, most, often, some, may,* and *sometimes,* are usually correct.

f   Answers with absolute words, such as *all, always, everyone, everybody, never, no one, nobody, none,* and *only,* are usually incorrect.

Hint _____   1. *True or false?* _____ Denial and intellectualization always reduce anxiety.

Hint _____   2. Newton's third law of motion is
   a. $x = 2y$.
   b.   "force equals mass times acceleration."
   c.   "for every force there is an opposing force of equal value."
   d.   a measure of inertia.

Hint _____   3. With a policy of exclusive market coverage, a manufacturer
   a.   expands the availability of a product.
   b.   restricts the availability of a product.
   c.   seeks multiple retail outlets.
   d.   advertises in low-circulation magazines.

Hint _____   4. *True or false?* _____ Too much thyroxin can often result in tenseness and agitation.

Hint _____   5. Charismatic authority is based on
   a.   law.
   b.   established behavior.
   c.   belief in the extraordinary personal qualities of the ruler.
   d.   religious beliefs.

Hint _____   6. Schizophrenics labeled *paranoid*
   a.   always display "waxy flexibility."
   b.   usually fear that they are being persecuted.
   c.   are invariably the children of schizophrenics.
   d.   always display multiple personalities.

Hint _____ 7. Prohibition
   a. was supported mainly by urban dwellers.
   b. caused a decrease in crime.
   c. was an unqualified success.
   d. failed because of widespread violations, an upsurge in crime, and inadequate enforcement.

Hint _____ 8. *True or false?* _____ A charged cloud may cause an induced charge in the earth below it.

Hint _____ 9. A covalent bond is
   a. a bond between two atoms made up of a shared pair of electrons.
   b. impossible in organic compounds.
   c. an extremely unstable chemical bond.
   d. the basis of all inorganic compounds.

Hint _____ 10. *True or false?* _____ The only factors influencing the decision of the United States to enter World War I were economic ones.

TAKING
ESSAY EXAMS

This chapter will show you:

- Two key steps in preparing for an essay exam
- Three key steps in writing an exam essay

Essay exams are perhaps the most common type of writing you will do in school. They include one or more questions to which you must respond in detail, writing your answers in a clear, well-organized manner. Many students have trouble with essay exams because they do not realize there is a sequence to follow that will help them do well on such tests. Here are five steps you should master if you want to write effective exam essays:

1 Anticipate probable questions.
2 Prepare and memorize an informal outline answer for each question.
3 Look at the exam carefully and do several things.
4 Prepare a brief, informal outline before answering an essay question.
5 Write a clear, well-organized essay.

Each step will be explained and illustrated on the pages that follow.

STEP 1: ANTICIPATE PROBABLE QUESTIONS

Because exam time is limited, the instructor can give you only a few questions to answer. He or she will reasonably focus on questions dealing with the most important areas of the subject. You can probably guess most of them.

Go through your class notes with a colored pen and mark those areas where your instructor has spent a good deal of time. The more time spent on any one area, the better the chance you'll get an essay question on it. If the instructor spent a week talking about the importance of the carbon molecule, or about the advantages of capitalism, or about key early figures in the development of psychology as a science, you can reasonably expect that you will get a question on the emphasized area.

In both your class notes and your textbooks, pay special attention to definitions and examples and to basic lists of items (enumerations). Enumerations in particular are often the key to essay questions. For instance, if your instructor spoke at length about the causes of the Great Depression, or about the long-range effects of water pollution, or about the advantages of capitalism, you should probably expect a question such as "What are the causes of the Great Depression?" or "What are the wide-range effects of water pollution?" or "What are the advantages of capitalism?"

If your instructor has given you study guides, look for probable essay questions there. (Some teachers choose their essay questions from among those listed in a study guide.) Look for clues to essay questions on any short quizzes that you may have been given. Finally, consider very carefully any review that the instructor provides. Always write down such reviews—your instructor has often made up the test or is making it up at the time of the review and is likely to give you valuable hints about the test. Take advantage of them! Note also that if the instructor does not offer to provide a review, do not hesitate to *ask* for one in a friendly way. Essay questions are likely to come from areas the instructor may mention.

- *Complete the following sentence:* Very often you can predict essay questions,

  for they usually concern the most ＿＿＿＿＿＿＿＿ areas of a subject.

STEP 2: PREPARE AND MEMORIZE AN INFORMAL OUTLINE ANSWER FOR EACH QUESTION

Write out each question you have made up and, under it, list the main points to be discussed. Put important supporting information in parentheses after each main point. You now have an informal outline that you can go on to memorize.

If you have spelling problems, make up a list of words you might have to spell in writing your answers. For example, if you are having a psychology test on the principles of learning, you might want to study such terms as *conditioning, reinforcement, Pavlov, reflex, stimulus,* and so on.

An Illustration of Step 2:   One class was given a day to prepare for an essay exam on the note-taking hints on pages 41–48. The students were told that the question would be, ''Describe seven helpful hints for taking classroom notes.'' One student, Carl, made up the following outline answer for the question:

Hints to remember when taking class notes:

1 Read (text) in advance (understand more, take better notes)
2 (Signals of) importance (defs. + enumerations, emphasis words, repeats, tone of voice, blackboard)
3 Write (connections) between ideas (need for full understanding; also, previews + reviews)
4 Written (record) of class (80% forgetting in 2 weeks)
5 (Outline) form (main points at margin, skip line)
6 (Discussion) notes (may not cover later main ideas that arise)
7 (Review) soon after class (gaps, organization)

TSCRODR (Tom Smothers's cat ran outside dressing room)

Activity

Complete this explanation of what Carl did to prepare for the essay question.

First, Carl wrote down the heading and then numbered the seven hints under it. Also, in parentheses beside each point he added _____. Then he picked out and circled a key _____ in each hint, and he wrote down the first _____ of each key word underneath his outline. Carl then used the first letter in each key word to make up a catchphrase that he could easily remember. Finally, he _____ himself over and over until he could recall all seven of the words that the first letters stood for. He also made sure that each word he remembered truly stood for an _____ in his mind and that he recalled much of the supporting material that went with each idea.

STEP 3: LOOK AT THE EXAM CAREFULLY
AND DO SEVERAL THINGS

1 Get an overview of the exam by reading *all* the questions on the test.

2 Note the direction words (*compare, illustrate, list,* and so on) for each question. Be sure to write the kind of answer that each question requires. For example, if a question says ''illustrate,'' do not ''compare.'' The list on the following page will help clarify the distinctions among various direction words. Notice that, ordinarily, you are not asked for your opinion. Instead, essay questions ask you to give back information you have learned about a given topic.

3 Budget your time. Write in the margin the number of minutes you should spend for each essay. For example, if you have three essays worth an equal number of points and a one-hour time limit, figure twenty minutes for each one. Make sure you are not left with only a couple of minutes to do a high-point essay.

4 Start with the easiest question. Getting a good answer down on paper will help build up your confidence and momentum. Number your answers plainly so that your instructor will know which question you answered first.

An Illustration of Step 3:   When Carl received the exam, he circled the direction word *describe,* which meant that he should explain in detail each of the seven hints. He also jotted a 30 in the margin when the teacher said that students would have a half hour to write the answer.

Activity

Complete the short matching quiz below. It will help you review the meanings of some of the direction words shown on the next page.

1. List _____
2. Contrast _____
3. Define _____
4. Summarize _____
5. Describe _____

a. Tell in detail about something.
b. Give a series of points and number them 1, 2, 3. . . .
c. State briefly the important points.
d. Show differences between two things.
e. Give the formal meaning of a term.

Direction Words Used in Essay Questions

Compare	Show similarities between things.
Contrast	Show differences between things.
Criticize	Give the positive and negative points of a subject as well as evidence for these positions.
Define	Give the formal meaning of a term.
Describe	Tell in detail about something.
Diagram	Make a drawing and label it.
Discuss	Give details and, if relevant, the positive and negative points of a subject as well as evidence for these positions.
Enumerate	List points and number them 1, 2, 3. . . .
Evaluate	Give the positive and negative points of a subject as well as your judgment about which outweighs the other and why.
Illustrate	Explain by giving examples.
Interpret	Explain the meaning of something.
Justify	Give reasons for something.
List	Give a series of points and number them 1, 2, 3. . . .
Outline	Give the main points and important secondary points. Put main points at the margin and indent secondary points under the main points. Relationships may also be described with symbols, as follows:

    1. _____

        a. _____

        b. _____

    2. _____

Prove	Show to be true by giving facts or reasons.
Relate	Show connections among things.
State	Give the main points.
Summarize	Give a condensed account of the main points.
Trace	Describe the development or history of a subject.

STEP 4: PREPARE A BRIEF, INFORMAL OUTLINE
BEFORE ANSWERING AN ESSAY QUESTION

Use the margin of the examination or a separate piece of scratch paper to jot down quickly, as they occur to you, the main points you want to discuss in each answer. Then decide in what order you want to present these points in your response. Put *1* in front of the first item, *2* beside the second item, and so on. You now have an informal outline to guide you as you answer your essay question.

If there is a question on the exam that is similar to the questions you anticipated and outlined at home, quickly write down the catchphrase that calls back the content of the outline. Below the catchphrase, write the key words represented by each letter in the catchphrase. The key words, in turn, will remind you of the concepts they represent. If you have prepared properly, this step will take only a minute or so, and you will have before you the guide you need to write a focused, supported, organized answer.

An Illustration of Step 4:   Carl immediately wrote down his catchphrase ''Tom Smothers's cat ran outside dressing room.'' He next jotted down the first letters in his catchphrase and then the key words that went with each letter. He then filled in several key details. At that point, he was ready to write his actual essay answer.

Here is what Carl's brief outline looked like:

Tom Smothers's cat ran outside dressing room

T   Text—read in advance
S   Signals (defs. + enumerations, repeats, voice, emphasis words)
C   Connections between ideas
R   Record of the class (80% forgotten in 2 weeks)
O   Outline
D   Discussion notes
R   Review after class

STEP 5: WRITE A CLEAR, WELL-ORGANIZED ESSAY

If you have followed the suggestions to this point, you have done all the preliminary work needed to write an effective essay. Be sure not to wreck your chances of getting a good grade by writing carelessly. Instead, as you prepare your response, keep in mind the principles of good writing: unity, support, organization, and clear, error-free sentences.

First, start your essay with a sentence that clearly states what it will be about. Then make sure that everything in your essay relates to your opening statement.

Second, though you must obviously take time limitations into account, provide as much support as possible for each of your main points.

Third, use transitions to guide your reader through your answer. Words such as *first, next, then, however,* and *finally* make it easy for the reader to follow your train of thought.

Last, leave time to proofread your essay for sentence-skills mistakes you may have made while you concentrated on writing your answer. Look for illegible words; for words omitted, miswritten, or misspelled (if possible, bring a dictionary with you); for awkward phrasings or misplaced punctuation marks; for whatever else may prevent the reader from understanding your thoughts. Cross out any mistakes and make your corrections neatly above the errors. If you want to change or add to some point, insert an asterisk at the appropriate spot, put another asterisk at the bottom of the page, and add the corrected or additional material there.

An Illustration of Step 5: Read through Carl's answer, on the opposite page, and then do the activity below.

Activity

The following sentences comment on Carl's essay. Fill in the missing word or words in each case.

1. Carl begins with a sentence that clearly signals what his paper _____. Always begin with such a clear signal!

2. Notice the various _____ that Carl made when writing and proofreading his paper. He crossed out awkward phrasings and miswritten

   words; he used his _____ after he had finished the essay to correct misspelled words; he used insertion signs (∧) to add omitted words; and he used an asterisk to add omitted details.

3. The transition words that Carl used to guide his reader, and himself, through the seven points of his answer include

   _____   _____   _____

   _____   _____   _____

   _____

The seven hints that follow are helpful to remember when taking classroom notes. ~~he~~ First, read the textbook in advance. This way you should understand more of the material given in class. Also, you may be able to organize your notes better. ~~A~~ Second, be ready for signals of importance. These ~~un~~ include definitions and enumerations, emphasis words ("the chief cause . . .") the teacher's tone of voice.* Next, write down the connections between ideas so that you will be able to tie together and fully understand your ideas later. Write down any ~~previous~~ previews or reviews the teacher gives as well. A fourth hint is ~~a written~~ to make sure you get a written record of the class. This must be done because in only ~~too~~ two weeks we forget 80% of what we hear. In added time we ~~about~~ forget just about everything. Another hint is to try to outline notes when you can. Keep the main points at the margin and indent supporting ~~info below~~ information under main points. Also use white space to show when the teacher has moved from one topic to another. A sixth hint is to keep taking notes during discussion periods. Important ideas may come up here that the teacher will not come back to later. Finally, review your notes soon after class, when you still remember enough to add to the ~~matri~~ material. You can also make the organization clearer to yourself, if necessary.

*and everything the teacher puts on the board.

PRACTICE IN PREPARING FOR AND TAKING ESSAY EXAMS

Activity 1

Evaluate your present skills in preparing for and taking essay tests. Put a check mark beside each of the following steps that you already practice. Then put a check mark beside those steps that you plan to practice. Leave a space blank if you do not plan to follow a particular point.

Now   Plan
Do   to Do

____ ____   1. List ten or so probable questions.
____ ____   2. Prepare a good outline answer for each question and memorize the outline.
            3. Look at the exam carefully and do the following:
____ ____   a. Read *all* the questions.
____ ____   b. Note direction words.
____ ____   c. Start with the easiest question.
____ ____   4. Outline an answer before writing it.
            5. Write a well-organized answer by doing the following:
____ ____   a. Have a main-idea sentence.
____ ____   b. Use transitions throughout the answer.
____ ____   c. Write complete sentences.
____ ____   d. Proofread paper for omitted words, miswritten words, unclear phrasing, punctuation problems, and misspellings.

Activity 2

The student paragraph that follows was written in response to the essay question "Describe seven helpful hints to remember when taking classroom notes." On separate paper, rewrite the paragraph, expanding and correcting it. Begin with a clear opening statement, use transitions throughout your answer, and make sure that each point and the supporting details for that point are clearly presented.

	One of the first things is to be in class. Attending class is
	often the chief to doing well in a course. Read your text book
	to help notetaking. Always write down examples they are
	good for you and can help you very much. Remember that
	forgetting sets it almost immediate. In two week we forget
	80% of what we hear. Always try to review your notes after
	class still fresh in your mind. Next, the connections between
	ideas—label PREVIEW or REVIEW. Last, notes at the end
	of a class are important.

Activity 3

Spend a half hour getting ready to write a one-paragraph essay on the question "Describe seven steps you can take to improve your memory." (Refer to pages 192–199.) Prepare for the test by following the advice given in step 2 on page 221.

Activity 4

Prepare five questions you might be expected to answer on an essay exam in one of your courses. Make up an outline answer for each of the five questions. Memorize one of the outlines, using the technique of repeated self-testing (see page 194). Finally, write a full essay answer, in complete sentences, to one of the questions. Your instructor may ask you to hand in your five outlines and the essay.

USING
THE LIBRARY

This chapter will show you how to use the library and its:

- Main desk
- Book file
- Book stacks
- Magazine file
- Magazine holdings area

Introductory Project

Consider this study situation:

> Pete had been out of school for ten years before he enrolled in college. During his first semester, his sociology instructor asked him to "compile a list of ten books and articles about single-parent families." In addition, Pete's business instructor asked him to do a research paper on "benefits of the Japanese quality circle in American companies." Pete dreaded these projects because he had no idea where or how to begin them. Before class one night, he walked into his college library and wandered around for a while, aimlessly and shyly. He felt especially intimidated by the people who sat typing in front of computer screens and seemed to know exactly what they were doing. Pete felt completely out of his element—like a visitor in a foreign land. He didn't even know what questions to ask about how to use the library.

This chapter will explain exactly how Pete, or anyone, can use the library to get the information needed for course work. But take a few minutes first to examine your own ideas. What do you think are two specific things that Pete could do to get the information he needs?

This chapter provides the basic information you need to use your college library with confidence. It also describes the basic steps you should follow in researching a topic.

Most students seem to know that libraries provide study space, typing facilities, and copying machines. They also seem aware that a library has a reading area, which contains recent copies of magazines and newspapers. But the true heart of a library consists of the following: a *main desk,* a *book file, book stacks,* a *magazine file,* and a *magazine storage area.* Each of these will be discussed on the pages that follow.

PARTS OF THE LIBRARY

Main Desk

The main desk is usually located in a central spot. Check at the main desk to see if there is a brochure that describes the layout and services of the library. You might also ask if the library staff provides tours of the library. If not, explore your library to find each of the areas described below.

Activity

Make up a floor plan of your college library. Label the main desk, card file, book stacks, magazine file, and magazine storage area.

Book file

The book file will be your starting point for almost any research project. The book file is a list of all the books in the library. It may be an actual card catalog: a file of cards alphabetically arranged in drawers. Increasingly, however, the book file is computerized, and it appears on a number of computer terminals located at different spots in the library.

Finding a Book: Author, Title, and Subject: Whether you use an actual file of cards or a computer terminal, it is important for you to know that there are three ways to look up a book: you can look it up according to *author, title,* or *subject.* For example, suppose you want to see if the library has *The Population Explosion* by Paul R. Ehrlich and Anne H. Ehrlich. You could check for the book in any of three ways:

1 You could go to the *title* section of the book file and look it up there under ''P.'' Note that you always look up a book under the first word in the title, excluding the words *A, An,* and *The.*

2   You could go to the *author* section of the book file and look it up there under "E." An author is always listed under his or her last name. Here is the author entry in a card catalog for Ehrlich's book *The Population Explosion:*

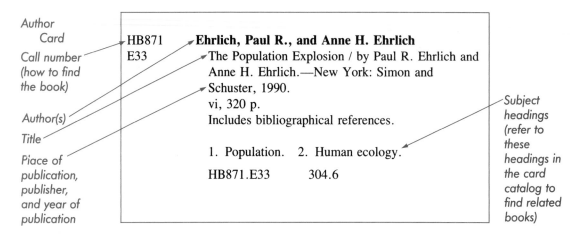

Author
Card

Call number
(how to find
the book)

Author(s)

Title

Place of
publication,
publisher,
and year of
publication

HB871
E33

Ehrlich, Paul R., and Anne H. Ehrlich
The Population Explosion / by Paul R. Ehrlich and
Anne H. Ehrlich.—New York: Simon and
Schuster, 1990.
vi, 320 p.
Includes bibliographical references.

1. Population.   2. Human ecology.

HB871.E33   304.6

Subject
headings
(refer to
these
headings in
the card
catalog to
find related
books)

3   Or, since you know the subject that the book deals with—in this case the subject is obviously "population"—you could go to the *subject* section of the book file and look it up under "P."

Generally, if you are looking for a particular book, it is easier to use the *author* or *title* section of the book file.

On the other hand, if you hope to find other books about population, then the *subject* section is where you should look. You will get a list of all the books in the library that deal with population. You'll also be given related subject headings under which you might find additional books about the subject.

Using a Computerized Book File: Recently, I visited a local library that had just been computerized. The card catalog was gone, and in its place was a table with ten computer terminals. I approached a terminal and looked, a bit uneasily, at the instructions placed nearby. The instructions turned out to be very simple. They told me that if I wanted to look up the author of a book, I should type "A = " on the keyboard in front of the terminal and then the name of the author. I typed "A = Ehrlich," and then (following the directions) I hit the Enter/Return key on the keyboard.

In two seconds a new screen appeared showing me a numbered list of several books by Paul R. Ehrlich, one of which was *The Population Explosion*. This title was numbered "3" on the list, and at the bottom of the screen was a direction to type the number of the title I wanted more information about. So I typed the number "3" and hit the Enter/Return key. I then got the screen shown on the next page.

```
AUTHOR:      Ehrlich, Paul
TITLE:       The Population Explosion
PUBLISHER:   Simon and Schuster, 1990.
SUBJECTS:    Population. Human ecology.


Call Number    Material    Location      Status

362.5097       Book        Cherry Hill   Available
```

I was very impressed. The terminal was easier and quicker to use than a card catalog. The screen gave me the basic information I needed to know about the book, including where to find it. In addition, the screen told me that the book was "Available" on the shelves. (A display card nearby explained that if the book was not on the shelves, the message under "Status" would be "Out on loan.") I noticed other options. If the book was not on the shelves at the Cherry Hill location of the library, I would be told if it was available at other libraries nearby, by means of interlibrary loan.

The computer gave me two other choices. I could type "T = " plus a name to look up the title of a book. Or I could type "S = " plus the subject to get the names of any books that the library had dealing with the subject of population.

Using Subject Headings to Research a Topic: Whether your library has a card catalog or a computer terminal, it is the subject section that will be extremely valuable to you when you are researching a topic. If you have a general topic, the subject section will help you find books on that general topic and also on more specialized topics within that subject.

For example, I typed "S = Population" to see how many book titles there were dealing with the subject of population. In seconds, a screen came up showing me thirty-three different titles! In addition, the screen informed me of related headings under which I could find dozens of other books about population. These related headings included "human ecology," "environmental health," "contraception," "conservation of nature," and "bioengineering." With the help of all these headings and titles, a student could really begin to think about a limited research topic to develop within the general subject of population.

There are two points to remember here: (1) Start researching a topic by using the subject section of the book file. (2) Use the subtopics and related topics suggested by the book file to help you begin to narrow your topic. Chances are you will use the library to do research on a paper of anywhere from five to twenty pages or so. You do not want to choose a topic so broad that it could be covered only by an entire book or more. Instead, you want to come up with a limited topic that can be covered adequately in a relatively short paper.

Activity

Part A: Answer the following questions about the card catalog.

1. Is your library's book file an actual file of cards in drawers, or is the book file on computer terminals? _____

2. What are the three ways of looking up a book in the library?

   a. _____

   b. _____

   c. _____

3. Which section of the book file will help you research and limit a topic?

   _____

Part B: Use your library book file to answer the following questions.

1. What is the title of one book by Ellen Goodman?

   _____

2. What is the title of one book by John Updike?

   _____

3. Who is the author of *The Organization Man?* (Remember to look up the title under *Organization,* not *The.*)

   _____

4. Who is the author of *The Lord of the Flies?* _____

5. List two books dealing with the subject of day care, and note their authors.

   a. _____

   _____

   b. _____

   _____

6. List two books dealing with the subject of Robert Kennedy, and note their authors.

   a. _____

   _____

   b. _____

   _____

7. Look up a book titled *Among Schoolchildren* or *What Color Is Your Parachute?* or *The Art of Loving* and give the following information:

   a. Author _____

   b. Publisher _____

   c. Date of publication _____

   d. Call number _____

   e. Subject headings: _____ _____

8. Look up a book written by Dr. Joyce Brothers or Jonathan Kozol or Rachel Carson and give the following information:

   a. Title _____

   b. Publisher _____

   c. Date of publication _____

   d. Call number _____

   e. Subject headings: _____

Book Stacks

The book stacks are the library shelves where books are arranged according to their call numbers. The call number, as distinctive as a social security number, always appears on a call file for any book. It is also printed on the spine of every book in the library.

If your library has *open stacks* (ones that you are permitted to enter), follow these steps to find a book. Suppose you are looking for *The Population Explosion*, which has the call number HB871.E33 in the Library of Congress system. (Libraries using the Dewey decimal system have call letters made up entirely of numbers rather than letters and numbers. However, you use the same basic method to locate a book.) You go to the section of the stacks that holds the H's. After you locate the H's, you look for the HB's. After that, you look for HB871. Finally, you look for HB871/E33, and you have the book.

If your library has *closed stacks* (ones you are not permitted to enter), you will have to write the title, author, and call number on a slip of paper. (Such slips of paper will be available near the card catalog or computer terminals.) You'll then give the slip to a library staff person, who will locate the book and bring it to you.

Activity

Use the book stacks to answer one of the following sets of questions. Choose the set of questions related to the classification system of your library.

Library of Congress System (Letters and Numbers)

1. Books in the BF21-BF204 area deal with
   - a. biology.
   - b. sociology.
   - c. psychology.
   - d. theology.
2. Books in the DS705-DS778 area deal with
   - a. Japan.
   - b. Vietnam.
   - c. India.
   - d. China.
3. Books in the PR502-PR610 area deal with
   - a. poetry.
   - b. drama.
   - c. novels.
   - d. essays.
4. Books in the ML55-MT200 area deal with
   - a. art.
   - b. music.
   - c. painting.
   - d. weaving.

Dewey Decimal System (Numbers)

1. Books in the 610 area deal with
   - a. dentists.
   - b. nurses.
   - c. lawyers.
   - d. doctors.
2. Books in the 747 area deal with
   - a. landscape design.
   - b. home decorating.
   - c. camping.
   - d. bird-watching.
3. Books in the 649.1 area deal with
   - a. child rearing.
   - b. study skills.
   - c. adoption.
   - d. senior citizens.
4. Books in the 510–512 area deal with
   - a. volcanos.
   - b. deserts.
   - c. numbers.
   - d. poetry.

Magazine File

The magazine file is also known as the *periodicals* file. *Periodicals* (from the word *periodic,* which means "at regular periods") are magazines, journals, and newspapers. In this chapter, the word *magazine* stands for any periodical.

The magazine file often contains recent information about a given subject, or very specialized information about a subject, that may not be available in a book. It is important, then, to check magazines as well as books when you are doing research.

Just as you use the book file to find books on your subject, you use the magazine file to find articles on your subject in magazines and other publications. There are two files in particular that should help:

Readers' Guide to Periodical Literature: The familiar green volumes of the *Readers' Guide,* found in just about every library, list articles published in almost 200 popular magazines, such as *Newsweek, Health, People, Ebony, Redbook,* and *Popular Science.* Articles are listed alphabetically under both subject and author. For example, if you wanted to learn the titles of articles published on the subject of child abuse within a certain time span, you would look under the heading "Child abuse."

Here, for example, is a typical entry from the *Readers' Guide:*

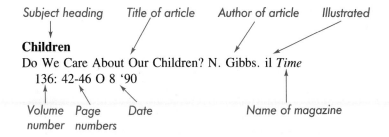

Note the sequence in which information is given about the article:

1 Subject heading.
2 Title of the article. In some cases, there will be bracketed words [like these] after the title that help make clear just what the article is about.
3 Author (if it is a signed article). The author's first name is always abbreviated.
4 Whether the article has a bibliography (*bibl*) or is illustrated with pictures (*il*). Other abbreviations sometimes used are shown in the front of the *Readers' Guide.*
5 Name of the magazine. A short title like *Time* is not abbreviated, but longer titles are. For example, the magazine *Popular Science* is abbreviated *Pop Sci.* Refer to the list of magazines in the front of the index to identify abbreviations.

6   Volume number of the magazine (preceding the colon).
7   Page numbers on which the article appears (after the colon).
8   Date when the article appeared. Dates are abbreviated: for example, *Mr* stands for *March, Ag* for *August, N* for *November*. Other abbreviations are shown in the front of the *Readers' Guide*.

The *Readers' Guide* is published in monthly supplements. At the end of a year, a volume is published covering the entire year. You will see in your library large green volumes that say, for instance, *Readers' Guide 1988* or *Readers' Guide 1990*. You will also see the small monthly supplements for the current year.

The *Readers' Guide* is also now available in a much more useful form, on a computer. I was amazed to see at my local library that I could now sit down at a terminal and quickly search for an article on almost any subject published in the last seven years. Searching on the computer was much easier than having to go through seven or so different paper volumes of the *Readers' Guide*.

Magazine Index: The *Magazine Index* is an automated system that lists articles in about four hundred general-interest magazines. Given a choice, you should always use this system rather than the *Readers' Guide:* it lists articles from twice as many sources as the *Guide* and is both fast and easy to use.

You sit in front of what looks like a large television screen that is already loaded with a microfilmed index. By pushing the first of two buttons, you quickly advance the film forward from A to B to C and so on. By pushing the other button, you move in the opposite direction. It really is as simple as that! The entries on the screen look just like the entries in the *Readers' Guide*. You'll note that the most recent articles on a topic are given first. This machine is an excellent research tool that is finding its way into more and more libraries.

Activity 1

At this point in the chapter, you know the two basic steps in researching a topic in the library. What are the steps?

1. _____

2. _____

Activity 2

Use the excerpt below from the *Readers' Guide* to answer the questions that follow on page 240.

MARRIAGE
    See also
    Adultery
    Childlessness
    Divorce
    Family
    Farm marriage
    Honeymoon
    Husbands
    Married couples
    Married women
    Remarriage
    Weddings
    Wife abuse
    Wives
Can this marriage be saved? See issues of Ladies' Home Journal
Clear-thinking couples [views of Aaron Beck] S. McKee. il *American Health* 9:99 My '90
An excerpt from Love and other infectious diseases [illness of A. Sarris] M. Haskell. il pors *American Health* 9:66-8+ My '90
How does your marriage grow? N. Rubin. il *Parents* 65:83-6 Ap '90
Ingredients of a happy marriage. A. Stoddard. *McCall's* 117:140 Je '90
Long time love. il *Essence* 21:139-40+ My '90
Love and marriage [questions and answers] C. Deutsch. See issues of Parents
Married with children . . . and still in love. A. Mayer. il *Ladies' Home Journal* 107:110 Je '90
My husband wouldn't talk to me. il *Good Housekeeping* 210:36+ Ap '90
A separate peace [interview with A. Sarris and M. Haskell] J. W. Ellison. il pors *American Health* 9:64-8 My '90
When Peter met Elysa [pretending to be married for two weeks; with reply by E. Lazar] P. Gethers. il pors *Esquire* 113:182-88+ Je '90
    Anecdotes, facetiae, satire, etc.
Do you take this man? And how! M. G. Stoddard. il *The Saturday Evening Post* 262:56-7+ Ap '90
    Annulment (Catholic Church)
Annulment: a personal reflection. R. C. Haas. *America* 162:499-501+ My 19 '90
    Catholic Church
    See also
    Marriage—Annulment (Catholic Church)
    United States
    See Marriage
MARRIAGE CONTRACTS
From wedlock to deadlock? How to negotiate a prenup. L. N. Vreeland. il *Money* 19:21 Je '90
Great expectations [prenuptial contracts] T. Young. *Vogue* 180:274 Je '90
MARRIAGE COUNSELING
Can this marriage be saved? See issues of Ladies' Home Journal
MARRIAGE CUSTOMS AND RITES
    See also
    Weddings
        Japan
    Photographs and photography
Wedding pros Japan style. M. Ono. il *Petersen's Photographic Magazine* 19:20-3+ My '90

MARRIAGE LAW
    See also
    Marriage contracts
MARRIED COUPLES
It's you and me, babe, against flab [S. and M. Blair winners of Husband/Wife Body Makeover Contest] P. Shimer. il pors *Prevention (Emmaus, Pa.)* 42:96+ Je '90
Marriage with a Midas touch [billionaire couples; cover story; special section] E. Sporkin. il *People Weekly* 33:150-4+ My 7 '90
Together, you and me [finances of Quinn and Lisa Ellner] il *Changing Times* 44:32-3 Ap '90
What makes a couple happy? [results of survey] A. M. Pines. il *Redbook* 174:102-3+ Ap '90
    Anecdotes, facetiae, satire, etc.
'Til running do us part [running with husband] L. Clyne. il *Runner's World* 25:112 Je '90
    Attitudes
Faithful attraction [excerpts] A. M. Greeley. il *Good Housekeeping* 210:132+ Je '90
    Employment
    See also
    Children of working parents
Mixing marriage and business. S. Nelton. il *Nation's Business* 78:36 My '90
Successful relocation: it's all in the family. M. Olivero. *Working Woman* 15:24+ Ap '90
When you're more ambitious than your husband. E. Davidowitz. il *Ladies' Home Journal* 107:120+ Ap '90
Wives and husbands who work together. D. Narine. il *Ebony* 45:34+ Mr '90
    Quarrels
    See Quarrels
    Sexual behavior
Bring out the lover in your spouse [condensed from How to stay lovers while raising your children] A. Mayer. il *Reader's Digest* 136:131-4 Je '90
Don't be his mother. 6 don'ts for loving wives with dull sex lives [excerpt from Secrets about men every woman should know] B. De Angelis. *Redbook* 174:130-1+ Mr '90
Don't settle—sizzle! D. G. Weiss. il *Redbook* 175:120-1+ My '90
Lovetalk: the quickest way to better sex [results of survey] S. Carter and J. Sokol. il *Redbook* 174:108-9+ Ap '90
Sex and the single bed. Q. Crisp. il *House & Garden* 162:178-81 My '90
MARRIED WOMEN
    See also
    Mothers
Affairs of the heart [fantasizing about other men] K. McCoy. il *Redbook* 175:128-9+ My '90
    Employment
    See also
    Mothers—Employment
Trouble at work? Work on your marriage. A. M. Pines. *Redbook* 174:103 Ap '90

1. Who is the author of an article titled "Wives and Husbands Who Work Together"?

   _____

2. What is the title of an article by L. N. Vreeland?

   _____

3. How many articles are listed that deal with sexual behavior in marriage?

   _____

4. In what issue of *McCall's* is there an article about the ingredients of a happy marriage?

   _____

5. On what pages of *American Health* is the article "A Separate Peace"?

   _____

Activity 3

1. Look up a recent article on stress in the *Readers' Guide* or the *Magazine Index* and fill in the following information:

   a. Article title

   _____

   b. Author (if given)

   _____

   c. Name of magazine

   _____

   d. Pages _____ e. Date _____

2. Look up a recent article on adoption in the *Readers' Guide* or the *Magazine Index* and fill in the following information:

   a. Article title

   _____

   b. Author (if given)

   _____

   c. Name of magazine

   _____

   d. Pages _____ e. Date _____

Specialized Indexes: Once you know how to use the *Readers' Guide,* and the *Magazine Index,* you will find it easy to use some of the more specialized indexes in most libraries. Here are three helpful ones:

- *New York Times Index.* This is an index to articles published in the *New York Times.* After you look up a subject, you'll get a list of articles published on that topic, with a short summary of each article.

- *Business Periodical Index.* The articles here are from over three hundred publications that generally treat a subject in more detail than it would receive in the popular magazines indexed in the *Readers' Guide.* At the same time, the articles are usually not *too* technical or hard to read.

- *Social Sciences Index.* This is an index to articles published by journals in the areas of anthropology, environmental science, psychology, and sociology. Your teachers in these areas may expect you to consult this index while doing a research project on any of these subjects.

Other specialized indexes that your library may have include the following:

Art Index	*General Science Index*
Applied Science and Technology	*Humanities Index*
Index	*Nursing Index*
Biological and Agricultural Index	*Religious Periodical Literature*
Book Review Digest	*Index*
Education Index	

Depending on the subject area you are researching, you may want to consult the appropriate index. Some libraries have most of these indexes on a computer.

Activity

1. Check the magazine area in your library. (It might be known as the *periodicals* area.) Place a check by each of the indexes that it includes:

    _____ Readers' Guide Index   _____ Social Sciences Index
    _____ Business Periodicals Index   _____ New York Times Index
    _____ Magazine Index

2. Are any of these indexes available on a computer as well as in paperbound volumes? _____ If so, which ones? _____

    _____

3. What are two other indexes in this area of your library besides the five mentioned above? _____

    _____

A Note on Other Reference Materials: Every library has a reference area, often close to the place where the *Readers' Guide* is located, in which other reference materials can be found. Such general resource materials include dictionaries, encyclopedias, atlases, yearbooks, almanacs, a subject guide to books in print (this can help in locating books on a particular subject), anthologies of quotations, and other items.

You may also find in the reference area a series of filing cabinets called the *pamphlet file.* This will consist of a series of file cabinets full of pamphlets, booklets, and newsletters on a multitude of topics. One file drawer, for example, may include all the pamphlets and the like for subjects that start with "A." I looked in the "A" drawer of the pamphlet file in my library and found lots of small pieces about subjects like abortion, adoption, and animal rights, along with many other topics starting with "A." On top of these filing cabinets may be a booklet titled "Pamphlet File Subject Headings"; it will quickly tell you if the file includes material on your subject of interest.

Activity

1. What is one encyclopedia that your library has?

   _____

2. What unabridged dictionary does your library have?

   _____

3. Where is your library's pamphlet file located?

   _____

4. Is there a booklet or small file that tells you what subject headings are included in the pamphlet file? _____ Where is it? _____

Magazine Storage Area

Near your library's *Readers' Guide* or *Magazine Index,* you'll probably notice slips of paper. Here, for instance, is a copy of the slip used in my local library:

PERIODICAL REQUEST

Name of Magazine _____

Date of Magazine _____

(For your reference: Title and pages of article:)

_____

As you locate each magazine and journal article that you would like to look at, fill out a slip. When you are done, take the slips to a library staff person working nearby. Don't hesitate to do this: helping you obtain the articles you want is part of his or her job.

Here's what will probably happen next:

- If a magazine that you want is a very recent one, it may be on open shelves in the library. The staff member will tell you, and then you can go find it yourself.

- If the magazine you want is up to a year or so old, it may be kept in a closed area of the library. In that case, the staff person will go find it and bring it to you.

- Sometimes you'll ask to see an article in a magazine that the library does not carry. You'll then have to plan to use other articles, or go to a larger library. However, most college libraries or large county libraries should have what you need.

- Very frequently, especially with older issues, the magazine will be on microfilm or on microfiche. (*Microfilm* is a roll of film on which articles have been reproduced in greatly reduced size; *microfiche* is the same thing, but it is on easily handled sheets of film rather than on a roll.) The staff person will bring you the film or fiche and at your request will then show you how to load this material onto a microfilm or microfiche machine nearby, so that it can be read.

    Faced with learning how to use a new machine, many people are intimidated and nervous. I know I was. What is important is that you ask for as much help as you need. Have the staff person demonstrate the machine and then watch you as you try it. (Remember that this person is being paid by the library to help you learn how to use the resources in the library, including the machine.) While the machine may seem complex at first, in fact most of the time it turns out to be easy to use. Don't be afraid to insist that the person give you as much time as you need to learn how to use the machine.

    After you are sure you can use the machine to look up any article, check to see if the machine will make a copy of the article. Many will. Make sure you have some change to cover the copying fee, and then go back to the staff person and ask him or her to show you how to use the print option on the machine. You'll be amazed at how quickly and easily you can get a printed copy of almost any article you want.

Activity

1. Use the *Readers' Guide* or *Magazine Index* to find an article on divorce that was published in the last three months. Write the name of the magazine and the date on a slip of paper and give it to a library staff person. Is the article available in the actual magazine? _____ If so, is it on an open shelf or is

   it in a closed area where a staff person must bring it to you? _____

   _____

2. Use the *Readers' Guide* or *Magazine Index* to find an article on divorce that was published more than one year ago. Write down the name of the magazine and the date on a slip of paper and give it to a library staff person. Is the article available in the actual magazine, or is it available on microfiche or microfilm?

   _____

   _____

3. Place a check if your library has:

   _____ Microfiche machine   _____ with a print option
   _____ Microfilm machine   _____ with a print option

A Summary of Library Areas

You now know the five areas of the library that will be most useful to you in doing research:

1 *Main desk.*
2 *Book file.* In particular, you can use the *subjects* section of the card file to get the names of books on your subject, as well as suggestions about other subject headings under which you might find books. It is by exploring your general subject in books and then in magazine articles that you will gradually be able to decide upon a subject limited enough to cover in your research paper.
3 *Book stacks,* where you will get the books themselves.
4 *Magazine files and indexes.* Once again, you can use the *subjects* sections of these files to get the names of magazine and journal articles on your subject.
5 *Magazine storage area,* where you will get the articles themselves.

PRACTICE IN USING THE LIBRARY

Activity

Use your library to research a subject that interests you. Select one of the following areas or (with your teacher's permission) one of your own choice:

Marriage contracts	New remedies for allergies
Food poisoning (salmonella)	Censorship in the 1990s
Greenhouse effect	New prison reforms
Medical care for the aged	Drug treatment programs
Pro-choice movement	Sudden infant death syndrome
Pro-life movement	New treatments for insomnia
Health insurance reform	Organ donation
Drinking water pollution	Safe sex
Problems of retirement	Voucher system in schools
Cremation	Sexual harassment in business
Day care programs that work	Gambling and youth
Noise control	Nongraded schools
Drug treatment programs for adolescents	Earthquake forecasting
Fertility drugs	Ethical aspects of hunting
Witchcraft in the 1990s	Euthanasia
New treatments for AIDS	Recent consumer frauds
Changes in immigration policy	Stress reduction in the workplace
Video display terminals—health aspects	Sex on television
Hazardous substances in the home	Everyday addictions
Airbags	Toxic waste disposal
Capital punishment	Self-help groups
Prenatal care	Telephone crimes
Acid rain	Date rape
New aid for the handicapped	Heroes for the 1990s

Now turn to the instructions on the next page.

Research the topic first through the *subjects* section of the book file and then through the *subjects* section of one or more magazine files and indexes. On a separate sheet of paper, provide the following information:

1. Topic.

2. Three books that cover the topic directly or at least touch on the topic in some way. Include these items:

   Author
   Title
   Place of publication
   Publisher
   Date of publication

3. Three articles on the topic published in 1990 or later from the *Readers' Guide* or the *Magazine Index.* Include these items:

   Title of article
   Author (if given)
   Title of magazine
   Date
   Page(s)

4. Three articles on the topic published in 1990 or later from other indexes (such as the *New York Times Index, Business Periodical Index, Social Sciences Index,* or *Humanities Index.*) Include these items:

   Title of article
   Author (if given)
   Title of magazine
   Date
   Page(s)

5. Finally, include a photocopy of one of the three articles. Note whether the source of the copy was the article on paper, on microfiche, or on microfilm.

PART THREE

A BRIEF GUIDE TO IMPORTANT WORD SKILLS

PREVIEW

In Part Three, the chapter "Understanding Word Parts" will help you review sixty of the most common word parts used in forming English words. The explanations and activities in "Using the Dictionary" will explain the most important kinds of information about words that a good dictionary provides. "Word Pronunciation" describes several basic rules you can use to pronounce unfamiliar words, including the specialized terms you will meet in your different college subjects. "Spelling Improvement" suggests techniques and provides spelling rules and a word list to make you a better speller. Finally, "Vocabulary Development" explains three approaches that can increase your word power.

AN IMPORTANT NOTE

Part Three provides a concise review of important word skills, some of which you may remember from earlier school years. All these skills can be supplemented by the extensive materials usually available in college learning centers. With the basic information in Part Three, you can quickly brush up on word skills or refer to them when needed. You can also discover which skills you may want to work on at greater length in your school learning center.

UNDERSTANDING WORD PARTS

This chapter will help you recognize and spell:

- ▪ Twenty common prefixes
- ▪ Twenty common suffixes
- ▪ Twenty common roots

One way to improve your pronunciation and spelling of words is to increase your understanding of common word parts. These word parts—also known as *prefixes, suffixes,* and *roots*—are building blocks used in forming many English words. The activities in this section will give you practice in sixty of the most common word parts. Working with them will help your spelling, for you will realize how many words are made up of short, often-recurring, easily spelled parts. Increasing your awareness of basic word parts will also help you to pronounce many unfamiliar words and, at times, to unlock their meanings.

PREFIXES

A *prefix* is a word part added to the beginning of a word. The prefix changes the meaning of some words to their opposites. For example, when the prefix *in-* is added to *justice,* the result is *injustice;* when the prefix *mis-* is added to *understanding,* the result is *misunderstanding.* A prefix need not change a word to its opposite, but it will alter the meaning of the word in some way. For instance, when the prefix *re-* (meaning *again*) is added to *view,* the result is *review,* which means *to view again.* When the prefix *mal-* (meaning *bad*) is added to *practice,* the result is *malpractice,* which means *bad* or *improper practice.*

In the following activities, look carefully at the meanings of the two prefixes presented. Then add the appropriate prefix to the base word (the one in *italics*) in each of the five sentences *a* to *e.* Write your word in the space provided. You will know which prefix to choose in each case if you consider both its meaning and the general meaning of the sentence. Next, you'll see two groups of words separated by a slash line (/). In the spaces provided, write a sentence using one word from the first group and a sentence using one word from the second group.

1   mono   alone, one
2   trans   across, over, beyond

> Example: After the full moon rose, Lawrence Talbott was (. . . *formed*)
>   *transformed*   into the Wolfman.

a. The interpreter (. . . *lated*) _____ the speech into sign language.

b. She hates the student in her psychology course who tries to (. . . *polize*) _____ the class discussion time.

c. As soon as they (. . . *ported*) _____ the stolen cigarettes across the state line, they were guilty of a federal offense.

d. A (. . . *poly*) _____ occurs when one person or group assumes an unfair amount of control over others.

e. Some people use yoga or other Eastern disciplines to try to (. . . *cend*) _____ everyday cares and difficulties.

Now write a sentence using one of the words before the slash line and a sentence using one of the words that appear after the slash.

monologue   monotony   mononucleosis   /   transplant   transition   transparent

_____

_____

3   dis   apart, away
4   pre   before

a. She (. . . *cards*) _____ friends the way some people throw away an item of clothing they no longer want.

b. I would be frightened to go to a fortune-teller if he or she truly had the ability to (. . . *dict*) _____ the future.

c. The speaker was (. . . *composed*) _____ by the conversations that went on during his talk.

d. I sometimes have a tendency to (. . . *judge*) _____ people; only when I meet them do I find out how biased I've been.

e. I worry about germs taking over the house if I don't (. . . *infect*) _____ the bathroom once a week.

disorient   dispassionate   dissatisfied   /   presume   preliminary   prevention

_____

_____

5   inter   between, among
6   sub   under, below

a. During the halftime (. . .*val*) _____ of the football game, I ran out to get a pizza.

b. Cold medicines will (. . . *due*) _____ a cold, but they won't cure it.

c. She has the bad habit of (. . . *rupting*) _____ people when they are in the midst of making a point.

d. Seeing whether and how (. . . *heads*) _____ relate to main heads in a text is an important reading skill to develop.

e. My mother would constantly (. . . *fere*) _____ in the relationship I had with my first girlfriend, who lived next door to me.

interact   interject   intercom   /   subdivide   subvert   submerged

_____

_____

7   ex   out
8   mis   badly, wrong

a. In grade school I shunned the pursuit of grades and majored in (. . . *conduct*) _____.

b. In his autobiography, Howard Cosell claims that he has been (. . . *represented*) _____ by the press.

c. If a football player doesn't learn how to (. . . *ecute*) _____, or carry out a play properly, he will soon lose his job.

d. One day he suddenly realized that he (. . . *treated*) _____ his children in the same way his father had been unfair to him.

e. When Raid wasn't enough, I called in an (. . . *terminator*) _____ to battle the roaches.

exorcist exhaust exclamation / misspelling mismatch misunderstanding

_____

_____

9 **con**   together, with
10 **post**   after, following, later

a. A (. . . *mortem*) _____ examination was not needed to reveal the obvious cause of death: a wooden stake through the heart.

b. He could hardly walk across the attic floor because of the (. . . *glomera-tion*) _____ of items piled there.

c. His (. . . *operative*) _____ condition was poor, and so he was put in the intensive care unit.

d. Part of me often wants to (. . . *form*) _____ with the group; the other part of me wants to follow the beat of my own drummer.

e. She feels persecuted and believes that everyone is (. . . *niving*) _____ against her.

congested   concur   conflict   /   postnasal   postpone   postscript

_____

_____

11 **anti**   against
12 **pro**   before; for (in favor of)

a. The (. . . *posal*) _____ to legalize gambling was placed on the state ballot.

b. Because I had forgotten to put in (. . . *freeze*) _____, my car's radiator turned into a block of ice one frigid winter morning.

c. The main purpose of marriage, according to some religions, is the (. . . *cre-ation*) _____ of children.

d. Even though the new cold remedy was no more effective than others on the market, millions of dollars were spent to (. . . *mote*) _____ it.

e. If an (. . . *dote*) _____ is not given minutes after the bite of a cobra, death is almost a certainty.

antiseptic   antipathy   antithesis   /   proponent   promise   progress

_____

_____

13 **un** not, reverse
14 **ad** to, toward

a. The (. . . *hesive*) _____ tape stuck to his fingers more than it stuck to the package.

b. Because she finds it difficult to tolerate (. . . *certainty*) _____, she quickly closes her mind on many issues.

c. (. . . *diction*) _____ to alcohol or other drugs is a major problem in our country.

d. The dog continued to run around the neighborhood (. . . *restrained*) _____, and so someone decided to call the police.

e. People who feel very depressed are likely to have (. . . *productive*) _____ workdays.

unreasonable unfamiliar uncompromising / address advise advocate

_____

_____

15 **in**   not, within
16 **extra** more than

a. The school principal showed an (. . . *ordinary*) _____ amount of composure when the first grader threw a rock at him.

b. Students who do well in (. . . *curricular*) _____ activities but earn poor grades are mistaking the sideshow for the main event.

c. Because of (. . . *adequate*) _____ funds, the school athletic program was canceled.

d. The old father in the play was driven mad by the (. . . *gratitude*) _____ of his daughters.

e. The teacher explained that the class would be run in an (. . . *formal*) _____ way, for she wanted students to be relaxed.

incompetent inaudible insatiable / extrasensory extravagance extramarital

_____

_____

17 re   again, back
18 mal bad

a. In many poor families in Appalachia, you will find children and adults suffering from (. . . *nutrition*) _____.

b. After her (. . . *covery*) _____ from a pulled leg muscle, the tennis pro went on to have a great year.

c. The politician was convicted of (. . . *feasance*) _____ in office and was sentenced to a one-week jail term.

d. Most students agree that they should (. . . *view*) _____ their notes right after class, but few take the time to do so.

e. Psychologists advise parents to give children (. . . *inforcement*)

_____—compliments and rewards for doing well.

relapse   recount   reflect   /   malpractice   malfunction   maladjusted

_____

_____

19 com with, together with
20 de   down, from

a. (. . . *munal*) _____ living is difficult for someone who feels a strong need for privacy.

b. An entire block of houses had been (. . . *molished*) _____

_____ in order to build the shopping center.

c. The man who stopped to help us change our flat tire (. . . *meaned*)

_____ himself afterward by asking for $5.

d. If I did not (. . . *ply*) _____ with my parents' household orders, I would be punished quickly.

e. Homes quickly (. . . *preciated*) _____ in value when plans for a nearby airport were publicized.

compatible   combine   companion   /   descend   deplore   detract

_____

_____

SUFFIXES

A *suffix* is a word part added to the end of a word. While a suffix may affect a word's meaning slightly, it is more likely to affect how the word is used in a sentence. For instance, when the suffix *-ment* is added to the verb *measure,* the result is the noun *measurement.* When the suffix *-less* is added to *measure,* the result is the adjective *measureless.* Very often, one of several suffixes can be added to a single word. Understanding common suffixes is especially helpful when you are learning new words. If you note the suffixes that can be added to a new word, you will learn not just a single word but perhaps three or four other forms of the word as well.

In the following activities, decide from the context which suffix in each pair should be added to the base word (the one in *italics*) in sentences *a* to *e.* Then write the entire word in the space provided. Alternative forms of some suffixes are shown in parentheses, but you will not have to use alternative forms to complete the spelling of any of the base words. Next, you'll find two groups of words separated by a slash line (/). In the spaces provided, write a sentence using one word from the first group and a sentence using one word from the second group.

1 ion (tion)
2 less

a. Heartburn and a knotted feeling in the stomach often develop when people are under a lot of (*tens* . . .) _____.

b. The panhandler who everyone thought was (*penni* . . .) _____ turned out to have a $50,000 bank account.

c. The dealer I bought the junk car from is a master in the art of (*persuas* . . .) _____.

d. One type of (*care* . . .) _____ driver is the person who neglects to signal before making a turn.

e. The squirrel sat (*motion* . . .) _____ on the tree trunk, as if made of stone.

Now write a sentence using one of the words before the slash line and a sentence using one of the words that appear after the slash.

corruption   election   confusion   /   worthless   speechless   restless

_____

_____

3 ant (ent)
4 ness

a. Men seem to have more difficulty admitting vulnerability and (*sad . . .*) _____ than women do.

b. Popeye was (*reluct . . .*) _____ to swallow the spinach, for he wanted to give his opponent a fighting chance.

c. He refuses to use (*deodor . . .*) _____ because he believes that sweating is a natural process.

d. The storm broke with such (*sudden . . .*) _____ that the floors were wet before all the house windows were closed.

e. (*Abund . . .*) _____ practice is the best way of mastering a skill.

apparent   convenient   dependent   /   togetherness   happiness   loneliness

_____

_____

5 en
6 ize (ise)

a. Some people do not know how to (*memor . . .*) _____ material efficiently.

b. He saw her eyes (*soft . . .*) _____ as she greeted him, and he realized that she loved him.

c. To (*strength . . .*) _____ and tone her muscles, she began doing the Royal Canadian Air Force exercises.

d. The sky began to (*dark . . .*) _____, the wind picked up, and the rain hurtled down.

e. For some people, having children is a way to (*immortal . . .*) _____ themselves.

fasten   weaken   risen   /   theorize   materialize   compromise

_____

_____

7 age
8 ist

a. Approximately one week after their (*marri . . .*) _____, they realized they had made a mistake.

b. At one time in this country, people lost their jobs if they were accused of belonging to the (*Commun . . .*) _____ Party.

c. He was reluctant to go to a medical (*special . . .*) _____, for he was afraid of the expense.

d. Because the bathtub was not caulked, there was water (*leak . . .*) _____ occurring on the floor below.

e. His favorite things to read in the newspaper are the sports and "Dear Abby," the advice (*column . . .*) _____.

overage   breakage   mileage   /   tourist   capitalist   pharmacist

_____

_____

9 ment
10 ful

a. Many people are demanding reforms in the tax system of our (*govern . . .*) _____.

b. My (*forget . . .*) _____ brother did not leave me the key to the house, and I was locked out.

c. She felt both nervousness and (*excite . . .*) _____ when she took her driver's test; her face was flushed and her knees trembled.

d. The ten-year-old girl felt (*grate . . .*) _____ to her uncle, who spoke to her as though she were an adult, not a little child.

e. As he saw the (*improve . . .*) _____ in his grades, he began to study more; success bred success.

replacement   establishment   movement   /   helpful   useful   hopeful

_____   _____

_____

11 ship
12 able (ible)

a. People who are part of an assembly line seldom have pride in their (*workman . . .*) _____.

b. She is not (*comfort . . .*) _____ until she takes off her working shoes and clothes and puts on slippers and a bathrobe.

c. Many persons describe their first goal in life as achievement in their work; their second goal is love and (*friend . . .*) _____.

d. More and more companies put their products in plastic bottles, even though plastic is not always (*recycl . . .*) _____.

e. She never forgot the poverty and (*hard . . .*) _____ her family went through when she was a little girl.

membership   apprenticeship   leadership   /   capable   noticeable
changeable

_____

_____

13 ence (ance)
14 ify (fy)

a. She attempted to achieve (*excell . . .*) _____ in whatever she did.

b. He was cooperative and courteous to his demanding boss because he wanted to use him later as a (*refer . . .*) _____.

c. Many   students   are   afraid   to   ask   questions   to   (*clar . . .*) _____ a teacher's point.

d. The landlord was not able to (*just . . .*) _____ his neglect of the slum properties that he owned.

e. An animal's (*depend . . .*) _____ on its mother for survival varies from several days to several years.

continuance   acquaintance   assistance   /   verify   notify   rectify

_____

_____

15 ate
16 ly

a. There was not enough good topsoil on their lawn for them to (*cultiv . . .*)
    _____ a healthy crop of grass.

b. I ate my meal too (*quick . . .*) _____, and my stomach
    suffered as a consequence.

c. Education is one means of breaking the vicious circle in which slums
    (*perpetu . . .*) _____ more slums.

d. The restaurant waiter (*final . . .*) _____ served their dinner,
    but they were so angry at waiting so long that they decided to leave.

e. The television show did not (*gener . . .*) _____ enough
    interest to keep him awake.

    fortunate   populate   aggravate   /   obviously   apparently   carefully

    _____

    _____

17 ious (ous)
18 or (er)

a. They went to a marriage (*counsel . . .*) _____ to try to
    improve their marriage.

b. He had a troubling dream in which he saw a (*myster . . .*)
    _____ stranger in a dark robe standing by a lake.

c. The fact that many students don't follow test directions is an example of how
    we often overlook the (*obv . . .*) _____.

d. Ben Franklin was an (*invent . . .*) _____, a statesman, a
    philosopher, and a businessman.

e. After three years as an unemployed (*act . . .*) _____, I decided
    on another career.

    dangerous   jealous   glamorous   /   builder   teacher   employer

    _____

    _____

19 ism
20 ery (ary)

a. Her (*tomfool . . .*) _____ in grade school classes kept her from getting good marks.

b. Some people believe that (*terror . . .*) _____ in the form of kidnapping deserves the death penalty.

c. For a long time, (*alcohol . . .*) _____ was regarded as a vice rather than a physical disease.

d. It was cold in the (*cemet . . .*) _____, so Dracula decided to move his coffin to a Howard Johnson motel.

e. The teacher stopped assigning research projects when she realized that most of her students resorted to (*plagiar . . .*) _____, or stealing, to do their papers.

realism   socialism   baptism   /   imaginary   dictionary   library

_____

_____

ROOTS

A *root* is a basic word part to which prefixes, suffixes, or both are added. For example, to the root word *port* (meaning *carry*), the prefix *trans-* (meaning *across*) could be added; the resulting word, *transport*, means *to carry across*. Various suffixes could also be added, among them *-ed* (*transported*), *-able* (*transportable*), and *-ation* (*transportation*).

In the following activities, decide from the context which root in each pair should be added to the word part or parts in italics in sentences *a* to *e*. Then write the entire word in the space provided. Some common roots at times change their spelling slightly, especially in the last one or two letters. Alternative spellings of such roots are shown in parentheses. Note, however, that you will not have to use the alternative spellings to complete any of the following sentences.

Next, you'll find two groups of words separated by a slash line (/). In the spaces provided, write a sentence using one word from the first group and a sentence using one word from the second group.

1 duc (duct) take, lead
2 mit (miss) send, let go

a. The preface at the beginning of a book often serves as an (*intro . . . tion*)
    _____, or lead-in, to a subject.

b. Copper wire is an excellent (*con . . . tor*) _____ of electricity.

c. The collection agency warned me that if I did not (*re . . .*)
    _____ my payment, I would be harassed day and night.

d. News is (*trans . . . ted*) _____ over the Teletype.

e. The only decision that the (*com . . . tee*) _____
    made during the meeting was to call another meeting.

Now write a sentence using one of the words before the slash line and a
sentence using one of the words that appear after the slash.

reduce   abduct   conducive   /   submit   missile   commission

_____

_____

3 port   carry
4 voc (vok) call

a. He decided that his (*. . . ation*) _____ in life was to be a
    plumber, but his guidance counselor wanted him to apply to law school.

b. She is an (*ad . . . ate*) _____ of the death penalty; her husband
    is not.

c. I am going to buy a (*. . . able*) _____ television that I can
    carry from the living room to the bedroom.

d. (*Re . . . ers*) _____ channel the news from its source to the
    general public.

e. She began reading faster when she learned the difference between main ideas
    and (*sup . . . ing*) _____ details.

export   supporter   transport   /   vocal   revoke   avocation

_____

_____

5 tract (trac)   draw
6 auto   self

a. He wore his leather jacket and tight pants, for he wanted to (*at . . .*) _____ girls at the dance.

b. The television, stereo, and phone in her room are such strong (*dis . . . ions*) _____ that they pull her away from her studies.

c. He loves to read (*. . . biographies*) _____, for he is curious about what other people write about themselves.

d. The Mediterranean design of the console (*de . . . s*) _____ from the country style in the rest of the room.

e. Because the thirteen American colonies wanted to form their own (*. . . nomous*) _____ government, they rebelled against British rule.

attraction   traction   retract   /   automobile   automation   autograph

_____

_____

7 path   feeling
8 cept (capt)   take, seize

a. The audience felt an embarrassed (*sym . . . y*) _____ for the young comedian who had to continue his performance even though no one was laughing.

b. Both political candidates seemed so inferior that many voters were completely (*a . . . etic*) _____ about the election.

c. Everyone (*ex . . .*) _____ me seemed to understand the directions for the test, so I was afraid to ask the teacher to clarify them.

d. The good cowboys were greeted with a (*re . . . ion*) _____ of bullets by the bad cowboys.

e. The parents were gratified that their own children quickly (*ac . . . ed*) _____ the foster child they had decided to adopt.

pathos   telepathy   pathetic   /   deception   interception   except

_____

_____

9 dict (dic)   say, tell, speak
10 script (scrib)   write

a. The article's vivid (*de . . . ion*) _____ of the beauties of Switzerland made her want to visit there.

b. They bought the magazine because it contained an astrologer's (*pre . . . ions*) _____ for the coming year.

c. The (*manu . . .*) _____ was damaged in the mail; fortunately, she had made a Xerox copy.

d. One does not (*contra . . .*) _____ him, or he will blow up entirely.

e. The (*in . . . ion*) _____ on the tombstone of Henry David Thoreau is simply ''Henry.''

    diction   indicate   dictator   /   postscript   scripture   subscribe

_____

_____

11 vers (vert)   turn
12 tang (tact)   touch

a. Children's ideas often get (*. . . led*) _____ together, and they try to say several things at once.

b. She is a (*. . . atile*) _____ athlete, able to perform in different sports with ease.

c. The judge dismissed the case for lack of (*. . . ible*) _____ evidence; everything was hearsay.

d. He had been down on his luck for so long that he felt he deserved a (*re . . . al*) _____ in fortune.

e. While spending ten hours as a security guard in a lonely warehouse, he does crossword puzzles for (*di . . . ion*) _____.

    reversal   subversive   introvert   /   tangent   tactless   tactics

_____

_____

13 cess (ced) go, move, yield
14 sist   stand

a. Almost more than any other quality, (*per . . . ence*) _____ is needed for college success.

b. When the infamous Dr. Frankenstein was killed, his (*as . . . ant*) _____, Igor, got a job as a medical lab technician.

c. The only part of her grade school days that she enjoyed was (*re . . .*) _____ period.

d. With the help of a police escort, the long funeral (*pro . . . ion*) _____ was able to proceed (*suc . . . fully*) _____ through the midday traffic.

e. An expensive paint is likely to be more weather-(*re . . . ant*) _____ than a cheap paint would be.

precede   intercession   concede   /   consistent   subsistence   insist

_____

_____

15 gress   go
16 pend (pens) hang, weigh

a. To succeed in many businesses, you must be a highly (*ag . . . ive*) _____ person.

b. The ruby (*. . . ant*) _____ around her neck was her mother's.

c. Our teacher has a tendency to go off on (*di . . . ions*) _____ from his topic that are interesting but not helpful to us.

d. Because of the (*im . . . ing*) _____ divorce trial, he was unable to sleep at night.

e. He is thirty-two years old but is still entirely (*de . . . ent*) _____ on his mother.

progress   transgress   regression   /   appendix   suspend   pending

_____

_____

17 psych   mind
18 vid (vis)   see

a. It was (*e . . . ent*) _____ from the instant replay that the umpire's call on the play had been correct.

b. When she could no longer get out of bed in the morning to face her day, she realized she was suffering from a severe (*. . . osis*)

_____ .

c. The teenagers in our family spend much of their time watching the music (*. . . eo*) _____ television channel.

d. A neighbor of mine who claims to have (*. . . ic*) _____ powers has predicted the end of the world on two occasions.

e. Some people try to use pills for body pains that are (*. . . osomatic*)

_____ in origin.

psychology   psychotherapy   psychedelic   /   visual   vision   visibility

_____

_____

19 spec (spic)   look
20 graph   write

a. In (*retro . . . t*) _____, he realized that his decision to go on to college right after high school had been a mistake.

b. She hated her job as a stocking (*in . . . tor*) _____ at the knitting mill.

c. She believes (*re . . . t*) _____ is something you buy with money rather than earn with deeds.

d. Some companies insist on giving regular (*poly . . .*) _____ tests to check on their employees' honesty.

e. The two essential steps in writing an effective (*para . . .*)

_____ are to make a point and to support that point.

perspective   spectator   respectable   /   photography   biography
stenographer

_____

_____

PRACTICE IN UNDERSTANDING WORD PARTS

Activity 1

Draw a single line under the prefix and a double line under the suffix in each of the following words:

transparent	antiseptic	replacement
disorient	malpractice	conductive
preliminary	extrasensory	deceptive
subdivision	compatible	reversal
exclamation	confusion	interpretation

Activity 2

Your instructor will give you a spelling test on all the words used in the prefix activities on pages 250–254. You will be expected to spell correctly the *prefix part of the word* and to do your best with the spelling of the rest of the word. (The word will be marked wrong only if the prefix is spelled incorrectly.) Study carefully, then, the spelling of the twenty prefix parts. You will find that knowing the spelling of a prefix will help you considerably in the spelling of an entire word.

Activity 3

The same instructions apply that were given for Activity 2, except that the test will be on the twenty suffixes on pages 255–260.

Activity 4

The same instructions apply that were given for Activity 2, except that the test will be on the twenty roots on pages 261–265.

USING THE DICTIONARY

This chapter will help you use the dictionary to:

- Look up the spelling of words
- Find the syllable divisions in a word
- Pronounce an unfamiliar word
- Obtain other information about words

The dictionary is a valuable tool. To take advantage of it, you need to understand the main kinds of information that a dictionary gives about a word. Look at the information provided for the word *disdain* in the following entry from *The American Heritage Dictionary*, paperback edition.*

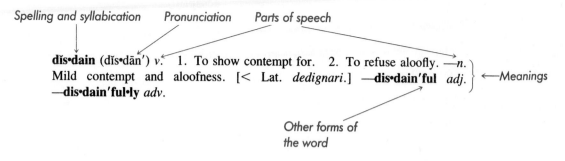

Spelling and syllabication   *Pronunciation*   *Parts of speech*

dis•dain (dĭs•dān′) *v.* 1. To show contempt for. 2. To refuse aloofly. —*n.* Mild contempt and aloofness. [< Lat. *dedignari*.] —**dis•dain′ful** *adj.* —**dis•dain′ful•ly** *adv.*   ←—Meanings

Other forms of the word

---

* Dictionary excerpts in this chapter and in the Mastery Tests © 1983 by Houghton Mifflin Company. Reprinted by permission from *The American Heritage Dictionary of the English Language*, paperback edition.

SPELLING

The first bit of information, in the boldface (heavy-type) entry itself, is the spelling of *disdain*. At times you may have trouble looking up words that you cannot spell. Be sure to pronounce each syllable in the word carefully and write it down the way you think it is spelled. If you still cannot find it, proceed as follows:

1 Try the other vowels. For example, if you think the vowel is *e*, try *a, o, i, u,* and *y.*

2 Try doubling consonants. If you think the letter is one *c*, try *cc*; if one *m*, try *mm*; if one *t*, try *tt*; and so on. On the other hand, if you think the word has double letters, try a single letter.

3 If you think a word has the letter or letter combination in the first column of each group that follows but you can't find the word in the dictionary, try looking at the letter or letters in the second column of each group.

c	k, s	g, j	j, g	s	c, z, sh
er, re	re, er	ie, ei	ei, ie	sh, ch	ch, sh
f	v, ph	k	c, ch	shun	tion, sion
		oo	u	y	i, e

Use your dictionary and the preceding hints to correct the spelling of the following words.

guidence	_____	acomplish	_____
writting	_____	acsept	_____
agresive	_____	enviroment	_____
plesent	_____	particuler	_____
akomodate	_____	conscous	_____
progrem	_____	artical	_____
disese	_____	nesessary	_____
begining	_____	chalenge	_____

SYLLABICATION

The second bit of information that the dictionary gives, also in the boldface entry, is the syllabication of *disdain*. Note that a dot separates each syllable (or part) in the word. The syllable divisions help you pronounce a word and also show you where to hyphenate a word as needed when writing a paper.

Use your dictionary to mark the syllable divisions in the following words. Also indicate how many syllables are in each word.

s p a r k l e   (_____ syllables)

h y p n o t i z e   (_____ syllables)

e x o r c i s m   (_____ syllables)

o p p o r t u n i s t i c   (_____ syllables)

PRONUNCIATION

The third bit of information in the dictionary entry is the pronunciation of *disdain:* (dĭs-dān'). You may already know how to pronounce *disdain,* but if you didn't, the information within the parentheses would serve as your guide. Use your dictionary to complete the following exercises that relate to pronunciation.

Vowel Sounds

You will probably use the pronunciation key in your dictionary mainly as a guide to pronouncing different vowel sounds (vowels are the letters *a, e, i, o,* and *u*). Here is the pronunciation key that appears on every other page of the paperback *American Heritage Dictionary:*

ă pat ā pay â care ä father ĕ pet   ē be ĭ pit ī tie î pier ŏ pot ō toe ô paw, for oi noise oo took o͞o boot ou out th thin *th* this ŭ cut û urge yo͞o abuse zh vision ə about, item, edible, gallop, circus

The key tells you, for example, that the sound of the short *a* is pronounced like the *a* in *pat,* the sound of the long *a* is like the *a* in *pay,* the sound of the short *i* is like the *i* in *pit,* and so on.

Now look at the pronunciation key in your dictionary. The key is probably located in the front of the dictionary or at the bottom of every page. What common word in the key tells you how to pronounce each of the following sounds?

ĕ _____   ō _____

ī _____   ŭ _____

ŏ _____   o͞o _____

(Note that the long vowel always has the sound of its own name.)

The Schwa (ə)

The symbol ə looks like an upside-down *e*. It is called a *schwa,* and it stands for the unaccented sound in such words as *ago, item, edible, gallop,* and *circus.* More approximately, it stands for the sound *uh*—like the *uh* speakers may make when they hesitate in their speech. Perhaps it would help to remember that *uh,* as well as ə, could often be used to represent the schwa sound.

Here are some of the many words in which the sound appears: *recollect* (rĕk'ə-lĕkt' *or* rĕk'uh-lĕkt'); *hesitate* (hĕz'ə-tāt *or* hĕz'uh-tāt); *courtesy* (kûr'tə-sē *or* kûr'tuh-sē). Open your dictionary to any page and you will almost surely be able to find three words that make use of the schwa in the pronunciation in parentheses after the main entry. Write each of the three words and their pronunciations in the following spaces:

1. _____   (_____)

2. _____   (_____)

3. _____   (_____)

Accent Marks

Some words contain both a primary accent, shown by a heavy stroke ('), and a secondary accent, shown by a lighter stroke ('). For example, in the word *discriminate* (dĭs krĭm'ə-nāt'), the stress, or accent, goes chiefly on the second syllable (krĭm') and to a lesser extent on the last syllable (nāt').

Use your dictionary to add accent marks to the following words:

connote (kə nōt)
admonish (ăd mŏn ĭsh)
behemoth (bĭ hē məth)
reciprocal (rĭ sĭp rə kəl)
extravaganza (ĕk străv ə găn zə)
polyunsaturated (pŏl ē ŭn săch ə rā tĭd)

Full Pronunciation

Here are ten pronunciations of familiar words. See if you can figure out the correct word in each case. Confirm your answers by checking your dictionary. One is done for you as an example.

kwĭz	*quiz*	kwĕs′chən	_____
tĭk′əl	_____	ĕg′zĭt	_____
wûr′ē	_____	kē′bôrd′	_____
dĭ-zûrt′	_____	fĭk-tĭsh′əs	_____
mēt′bôl′	_____	lŭg′zhə-rē	_____

Now use your dictionary to write out the full pronunciation (the information given in parentheses) for each of the following words:

1. cogent _____   6. lucrative _____
2. fiasco _____   7. nemesis _____
3. rationale _____   8. deprecate _____
4. atrophy _____   9. lethargy _____
5. trenchant _____ 10. rapacious _____

Now practice *pronouncing* each word. Use the pronunciation key in your dictionary as an aid to sounding out each syllable. Do *not* try to pronounce a word all at once; instead, work on mastering *one syllable at a time.* When you can pronounce each of the syllables in a word successfully, say them in sequence, add the accent, and pronounce the entire word.

OTHER INFORMATION ABOUT WORDS

Parts of Speech

The next bit of information that the dictionary gives about *disdain* is *v*. This label, as the key in the front of your dictionary explains, indicates the *part of speech* and is one of the abbreviations given in the dictionary.

Fill in any meanings that are missing for the following abbreviations:

v. = verb

n. = _____

adj. = adjective

pl. = _____

sing. = _____

Principal Parts of Irregular Verbs

Disdain is a regular verb and forms its principal parts by adding *-ed*, *-ed*, and *-ing* to the stem of the verb. When a verb is irregular, the dictionary lists its principal parts. For example, with *write* the present tense comes first (the entry itself, *write*). Next comes the past tense (*wrote*) and then the past participle (*written*), the form of the verb used with such helping words as *have*, *had*, and *was*. Then comes the present participle (*writing*)—the *-ing* form of the verb.

Look up the parts of the following irregular verbs and write them in the spaces provided. The first one has been done for you.

Present	Past	Past Participle	Present Participle
write	wrote	written	writing
begin			
steal			
eat			

Plural Forms of Irregular Nouns

The dictionary supplies the plural forms of all irregular nouns (regular nouns form the plural by adding -s or -es). Give the plurals of the following nouns. If two forms are shown, write both.

apology   _____

wife   _____

hypothesis   _____

formula   _____

passer-by   _____

Meanings

When there is more than one meaning to a word, the meanings are numbered in the dictionary, as with *disdain*. In many dictionaries, the most common meanings are presented first. The introductory pages of your dictionary will explain the order in which meanings are presented.

Use the sentence context to try to explain the meaning of the italicized word in each of the following sentences. Write your definition in the space provided. Then look up and record the dictionary meaning of the word. Be sure you pick out the meaning that fits the word as it is used in the sentence.

1. *Effervescent* drinks like soda appeal to children; they enjoy the bubbles that burst below their noses.

   Your definition: _____

   Dictionary definition: _____

2. The actress's *effervescent* personality saved the show from being a disaster.

   Your definition: _____

   Dictionary definition: _____

3. The small border skirmish was merely a *prelude* to the full-scale war that followed.

   Your definition: _____

   Dictionary definition: _____

4. The pianist began the *prelude* in a hesitant manner; then he relaxed and gained confidence.

   Your definition: _____

   Dictionary definition: _____

Etymology

Etymology refers to the history of a word. Many words have origins in foreign languages, such as Greek (Gk) or Latin (L). Such information is usually enclosed in brackets and is more likely to be present in a hardbound desk dictionary than in a paperback one. Good desk dictionaries include the following:

American Heritage Dictionary   *Webster's New Collegiate Dictionary*
Random House College Dictionary   *Webster's New World Dictionary*

A good desk dictionary will tell you, for example, that *maverick* derives from the name of a Texas rancher who refused to brand his calves. The word is now a general term used to describe someone who does not conform or "follow the herd."

See whether your dictionary gives the origins of the following words:

sandwich _____   breakfast _____

Usage Labels

As a general rule, use only standard English words in your writing. If a word is not standard English, your dictionary may give it a usage label such as one of the following: *informal, nonstandard, slang.* Look up the following words and record how your dictionary labels them. Note that a recent hardbound desk dictionary will be the best source of information about usage.

rough (meaning *difficult*)   _____

finagle   _____

hang-up (meaning *inhibition*) _____

ain't   _____

cool (meaning *composure*)   _____

PRACTICE IN USING THE DICTIONARY

Activity 1

Use your dictionary to write the full pronunciation for the following words.

1. encomium _____   6. verbatim _____

2. caustic _____   7. amorphous _____

3. conjecture _____   8. primeval _____

4. pernicious _____   9. machination _____

5. Roquefort _____   10. disingenuous _____

Activity 2

Refer to the excerpt below from the paperback *American Heritage Dictionary* to answer the questions that follow.

expertise/exposure

ex·per·tise (ex'spər-tez') *n.* Expert skill or knowledge. [< OFr.]

ex·pi·ate (ĕk'spē-āt') *v.* **at·ed, -at·ing.** To atone or make amends for. [< Lat. *expiare*.]—**ex·pi·a·tion** *n.* —**ex·pi·a'tor** *n.* —**ex·pi·a·to'·ry** (-ə-tôr'ē, -tōr'ē) *adj.*

ex·pire (ĭk-spīr') *v.* **-pired, -pir·ing. 1.** To come to an end; terminate. **2.** To die. **3.** To breathe out; exhale. [< Lat. *exspirare*.] —**ex'·pi·ra'tion** *n.*

ex·plain (ĭk-splān') *v.* **1.** To make plain or comprehensible. **2.** To offer reasons for; account for. [< Lat. *explanare*.] —**ex·plain'·a·ble** *adj.* —**ex·plain'er** *n.* —**ex'pla·na'tion** *n.* **ex·plan'a·to'ri·ly** *adv.* —**ex·plan'a·to·ry** (-splăn'-ə-tōr'ē, -tōr'ē) *adj.*

ex·ple·tive (ĕks'plĭ-tĭv) *n.* An exclamation or oath. [LLat. *expletivus*.]

ex·pli·ca·ble (ĕk'splĭ-kə-bəl) *adj.* Capable of being explained.

ex·pli·cate (ĕks'splĭ-kāt') *v.* **-cat·ed, -cat·ing.** To explain, esp. in detail. [Lat, *explicare*. to unfold.] —**ex'pli·ca'tion** *n.* —**ex'pli·ca'tive** *adj.* —**ex'pli·ca'tor** *n.*

ex·plic·it (ĭk-splĭs'it) *adj.* Clearly defined; specific; precise. [< Lat. *explicitus*, p.p. of *explicare*, to unfold.] —**ex·plic'it·ly** *adv.* — **ex·plic'it·ness** *n.*

Syns: explicit, categorical, clear-cut, decided, definite, express, positive, precise, specific, unequivocal **adj.**

Usage: Explicit and *express* both apply to something clearly stated rather than implied. *Explicit* applies more particularly to that which is carefully spelled out: *explicit instructions. Express* applies particularly to a clear expression of intention: *an express promise.*

ex·po·nent (ĭk-spō'nənt) *n.* **1.** One who explains, interprets, or advocates. **2.** A number or symbol, as *3* in $(x + y)^3$, placed to the right of and above another number, symbol, or expression, denoting the power to which the latter is to be raised [< Lat. *exponere*, to expound.] —**ex'po·nen'tial** (-nĕn'shəl) *adj* —**ex'po·nen'tial·ly** *adv.*

ex·port (ĭk spôrt', -spōrt', ĕk'spôrt', -spōrt') *v.* To send or carry abroad, esp. for sale or trade —*n.* (ĕk'spôrt, -spōrt'). **1.** The act of exporting. **2.** Something exported. [Lat. *exportare*.] —**ex·port'a·ble** *adj.* —**ex'por·ta'tion** *n.*—**ex·port'er** *n.*

ex·pose (ĭk-spōz') *v.* **-posed, -pos·ing. 1.** To uncover; lay bare. **2.** To lay open or subject, as to a force, influence, etc. **3.** To make visible or known; reveal. **4.** To subject (a photographic film or plate) to the action of light [< Lat. *exponere*.] —**ex·pos'er** *n.*

ex·po·sé (ĕk'spō-zā') *n.* A public revelation of something discreditable. [Fr.]

ex·po·si·tion (ĕk'spə-zĭsh'ən) *n.* **1.** A setting forth of meaning or intent. **2.** The presentation of information in clear, precise form. **3.** A public exhibition of broad scope. —**ex·pos'i·tor** *n.* —**ex·pos'i·to'ry** (-tôr'ē, -tōr'ē) *adj.*

ex post fac·to (ĕks' pōst făk'tō) *adj.* Formulated, enacted, or operating retroactively [Med. Lat., from what is done afterwards.]

ex·pos·tu·late (ĭk-spŏs'chə-lāt') *v.* **-lat·ed, -lat·ing.** To reason earnestly with someone, esp. to dissuade. [Lat. *expostulare*, to demand strongly.] —**ex·pos'tu·la'tion** *n.* —**ex·pos'tu·la'tor** *n.*—**ex·pos'tu·la·to'ry** *adj.*

ex·po·sure (ĭk-spō'zhər) *n.* **1.** An act or example of exposing. **2.** The condition of being exposed. **3.** A position in relation to direction of weather conditions. **4. a.** The act or time of exposing a photographic film or plate. **b.** A film or plate so exposed.

ă pat ā pay â care ä father ĕ pet   ē be ĭ pit ī tie î pier ŏ pot ō toe ô paw, for oi noise o͞o took o͞o boot ou out th thin *th* this ŭ cut û urge yoo abuse zh vision ə about, item, edible, gallop, circus

1. How many syllables are in the word *expostulate?*_____

2. Where is the primary accent in the word *exposition?* _____

3. Where is the primary accent in the word *exposé?* _____

4. What word in the pronunciation key tells you how to pronounce the *a* in *ex post facto?* _____

5. In the word *exponent,* the *o* is pronounced like the *o* in
   a. boot.
   b. hot.
   c. drop.
   d. toe.

6. In the word *expiate,* the *i* is pronounced like a
   a. long *i.*
   b. short *i.*
   c. schwa.
   d. long *e.*

7. In the word *explicate,* the *a* is pronounced like a
   a. long *a.*
   b. long *i.*
   c. schwa.
   d. short *a.*

8. *True or false?* _____ The word *exposé* is a verb.

9. *True or false?* _____ *Exponent* is a word with a specific meaning in mathematics.

10. Which word in the excerpt is followed by a list of synonyms and a note on usage? _____

11. In the sentence "Our free pass to the movie theater will *expire* if we do not use it within the next month," which meaning of *expire* applies?
    a. Meaning 1
    b. Meaning 2
    c. Meaning 3

12. In the sentence "I don't quite understand how a kernel of corn pops into popcorn. Can you *explain* it to me?" which meaning of *explain* applies?
    a. Meaning 1
    b. Meaning 2

13. In the sentence "People in other countries learn about the United States through one of our major *exports*: movies," which meaning of *export* applies?
    a. Noun meaning 1
    b. Noun meaning 2

14. In the sentence "In the agricultural *exposition* at our state fair, I saw a purple cabbage that weighed fifty pounds," which meaning of *exposition* applies?
    a. Meaning 1
    b. Meaning 2
    c. Meaning 3

WORD PRONUNCIATION

This chapter will help you:

- Review the two major rules for dividing words into syllables
- Apply the two rules to specialized terms in different subjects
- Review other rules relating to word division and pronunciation

WHY YOU NEED TO LEARN PRONUNCIATION

You will meet many specialized terms in your various academic subjects. Knowing how to *pronounce* the terms will help you master their meanings. You can often locate difficult-to-pronounce words in the dictionary. But in other cases the words may be too technical to appear in a desk dictionary—or you will simply not have the time to look up every pronunciation.

Another problem related to word pronunciation is that there are probably more words in your *listening* vocabulary than in your *sight* vocabulary. That is, you probably recognize more spoken words than written ones. Learning how to sound out and pronounce unfamiliar words will help narrow any gap between your listening and sight vocabularies.

Using the two major rules provided in this section, you should be able to divide most unfamiliar words into syllables—and so pronounce them without having to refer to the dictionary. The rules hold true most of the time; with them, you will never be far from correct word pronunciation.

BACKGROUND INFORMATION

Before looking at the rules, be sure you understand the necessary background information that follows. First of all, remember that the vowels are *a, e, i, o, u,* and sometimes *y;* the consonants are all the other letters.

It is also important to remember that each syllable is a different general sound in a word. If a word has two syllables, it has two sounds; three syllables, three sounds; and so on. For example, in the word *impacted* (as in "impacted wisdom tooth"), there are three syllables (im pact ed) and three sounds. How many syllables (and sounds) are there in the following words?

nostril	(_____ syllables)
Frankenstein	(_____ syllables)
contemporary	(_____ syllables)

After you use the rules below to divide a word into syllables, work on pronouncing *one syllable at a time.* Only when you can pronounce each syllable in a word separately should you put the sounds together in succession. Then, when you can correctly pronounce all the sounds in the word in succession, you should add the accent (stress) where it sounds right. If the word doesn't "sound right," or if it is hard or awkward to say, change the accent or the pronunciation (or both) slightly until it does sound right to your ear. Remember that the rules given below will get you close to the correct pronunciation, but they are not always exact. You may have to make final adjustments.

THE TWO MAJOR RULES FOR DIVIDING WORDS INTO SYLLABLES

Rule 1: Divide between Double Consonants

Here are examples of rule 1:

mes/sage   dis/tance   fun/gus

In each case the division is between the double consonants: the *ss* in *message,* the *st* in *distance,* and the *ng* in *fungus.*

At times, the division will occur between a consonant and a *consonant blend*—two or more consonants that blend together to form one sound. Here are examples:

mor/phine   con/struct   sub/stance

The syllable division in *morphine* is between the consonant *r* and the consonant blend *ph;* in *construct,* between the consonant *n* and the consonant blend *str;* in *substance,* between the consonant *b* and the consonant blend *st.*

Activity

Use a slash line to divide the following words into syllables at the point where double consonants occur.

1. center
2. pollen
3. horrid
4. twitter
5. pressure

6. umber
7. acrid
8. germane
9. stencil
10. turbid

11. fervent
12. spectral
13. gremlin
14. viscous
15. transvestite

Pronunciation Hint: The vowel before double consonants usually has a short sound. For example, the *u* in *umber* has a short sound, like the *u* in *cut*.

Rule 2: Divide before a Single Consonant

Here are examples of rule 2:

lo/cal   vi/per   bla/tant

In each case, the syllable division is before the single consonant: before the *c* in *local*, before the *p* in *viper*, and before the first *t* in *blatant*.

At times, the division will occur before a consonant blend. For example, in the word *preclude*, the division occurs before the consonant blend *cl: pre/clude*.

Activity

Use a slash line to divide the following words into syllables before single consonants.

1. cogent
2. evoke
3. humid
4. lethal
5. savor

6. suture
7. irate
8. solace
9. pathos
10. frugal

11. declaim
12. mimosa
13. luminous
14. matron
15. cremation

Pronunciation Hint: The vowel before a division at a single consonant usually has a long sound. For example, the *o* in *cogent* has a long sound, like the *o* in *go*.

■ **Review Test**

Divide these words into syllables by applying either or both of the two rules.

1. advocate	6. sinecure	11. cursory
2. desist	7. reprimand	12. scrutinize
3. condolence	8. patella	13. colostomy
4. festival	9. inconclusive	14. incontrovertible
5. nonpartisan	10. lassitude	15. phenobarbital

OTHER HELPFUL RULES FOR DIVIDING WORDS INTO SYLLABLES

Rule 3: Always Divide Compound Words between the Words That Form the Compound

Divide the following words:

straightforward	evergreen	stronghold
wholesale	monkeyshine	newsprint

Rule 4: Divide between Prefixes and Suffixes

Common prefixes include: *anti, trans, non, re, post, con, mis, ex, de, inter, sub, ad, dis, ante, ultra, bi, syn, ab, tri, in, pre.* Common suffixes include: *en, ize, ess, ism, able, ible, ward, ment, ry, ic, ist, less, ship, ance, age, ful, ness, ier, ious, ition, ion, ing.*

Divide the following words at prefix or suffix divisions:

heading	exhume	syndrome
spineless	discontent	submerge
statement	majority	antibiotics

Rule 5: Two Vowels Together May Represent Separate Sounds and Be in Separate Syllables

Use this rule to divide and pronounce the following words:

neon	cooperate	duodenum
obvious	venereal	actuary

Note: Only some vowel pairs divide into separate syllables. There are many vowel pairs in English that have only one syllable, usually with the first vowel long and the second vowel silent. For example: *please, chain, road,* and *dream.*

PRACTICE IN WORD PRONUNCIATION

Activity 1

Divide the words that follow these instructions into syllables. When you have done so, you should be able to sound out and pronounce each separate syllable and then the whole word.

Remember that the chief rules for syllable division are to (1) divide between double consonants and (2) divide before a single consonant.

> Example: dis/con/so/late
> (The word has four syllables. The first two divisions are between double consonants—*sc* and *ns;* the third division is before the single consonant.)

1. detergent
2. voracious
3. bulwark
4. prognosticate
5. fulsome
6. furtive
7. vicissitude
8. consummate
9. fabricate
10. cajole
11. nuance
12. salient
13. embellish
14. inadvertent
15. repudiate
16. postprandial
17. alacrity
18. abortive
19. pugnacious
20. promulgate
21. castigate
22. octogenarian
23. abstemious
24. scurrilous
25. aspirant

Note: After you divide a word into syllables, place the stress, or accent, on the syllable that makes the word easier to pronounce. The stress that sounds the most natural is generally the correct one. For instance, the word *disconsolate* is most easily emphasized on the second syllable—*dis **con** so late*—and that accent is the correct one.

Activity 2

The following lists are made up of specialized terms you can expect to encounter in your various content courses. You should be able to divide the words into syllables and pronounce them correctly (or come close to the correct pronunciation) using chiefly the two basic rules for syllable division.

Terms from Psychology

1. engram
2. sensory
3. germinal
4. prenatal
5. aversive

6. sibling
7. libido
8. visceral
9. olfactory
10. sublimation

Terms from Sociology

1. marginal
2. dissenter
3. accommodation
4. kibbutz
5. amalgamation

6. demography
7. hallucinogen
8. gesellschaft
9. hospice
10. compartmentalization

Terms from Biology and Other Sciences

1. cortex
2. mitosis
3. rubella
4. peptide
5. histamine

6. insulin
7. estrogen
8. dermatitis
9. hematoma
10. placenta

Terms from Business and Economics

1. surtax
2. fiscal
3. mercantile
4. convergence
5. indenture

6. consumption
7. merger
8. aggregate
9. Malthusian
10. decentralization

SPELLING IMPROVEMENT

This chapter will show you how to improve your spelling by using:

- A dictionary
- Electronic aids
- A personal spelling list
- Lists of specialized words
- A list of common English words
- Four basic spelling rules

Poor spelling often results from bad habits developed in early school years. With work, such habits can be corrected. If you can write your name without misspelling it, there is no reason why you can't do the same with almost any word in the English language. The six steps that you can follow to improve your spelling are discussed starting on the next page.

USING THE DICTIONARY

Get in the habit of using the dictionary. When you write a paper, allow yourself time to look up all those words whose spelling you are unsure about. Do not overlook the value of this step just because it is such a simple one. Through using the dictionary, you will probably improve your spelling 95 percent almost immediately.

USING ELECTRONIC AIDS

There are three electronic aids that may help you with spelling. First, many *electronic typewriters* on the market today will automatically beep when you misspell or mistype a word. They include built-in dictionaries that will then give you the correct spelling. Smith-Corona, for example, has a series of portable typewriters with an ''Auto-Spell'' feature that start at around $150 at discount stores.

Second, a *computer with a spell-checker* will identify incorrect words and suggest correct spellings. If you know how to write on a personal computer, you will have no trouble learning how to use the spell-check feature.

Finally, *electronic spell-checkers* are pocket-size spelling aids. They look much like the pocket calculators you may carry to your math class, and they are the latest example of how technology can help the learning process. Electronic spellers can be found in the typewriter or computer section of any discount store, at prices in the range of $100. The checker has a tiny keyboard on which you type out a word the way you think it is spelled; the checker then quickly provides you with the correct spelling of related words. Some of the checkers even *pronounce* the word for you.

KEEPING A PERSONAL SPELLING LIST

Either in a separate notebook for spelling or in a specific section in your English or reading and study skills notebook, keep a list of words that you misspell.

To master such words, do the following:

1 Look at the first word, say it, and spell it. Then look away and try to spell it. When you can, go on and work on the next word until you can spell it without looking at it. Then go back and test yourself on the first word. After learning each new word, go back and review all the preceding ones. *This review and repeated self-testing are the keys to effective learning.*

2   As a reinforcement, you may want to write out difficult words several times or ''air-write'' them with your finger in large, exaggerated motions. Also, you may want to capitalize the letters you confuse in a word when you write it out. For example, if you tend to spell *resources* as *resorces,* you might want to write *resOURces.*

3   With long words, divide the word into syllables and try to spell the syllables. For example, *misdemeanor* can be spelled easily if you can hear and spell in turn its four syllables: *mis de mean or.* Again, the word *formidable* can be spelled easily if you hear and spell in turn its four syllables: *for mi da ble.* Even a very long word like *antidisestablishmentarianism* becomes simple if you first break it down into syllables: *an ti dis es tab lish men tar i an is m.* Remember, then: Try to see, hear, and spell long words in terms of their syllable parts.

Activity

Use the space that follows as a starter for words that you misspell. As you accumulate additional words, you may want to jot them down on a back page of this book or your English or reading notebook.

Incorrect Spelling	Correct Spelling	Points to Remember
alot	a lot	two words
writting	writing	one ''t''
alright	all right	two words

LEARNING KEY WORDS IN MAJOR SUBJECTS

Make up lists of words central to the vocabulary of your major subjects. For example, a list of key words in business might include *economics, management, resources, scarcity, capitalism, decentralization, productivity, enterprise,* and so on; in psychology: *behavior, investigation, experimentation, frustration, cognition, stimulus, response, organism,* and so on. Set aside a specific portion of your various course notebooks to be used only for such lists and study them using the method for learning words described on page 285.

Activity

Write in the space below the name of one of your subjects and fifteen repeatedly used terms which you should learn to spell for that subject.

Subject _____

1. _____
2. _____
3. _____
4. _____
5. _____
6. _____
7. _____
8. _____
9. _____
10. _____
11. _____
12. _____
13. _____
14. _____
15. _____

STUDYING A BASIC WORD LIST

Master the spellings of the words in the following list. They are some of the most often used words in English. Your instructor may assign twenty-five or fifty words for you to study at a time and give you a series of quizzes until you have mastered the list.

ability	attempt	chief	education
absent	attention	children	either
accept	awful	church	English
accident	awkward	cigarette	enough
across	back	clothing	entrance
address	balance	collect	everything
advertise	bargain	color	examine
advice	beautiful	comfortable	exercise
after	because	company	expect
again	become	condition	family
against	been	conversation	flower
all right	before	daily	foreign
almost	begin	danger	friend
a lot	being	daughter	from
also	believe	death	garden
always	between	deposit	general 100
although	bottom	describe	grocery
among	brake	different	guess
amount	breathe	direction 75	handkerchief
angry	building	distance	happy
animal	business	does	heard
another	came 50	doubt	heavy
answer	careful	dozen	himself
anxious	careless	during	holiday
apply 25	cereal	each	house
approve	certain	early	however
argue	change	earth	hundred
around	cheap	easy	hungry

instead	noise	ready	thought
intelligence	none	really	thousand
interest	nothing 150	reason	through
interfere	number	receive	ticket
kindergarten	ocean	recognize	tired
kitchen	offer	remember	today
knowledge	often	repeat	together
labor	omit	restaurant	tomorrow 225
language	only	ridiculous	tonight
laugh	operate	right	tongue
learn	opportunity	said	touch
length	original	same	travel
lesson 125	ought	sandwich	truly
letter	pain	sentence	under
listen	paper	several	understand
loneliness	peace	should	until
making	pencil	since	upon
marry	people	sleep 200	usual
match	perfect	smoke	value
matter	period	something	vegetable
measure	person	soul	view
medicine	picture	state	visitor
middle	place	straight	voice
might	pocket	street	warning
million	possible	strong	weather
minute	potato	student	whole
mistake	president	studying	window
money	pretty 175	suffer	without
month	promise	summer	would
morning	psychology	sweet	writing
mountain	public	teach	written
much	quick	telephone	yesterday
needle	quiet	than	your 250
neither	quite	there	
newspaper	raise	thing	

LEARNING BASIC SPELLING RULES

A final way to improve your spelling is to learn and practice the four often-used rules that follow. While the rules have exceptions, they usually hold true.

Rule 1: *I* before *E*

Use *i* before *e* except after *c*. For example:

believe	deceive	yield
chief	receive	receipt
field	perceive	piece
grief	ceiling	priest
cashier	conceited	deceit

Activity

Fill in *ie* or *ei* in each of the following words:

1. fr_____nd
2. c_____ling
3. br_____f
4. misch_____f
5. retr_____ve
6. rel_____ve
7. rec_____ve
8. th_____f
9. ach_____ve
10. hyg_____ne

Note: Here are some exceptions to the rule: *height, either, leisure, seize, weird, neighbor, efficient, science.*

Rule 2: Final *E*

Drop a final *e* when adding a suffix that begins with a vowel. Keep the final *e* when adding a suffix that begins with a consonant. Some background information will help make this rule clear to you.

- There are two kinds of letters in the alphabet: vowels (*a, e, i, o, u,* and sometimes *y*) and consonants (all the other letters).

- Suffixes are common endings on many English words. Here are some suffixes that begin with vowels: *en, ize, ess, ism, able, ible, ic, ist, ance, age, ier, ation, ition, ion, ing, ed.* Here are some suffixes that begin with consonants: *ward, ment, ry, ship, ful, ness.*

- In the following examples, the final *e* is dropped before a suffix beginning with a *vowel:*

  hope   + ing = hoping   sense + ible = sensible
  excite + ed   = excited   create + ive = creative
  believe + able = believable   fine   + est = finest

- In the following examples, the final *e* is retained before a suffix beginning with a *consonant:*

  hope   + less = hopeless   use   + ful = useful
  excite + ment = excitement   life   + like = lifelike
  extreme + ly   = extremely   apprentice + ship = apprenticeship

Activity

Use the *final e* rule with the following words:

1. describe + ing   = _____

2. lone   + er   = _____

3. care   + ing   = _____

4. immense   + ly   = _____

5. like   + ness = _____

6. arrive   + al   = _____

7. use   + able = _____

8. peace   + ful   = _____

9. service   + ing   = _____

10. retire   + ment = _____

Rule 3: *Y* to *I*

When a word ends in a consonant plus *y*, change the *y* to *i* when you add a suffix. Here are some examples:

reply + es = replies	carry + age = carriage	
angry + ly = angrily	marry + es = marries	
lazy + ness = laziness	defy + ed = defied	
happy + er = happier	penny + less = penniless	

■ *Complete this sentence:* The letter before *y* in all the preceding examples is

a _____. Therefore, you change the _____ to _____ before adding the suffix.

Activity

Use the *y*-to-*i* rule with the following words:

1. fly + es = _____
2. hurry + ed = _____
3. empty + ness = _____
4. easy + er = _____
5. try + ed = _____
6. worry + es = _____
7. ready + ness = _____
8. baby + es = _____
9. pretty + er = _____
10. beauty + ful = _____

Note: Do not worry about the following exceptions. They are here simply to make the rule complete. One exception is that you do not change the *y* when you add -*ing*. For example, *play + ing = playing*. A second exception is that you do not change the *y* when a word ends in a vowel plus *y* (rather than a consonant plus *y*). For example, *employ + ed = employed*.

Rule 4: Doubling

Double the final consonant of a word when all of the following apply:

1   The word is one syllable or is accented on the last syllable.
2   The word ends with a consonant preceded by a vowel.
3   The suffix you are adding begins with a vowel.

Here are some examples:

■   If you are adding *-ing* to *drop,* you double the final consonant because:

Drop is one syllable.
Drop ends with a consonant preceded by a vowel.
The suffix (*ing*) being added begins with a vowel.

■   If you are adding *-able* to *control,* you double the final consonant because:

Control is accented on the last syllable.
Control ends with a consonant preceded by a vowel.
The suffix (*able*) being added begins with a vowel.

■   If you are adding *-ed* to *happen,* you do *not* double the final consonant, because *happen* is accented on the first rather than the last syllable.

Activity

Use the doubling rule with the following words.

1. big   + er   = _____
2. shop   + ed   = _____
3. swim   + ing   = _____
4. compel   + ed   = _____
5. begin   + ing   = _____
6. forget   + ful   = _____
7. equip   + ed   = _____
8. repel   + ent   = _____
9. commit   + ed   = _____
10. ship   + ment   = _____

■ Final Activity

Use the four rules to spell the following words.

1. regret   + ing   = _____
2. sip   + ed   = _____
3. dec_____t
4. study   + es   = _____
5. mere   + ly   = _____
6. rely   + ed   = _____
7. rob   + ery   = _____
8. rec_____pt
9. forgot   + en   = _____
10. nerve   + ous   = _____

On the lines below, explain which rule you applied to spell each word.

1. _____
2. _____
3. _____
4. _____
5. _____
6. _____
7. _____
8. _____
9. _____
10. _____

VOCABULARY DEVELOPMENT

This chapter will explain how you can develop your vocabulary by:

- Regular reading
- Using context clues
- Systematically learning new words

A good vocabulary is a vital part of effective communication. A command of many words will make you a better writer, speaker, listener, and reader. In contrast, a poor vocabulary can seriously slow your reading speed and limit your comprehension. Studies have shown that students with strong vocabularies and students who work to improve limited vocabularies are more successful in school. And one research study found that *a good vocabulary, more than any other factor, was common to people enjoying successful careers in life.*

The question, then, is not whether vocabulary development is helpful but what the best ways are of going about it. This section will describe three related approaches you can take to increase your word power. Remember from the start, however, that none of the approaches will help unless you truly decide in your own mind that vocabulary development is an important goal. Only when you have this attitude can you begin doing the sustained work needed to improve your word power.

- *Complete the following sentence:* Most people who enjoy successful careers in life have in common a _____.

REGULAR READING

The best way to learn words is by experiencing them a number of times in a variety of sentences. Repeated exposure to a word will eventually make it a part of your working language. This method of learning words requires that *you make reading a habit.* You should, first of all, read a daily newspaper. You do not have to read it from first page to last. Instead, you should read the features that interest you. You might, for instance, read the movie and television pages, the sports section, columns on consumer tips, and any news articles or features that catch your eye. Second, you should subscribe to one or more weekly magazines such as *Newsweek, Time,* or *People,* as well as monthly magazines suited to your interests. Among monthlies, you might choose from such magazines as *Sports Illustrated, Cosmopolitan, Science Digest, Consumer Reports, Ladies' Home Journal, Ebony, Personal Computing, Glamour, Redbook,* and many others.

Finally, you should, if possible, try to fit reading for pleasure into your schedule. A number of interesting books are included in the selected book list on page 525. You may find such reading especially difficult when you also have textbooks to read. Try, however, to redirect a half hour to an hour of your recreational time to reading books on a regular basis instead of watching television, listening to music, or the like. By doing so, you may eventually reap the rewards of an improved vocabulary *and* discover that reading can be truly enjoyable.

- *Complete the following sentence:* The best way to learn a word is by seeing it in several different _____.

- Put a check next to each step that you can realistically take to make reading a part of your life.

_____ Begin a subscription to a daily newspaper. What newspaper would be a good choice for you? _____

_____ Begin a subscription to a weekly magazine. What magazine might you want to subscribe to? _____

_____ Go to the library or bookstore and pick out a book you will read for pleasure. (You may want to look at the list of recommended books starting on page 525.) What book might you want to try first?

_____

_____ Find a time and place that will be suitable for quiet reading. (I, for example, read in bed for a half hour or so before I go to sleep. That's an ideal quiet time for me.) What is one possibility?

_____

Activity 1

Read through a daily newspaper. Record below the name and date of the paper and the titles and authors (when their names are given) of five different features or articles that you found interesting to read.

Name of newspaper: _____ Date: _____
Articles read:

1. _____

2. _____

3. _____

4. _____

5. _____

Bring one of the articles to class and give a three-minute talk on it to a small group of other students. Do not read the article to them. Instead, explain what you felt was the main point of the article (the title will often provide a clue). Also, express in your own words some of the details used to support or develop the main point.

Activity 2

Go through a weekly or monthly magazine and read at least five articles that seem interesting to you. Record the following information:

Name of magazine: _____ Date: _____
Articles read (title and author):

1. _____

2. _____

3. _____

4. _____

5. _____

Prepare a three-minute report on one of the articles, to be presented to a small group of students.

In your report for Activity 2, do the following:

- Explain briefly the main point of the article (again, the title often provides a clue to the author's main idea).
- Then present to the group the chief details that are used to support or develop that point.
- As you provide details, quote several sentences (no more than three) from the article.

Activity 3

Obtain one of the books listed on pages 525–530. Fill in the following information about the book:

Title: _____ Author: _____

Place of publication: _____ Publisher: _____ Year: _____

Read a minimum of fifty pages in the book. Prepare a ten-minute oral report on the fifty-odd pages for a small group of your peers. Your purpose in this report is to give them a good sense of the flavor of the book. To do this, you should explain and summarize in your own words how the book begins, who the main characters are, and what specific problems or conflicts are developed. Read at least two passages you like from the book as part of your report. The passages you read should be no more than 20 percent of your entire report.

Alternatively, prepare a written report that you will hand in to your instructor. Follow the same instructions that were given for the oral report. Set off quoted passages longer than three sentences by single-spacing them and by indenting them ten spaces in from the left margin of your paper.

Some Final Thoughts about Regular Reading

Keep in mind that you cannot expect to make instant habits of newspaper, magazine, and book reading. Also, you should not expect such reading to be an instant source of pleasure. You may have to work at becoming a regular reader, particularly if you have done little reading in the past. You may have to keep reminding yourself of the enormous value that regular reading can have in developing your language, thinking, and communication power. Remember that if you are determined and if you persist, reading can become a rewarding and enjoyable activity.

USING CONTEXT CLUES

When asked how they should deal with an unknown word they meet in reading, many people answer, "Use the dictionary." But stopping in midsentence to pull out a dictionary and look up a word is seldom a practical—or necessary—solution. You can often determine the meaning of an unknown word by considering the context in which the word appears. The surrounding words and sentences frequently provide clues to the meaning of the word. Notice the italicized word in the following selection:

> A poll showed that the senator's *candor* was appreciated even by the voters who did not agree with him. "I don't go along with some of his views," one voter said. "But it's refreshing to have a politician tell you exactly what he believes."

Even if you do not know the meaning of *candor,* the context helps you realize that it means *openness,* or *honesty.* Much of the time, such context clues in surrounding words or sentences will help you make sense of unknown words in your reading.

If you are a regular reader, you will use context clues on repeated occasions to determine the meaning of a word. Perhaps another time you will read:

> Tony appreciated Lola's *candid* remark that his pants were baggy. And he was pleased with himself for not getting upset when faced with an unflattering truth.

Again, context helps you understand and learn the word. And through repeated use of such context clues to understand an unfamiliar word, you will make that word a natural part of your working vocabulary.

In combination with regular reading, the use of context clues is an excellent means to vocabulary improvement. Unfamiliar words, encountered often enough in context, eventually become part of one's natural working vocabulary. If you develop the habits of reading regularly and using context clues to guess the meanings of unknown words, you will turn many unfamiliar words into familiar ones.

- ■   Complete the following sentence: Instead of using a dictionary, you can often determine the meaning of an unknown word by looking at

  _____ .

Activity 1

Read each of the following sentences carefully. Then decide which of the four choices provided comes closest in meaning to the word in *italic* type. Circle the letter of your choice.

1. As a *naive* little boy, I thought elbow grease was something you bought in a store.
   a. Careless
   b. Serious
   c. Unknowing
   d. Easygoing

2. J. Paul Getty, the late billionaire, was so *frugal* that he had a pay telephone for the guests in his home.
   a. Honest
   b. Generous
   c. Sensitive
   d. Thrifty

3. Sue *affected* to like him only until she found a better-looking boyfriend.
   a. Decided
   b. Bothered
   c. Pretended
   d. Agreed

4. My Corvette's *voracious* appetite for gasoline made me decide to trade it in for an economy car, the Chevette.
   a. Huge
   b. Tiny
   c. Finicky
   d. Sensational

5. When I was called upon to give an on-the-spot speech in class, I was so surprised that I stood up and recited nothing but *gibberish*.
   a. Stories
   b. Jokes
   c. Nonsense
   d. Lies

6. My neighbors are hardly *gregarious;* they keep their blinds drawn and have put a high fence around their property.
   a. Hostile
   b. Lonely
   c. Strange
   d. Friendly

7. Ted is a *masochist;* he encourages people to criticize and hurt him.
   a. One who likes pleasure
   b. One who likes pain
   c. One who agrees with others
   d. One who feels angry

8. School council members often complain about the *apathy* of the student body; they ignore the fact that students have interests other than school government.
   a. Hostility
   b. Loneliness
   c. Discourtesy
   d. Indifference

9. I felt *vindictive* toward the sales clerk who rudely ignored me, so I decided to complain to the store manager.
   a. Apologetic
   b. Jealous
   c. Sorry
   d. Inclined to revenge

10. The instructor said my term paper had no *contemporary* references; I should have cited some up-to-date research on my topic.
    a. Recent
    b. Scholarly
    c. Local
    d. Clear

Activity 2

Use the sentence context to try to explain the italicized word in each of the following sentences. Then check your answers in a dictionary.

1. Sometimes I have *ambivalent* feelings toward my husband; I both love him and hate him.

   Your definition: _____

   Dictionary definition: _____

2. I tried to *emulate* my sister's success in school by studying as hard as she did.

   Your definition: _____

   Dictionary definition: _____

3. The doctor gave *placebos* to the overworried patient who imagined that she was not taking enough pills for her arthritis.

   Your definition: _____

   Dictionary definition: _____

4. I have never met anyone who has not made *disparaging* comments about certain national politicians.

   Your definition: _____

   Dictionary definition: _____

5. My theme was so *redundant* that my teacher asked me to reduce it by half.

   Your definition: _____

   Dictionary definition: _____

Activity 3

The sentences on the following pages are taken from widely used college textbooks. They should dramatize to you how context clues are a practical tool for helping you identify the meanings of words you may not know in your college work. Read each sentence carefully. Circle the letter of the choice that comes closest in meaning to the italicized word.

1. The move from stage to stage is not automatic, and Greeley indicates that *regression* to an earlier stage is always a possibility.
   a. Progress
   b. Advance
   c. Expansion
   d. Return

2. The *fallacy* of this approach is that it overlooks the extent to which every large organization is a network of small primary groups.
   a. Incorrectness
   b. Value
   c. Cause
   d. Result

3. Most of us are *deferential* toward those whose social position we believe to be above ours and look down on those whom we consider socially below us.
   a. Open
   b. Impolite
   c. Bitter
   d. Respectful

4. Like reward, punishment serves two major functions in discipline. It *deters* the repetition of socially undesirable acts, and it shows the adolescent what the social group considers wrong.
   a. Encourages
   b. Discourages
   c. Permits
   d. Organizes

5. The first stage is one of denial. The patient refuses to accept the *prognosis*, typically believing that it is a mistake, and consults other doctors or even faith healers.
   a. Medical forecast
   b. Therapy
   c. Medicine
   d. Bill

6. America has been called the "*affluent* society" because of its abundance of goods and services.
   a. Divided
   b. Middle-class
   c. Prosperous
   d. Anxious

7. For four years, Hitler had concentrated on making northern France the most *impregnable* wall of his fortress.
   a. Expensive
   b. Unconquerable
   c. Inconspicuous
   d. Interesting

8. Competition functions as one method of *allocating* scarce rewards. Other methods are possible. We might ration goods on some basis such as need, age, or social status. We might distribute scarce goods by lottery or even divide them equally among all people.
   a. Distributing
   b. Disputing
   c. Collecting
   d. Taxing

9. As artificial parts *proliferate,* the need for transplants lessens.
   a. Increase
   b. Become more expensive
   c. Decrease
   d. Break down

10. Catholic Democrats who were *adamant* that federal aid should go to parochial schools and Republicans who were *adamant* that aid not go to any school were locked in a stalemate that ended hopes for the passage of any bill.
    a. Set in a belief
    b. Flexible in a belief
    c. Reluctant
    d. Agreeable

SYSTEMATICALLY LEARNING NEW WORDS

Learning Technical Words

Some of the most important words you must learn and remember are the technical terms used in specific subjects. In a psychology course, for instance, you need to understand such terms as *behaviorism, stimulus, regression, cognition, neurosis, perception,* and so on. With an introductory course in particular, you must spend a good deal of time learning the specialized vocabulary of the subject. Mastering the language of the subject will be, in fact, a major part of mastering the subject.

Textbook authors often define a technical word at the same time they introduce it to you. Here are several examples:

> *Catharsis,* the release of tension and anxieties by acting out the appropriate emotions, has long been recognized as helpful to one's health.

> A *capitalist,* then, is an individual who invests money or other assets in a business, hoping to make a profit.

> The word *ulcer* is used to designate an open sore in the skin or in the alimentary canal.

If you should come upon a technical word that is not explained, look for its definition in the glossary of words that may appear in the back of the book. Or look for the word in the index that will probably be included in the back of the book. Once introduced and explained, many technical words may then recur frequently in a book. If you do not learn such words when they are first presented, it may be impossible for you to understand later passages where the words are used again. To escape being overwhelmed by a rising flood of unfamiliar terms, you should mark off and master important technical words as soon as they appear.

Your teacher may be your best source of information about important technical terms. He or she will probably introduce a number of these terms to you during class discussions and provide definitions. You should write down each definition and clearly set it off in your notes by underlining the term and perhaps putting *def* beside it in the margin. If you are responsible for textbook material, you should mark off and then write down definitions and other important ideas, as described on page 313. (If a teacher's definition of a term differs in wording from a text definition of the same term, you should study the one that is clearer for you.)

Some students find it helpful not only to set off definitions in their class and text notes but also to keep a list of such definitions at the back of their course notebooks. What is crucial is that you realize the importance of noting and mastering the definitions of key words in a subject. If you do not do this, you cannot expect to understand fully and master the subject.

The activities on pages 314–319 will give you practice in locating and writing down definitions of technical terms.

■ Complete the following sentences:

Courses such as sociology, psychology, and biology have their own specialized _____.

Technical terms are often _____ when they are first introduced; they may also be defined in a _____ or an _____ at the back of a textbook.

You may find it helpful to keep a list of important definitions at the back of _____.

Learning General-Interest Words

General-interest words are not technical terms but ones you might come upon in your everyday reading. Perhaps while reading a magazine you encounter the italicized word in the following sentence: "People who vacation in resort towns often have good reason to feel *exploited*." You may be able to guess the meaning of *exploited* from the context and so feel no need to consider the word any further. However, perhaps it is a word you have seen and been slightly puzzled about before, and a word you think it would be useful for you to master. You should have an organized method of learning words such as *exploited* so that you can not only recognize them but also use them in speaking and writing.

A Method of Learning New Words: To build your vocabulary, first mark off in your reading words that you want to learn thoroughly. If you are reading a newspaper or magazine, tear out the page on which the word appears and put the page in a file folder. If you are reading a book, jot down the word and the page number on a slip of paper which you have tucked into the book for that purpose. Then, every so often, sit down with a dictionary and look up basic information about each word. Put this information on a vocabulary word sheet like the one that follows.

Vocabulary Word Sheet

1 Word: _____*exploit*_____ Pronunciation: _____*(eks ploit')*_____

Meanings: _____ *v.*   *1 To take advantage of*

_____*2 To make use of selfishly*_____

Other forms of the word: ___*exploiter   exploitable   exploitative*___

Use of the word in context: ___*People who vacation in resort*___
towns often have good reason to feel exploited.

Your own sentence using the word: ___*I tried to exploit the fact*___
that my boss was my father-in-law by asking for a raise.

2 . . .

Study each word as follows:

- First, make sure you can correctly pronounce the word and its derivations. (Page 269 explains the dictionary pronunciation key that will help you pronounce each word properly.)

- Second, study the main meanings of the word until you can say them without looking at them.

- Finally, spend a moment looking at the example of the word in context.

You should then go on to follow the same process with the second word. Then, after testing yourself on the first and the second words, go on to the third word. Continue going back and testing yourself on all the words you have studied after you learn each new word. Such repeated self-testing is the key to effective learning.

An Alternative Method of Accumulating Words: Some people can effectively use three- by five-inch cards, rather than the word sheet shown before, to accumulate words. In this method, you prepare a card for each word, using the following format.

1 *Front of the card:* word; pronunciation; part of speech; forms of the word; example of the word in context.

```
exploit     (eks ploit') v.

exploiter   exploitable   exploitative

People who vacation in resort towns
   often have good reason to feel exploited.
```

2 *Back of the card:* different meanings of the word; check (√) beside the meaning that fits the context in which you found the word; sentence using the word.

```
√  1 To take advantage of
   2 To make use of selfishly

I tried to exploit the fact that my boss
was my father-in-law by asking for a
raise.
```

An advantage of this method is that the cards can be shuffled and the words can be studied in any order. A drawback of the method is that some people do not find it practical or convenient to keep handy a pack of vocabulary cards. Use whichever method you think will work for you.

Activity

Locate five words in your reading that you would like to master. Enter them on your vocabulary word sheet and fill in all the needed information. Your instructor may then check your word sheet and perhaps give you a quick oral quiz on selected words.

You may receive a standing assignment to add five words a week to a word sheet and to study the words. Note that you can create your own word sheets using loose-leaf paper, or your instructor may give you copies of the word sheet that follows.

1. Word: _____ Pronunciation: _____

    Meanings: _____

    _____

    _____

    _____

    Other forms of the word: _____

    Use of the word in context: _____

    _____

2. Word: _____ Pronunciation: _____

    Meanings: _____

    _____

    _____

    _____

    Other forms of the word: _____

    Use of the word in context: _____

    _____

3. Word: _____ Pronunciation: _____

    Meanings: _____

    _____

    _____

    _____

    Other forms of the word: _____

    Use of the word in context: _____

    _____

4. Word: _____ Pronunciation: _____

   Meanings: _____

   _____

   _____

   _____

   Other forms of the word: _____

   Use of the word in context: _____

   _____

5. Word: _____ Pronunciation: _____

   Meanings: _____

   _____

   _____

   _____

   Other forms of the word: _____

   Use of the word in context: _____

   _____

Learning through Vocabulary Study Books

A final systematic way of learning new words is to use vocabulary study books. The most helpful of these books present words in more than one sentence context and then provide several reinforcement activities for each word. The more you work with a given word in actual sentence situations, the better your chances of making it part of your permanent word base.

There may also be materials in your college learning center that take a ''word in context'' approach. The regular use of vocabulary study books and materials, combined with regular reading and with your own ongoing vocabulary word sheets, is a solid way to improve your vocabulary.

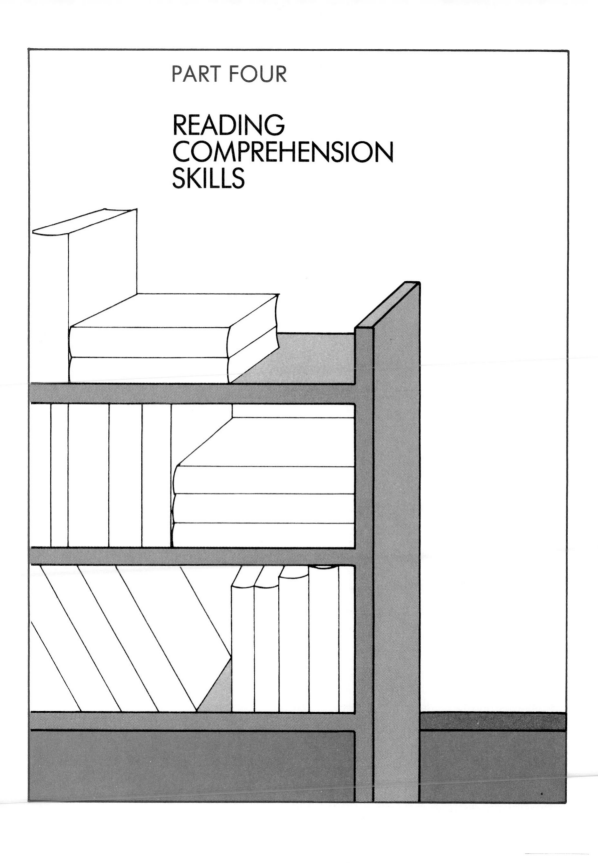

PART FOUR

READING COMPREHENSION SKILLS

PREVIEW

Part Four explains and offers practice in seven key reading comprehension skills. All these skills will help you read and take notes on your textbooks and other college materials. The first five skills involve the ability to recognize and use: (1) definitions and examples of definitions, (2) enumerations and their headings, (3) the relationship of headings to subheadings, (4) emphasis words and other signal words, and (5) main ideas in paragraphs and short selections. The last two skills involve the ability to outline and to summarize material you have read.

INTRODUCTION

One misleading idea that some students have about reading is that comprehension should happen all at once. They believe that a single reading of a textbook selection should result in a satisfactory understanding of that selection. But what such students do not realize is that good comprehension is usually a *process*. Very often, comprehension is achieved gradually, as you move from a general feeling about what something means to a deeper level of understanding.

SEVEN KEY SKILLS

The purpose of Part Four is to help you learn seven key skills that will increase your understanding of what you read. The first five skills include the ability to recognize and use important elements of written material; the last two skills are techniques that will help you take effective study notes:

1　Recognizing definitions and examples
2　Recognizing enumerations
3　Recognizing headings and subheadings
4　Recognizing signal words
5　Recognizing main ideas in paragraphs and short selections
6　Knowing how to outline
7　Knowing how to summarize

Your mastery of the seven basic skills will enable you to read and understand the important ideas in articles and textbook chapters.

■　*Complete the following statements:*
　　Good comprehension seldom happens all at once but is usually a

　　_____.

　　There are seven skills you can learn to improve your

　　_____.

COMPREHENSION AND RAPID READING

Another misleading idea that students sometimes have about reading is that an increase in reading *rate*—the purpose of the much-advertised speed-reading courses—means an automatic increase in reading comprehension. Speed-reading courses *may* increase the number of words your eyes take in and "read" per minute. And comprehension may improve because you tend to concentrate more as you read faster. However, with difficult material, understanding is likely to fall as rate rises. The surest way to reading speed *and* comprehension is to develop reading comprehension skills. Speed will automatically follow as you learn how to identify main ideas and then go quickly over lesser points and supporting details. Speed will also result as you learn how to vary your reading rate according to the nature of the material and your purpose in reading. In summary, by emphasizing comprehension rather than sacrificing it, you will make yourself a more efficient reader, and therefore a faster reader.

■   What are two misleading ideas that students sometimes have about reading?

_____

_____

■   What is the drawback of speed-reading courses?

_____

■   What is the surest way to develop reading speed *and* comprehension?

_____

SKILL 1: RECOGNIZING DEFINITIONS AND EXAMPLES

Definitions are often among the most important ideas in a selection. They are particularly significant in introductory courses, where much of your time is spent mastering the specialized vocabulary of the subject. You are, in a sense, learning the "language" of sociology or biology or whatever the subject might be.

Most definitions are abstract, and so they are usually followed by one or more examples that help clarify their meaning. Always select and mark off at least one example that helps make an abstract defintion clear for you.

In the following passage from a sociology textbook, underline the definition. Also, locate the two examples and write *ex* in the left-hand margin beside each of them.

INTUITION

Galen, a famous Greek physician of the second century, prepared an elaborate chart of the human body showing exactly where it might be pierced without fatal injury. How did he know the vulnerable spots? He just *knew* them. True, he had learned a good deal of human anatomy through his observations and those of his associates, but beyond this, he relied upon his intuition to tell him which zones were fatal. *Intuition* is any flash of insight (true or mistaken) whose source the receiver cannot fully identify or explain. Hitler relied heavily upon his intuition, much to the distress of his generals. His intuition told him that France would not fight for the Rhineland, that England would not fight for Czechoslovakia, that England and France would not fight for Poland, and that England and France would quit when he attacked Russia. He was right on the first two insights and wrong on the last two.

You may have realized that the first lines of the passage are not the definition of intuition but an example. The definition (''Intuition is any flash of insight'') is found midway through the paragraph. The examples (on Galen and Hitler) are found at the beginning and end of the paragraph. Underlining the definition and putting *ex* in the margin beside the examples will be helpful later when you are taking study notes on the passage.

■ How should you mark off definitions? _____

    _____

■ Why should you mark off examples? _____

    _____

■ If a text gives several examples of a definition, which one should you mark

   off, write down, or both? _____

    _____

Activity 1

Read quickly through the following selections, underlining each definition and writing *ex* in the left-hand margin beside an example of the definition. Some definitions will have several examples, but you need mark off only the example that makes the definition clear for you.

    Note that textbook authors often call attention to terms they are defining by setting them off in *italic* or **boldface** type.

1.   *Territoriality* refers to persons' assumptions that they have exclusive rights to certain geographic areas, even if these areas are not theirs by legal right. To take a common example: By the end of the first week of class most students consider a particular seat to be their territory and will show signs of distress or irritation if someone else sits in that seat. What is interesting, even for the simple example we cited, are the subtle ways in which strangers observe certain implicit territorial rights and the emotional mechanisms that regulate this behavior.

       Personal space refers not to a geographic area but to the space surrounding our body, a space that moves with us. Persons regard that space as private and try to prevent others from entering it. For example, persons sitting in a public reading room definitely seek to have at least one empty seat between themselves and the next reader. The phenomenon is also evident in less formal settings.

2.   We should not yield to the **allness fallacy**—the attitude that what we know or say about someone or something is all there is to know and say. The more we delve into some subjects, the more we realize there is so much more to learn and to consider. Even authorities on certain subjects humbly admit they don't know all the answers. Though they sometimes disagree among themselves on various topics, they continue to study all available facts. So do conscientious, open-minded business executives, government leaders, educators, students. Unfortunately, it is true of some people that "the less they know, the more sure they are that they know it all." Perhaps you have worked with such persons. A conspicuous example is that of the high school sophomore chatting casually with a man who (unknown to the student) was a distinguished scientist devoting his lifetime to studying botany. The smug sophomore commented, "Oh, botany? I finished studying all about that stuff last semester." As Bertrand Russell stated, "One's certainty varies inversely with one's knowledge."

3.   Matter can be said to have both potential and kinetic energy. Potential energy is stored-up energy or energy an object possesses due to its relative position. For example, a ball located twenty feet above the ground has more potential energy than another ball located ten feet above the ground and will bounce higher when allowed to fall. Water backed up behind a dam represents potential energy that can be converted into useful work in the form of electrical energy. Gasoline represents a source of stored-up chemical potential energy that can be released during combustion.

Kinetic energy is the energy that matter possesses due to its motion. When the water behind the dam is released and allowed to flow, its potential energy is changed into kinetic energy, which may be used to drive generators and produce electricity. All moving bodies possess kinetic energy. The pressure exerted by a confined gas is due to the kinetic energy of rapidly moving gas particles. We all know the results when two moving vehicles collide—their kinetic energy is expended in the "crash" that occurs.

4.   The fact that you have been going to school for so many years indicates society's faith that you will transfer your training from classroom situations to everyday life situations. There are two fundamentally different types of transfer: positive and negative. Suppose I have learned that in order to keep the attention of my class in introductory psychology, I must tell a joke every ten minutes or so. It seems to be a reasonably successful device, so I try it in my class in personality psychology, and it works there too. This is an example of *positive transfer:* What I have learned to do in one situation applies equally well in another situation. But suppose that I try to carry it one step further and use the technique in a talk that I give at the faculty club. Here I discover that my jokes fall flat and the talk is a failure. This is an example of *negative transfer:* What works in one situation is not applicable to another situation.

Activity 2

Mark off definitions and examples in the following sections. In addition, take brief study notes on each selection on separate paper. Your study notes should consist of the definition or definitions plus one example that makes the definition or definitions clear to you. In each case, try to summarize your example—that is, condense it into the fewest words possible that are still complete and clear. One selection is done for you as an example.

Example

Edwin Sutherland, who popularized the differential association theory discussed earlier, noted that certain crimes are committed by affluent, "respectable" individuals in the course of their daily business activities. Sutherland referred to such offenses as *white-collar* crimes. More recently, the term *white-collar crime* has been widened to include offenses by businesses and corporations as well as by individuals. A wide variety of offenses are included in this classification, such as income tax evasion, stock manipulation, consumer fraud, bribery and extracting "kickbacks," embezzlement, and misrepresentation in advertising.

White-collar crime—offenses by businesses and corporations as well as by "respectable" business individuals
Ex.—Income tax evasion

1. The effort to completely exterminate a people by killing all of them is called *annihilation*. It is ironic that the greatest annihilation in recorded history was conducted by a highly civilized Christian state. Between 1933 and 1945, the German Nazis killed about 4.5 million European Jews, marching many of them into gas chambers with a systematic bureaucratic efficiency. Other cataclysms in history may have produced more deaths, but we have no comparable example of such a deliberate, premeditated mass slaughter carried out as a government policy. Several instances of mass slaughter have transpired since then, perhaps the greatest of which accompanied the Hindu-Moslem clashes in India and Pakistan in 1948. Others include the slaughter of the Ibos in northern and western Nigeria in 1966 and of the Communists in Indonesia after their unsuccessful attempt to seize power in 1965.

2. Often, when faced with a conflict, we engage in the kind of behavior called vacillation—the tendency to be drawn first toward one possible resolution of the conflict, then toward another. Torn between studying and working and going out with friends, we may change our minds several times. At one moment we may lean strongly toward studying, at the next moment toward going out. In an extreme case of vacillation, we may take so long making up our minds that we wind up with very little time left for either of the possibilities.

3.   Behavior therapists have applied their knowledge of operant conditioning to large groups of hospitalized patients. The basic premise in this work is that patients should be treated as normal people capable of learning normal behavior if they are appropriately rewarded. Normal people are paid money for doing a job. They also receive attention and affection when they interact with other people. If they were not paid, they would not work; if they were ignored, they would not respond socially to others.

In the treatment method known as the **token economy**, hospitalized psychiatric patients receive rewards for performing "normal" behaviors. For example, one patient's job is to work in the hospital laundry each day. He receives fifty "tokens," usually in the form of poker chips, for each day's work. He can then trade in his tokens for his meals, a more comfortable bed than the hospital's standard equipment, weekend passes to leave the hospital, magazines, cigarettes, and so on.

4.   Throw a stone into a lake: water waves move outward from the splash. Clap your hands: sound waves carry the noise all around. Switch on a lamp: light waves illuminate the room. Water waves, sound waves, and light waves are very different from one another in important respects, but all have in common the basic properties of wave motion. A wave is a periodic disturbance—a back-and-forth change of some kind (of water height in the case of water waves, of air pressure in the case of sound waves, of electric and magnetic fields in the case of light waves)—that spreads out from a source and carries energy as it goes. Information, too, can be carried by waves, which is how sights and sounds reach us.

Activity 3

Working with a chapter or chapters in one of your textbooks, find five definitions *and* examples. Choose only definitions for which there are examples. Also, make sure each example is one that helps make the meaning of a definition clear to you. Use separate paper for this activity. Include the number of the page on which you find each definition and example, in case your instructor wants to refer to the text in reviewing your answers.

Here is a model for Activity 3:

Textbook _Understanding Psychology_ Author(s): _Feldman_
Definition: _Personal stressors—major life events that have immediate negative consequences that generally fade with time._
Example: _Death of a family member_

■ Review Test

Read these selections, noting definitions and examples of the definitions. In the space provided, write the number of the sentence that contains a definition. Then write the number of the *first* sentence that gives an example of the definition.

1.   ¹Rumors are both a form of collective behavior and an important element in other types of collective behavior. ²A rumor is a difficult-to-verify piece of information that people transmit to one another in relatively rapid fashion. ³Although many rumors are false, some are accurate, or contain a measure of truth (for instance, a local plant will close or a product will be discontinued). ⁴Rumors typically arise in times of tension and sagging economic conditions in which we lack information or distrust official sources of information. ⁵They are a substitute for hard news. ⁶Rumors regarding alleged contamination and conspiracy are quite common. ⁷Unfounded rumors have hurt the sales of some of the nation's largest corporations. ⁸For instance, McDonald's and Wendy's have had to fight rumors that they put earthworms in hamburgers (perhaps suggested by the fact that raw hamburger resembles red worms). ⁹Some people have seen a Communist connection in the bent-elbow, clenched fist symbol of Arm And Hammer, the baking soda. ¹⁰And Procter & Gamble removed its 135-year-old moon-and-stars trademark from its products when it was unable to dispel the rumor that the symbol is a sign of devil worship.

Definition: _____   Example: _____

2.   ¹You know what happens if you set out a pan of water: In time, the water will "disappear." ²The water did not boil. ³So what did happen? ⁴Remember, particles of matter are always in motion. ⁵Therefore, at the surface of a liquid, some particles will have enough kinetic energy to leave the liquid. ⁶It makes no difference what the temperature is. ⁷The particles that leave the surface are replaced by other particles. ⁸Some of these have enough kinetic energy to leave the surface. ⁹The process continues to go on. ¹⁰Finally, there is no liquid left. ¹¹This change from liquid to vapor (gas) is called *evaporation*.

Definition: _____   Example: _____

3.   ¹Phobias are fears that are out of proportion to the actual danger involved in a situation. ²Some people will not use elevators. ³Yes, the cable could break, the ventilation could fail, you could be stuck in midair awaiting repairs. ⁴But these problems are infrequent, and it would be foolhardy to walk forty flights twice daily to avoid them. ⁵Other people will not receive injections, even when quite ill. ⁶Injections can be painful, but these people would tolerate an even more painful pinch. ⁷Phobias can seriously interfere with our lives. ⁸People may know that a phobia is irrational yet still experience fear.

Definition: _____   Example: _____

4.   [1]Making up excuses or false attributions for potential failures is especially common when we think we might fail at something. [2]For example, a student fails to get enough sleep before an exam, an employee drinks too much at lunch with his boss, an investor says that he never has any luck in the stock market. [3]According to Edward Jones and Steven Berglas, these individuals are making up excuses so that they can blame some external thing if they fail. [4]The student can blame lack of sleep if she does poorly on the exam, the employee can blame drinking too much if he does not get his raise, and the investor can blame a run of bad luck if he loses money on the stock market. [5]Researchers Jones and Berglas call this tendency to make up an excuse for one's potential failure the use of a **self-handicapping strategy**. [6]By attributing to yourself all kinds of handicaps (missing sleep, drinking, bad luck), you can fail without having failure seem to be your own fault.

Definition: _____   Example: _____

SKILL 2: RECOGNIZING ENUMERATIONS

Like definitions, enumerations are keys to important ideas. Enumerations are lists of items that may actually be numbered in the text. More often, however, a list of items is signaled by such words as *first of all, second, moreover, next, also, finally,* and others. Typical phrases that introduce enumerations are: "There are three reasons why . . ."; "The two causes of . . ."; "Five characteristics of . . ."; "There are several ways to . . ."; and so on.

Activity

In the following selection, number 1, 2, and 3 the guidelines for constructive criticism. Note that each of the guidelines will be indicated by a signal word.

At times people need help so they can perform better. A necessary and yet far too often misused response is constructive criticism. *Constructive criticism* is evaluation of behavior—usually negative—given to help a person identify or correct a fault. Because criticism is such an abused skill, we offer several guidelines that will help you compose criticism that is both constructive and beneficial. First, make sure that the person is interested in hearing the criticism. The safest rule to follow is to withhold any criticism until it is asked for. It will be of no value if a person is not interested in hearing it. Another guideline is make the criticism as specific as possible. The more detailed the criticism, the more effectively the person will be able to deal with the information. Finally, show the person you are criticizing what can be done to improve. Don't limit your comments to what a person has done wrong. Tell him or her how what was done could have been done better.

You should have put a 1 in front of ''make sure that the person is interested in hearing the criticism'' (signaled by *First*), a 2 in front of ''make the criticism as specific as possible'' (signaled by *Another guideline*), and a 3 in front of ''show the person you are criticizing what can be done to improve'' (signaled by *Finally*). Develop the habit of looking for and numbering all the enumerations in a chapter.

When you take study notes on enumerations, be sure to include a heading that explains what a list is about. For example, because the following list does not have a descriptive heading, the notes are not as clear:

1: Make sure the person is interested in hearing the criticism
2: Make the criticism as specific as possible
3: Show the person you are criticizing what can be done to improve

Your notes will be clear and helpful if they include, as the following notes do, a heading describing what the list is about:

Guidelines for Constructive Criticism

1: Make sure the person is interested in hearing the criticism
2: Make the criticism as specific as possible
3: Show the person you are criticizing what can be done to improve

■ Why should you look for and number enumerations? _____

_____

_____

■ What do phrases such as *Two effects of, Three important results are, Five factors to note* tell you? _____

_____

_____

The activities that follow will give you practice in the skill of locating and marking off enumerations.

Activity 1

In the selections that follow, number 1, 2, 3, and so on, the items in each list or enumeration. Remember that words such as *first, another, also,* and *finally* often signal an enumeration. Also, in the space provided, write a heading that explains what each list is about. Look first at the example and the hints.

Example

Heading: _____ *Rewards of Schooling* _____

In strictly pragmatic terms, schooling yields three rewards, and the amount of each reward increases in proportion to the amount of schooling. First, the individual who is well schooled stands the [1]best chance of getting any job, other things being equal. Thus, the chance of unemployment is reduced. Second, the individual with a good background is the [2]one chosen for advancement and promotion, thus enabling him or her to earn more over the long run. Third, because of rewards one and two, the educated individual has [3]more personal freedom. Such a person will have more job opportunities from which to choose, is less threatened with unemployment, and can be freer economically because of his or her higher earning power. The decision in favor of further schooling needs to be encouraged if only for the above listed pragmatic reasons.

Hints

a   A selection often contains a phrase that introduces the enumeration. The introductory phrase in the preceding passage is "schooling yields three rewards." Look for such introductory phrases; they will help you write your heading.

b   Every heading that you write should begin with a word that ends in *s*, as in "Reward*s* of Schooling." As a reminder, the *s* has been added to each of the heading spaces that follow.

1. Heading: _____ *s* _____

An American worker can be said to earn several types of income. Money income is the amount a person receives in actual cash or checks for wages, salaries, rents, interest, and dividends. Real income is what the money income will buy in goods and services; it is purchasing power. If a person's money income rises 5 percent in one year but the cost of purchases increases 8 percent on the average, then real income decreases about 3 percent. Psychic income is an intangible but highly important income factor related to comfortable climate, a satisfying neighborhood, enjoyment of one's job, and so on. Some people prefer to take less real income so they can live in a part of the country with a fine climate and recreation opportunities—greater psychic income.

2. Heading: _____ s _____

Networking is the way people find out about jobs that aren't advertised in the newspaper; it is the way they learn about valuable new developments in their field before the crowd does. There are three main elements in networking. The first is *visibility*, making your presence known. The more people who meet you, the more who are likely to remember you. The second element is *familiarity*, letting people get to know you. It takes courage to expose your skills, attitudes, and opinions, but people are more likely to deal with you if they have some idea of how to think and react. The third element, *image*, means giving people the impression that you are competent and pleasant to deal with. An optimistic, enthusiastic approach to business—and to life—is magnetic.

3. Heading: _____ s _____

In 1747, Lord Chesterfield wrote to his son:

I always naturally hated drinking; and yet I have often drunk, with disgust at the time attended by great sickness the next day, only because I then considered drinking as a necessary qualification for a fine gentleman and a Man of Pleasure.

Chesterfield's motivation is clear. But what are the motivations of contemporary drug abusers, including many who, like Chesterfield, get no pleasure from drug use? Researchers such as Graham Blaine, Norman J. Levy, Leon Wurmser, and Farnsworth have suggested a number of common motivations:

Escape: Drug users often want to escape from the pressures of school, job, family; from responsibility, from doing something they really don't want to do (going to college, staying home with a baby); from fear of not being able to live up to their own expectations or those of others; or from an inability to "feel," to respond to the world around them.
Rebellion: Some need to rebel against the establishment, parents, school, society in general, or what they consider the hypocrisy of drug laws.
Getting even: Some want to take revenge on parents or others.
Substitute for sexual experience: Some people, especially males whose sex lives are not satisfactory, use drugs as a substitute.
Experimentation: Sometimes drug users feel they have found a way of saying, "I'm not afraid, I'm invincible; nothing can happen to me," of winning a badge of courage that is difficult to achieve in a society they believe to be devoid of the challenges and excitement of new frontiers.
Self-destruction: Drug use can be a form of risk taking that says, "I don't care what happens to me!"

4. Heading: _____ _s_ _____

Three reasons for the existence of stereotypes will be noted. First, they simplify explanations of human behavior. The crudest way to explain a phenomenon is to classify it. Aristotle was asked, for example, "Why do stones fall to Earth?" He answered that stones belong to the class Earth, and objects yearn to return to the class to which they belong. The explanation seems rather foolish in the light of modern physics. However, if you saw someone behaving oddly in a mental hospital, you might inquire of a psychiatrist, "Why does he behave that way?" The psychiatrist might answer, "He is a schizophrenic." You would probably be satisfied. But the answer is no explanation at all. Why is he diagnosed as a schizophrenic? The answer to this question is: Because he acts oddly—in ways characteristic of schizophrenic patients. Explanations by classification all have this quality of circularity. Nonetheless, explanations by classification often put curiosity to rest. Therefore, stereotypes are sometimes comforting pseudo-explanations.

Second, stereotypes often provide a scapegoat for aggressions. A scape-goat is a target for abuse. Scapegoats may actually be innocent, but because they can't fight back, they have all sorts of abuse heaped upon them. Minority groups are often unable to fight back, and they serve as an easy target for angry feelings that may have their real roots in other sources. A man who is angry at his boss may pick a fight with his wife; she becomes the scapegoat for his hostile feelings toward his boss. In the same way, it has been argued that the Nazis offered the Jew as a scapegoat to the German people. Prior to World War II, Germany had numerous economic problems. There was widespread frustration and latent anger. The Jew was blamed for Germany's problems.

Third, stereotypes give members of a dominant group a sense of superior-ity. The members of the larger group can look at the members of the minority group and say to themselves, "I'm better than they are." These thoughts help individuals compensate for any dominant feelings of inferiority they themselves may possess. To illustrate, poor white Southern sharecroppers, feeling inade-quate and incompetent in many ways, can look at black people and feed their egos by thinking, "We're white and they're black."

From the three reasons postulated for the creation of stereotypes, it seems clear that stereotypes exist for very real reasons. They meet human needs for explanation, aggression, and superiority.

Activity 2

In the following selections, number 1, 2, 3, and so on the items in each list and underline the words that introduce the list. In addition, take brief study notes on each selection on separate paper. Your notes should consist of a numbered list of items and an accurate heading for that list. Try to summarize the items in each list—that is, condense them to the fewest words possible that are still complete and clear. One selection is done for you as an example.

Example

Studies have indicated <u>a number of values to reading and reciting</u>, as opposed to reading alone. For one thing, when you read something with the knowledge that you must soon recite what you have read, you are [1]more likely to be motivated to remember and less likely to become inattentive. Moreover, recitation provides [2]immediate knowledge of results, so that you can see how well you are doing and adjust and modify your responses accordingly. Finally, recitation provides [3]active practice in recalling the material you wish ultimately to retain.

Values of Reading and Reciting
1. More motivation to remember
2. Immediate knowledge of results
3. Active practice in recalling material

1.   Private property serves two important functions in capitalism. First, it places in the hands of individuals power over the use of productive resources. Economic activity cannot occur unless someone makes decisions about which goods are to be produced and when and how they are to be produced. The more complex the method of production, the more crucial is the decision-making process. The owners of resources may delegate part of their powers to others, but for there to be capitalism, the owners must have the final say as to how resources are used. Second, private property serves as an incentive for the accumulation of wealth. This incentive is necessary if the stock of capital in the economy is to grow. The right of property owners to benefit from the use of their property in the productive process encourages them to save and invest in capital goods.

2.   Physical punishment is a less efficient means of shaping behavior than is reinforcement. Spanking a child for hitting another child may have negative results. First, the child's main response to the spanking may be one of anger and frustration—reactions that are incompatible with learning other, more socially acceptable responses. Second, the feelings aroused by the spanking may lead to aggressive acts against "safe," nonpunishing objects in the environment. Third, the punishment effects may extend only to behavior in the presence of the parents: Children may refrain from hitting while their parents are with them, but as soon as the parents are out of sight, the children will do what they want.

3.   Approaching the choice of a marriage partner rationally may seem coldly calculating—more like choosing a car than a spouse. But consider: Which is the more important decision? Here are some points worth exploring. First of all, consider background. Husbands and wives who share common racial, religious, ethnic, educational, and socioeconomic backgrounds and experiences bring similar expectations about marriage to the relationship. They are more likely to hold the same values and desire the same life-styles than are

those from differing backgrounds. A second point to explore in selecting a mate is goals. Two people should understand and accept one another's goals for life as well as for marriage and family. If they value the same things, they will increase the odds for marital success. Last, look at the potential spouse's personality. How does the would-be mate treat his or her family? (Once married, you will be family, too.) How does he or she treat the waitress, the service station attendant, salespeople, friends? Does he or she make mountains out of molehills? Is he or she honest? Is the prospective partner always right? Is someone else always to blame? Does he or she have a sense of humor (a difficult trait to live without)? Look carefully for as many tips as you can find about what it will be like to live on an everyday basis with the person.

4.   We have defined directed thinking as being aimed at the solution to a specific problem, and logical thinking as one method of getting to such a solution. But in concrete terms, what are the actual steps we go through when we have a complex problem to solve?

It is first necessary to *identify* the problem—to know that it exists and then to pinpoint and delineate it in order to see how you will direct your thinking to solve it. You first become aware of a problem as an obstacle or frustration—not always an unpleasant one, certainly, or sports and puzzles would not exist. Say you have just made a date to play tennis. After hanging up the phone, you realize that you have a dental appointment for exactly the same time. The problem is now identified—you are committed to being at two different places at one-thirty tomorrow afternoon.

After this, you begin to *search* for possible solutions. With some problems this search can be as simple as random trial and error, like fitting one key after another into a lock until you find the one that works. If you stumble upon the right solution by the trial-and-error method, of course, you need go no further. But many problems do not yield to such a mechanical solution, and trying every possible alternative is not a very economical approach. Still, to some extent trial and error probably does enter into your search for a solution. First you start restricting your alternatives. Can you simply not turn up at the dentist's? No. Not show up at the tennis court? Not a good idea, either. Perhaps you had better call your friend back. Next, you *analyze* the situation: If you explain to your friend what the difficulty is, maybe you can work out another time for the tennis game.

You then move to the *attack* itself. You telephone your friend, and you agree to meet on the courts at four o'clock instead of one-thirty. You no longer have to be in two places at once, and your problem is solved.

Sometimes, of course, the interval between the appearance of a problem and its solution is short enough that you think of it as all having happened in a single step. What has really happened is that these four steps have occurred so rapidly that the solution seemed to come instantaneously. Other times—if the problem is a very complicated one, such as finding a cure for cancer—the single problem must be broken down into many parts, and the steps must be gone through, over and over, by many people.

Activity 3

Using one of your textbooks, find and record five separate enumerations. Write a heading for each list. There should be at least three items under each heading.

At the top of the first sheet of paper on which you do this activity, give the name of the textbook you are using and the authors. Also include the number of the page on which you find each enumeration, in case your instructor wants to refer to the text in reviewing your answers. A model follows.

Model

Textbook: *Alive and Well*   Authors: *A. & H. Eisenberg*

Heading: *Problems of the Elderly*   Pages: *542-544*

(1) Retirement

(2) Health

(3) Finances

■ Review Test

Locate and number the enumeration in each selection that follows. Then, in the space provided, summarize the points in each enumeration. Also, write a heading that accurately describes what the enumeration is about.

1. There are at present three approaches to treating the allergic patient. One approach is to control the environment by removing the offending substances. Such control could be achieved, for example, by keeping the home—especially the bedroom—free of carpeting, upholstery, clutter, and other dust collectors. Another approach to treating the allergic patient is to use drug therapy or chemotherapy. Antihistamine drugs are the most widely used of all allergy drugs. Most effective for nasal allergies, they are often useful in skin and other allergies as well. Corticosteroids, used since 1949 for asthmatic attacks, have many adverse effects and are usually recommended only for life-threatening attacks and for short-term use. Finally, when environmental control and antihistamines fail to bring relief, the physician may consider "desensitizing" the patient. This is accomplished by a series of injections of the allergen in increasing amounts. Unfortunately, even a successful hyposensitization may wear off with time and need to be repeated.

    Heading: _____

    (1) _____

    (2) _____

    (3) _____

2.   The major weapon of the Reform New Deal's war on poverty was the Social Security Act of 1935. The first feature of this milestone legislation was the creation of a system of unemployment insurance based on contributions by employers into a fund administered by the states. Second, the legislation granted small federal stipends for dependent persons such as parentless children, the blind, the deaf, the mute, and the crippled. Third, it created an old-age pension program. To be sure, it provided far less than Francis Townsend had demanded, but it constituted a beginning. The plan called for establishment of a pension fund on the basis of regular contributions from employers and employees. After the age of sixty-five, workers were eligible for modest old-age pensions, depending on the size of their contributions.

Heading: _____

(1) _____

(2) _____

(3) _____

3.   Most warfare is confined within the tribe itself and is part of a series of forms of patterned violence. At the lowest level is the chest pounding duel. This occurs between villages that are in alliance and occurs in response to accusations of cowardice or excessive demands for food or women. Here a man represents his village at feasts and offers his chest to be beaten upon. Someone from the "insulting" village takes up the challenge. "Fierce fighters will take as many as four blows before demanding to hit the opponent. The recipient of the blows has a chance to hit the first man as many times as he was hit, unless he knocks him unconscious before delivering all the blows." Serious injury or unconsciousness terminates the matter, and the disputants usually patch up the quarrel. This, then, is legal violence. The second form of patterned violence is the club fights that occur between and within villages over adultery and theft of food. Here the offended party takes a long pole (club) and insults his opponent, who then comes with his own pole, and they alternately strike each other in the head. At the first sight of blood these often turn into a free-for-all with other men joining both sides. Theoretically, the village headman, armed with bow and arrows, will shoot anyone deliberately trying to kill his opponent or escalating the violence level. Often, however, a village may split into permanent factions over this, or the different villages will terminate their alliance. The club fight is regulated combat. The final violence level, that of the raid, is actual warfare. It takes place between unrelated villages and those who have broken their alliances. Here a war party practices throwing spears into a grass dummy representing the enemy, and before leaving they "psyche" themselves up by singing their war song ("I am a meat-hungry buzzard"). They attack early in the morning, trying to pick off and kill some one individual and then retreat back to their home territory without being detected.

Heading: _____

(1) _____

(2) _____

(3) _____

4.   Traditionally, journalists have been taught that an event becomes news or newsworthy if it fulfills one or more of five basic criteria. The first quality, *prominence,* refers to the concept that some people are simply better known than others; hence, they become the newsmakers. Who might make the national news with the birth of a child: a well-known film star or your authors? If someone is well known, what he or she does or accomplishes becomes of interest to readers. The second quality, *proximity,* serves as a measurement of the closeness of a story to the newspaper's readers. The local newspaper will cover local fires and accidents, but an accident that occurs in another state or country will have to be quite unusual or affect the future of readers if it is to be picked up outside of the locale in which it took place. This brings us to the third quality, *consequence;* consequence refers to whether an event will significantly affect the lives of the newspaper's readers. For example, usually events leading up to war are judged to be more newsworthy than are events that lead up to a supermarket opening. The fourth quality, *timeliness,* is that which makes news "news" and not "olds." Current happenings and trends fall into this category. As Ben Bagdikian points out, however, our system of news reporting actually favors older information at times. This is because the earlier the story reaches an editor, the better the story's chances of being used. Thus, if you were planning to run a press conference in a community that had an afternoon newspaper, it would be better to schedule it for 10 A.M. than for 4 P.M. The fifth quality, *human interest,* relates to whether a story is emotionally appealing or unusual. The fact that four thousand students at a local college go diligently about their studies is not news; the fact that they riot is, however. Stories that are heart tuggers, or that reveal the human side of events, usually also find eager readers.

Heading: _____

(1) _____

(2) _____

(3) _____

(4) _____

(5) _____

SKILL 3: RECOGNIZING HEADINGS AND SUBHEADINGS

Headings and subheadings are important visual aids that give you a quick idea of how the information in a chapter is organized. The model below shows a typical use of heads in a selection.

CHAPTER TITLE

The chapter title is set off in the largest print in the chapter. The title represents the shortest possible summary of what the entire chapter is about.

THIS IS A MAIN HEADING

Appearing under the chapter title are a series of main headings. Main heads may be centered or may start at the left margin; they are often set off with capital letters and, sometimes, a different color of ink. They represent a breakdown of the main topics covered in the chapter.

This Is a Subheading

Set off under the main headings are subheadings. They are in smaller type; sometimes they are underlined, italicized, or set in from the left margin. The subheadings represent a breakdown of the different ideas that are explained under the main headings.

Activity

1. Look at the first chapter of this book (pages 11–19).

    How many main heads are there in the chapter? _____

    How many subheads are there? _____

    How do the main heads differ from the subheads? _____

    _____

    _____

    _____

2. Look at the excerpt from a textbook chapter on pages 156–168. The main head is ''Courtship, Marriage, and Children.''

    How many subheads fit under that main head? _____

    One of the subheads is ''Marriage and Children.'' How many subsubheads

    fit under it? _____

    Another of the subheads is ''Dual-Earner and Dual-Career Families.'' How

    many subsubheads fit under it? _____

    How do the subsubheads differ from the subheads? _____

    _____

    _____

    _____

3. Look at a chapter in one of your other textbooks.

    How many main heads are there in the chapter? _____

    How many subheads are there? _____

    How do the subheads differ from the main heads? _____

    _____

    _____

    _____

USING HEADINGS TO LOCATE IMPORTANT IDEAS

There are two methods for using headings to locate key ideas. Each method is explained and illustrated on the following pages.

Method 1: Change Headings into Basic Questions

Change a heading into one or more basic questions. A basic question can be general, starting with the word *What, Why,* or *How.* Or it can be specific, starting with the word *When, Where,* or *Who.* Use whatever words seem to make sense in terms of the heading and the passage that follows it. Consider, for example, the following textbook selection:

DECLINE OF THE PURITAN WORK ETHIC

The Puritan concept of work as necessary for survival and as a duty and virtue in and of itself long dominated our culture. Work, obedience, thrift, and the delay of gratification were valued highly, and people's righteousness was often judged according to how hard they worked and how much they accomplished.

These views have changed, however, at an accelerated pace. Today's workers, particularly young workers, demand much more of themselves and their jobs than simply "filling a slot" and earning a living. The search for a meaningful, fulfilling job has become crucial. Workers increasingly desire to have responsibility and autonomy, to have a voice, and to demand not merely good physical working conditions but also good psychological working conditions. Rigid, authoritarian work structures are increasingly rejected as workers look to their jobs as a significant source of creative self-expression.

■ What are two questions that could be made out of the heading "Decline of the Puritan Work Ethic"?

_____

_____

The title could be changed into the two basic questions: "What is the Puritan work ethic?" "Why has the Puritan work ethic declined?" The answer to the second question especially (the Puritan work ethic has declined because today's workers want meaningful, personally fulfilling jobs) forms the main idea of the passage. This technique of turning headings into basic questions often helps you cut through a mass of words to get to the heart of the matter. Develop the habit of using such questions.

Method 2: See How Subheads Relate to Main Heads

If subheads follow a main head, determine how they are related to the main head. For example, suppose you noted the following main head and subheads spaced out over three pages of a business text:

ADVANTAGES OF THE PRIVATE ENTERPRISE SYSTEM

Freedom of Choice by Consumers
Decentralized Decision Making
High Productivity

Without having read a word of the text, you will have found one of the main ideas: The private enterprise system has three advantages—(1) freedom of choice, (2) decentralized decision making, and (3) high productivity.

Often the relationship between headings and subheads will be as clear and direct as in this example. Other times, however, you must read or think a bit to see how a heading and its subheads relate. For instance, in the excerpt from a speech text on page 119, following the main head "How to Become a Better Listener" are the subheads "Take Listening Seriously," "Resist Distractions," and so on. When you realize that the subheads are a list of the different ways to become a better listener, you have found one of the most important ideas on those pages—without having read even a word of the text. Sometimes there will be no clear relationship between the heading and the subheads. You want to be ready, though, to take advantage of a relationship when it is present.

- Why should you change headings into a basic question or questions?

  _____

- Why should you check to see how subheads relate to the main heads?

  _____

- Look at the excerpt from the speech text starting on page 121. How many subsubheads appear under the subhead "Focus Your Listening"? _____
  What is the relationship between "Focus Your Listening" and the three subsubheads?

  _____

- Look at the excerpt from the communications text starting on page 123. How many subheads appear under the heading "Methods of Dealing with Conflict"? _____
  What is the relationship between "Methods of Dealing with Conflict" and the subheads?

  _____

Activity 1

Read the following selections to find the answer or answers to the basic question or questions asked. Write your answer or answers in the space provided.

1. *Question:* What is an important difference between writing and talking?

AN IMPORTANT DIFFERENCE BETWEEN WRITING AND TALKING

In everyday conversation, you make all kinds of points or assertions. You say, "I'm not going out with him anymore," or "She's really generous," or "I hate my job," or "That was a tremendous party." The people you are talking to don't always challenge you to give reasons for your statements. They may know why you feel as you do, or may already agree with you, or may simply not want to put you on the spot, so they don't always ask "Why?" But the people who *read* what you write may not know you, agree with you, or feel in any way obligated to you. So if you want to communicate effectively with them, you must provide solid evidence for any point that you make. In writing, any idea that you advance must be supported with specific reasons or details.

Answer: _____

_____

2. *Questions:* What is selfish learning? What is an example of selfish learning?

SELFISH LEARNING

How can one explain the star football player who knows fifty plays by heart and the individual movements of all eleven players for most of the plays yet seems incapable of remembering a simple verb conjugation? Then there is the boy who hears the lesson instructions repeated four times yet fails to do the lesson correctly even though he can remember the pretty girl's phone number that he heard only once. At least some of the answers to the problems posed rest in what the author terms "selfish learning." In its simplest form, selfish learning refers to learning that the student accomplishes only for himself or herself—for his or her own ends with little or no regard for extrinsic, or external, reasons (requirements, grades) for the learning. The boy who knows fifty football plays by heart yet cannot conjugate a verb does not suffer from some impairment of his learning process, nor will general learning theory explain this apparent paradox. The explanation is to be found in those factors that activate or bring learning processes into action, namely, motivation, attention, and personal meaningfulness of the material once it is studied.

Answers: _____

_____

_____

3.   *Questions:* What is the Peace Corps? Why was the Peace Corps created?

THE PEACE CORPS

In the hope of winning back some of the friends the United States had alienated by the Bay of Pigs invasion, in September of 1961, President Kennedy created the Peace Corps, one of the most popular measures of his administration. The Peace Corps was composed of Americans of all ages who volunteered to work for token wages in virtually every nation outside the Communist bloc. Their task was to teach and to work with native citizens of the country in any way that would be of help. More than three thousand men and women, many of them idealistic young people, flocked to join the Peace Corps, which was directed by President Kennedy's brother-in-law Sargent Shriver. Their work and that of thousands of additional volunteers elicited an almost uniformly favorable response throughout the world and contributed significantly to restoring American prestige on the international scene.

Answers: _____

_____

_____

4.   *Questions:* How many people work in service jobs? Which services predominate?

SERVICE INDUSTRIES IN THE UNITED STATES

The United States is the world leader in service industries. It is estimated that more than 65 percent of the labor force in this country is engaged in providing services. Services are provided by government workers such as police officers, fire fighters, post office clerks, public schoolteachers, and state office employees. Services are also provided by those in the nonprofit private sector, such as employees in hospitals, museums, charities, churches, private schools, and private colleges. But the largest employment in service occupations is seen in profit-oriented and marketing-oriented businesses: airlines, banks, hotels and motels, consulting firms, restaurants, real estate agencies, insurance companies, beauty salons, amusements, caterers, and so on. And that listing continues to expand and increase.

Answers: _____

_____

_____

Activity 2

Following are chapter and section headings taken from a variety of college texts. Change each into a *meaningful* basic question or questions, using words like *what, why, who, which, when, in what ways, how*. Note the example.

Example: Alternatives to   a.   *What are alternatives to conflict?*
              Conflict   b.   *Which is the best alternative?*

Sociology

1. Primary and Secondary   a. _____
   Groups   b. _____

2. Prison Abuses and the   a. _____
   Reform Movement   b. _____

3. Barriers to Social   a. _____
   Knowledge   b. _____

4. Beneficial and Negative   a. _____
   Impacts of Cities   b. _____

Psychology

5. Loneliness in Modern Life   a. _____
                                b. _____

6. The Social Dropouts   a. _____
                                b. _____

7. Coping with Frustration   a. _____
                                b. _____

8. The Mentally Retarded   a. _____
                                b. _____

History and Political Science

9. The Dark Ages and the   a. _____
   Glimmer of Light   b. _____

10. The Two Terms of Theodore   a. _____
    Roosevelt   b. _____

11. The Fourteenth Amendment   a. _____
                                b. _____

12. The War of 1812   a. _____
                                b. _____

Business and Economics

13. Types of Economic Systems   a. _____

                                         b. _____

14. Pollution and Business   a. _____

                                         b. _____

15. Taft-Hartley Act   a. _____

                                         b. _____

16. Regulation of Business   a. _____

                                         b. _____

Biology and Other Sciences

17. Characteristics of Living Things   a. _____

                                         b. _____

18. Cell Development   a. _____

                                         b. _____

19. Energy   a. _____

                                         b. _____

20. Heart Disease   a. _____

                                         b. _____

Activity 3

Using a chapter from one of your textbooks, change five headings into basic questions. Then read the sections under the headings to find accurate and concise answers to the questions.

On a separate sheet of paper, indicate the headings, the questions you ask about the headings, and the answers to the questions. At the top of the first sheet on which you do this activity, give the name of the textbook, the author or authors, and the pages. Turn this activity in to your instructor.

Activity 4

Scrambled together in the list that follows are five textbook headings and four subheadings for each of them. Write the headings in the lettered blanks (A, B, C, D, E) and write the appropriate subheadings in the numbered blanks (1, 2, 3, 4).

Conquest of the Plains	The Cattle Kingdom	Frontier Farmers
Cells		Freewriting
Preparing a Scratch Outline	Tissues	Organ Systems
	Heart and Artery Disease	Kinds of Body Units
Urban Problems		
Removing the Indians	Pollution	Crowding
Organs	Brainstorming	Diabetes
Noncommunicable Diseases	Arthritis	Prospectors and Ranchers
	Making a List	
Techniques in the Writing Process	Strikes	Slums
	Cancer	

A. _____

   1. _____

   2. _____

   3. _____

   4. _____

B. _____

   1. _____

   2. _____

   3. _____

   4. _____

C. _____

   1. _____

   2. _____

   3. _____

   4. _____

D. _____

    1. _____

    2. _____

    3. _____

    4. _____

E. _____

    1. _____

    2. _____

    3. _____

    4. _____

Activity 5

Using one of your textbooks, find five sets of main heads and subheads that have a clear relationship to each other. Be sure to number the subheads and to find a minimum of two subheads in each case. Also, include the numbers of the pages on which you find your main heads and subheads, in case your instructor wants to refer to the text in reviewing your answers. A model follows.

Textbook: ___*Business Today*___ Authors: ___*Rachman and others*___

Main Head: ___*The Marketing Mix*___ *(pages 298–301)*

Subheads: ___*1. Product*___ ___*3. Place*___

              ___*2. Price*___ ___*4. Promotion*___

Following the main head "The Marketing Mix" are four subheads—titles in smaller print under the main heading. Each subhead, it is clear, is one of the ingredients in a marketing mix. By recognizing the relationship between the main head and the subheads, the reader has found an important idea—without having yet read a word of the text!

■ **Review Test**

Part A: Answer the basic questions that are asked about the selections below.

1. *Questions:* How much of a problem is teenage drinking? Who are the teenage drinkers?

TEENAGE DRINKING

Drinking patterns are often set in high school. Thus the growing use of alcohol by adolescents and even preadolescents and the high rate of misuse and abuse are of increasing concern. An estimated 1.3 million teenagers and preteens drink to excess. Though casual drinking is found among all groups of teenagers, problem drinking is found more often among students who also engage in other types of deviant behavior, who value and expect achievement less and esteem independence more than nondrinkers, and who are more tolerant of deviant behavior in others. Girls with drinking problems are likely to have parent problems.

Answers: _____

_____

_____

2. *Questions:* What is pollution? Why does it occur? How big a problem is it?

POLLUTION

Pollution involves the contamination of the environment by wastes or other substances that have a damaging effect upon public health and ecosystems. Within the United States, more than 71 billion gallons of waste chemicals from ammonia to zinc are generated by industry each year. According to the Environmental Protection Agency, up to 90 percent of this chemical debris is improperly disposed of in open pits and ponds or leaky barrels. A report of the Office of Technology Assessment says that more than ten thousand disposal sites for hazardous waste require cleanup on a priority basis to protect the public. It estimates that the total cost of cleaning up these sites could approach $100 billion. Hazardous sites contain toxic chemicals, metals, and other substances that contaminate water sources and pose health hazards. For example, some eight hundred families had to leave Niagara's Love Canal area in 1979 after health experts linked unusually high rates of illness and death there to chemicals leaking from an old industrial dump.

Answers: _____

_____

_____

Part B: Using words such as *what, why, who, which, in what ways,* and *how,* write two meaningful questions for each textbook head that follows.

Our Changing Life Span   a. _____

b. _____

Children of Divorce   a. _____

b. _____

Corporate Cover-Ups   a. _____

b. _____

Industrial Revolution   a. _____

b. _____

Part C: Scrambled together in the list that follows are three textbook headings and three subheadings for each of the headings. Write the headings in the lettered blanks (A, B, C) and write the appropriate subheadings in the numbered blanks (1, 2, 3).

Advertising Media	Drug Abuse	Hypnosis
Sleep	Problems of Adolescence	Juvenile
Dropping Out of	Meditation	Delinquency
School	Direct Mail	Altered States of
Television	Magazines	Consciousness

A. _____

(1) _____

(2) _____

(3) _____

B. _____

(1) _____

(2) _____

(3) _____

C. _____

(1) _____

(2) _____

(3) _____

SKILL 4: RECOGNIZING SIGNAL WORDS

Signal words help you, the reader, follow the direction of a writer's thought. They are like signposts on the road that guide the traveler. Common signal words show emphasis, addition, comparison or contrast, illustration, and cause and effect.

EMPHASIS WORDS

Among the most valuable signals for you to know are *emphasis words,* through which the writer tells you directly that a particular idea or detail is especially important. Think of such words as red flags that the author is using to make sure you pay attention to an idea. Look over the following list, which contains some typical words showing emphasis.

important to note	especially valuable	the chief factor
most of all	most noteworthy	a vital force
a significant factor	remember that	above all
a primary concern	a major event	a central issue
the most substantial issue	the chief outcome	a distinctive quality
a key feature	the principal item	especially relevant
the main value	pay particular attention to	should be noted

Activity

Circle the one emphasis signal in each of these selections. Note the example.

Example

The (safest and most effective solution) to the various approaches to sex education is obviously a course of compromise. Certain sexual needs should be permitted expression; unadorned information about the physiological and psychological aspects of sex should be presented to all; and the Judeo-Christian traditions within which we live must be understood and dealt with sensibly in the framework of present-day society.

1. Although the resources of our world are limited, the wants of people are not. Indeed, one of the most important assumptions of economics is that total human wants can never be satisfied. No matter how much we have, we seem to want more. As people's incomes increase, so does their desire for more and better goods and services.

2. Chronic air pollution is expensive to the American public, costing us dearly in terms of both money and health. Air pollution causes buildings and automobiles to deteriorate. Our poisoned air damages crops, livestock, roads, and metals and forces huge cleaning bills for everything from dusty draperies to soot-blackened buildings. It is especially in terms of health, however, that pollution hurts. It is estimated that breathing the air of New York City is the equivalent of smoking two packs of cigarettes a day.

3. To be happy, adolescents must be realistic about the achievements they are capable of, about the social acceptance they can expect to receive, and about the kind and amount of affection they will receive. Of the three, social acceptance is the most crucial. Well-accepted adolescents will automatically receive affection from those who accept them, and their achievements will win approval if not acclaim.

4. In practice, a deficiency of just one nutrient, such as protein, is not generally seen. More likely, a combination of protein and calorie malnutrition will occur. Protein and calorie deficiency go hand in hand so often that public health officials have given a name to the whole spectrum of disease conditions that range between the two—*protein-calorie malnutrition* (PCM). This is the world's most widespread malnutrition problem, killing millions of children every year.

ADDITION WORDS

Addition words tell you that the writer's thought is going to continue in the same direction. He or she is going to add on more points or details of the same kind. Addition words are typically used to signal enumerations, as described on pages 320–329.

Look over the following addition words.

also	first of all	last of all	and
another	for one thing	likewise	second
finally	furthermore	moreover	the third reason
first	in addition	next	

Activity

Read the selections that follow. Circle the *three* major addition words in the first passage and the *five* major addition words in the second passage.

1.   Despite favorable surface conditions, there were throughout the 1920s defects in the American economy. First, some major industries did not experience the general prosperity which characterized most of the economy. Meager farm income meant that farmers lacked purchasing power to buy their share of the increasing output of goods and services. Coal, textiles, and shoes were among other industries which suffered from low profit margins. Moreover, while employment rose during the 1920s, the biggest gains were in the low-paid service trades rather than in those industries where earnings were high. Furthermore, the condition of American foreign trade was not as healthy as it appeared.

2.   Here are ways to take some of the danger out of smoking. First of all, choose a cigarette with less tar and nicotine. The difference between brands (including those with filters) can be as much as two to one, even more. See how much you can reduce your tar and nicotine intake by switching. Also, don't smoke your cigarette all the way down. You get the most tar and nicotine from the last few puffs because the tobacco itself acts as a filter. Smoke halfway and you get only about 40 percent of the total tar and nicotine. The last half of the cigarette will give you 60 percent. Another help is to take fewer draws on each cigarette. Just reduce the number of times you puff on each cigarette and you'll cut down on your smoking without really missing it. In addition, you should reduce your inhaling. Remember, you're not standing on a mountain gulping in fresh air; so don't welcome it with open lungs. Don't inhale as deeply; take short shallow drags. Practice on a big cigar. Finally, you should smoke fewer cigarettes each day. For some people this is easy, but for others it may be the most difficult step of all. Don't think of it as cutting down; think of it as postponing. It's always easier to postpone a cigarette if you know you'll be having one later. Carry your cigarettes in a different pocket; at work, keep them in a desk drawer or a locker—any place where you can't reach for one automatically. The trick is to change your habit patterns.

COMPARISON OR CONTRAST WORDS

Comparison words signal that the author is pointing out a similarity between two subjects. They tell you that the second idea is like the first one in some way. Look over the following comparison words.

like	just as	in the same way	similarly
likewise	in like manner	alike	equally
just like	in a similar fashion	similarity	as

Contrast words signal a change in the direction of the writer's thought. They tell you that the author is pointing out a difference between two subjects or statements. Look over the following contrast words.

but	yet	variation	on the other hand
however	differ	still	conversely
in contrast	difference	on the contrary	otherwise

Activity

Circle the *one* comparison and the *one* contrast signal in each passage.

1.   Sleep has always been a fascinating topic. We spend about one-third of our adult life sleeping. Most animals sleep in a similar fashion—they collapse and relax their muscles. In contrast, birds and horses sleep upright, with their antigravity muscles at work.

2.   Between 1860 and 1910, some 23 million foreigners migrated to America. Just as before the Civil War, most of them came in search of better economic opportunities. But there were new forces at work in the United States and Europe which interacted to attract ever-increasing numbers of immigrants.

3.   Premarital sex does not always result from a desire for intimacy. Peer pressure also seems to be an important factor. For young males, sexual intercourse is often considered a way to prove their manliness. In like manner, young females believe that sexual intimacy will prove they are sexy and desirable. Several studies have found that young women with a poor self-image sometimes use sex as a way to feel better about themselves. On the other hand, females who plan to attend college are less likely to be sexually intimate than females who do not plan to go to college.

4.   The steadily increasing flow of women into the labor force was caused, then, by a number of economic factors. And just as these economic changes were occurring, attitudes were changing as well. Many women no longer felt that being a full-time homemaker was providing them with an adequate sense of fulfillment and self-worth. Still, many career ladders have remained frustratingly difficult for women to climb.

ILLUSTRATION WORDS

Illustration words tell you that an example or illustration will be given to make an idea clear. Such words are typically used in textbooks that present a number of definitions and examples of those definitions (see pages 313–319). Look over the following illustration words.

for example	specifically	for instance
to illustrate	once	such as

Activity

Circle the one illustration signal in each selection below.

1.   One purpose for incorporating sexual themes or pictorial material into advertisements is to attract consumers' attention to the ad. However, evidence suggests that use of such material may not always have an easily predictable or desired effect. For example, one study found nonsexual and sexual-romantic themes to have a greater influence on consumers' attention than did nudity.

2.   An interesting point about role playing is the way middle-years and adolescent youngsters play the role of being their age. One eight-year-old boy, for instance, avidly collected baseball cards and kept track of games and team standings in the sports pages in accordance with the mores of his neighborhood, even though he had never seen a baseball game or expressed the slightest interest in attending one.

3.   Many problems, of course, do not lend themselves to straightforward strategies but rely more on the use of flexible and original thinking. Psychologists sometimes refer to this type of thinking as *divergent* thinking, in contrast to *convergent* thinking. A problem such as a math problem requires convergent thinking—it has only one solution or very few solutions. Problems that have no single correct solution and require a flexible, inventive approach call for divergent thinking.

4.   Short-term memory is like your attention span. If you're distracted, you'll forget whatever is in short-term memory. This can be a nuisance sometimes, but it helps to preserve sanity. Suppose that you remembered every trivial transaction you were involved in all day long. Such information would interfere with your ability to go on with other activities and to take in new material. To illustrate, if you were waiting on tables and could not put the orders of the previous ten customers out of your mind after they had left the restaurant, you would have a hard time remembering the orders of your current customers.

CAUSE-AND-EFFECT WORDS

Cause-and-effect words signal that the author is going to describe results or effects. Look over the following cause-and-effect words.

because	reason	since
therefore	effect	as a result
so that	thus	if . . . then
cause	consequently	result in

Activity

Circle the *one* cause-and-effect word or words in each of the following passages.

1.   One study of the criminal justice system found that in one year over 800,000 felonies were committed in the city. About 104,000 people were arrested and only 1,000 were imprisoned. The great majority got off "scot free" because many victims refused to testify. When people call the police, they often do so to frighten the offender and show their anger; they cool off when it comes to giving testimony that will send the person to prison.

2.   Thirty years ago, coal miners and workers in cotton mills accepted cancer of the lung as part of life. In a vague way they knew that longtime workers got short of breath and coughed up blood, and they wrote folk songs about brown lung disease. But as a result of a new awareness about occupational diseases and a social movement against cotton dust and coal dust, an accepted fact of life was transformed into an unacceptable illness.

3.   "The hamburger end of the fast-food industry is facing the long-awaited problem of saturation," says analyst Michael Culp at the brokerage firm of Bache Halsey Stuart Shields. "It's increasingly difficult to open more restaurants, and it's harder to sell more hamburgers." Thus, to maintain their growth momentum, the industry's big names are moving aggressively to steal each other's customers, enlarge their menus, and spawn new fast-food concepts.

4.   There are several possible explanations why retail prices are set to end on certain odd or even numbers. The practice is supposed to have started many years ago when retailers priced products so that clerks were forced to record the sale and make change. This discouraged the clerks from pocketing the money from sales. Some people believe that the practice of odd-even pricing continues today because consumers view these prices as bargains. If the price of the shirt is only $14.95, then they are able to spend "less than $15 for a shirt."

PRACTICE IN RECOGNIZING SIGNAL WORDS

Activity 1

Below are some of the signal words that are most often used by writers. Place each word under its proper heading.

for example	in addition
therefore	for instance
moreover	just as
most important	consequently
but	most significant
also	however
differ	such as
alike	similarly
as a result	especially valuable

Emphasis

_____

_____

_____

Addition

_____

_____

_____

Comparison

_____

_____

_____

Contrast

_____

_____

_____

Illustration

_____

_____

_____

Cause and Effect

_____

_____

_____

Activity 2

Circle the signal words in the selections that follow. The number and kind of signal words you should look for are indicated at the start of each selection.

1. One cause-and-effect signal; one contrast signal.

Many of the restless and dissatisfied sons and daughters of these middle-, upper-middle-, and upper-class homes had never known want or poverty. Consequently, they could not understand their parents' emphasis upon money, status, and work. Parents, on the other hand, could not understand how some of their children could be indifferent, even hostile, to formal education and preparation for work.

2. One emphasis signal; one illustration signal; one contrast signal; one addition signal.

One of the most persistent desires of human beings has been to indulge in mood-changing and pleasure-giving practices. For instance, diverse cultures have engaged in the drinking of alcoholic beverages of all descriptions. But as with most pleasures, overindulgence can be harmful to oneself and others. Also, not everyone agrees that drinking or using other mood modifiers should be an accepted pleasure.

3. One emphasis signal; one contrast signal; one cause-and-effect signal.

The greatest value of play technique is in the study of personality. Children often cannot or will not explain themselves in the first person. However, they may reveal much of their inner lives in play. The child who will not tell about his or her own fears and conflicts may readily project these feelings onto dolls. Feelings of rejection, insecurity, mixed attitudes about parents, repressed hatred, fears, and aggressions may all be freely revealed in play. As a result, the play technique, when properly handled, offers opportunities for understanding the child that are otherwise difficult to create.

4. Two cause-and-effect signals; four addition signals; one contrast signal.

As you are well aware, bureaucracies, while designed for maximal efficiency, are notorious for their inefficiences. In practice, Weber's ideal form of bureaucracy is not achieved, for a number of reasons. First, human beings do not exist just for organizations. People track all sorts of mud from the rest of their lives with them into bureaucratic arrangements, and they have a great many interests that are independent of the organization. Second, bureaucracies are not immune to social change. When such changes are frequent and rapid, the pat answers supplied by bureaucratic regulations and rules interfere with a bureaucracy's rational operation. Third, bureaucracies are designed for the "average" person. However, in real life people vary in intelligence, energy, zeal, and dedication so that they are not in fact interchangeable in the day-to-day functioning of organizations. And fourth, in a bureaucracy each person considers anything that falls outside his or her province to be someone else's problem. Consequently, bureaucrats find it easy to evade responsibility.

■ **Review Test**

Signal words have been removed from each of the following textbook excerpts and placed above it. Fill in the missing signal word or words in the answer spaces provided.

Note that you will have to read each passage carefully to see which words logically fit in each answer space.

1. *As a result   For instance   Yet   also   However*

One of the most common and most inappropriate standards that we use for judging others is ourselves. _____, the policeman-father horrified at finding that his son's ambition is to be a poet is a common enough joke. We _____ hear a joke about the poet-father horrified to find that his son's ambition is to become a policeman. _____, the joke is not so funny to them. The father suffers the bitterness of having his expectations violated, and the son suffers the bitterness of being condemned by someone else's rules. Many of us know what it is like to be on the other side—to be declared a disappointment after choosing to be different from someone (a parent, say) who cared about us. _____ we often repeat the error in our own adulthood. We try to make people over into ourselves. We expect them to enjoy the music we enjoy, to support the political candidate we support, to see things *our* way. _____, we violate the other person's rights as an individual, and we condemn ourselves to frustration, for the other person can never be turned into a duplicate of ourselves.

2. *important   Consequently   However   For example*

Many Americans view gambling, prostitution, public drunkenness, and use of marijuana as victimless crimes in which there is no "victim" other than the offender. _____, there has been pressure from some groups to decriminalize certain activities. Such groups believe that decriminalization is an _____ step to freeing up the resources of the overburdened criminal justice system. _____, opponents of decriminalization insist that such offenses do indeed bring harm to innocent victims.

_____, a person with a drinking problem can become abusive to a spouse or children; a compulsive gambler may steal in order to pursue this obsession.

3. *One   For example   Because   Finally   Another   important*

In an ideal world, we could eliminate all physical and mental distractions.

In the real world, however, this is not possible. _____ we think so much faster than a speaker can talk, it's easy to let our attention wander while we listen. Whenever you find this happening, it is

_____ that you make a conscious effort to pull your mind back to what the speaker is saying. Then force it to stay there.

_____ way to do this is to think a little ahead of the speaker— try to anticipate what will come next. _____ way to keep your mind on a speech is to review mentally what the speaker has already said and

make sure you understand it. _____, listen between the lines and assess what a speaker implies verbally or says nonverbally with body

language. _____, suppose a speaker is introducing someone to an audience. The speaker says, "It gives me great pleasure to present to you my very dear friend, Mrs. Smith." But the speaker doesn't shake hands with Mrs. Smith. He doesn't even look at her—just turns his back and leaves the podium. Is Mrs. Smith really his "very dear friend"? Certainly not.

4. *Still   But   As a result   Yet   Second   First*

Adolf Hitler was a short, dark man who believed that the tall, blond "Aryan" race was infinitely superior to all others and had to maintain its

purity. _____ his view neglected some uncomfortable facts.

_____, there is no such thing as a "pure" race, and certainly

no such thing as an "Aryan" race. _____, it is a matter of scientific fact that interbreeding between different human populations is apt to produce offspring that are healthier than either parental stock.

_____, Hitler's theories fired Germany with a sense of national identity—and led to gas chambers and concentration camps, to the

murder of up to six million Jews, and to a global war. _____, racist ideology was made utterly disreputable, and few people or governments today, whatever their private attitudes, dare to openly endorse a racist

attitude. _____ it is worth noting that the United States fought Hitler with a racially segregated army and that German prisoners of war ate in canteens in which black American soliders were refused service.

SKILL 5: RECOGNIZING MAIN IDEAS IN PARAGRAPHS AND SHORT SELECTIONS

THE TWO BASIC PARTS OF A PARAGRAPH

Almost every effective communication of ideas consists of two basic parts: (1) a point is made, and (2) evidence is provided to support that point. The purpose of textbooks is to communicate ideas, and they typically do so by using the same basic structure: A point is advanced and then supported with specific reasons, details, and facts. You will become a better reader by learning to look for and take advantage of this basic structure used in textbooks.

Activity

To make sure that you understand the concept of two basic parts in the communication of ideas, take a few minutes to do the following. Make a point about anything at all and then provide at least two bits of specific evidence to support that point. Here are examples.

Point: I dislike the fast-food restaurant in my town.

Support: 1. The roast beef sandwiches have a chemical taste.
             2. Prices are high—for example, 80 cents for a small soda.

Point: My neighbors are inconsiderate.

Support: 1. They allow their children to play on my lawn.
             2. They often have their stereo on loud late at night.

Point: There are many inexpensive ways to save energy.

Support: 1. Install a water-saver plug in your showerhead.
             2. Turn down the thermostat of your hot water heater to 120 degrees.

Point: Marijuana should not be legalized.

Support: 1. Some people who don't use it now will begin using it because of its availability.
             2. Legalization will give a stamp of social approval that no mind-altering drug deserves.

Now write your own point and support for that point:

Point: _____

Support: 1. _____

             _____

             2. _____

             _____

Many textbook paragraphs that you read will be made up of the same two basic parts. The point is usually expressed in one sentence called a *main-idea,* or *topic, sentence.* The other sentences in the paragraph contain specific details that support or develop the main-idea sentence. Learning how to quickly recognize these two basic parts is sure to increase your reading comprehension.

Activity

Read the following textbook paragraph and see if you can identify the two major parts. Underline the main idea and put numbers in front of each reason that supports the main idea.

> Changes are occurring in the traditional nine-to-five workday. Many employers are exploring new options, such as flextime, compressed workweeks, and job sharing. With flextime, employees have a choice of starting and stopping times for their workdays. As long as they are present during a midday core period of six hours, they can choose to arrive any time between 7 and 9 A.M. and leave any time between 3 and 5 P.M. Compressed workweeks are another option. In this scheme, employees work longer shifts but fewer days. In one bank's computer department, employees work three twelve-hour days, at the end of which they have a four-day "weekend." Shared jobs are also becoming more popular. Two employees split the hours, work, and benefits of a single full-time job—a situation ideal for parents of young children and others who do not want a full-time job. Alternatives such as these may soon help solve the problems of rush-hour commuting and child care as well as increase employee morale.

The main idea is expressed in the first sentence, and the supporting ideas follow. The outline that follows shows clearly the two basic parts of the paragraph:

Changes are occurring in the traditional nine-to-five workday.
(1) Flextime
(2) Compressed workweeks
(3) Job sharing

THE VALUE OF FINDING THE MAIN IDEA

Finding the main idea is a key to understanding a paragraph or short selection. Once you identify the main idea or general point that an author is making, everything else in the paragraph should click into place. You will know what point is being made and what evidence is being provided to support that point. You will see the parts (the supporting material in the paragraph) in relation to the whole (the main idea).

If the main idea is difficult and abstract, you may want to read all the supporting details carefully to help increase your comprehension. If the main idea is easily understood, you may be able to skip the supporting details or read them over quickly, since they are not needed to comprehend the point.

The main idea is often located in the first sentence of a paragraph. You should thus pay special attention to that sentence when reading a paragraph.

However, the main-idea sentence may also be at the end, in the middle, or any other place in the paragraph. On occasion, the main idea of a paragraph may appear in slightly different words in two or more sentences in the paragraph—for example, in the first and last sentences. In other cases, the main idea in one paragraph will serve as the central thought for several paragraphs that follow or precede it. Finally, at times the main idea will not be stated directly at all, and the reader will have to provide it by combining parts of several sentences or by looking closely at the evidence presented.

One way to help yourself understand a paragraph or short selection is to look for two basic parts: (1) _____ . (2) _____ .

■ *Complete the following sentence:* The main idea most often appears in the _____ sentence of a paragraph.

PRACTICE IN FINDING THE MAIN IDEA

Activity 1

Locate and underline the main idea in each of the paragraphs that follow. The paragraphs are taken from a variety of articles and college textbooks.

To find the main idea, look for a general statement. Then ask yourself, *"Does most of the material in the paragraph support or develop the idea in this statement?"* Get into the habit of using this question as a test for a main idea.

1. During the Depression, money shortages produced important changes in the daily lives of people. Car owners often ran their automobiles until they simply defied repair. Children's college educations were postponed because parents could not pay even modest tuition charges of less than $100 in state-supported institutions. Trips to the doctor and dentist were delayed until a major emergency forced a family to seek medical attention. Even with federal food distribution after 1933, millions of families had inadequate diets. What made the lack of money and resulting poverty tolerable was that the condition was so widespread.

2. The very idea of a fire in a crowded building is enough to frighten most people. And with good reason: all too often, the cry of "Fire!" causes people to stampede to the nearest exit, trampling each other on the way. Fear seems to break down normal rational behavior. The result is unnecessary injury. Research studies have duplicated this panic behavior. In one experiment several people were given strings to hold, each of which was attached to a spool inside a bottle. The bottleneck was only large enough for one spool at a time to be removed. Told to get the spools out before the bottle filled with water, everyone tried to remove his or her spool at the same time. The resulting traffic jam kept everyone from getting the spool out in time. Even worse jams were produced when the experimenters threatened their subjects with electric shocks if they did not get their spools out before the bottle filled.

3. In 1980, more than 25 million people in the United States were sixty-five years of age or older, or 11.3 percent of our total population. Each census during this century has found the elderly to make up an increasingly larger share of the total population. In fact, this growth has far outpaced the percentage increase of the population generally, and if present trends continue, those fifty-five and over could account for 21 percent of the population by the year 2000. Thus, statistics negate a long-held concept that the United States is a nation of young people and is getting younger.

4. The term *integrity* essentially refers to being honest with oneself and others. But even on a simple level, being honest is not always easy. Suppose your friend asks you if you like her new hairstyle. Even though you may not think it becoming, it may not be very diplomatic to say, "If you really want to know, I think it looks awful." For such a statement would be far from reassuring and would be of little positive value. Perhaps a more diplomatic and supportive answer would be simply, "I would like to get used to it before I render an opinion." If your opinion remains negative, you can tell her your true feelings at a later time—perhaps suggesting an alternative hairstyle that you think would be more attractive. But even here, the answer is not easy; for the moment a person evades the truth, he or she tends to initiate a process of deception which may make a satisfying relationship impossible.

Activity 2

Following each paragraph below are four general statements. Circle the letter of the statement that best expresses the main idea of the paragraph. The statement you choose should be supported by all or most of the material in the paragraph.

1. Leaving no stone unturned in their search for the killer of two Atlanta boys in the early 1980s, the Atlanta police turned to psychics. But after hundreds of psychic visions had been scrutinized, the murderer remained at large until, later, the case was solved through tireless police work. Las Vegas casinos skim off only 1.4 percent of money bet at the tables. So a psychic who could beat chance by even 3 percent could make as much profit from the game as the house normally does. But casino owners who, in a sense, perform ESP experiments every night of the week, worry little about people who can predict or influence the roll of the dice. The casinos continue to operate, showing, as always, the expected return. Is there, in all the world, a single psychic who can discern the contents of a sealed envelope, move remote objects, or read others' minds? If so, magician James Randi will be surprised—and poorer. For nearly twenty years, he has been offering $10,000 to anyone who can perform just one such feat. To date, nearly six hundred would-be psychics have inquired, fifty-seven of whom submitted to a test. All have failed.

   a. Psychics who perform for profit are fakes.
   b. The use of psychics in police investigations has a history of failure.
   c. Scientists refuse to believe in the existence of ESP.
   d. Little scientific evidence exists to support a belief in ESP.

2. It has been estimated that over 98 percent of American households have at least one television set, and more than half have several. The average American household has the television turned on over six and three-quarters hours a day, or almost half of our waking day. Americans spend more time watching television than doing anything else except sleeping. For some, the time spent watching television equals or surpasses the time spent working. According to media personality and critic Robert MacNeil, "If you fit the statistical averages, by the age of twenty you will have been exposed to something like twenty thousand hours of television. You can add ten thousand hours for each decade you have lived after the age of twenty." By the time you are sixty-five, it is predicted that you will have spent about nine years of your life watching television. Sleeping habits are changed because of TV, mealtimes are altered because of TV, and leisure time is consumed. In fact, one study demonstrated that more than 40 percent of the leisure time we have available to us is spent watching television; that is almost three times the time we spend using all the other mass media.

a. Most American households have at least one TV set.
b. Some people actually watch TV for more hours than they work.
c. TV alters sleeping and eating habits.
d. To a great degree, TV has affected the structure and makeup of daily life.

3. What kind of illness would civilized people find so repulsive that they would reject the sufferers in the most barbaric fashion and brand them with a stigma that would remain even if a cure were achieved? These unfortunates— the mentally ill—used to be scorned and burned, but in more enlightened times we have built backwoods fortresses for them, presumably to protect ourselves from contagion. They have been executed as witches, subjected to exorcisms, chained, or thrown into gatehouses and prisons to furnish horrible diversion for the other prisoners. In some countries they were gathered together and placed on a "ship of fools" and shipped off to uninhabited lands where they were left to wander on their own. The methods recommended by Celsus, a first-century Roman scholar, established the pattern of treatment for the years to come: "When he [the mentally ill person] has said or done anything wrong, he must be chastised by hunger, chains, and fetters." In line with that approach, throughout human history the mentally ill have been subjected to misguided, cruel, sadistic, and fear-based treatment ranging from burning at the stake to banishment from society.

a. Mentally ill people are now treated in a humane way.
b. The Romans began the pattern of mistreating the mentally ill.
c. Mental illness is only now beginning to be understood.
d. The mentally ill have been mistreated throughout history.

4.   Some scientists consider hostility to represent a biological trait that makes aggressive behavior as inevitable a part of the human condition as fighting over territories is for baboons and other animals. Others, probably a majority, believe that hostility is learned and that it stems from the fact that the child cannot have everything he wants. Some of his desires are bound to be frustrated by the rules of society and by the conflicting desires of other people. He cannot always eat when he wants to. He has to learn to control his drive for elimination except when he is in the bathroom. He cannot have the toy that another child owns and is playing with. His mother cannot spend all her time catering to his whims. Other children, bigger than he, push him around.

a. Aggressive behavior is an inevitable part of the human condition.
b. Some scientists believe the hostility motive is biological, but many believe it is learned.
c. A child cannot always have everything he wants.
d. The hostility motive is learned.

Activity 3

Do one or both of the following assignments, as directed by your instructor.

1.   In the model textbook chapter on pages 141–185, locate four different paragraphs in which the main idea is clearly expressed in one sentence. On a separate sheet of paper, write down the page of this book on which each paragraph appears, the first five words of each paragraph you have chosen, and the full sentence within the paragraph that expresses the main idea.

2.   In an article or textbook, locate four different paragraphs in which the main idea is clearly expressed in one sentence. Make copies of the paragraphs (using the copying machine in your library), underline the main-idea sentences, and hand in the paragraphs to your instructor.

■ Review Test

Locate and underline the main-idea sentence in each selection. Then put the number of each main-idea sentence in the space provided at the left.

_____   1. ^{1}The San Francisco earthquake of 1906 was America's most deadly but not the strongest. ^{2}The "Good Friday earthquake" in 1964 in Alaska was one of the strongest ever recorded on earth. ^{3}Geologists estimate that this earthquake released energy about equal to that from the explosion of 31.5 million tons of TNT. ^{4}The Alaskan earthquake was so powerful that the tops of trees near the earthquake's center were snapped off. ^{5}Land was raised and lowered a meter or so (about three feet) over an area of 140,000 square kilometers (56,000 square miles). ^{6}Half of Alaska shook quite noticeably. ^{7}In Texas, water in swimming pools sloshed. ^{8}The entire earth vibrated slightly.

_____ 2.   [1]Education for handicapped children has come a long way since the family of deaf and blind Helen Keller had to travel to distant cities and eventually hire a private tutor for their daughter. [2]But many handicapped children still are not receiving the education that could help them to become fully functioning members of society. [3]It has been estimated that about half the nation's seven million handicapped youngsters are not being educated adequately. [4]These children—about 10 percent of the schoool-aged population—are deaf, blind, mentally retarded, physically deformed, emotionally disturbed, speech-impaired, or afflicted with other problems. [5]Some do not attend school at all because their local districts are unable or unwilling to meet their needs. [6]Some are placed in regular classes where they cannot keep up or are channeled into the wrong kind of special classes.

_____ 3.   [1]Of course, the disk jockey's job is far from easy. [2]DJs do much more than simply chatter idly. [3]They may also select recordings from a station playlist, manipulate turntables, carts, and audio boards, as well as ready commercial copy or scripts. [4]In addition, these days DJs' jobs are far from secure. [5]Each time a station changes its format, it usually also finds it necessary to hire new on-the-air personalities. [6]DJ hours are long; they are filled with repetition and can be tiring. [7]One young disk jockey lost his first job when after several hours on the air he could no longer stand to listen to a certain soft-drink commercial that he was playing constantly. [8]During one of his air checks, or talk sessions between records, he explained to his listening audience that that particular soft drink would eat the paint right off a car. [9]He was fired so swiftly that his replacement went on the air immediately after the next record!

_____ 4.   [1]You have probably had the experience of trying to obtain directions to a particular place in an unfamiliar neighborhood. [2]When you think you are at least in the right area, you stop a pedestrian and ask, "How do you get to the stadium from here?" [3]If he or she says, "Go three blocks north, turn to the right, and it's down a block or two on the left-hand side," you can probably process the information easily enough and will reach your destination with little difficulty. [4]But suppose you ask for directions and the local character says to you, "Well, let's see, go three blocks north, turn right at the diner, go five blocks until you come to a Texaco station, turn left until you hit the third stop sign, turn left again . . ." [5]If you are like most people, you will probably go part of the way, wonder where you are, and then seek new directions. [6]Regardless of how well you listen, you can be overloaded with details.

SKILL 6:
KNOWING HOW
TO OUTLINE

The five skills already discussed will help you locate and understand the main ideas in your textbooks. Outlining is another skill that will improve your reading comprehension as well as provide additional benefits. Outlining is an organizational skill that develops your ability to think in a clear and logical manner. It will help as you prepare textbook and classroom notes. It will also help as you plan speeches that you have to give or papers that you have to write. You have already learned a good deal about outlining in marking enumerations, noting relationships between heads and subheads, and identifying main ideas in paragraphs. You will now receive some direct practice in this important skill.

A SAMPLE OUTLINE

In an outline, you reduce the material in a selection to its main and supporting points and details. Special symbols are used to show how the points and details relate to one another.

To understand the outlining process, read the selection on the opposite page and study the outline of the selection. Then look carefully at the comments that follow.

All homeowners can take action if they are serious about saving on energy costs. Those with more than a hundred dollars to spend should consider any of the following steps. First, the sidewalls and especially the ceiling should be fully insulated. Proper insulation can save 30 percent or more of a heating or cooling bill. Next, storm windows and doors should be installed. They provide an insulating area of still air that may reduce energy loss by 10 percent or more. Finally, a homeowner might consider installing a solar water-heating system. Four factors in such a decision are geographic location, sunlight available, energy costs in the area, and the construction of the house.

Homeowners with less than a hundred dollars to spend can take many energy-saving steps as well. To begin with, two kinds of inexpensive sealers can be used to reduce energy leaks around the house. Caulking will seal cracks around outside windows and door frames, and at corners of the house. Weather stripping can be applied to provide a weathertight seal between the frame and moving parts of doors and windows. Another inexpensive step is to check that a home heating or cooling system is clean. A dirty or clogged filter, for example, can make a furnace or an air conditioner work much harder to heat or cool a house. Next, a "low-flow" shower head can be used to reduce hot water use. A special shower head can be purchased or a small plastic insert available at a hardware store can be added to a regular head to limit water flow. Finally, blinds and drapes can be used to advantage throughout the year. In winter they can be closed at night to reduce heat loss. In summer they can be closed during the day to keep the house cooler. These and other relatively inexpensive steps can produce large savings.

Title ————→ Ways to Save on Home Energy Costs

Main ————→ A. Spending more than a hundred dollars
points at
the margin   1. Insulate sidewalls and ceiling
      2. Add storm windows and doors
      3. Consider solar water-heating system depending on:

Supporting
ideas
indented   a. Geographic location
under main   b. Sunlight available
points   c. Energy costs
        d. Construction of house

   B. Spending less than a hundred dollars
Details   1. Sealers
indented
under   a. Caulking
supporting   b. Weather stripping
ideas   2. Clean heating or cooling system
      3. "Low-flow" shower head
        a. Special shower head
        b. Plastic insert
      4. Blinds and drapes
        a. Winter—close at night
        b. Summer—close during day

POINTS TO NOTE ABOUT OUTLINING

First: The purpose of an outline is both to summarize material and to show the relationships between different parts of the material. An outline is a summary in which letters and numbers are used to mark the main and supporting points and details.

In outlining, a sequence of symbols is used for the different levels of notes. In the outline above, capital letters (A and B) are used for the first level, numbers (1, 2, 3 . . .) are used for the second level, and small letters (a, b, c . . .) for the third level.

Second: Put all the headings at any particular level at the same point in relation to the margin. In the outline above, A and B are both at the margin; 1, 2, and 3 are all indented an equal amount of space from the margin; and a, b, and c are all indented an equal, greater amount of space from the margin.

Third: Most outlines do not need more than two or three levels of symbols. In textbook note-taking, two levels will often do. Use a sequence like the following, with subpoints indented under main points.

1. _____

    a. _____

    b. _____

    c. _____

    d. _____

2. _____

3. _____

    a. _____

    b. _____

    c. _____

4. _____

    a. _____

    b. _____

Fourth: Every outline should have a title (such as "Ways to Save on Home Energy Costs") that summarizes the information in the outline.

Activity

To check your understanding of outlining, answer question 1 and complete the statements in items 2 and 3.

1. Why do you think you should always begin main ideas at the margin?

   _____

   _____

   _____

   _____

2. Supporting ideas must always be _____ main ideas.

3. The material that appears in an outline is summarized in its _____

   _____.

DIAGRAMING

Many students find it helpful at times to use *diagraming* (also known as *mapping*) rather than outlining. In diagraming, you create a visual outline of shapes as well as words. Diagrams usually use circles or boxes that enclose major ideas and supporting details. The shapes are connected with lines to show the connections between ideas.

On the following page are two diagrams of the selection "Ways to Save on Home Energy Costs."

Notice that in the balloon diagram, the main idea is written in the large circle that anchors the entire outline. Each supporting idea occupies one of the balloons attached to the main idea. In the box diagram, the main idea is written in the long box at the top. Below the long box are smaller boxes that contain the supporting ideas.

Activities in this chapter will ask you to use diagrams as well as outlines to make relationships between ideas visually clear. Then, in your own note-taking, you will be able to use either diagrams or outlines, whichever you find more helpful.

Balloon Diagram

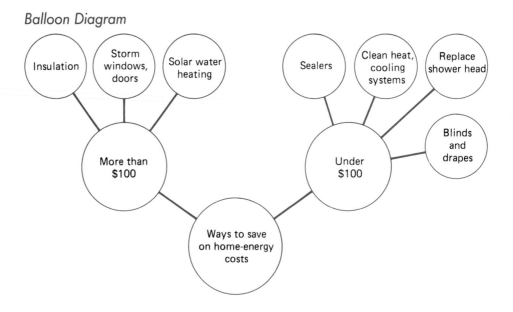

Box Diagram

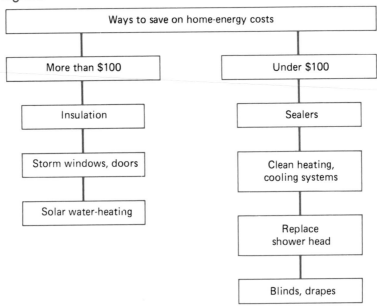

PRACTICE IN OUTLINING AND DIAGRAMING

The following pages provide a series of exercises that will develop your ability to outline and diagram effectively.

Activity 1:
Completing Outlines

Read each of the following selections. Then complete the outline that comes after each selection. Certain items in some outlines have already been added.

Note: In the chapter "Recognizing Enumerations," you practiced making one-level outlines. Here you will practice making two-or-more-level outlines as well.

Selection 1

World War I introduced weapons that were more destructive and more horrifying than any that had ever been known. Aerial bombardment, with planes and zeppelins, was a frightening new invention. In 1903, the Wright brothers' airplane had flown only 120 feet at thirty-five miles per hour; only fifteen years later, airplanes with two-man crews were dropping bombs and firing machine guns from heights of two miles at ninety-five miles per hour. Another new weapon was the tank. The British developed this "secret weapon" in 1916. When it was in the experimental stage, the new weapon was shipped around England disguised as a water tank—the name "tank" stuck. Long-range guns were another deadly development. By 1918, the Germans had a gun that could shell the city of Paris from a distance of seventy-five miles. Poison gas, another innovation, drifted across the fields of trench warfare. New submarines and destroyer ships attacked each other with torpedoes and depth charges. All these new weapons of war made possible a more impersonal style of combat. The soldier of World War I, in many cases, no longer had to face his enemy eye to eye. He could kill the enemy (often including women and children) long-distance.

_____

1. _____

2. _____

3. _____

4. _____

5. _____

Selection 2

The purchase price of a house is not the only cost that buyers must consider. Buying a house is a major transaction that involves search of title, closing costs, property insurance, and special assessments. A title search is done by a title guaranty company in order to see if a piece of property has any encumbrances. When a title search is done, the history of the property is traced back to the original owners to find out if anyone else has a claim to the property. For example, a power company may have obtained the right to place poles on the property. Any restrictions like this are called encumbrances. Closing costs occur when settlement is made on a piece of property. Costs may include lawyers' fees, the commission due a real estate agent, certain taxes that must be paid in advance, and the expenses in filing records. Property insurance is also essential when purchasing a house. Insurance policies are available for flood, fire, and burglary protection. Insurance is also needed to protect the homeowner against lawsuits, especially if someone is injured on the property. Finally, home buyers may have special assessments that will be charged at settlement. They may have to pay for such services as sewers and sidewalks and community parks.

Special Costs in Buying a House

1. _____
2. _____

    a. _____
    b. _____
    c. _____
    d. _____

3. _____

    a. _____
    b. _____
    c. _____
    d. _____

4. _____

    a. _____
    b. _____
    c. _____

Selection 3

Buying toys for children can be somewhat confusing and frustrating for parents as well as for gift givers. Children can show baffling preferences in toys; a favorite is not necessarily expensive or unique or "in." Matching toys carefully to a child's age, however, can help in this dilemma. Children usually fall into several different "toy-preference" age groups. Infants under eighteen months go through two stages. Before they can sit up, they enjoy toys that appeal to the senses, such as colorful mobiles, squeaky rubber toys, or big chewable beads. After they can sit up, babies like "graspable" things like blocks, nesting and stacking toys, and cloth picture books. Children from eighteen months to three years (toddlers) like toys that move (as they're learning to do). Push-pull toys and small tricycles and wagons interest toddlers. Toddlers also like to use their hands. They enjoy modeling clay, finger painting, scribbling with chalk, and banging on toy musical pianos. Between ages three and six, children prefer the fantasy of "make-believe." Costumes, toy theaters, hand puppets, mini-shopping carts with pretend food, play stores, money, and cash registers appeal to this age. From six to nine years, children become interested in the world of work; they like fashion dolls, action figures, and craft and science kits. This is also a good time for action toys—bigger bikes, roller skates, or sleds. Finally, older children from nine to twelve develop specific hobbies and skills. Pick out appropriate model kits, or magic sets, or handicraft kits. For all ages, though individual children may vary, these guidelines should guarantee a toy that is a success.

Toy Preferences of Children _____

1. _____

    a. _____

    b. *After sitting up—"graspable" things* _____

2. *Eighteen months to three years* _____

    a. _____

    b. _____

3. *Three to six—"make-believe" toys* _____

4. _____

    a. _____

    b. _____

5. _____

Activity 2:
Completing Diagrams

Read each of the following selections. Then complete the diagram that comes after each selection.

Selection 1

There are several easy ways to lose weight without feeling deprived. If you drink three cups of coffee a day, simply eliminating milk and sugar from the coffee will save approximately two hundred calories a day. If you cut out two hundred calories a day, you'll lose seventeen pounds in a year! Another way to avoid unnecessary calories is to use nonstick pots and pans. You can melt a large pat of butter to cook your eggs, thereby adding one hundred calories. Or, you can use a nonstick pan and eliminate those calories. Avoiding calorie-laden salad dressings is another easy way to lose weight. One small spoonful of creamy Russian or blue cheese dressing adds up to over one hundred calories. And how many of us are content with just one small spoonful? That "low-calorie" salad can quickly turn into a diet disaster. Substituting diet dressings, or a dash of lemon and pepper, is an easy way to slash calorie intake. One final way to avoid calories is to substitute broiling or baking for frying. The oil used in frying is absorbed by the food, and oil is high in calories. Broiled or baked chicken, for example, is as delicious as fried chicken, and the calorie savings are enormous.

Selection 2

Research psychologists have identified three different kinds of depression. Few of us have not at some time experienced "the blues" because of crises in our lives. This is *normal depression*. Such depression usually clears up by itself in a very short time. But an estimated ten million Americans react to life's problems—most often a loss, disappointment, change, frustration, or threat to identity—with depression deep enough or long-lasting enough to interfere with their functioning. This is *neurotic depression*. Symptoms usually disappear when stress is lifted.

Another six to eight million have medically triggered depression that appears out of the blue, apparently unrelated to life's problems. It may be caused by hereditary factors, hormonal or chemical imbalance, dietary deficiency, or drug or allergic reaction. This *psychotic depression* is more serious and more complex. It is usually divided into two main types: (1) *bipolar depressive disease*, also known as manic-depressive psychosis, in which the individual swings from deep depression to unexplained "highs," during which he or she feels all-powerful and all-wise and becomes difficult to control; (2) *unipolar depressive disease*, in which the patient has bouts of depression and is severely withdrawn and uncommunicative or behaves in an extremely agitated fashion.

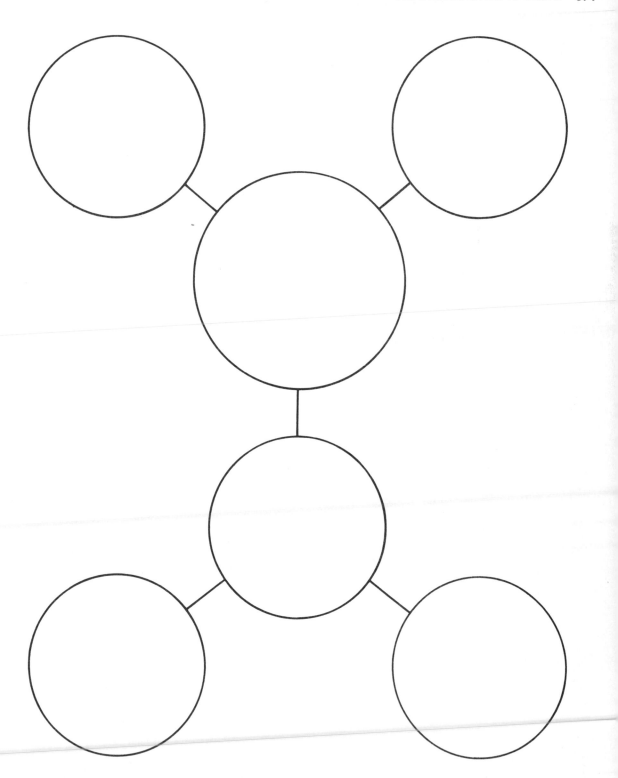

Selection 3

People are becoming more and more reluctant to pay full price for anything. Instead, they have adopted a number of strategies for saving money on their purchases. One is shopping at discount stores. They will patronize catalog showrooms that are like department stores, selling everything for the home or office at 20 to 40 percent off. Or they will go to a specialized cut-rate store that carries anything from cosmetics and over-the-counter drugs to records and tapes to major appliances. Another shopping strategy is visiting factory outlets. People will drive many miles to reach an outlet that features last season's goods. In such stores, first-quality clothing or dinnerware is available at half price. Or they will travel to outlets that feature irregular or damaged merchandise, hoping for even greater savings. Those shoppers who don't go to discount houses or factory outlets wait for sales. Retail establishments, realizing they must attract clientele, now have special weekly sales. They may be called "twelve-hour sales" or "assistant buyers' days," and they offer special markdowns. Another kind of sale centers on holidays. Every holiday, from Lincoln's birthday to Thanksgiving, is marked by a sale to attract parents and children who have the day off from work or school. Finally, there are still the end-of-season clearance sales, when unwanted items are practically given away at 50 to 80 percent reductions. In these ways, shoppers are getting more mileage out of their hard-earned dollars.

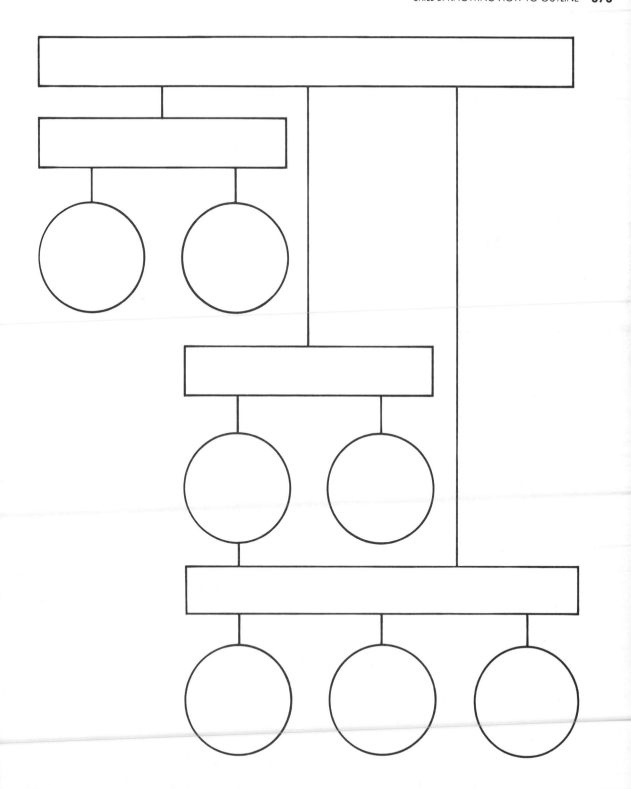

■ **Review Test**

Complete the diagram or outline for each of the following selections.

Selection 1

By the time students reach junior high school (their eighth or ninth year of formal education), they are usually well entrenched in a world of their peers. Parents and teachers assume a secondary place as a source of significant values. What is important is what one's crowd thinks. At this age and on through high school, the crowd is primarily fellow students. Burton R. Clark identifies three types of subcultures to which almost every junior and senior high school student belongs. First is the so-called *fun subculture,* which places utmost emphasis on having a good time. In this subculture, one must have a "good personality" and *savoir-faire* about clothes, automobiles, hangouts, and sports. Books and learning represent drudgery and low status. The second subculture is the *academic,* which places value on being a good student, discussing serious questions and interests of the day, and high educational achievement. This subculture is considerably less popular in most secondary schools than is the fun subculture. The least popular but most publicized student subculture is the *delinquent.* Members of this group have contempt for the school and its faculty in addition to a defiant attitude toward any form of regulation and toward anybody not approved by their crowd.

_____

1. _____

2. _____

3. _____

Selection 2

Most Americans use prescription drugs, and most Americans are extremely careless in their use. To use prescription drugs intelligently, several steps should be followed. First, it is important to know how to store drugs. Different medications should never be mixed in a single container. Even if pills can be distinguished by shape or color, storing them together may lead to dangerous mix-ups in dosage, kind, or amount. Also, cotton should be removed from containers, for it can absorb some of the chemicals in the drugs. High temperatures, too, can damage drugs, so do not store medicines in automobile glove compartments or on sunny windowsills. Consumers should also be aware of the side effects of many prescription medications. Harmful side effects may occur when drugs are mixed with alcohol, for example. Vitamin deficiencies, too, are linked to certain drugs. Most important, perhaps, consumers should not hesitate to ask questions about their prescriptions. They should ask about the drug's generic name as well as its brand name; in many cases, generic drugs are cheaper. They should ask if the medication may be taken simultaneously along with other medications. Many consumers, unaware of drug interactions, do not inform their doctors about previous prescriptions. Finally, they should ask about any precautions that should be taken while using the drug. Is it all right to drive while taking the drug? Should alcohol or certain foods be avoided? Careful use of prescription medicines can allow a drug to help, not hurt, you.

_____

A. _____

    1. _____

    2. _____

    3. _____

B. _____

    1. _____

    2. _____

C. _____

    1. _____

    2. _____

    3. _____

        a. _____

        b. _____

Selection 3

There are two types of smog. The first is a *combination of smoke and fog.* Such combinations occur in cities that burn lots of coal. The droplets of fog combine with the smoke particles. The fog acts like a giant sponge in creating this type of smog. The second type of smog is more common. It is properly called *photochemical smog* and is caused by sunlight reacting with certain pollutants. The chemicals in the exhausts of automobile engines are the biggest troublemakers. One of these chemical pollutants is carbon monoxide. In concentrated form, this odorless, colorless gas is a deadly poison. Another pollutant is nitrogen dioxide, a yellow-brown gas that gives photochemical smog its color. Nitrogen dioxide has a sharp odor that is described as "sweetish." Ozone is the other pollutant that results from the photochemical process. Ozone is colorless, but it has a sharp odor. You may have smelled ozone during an electrical storm or when a piece of electrical equipment short-circuited.

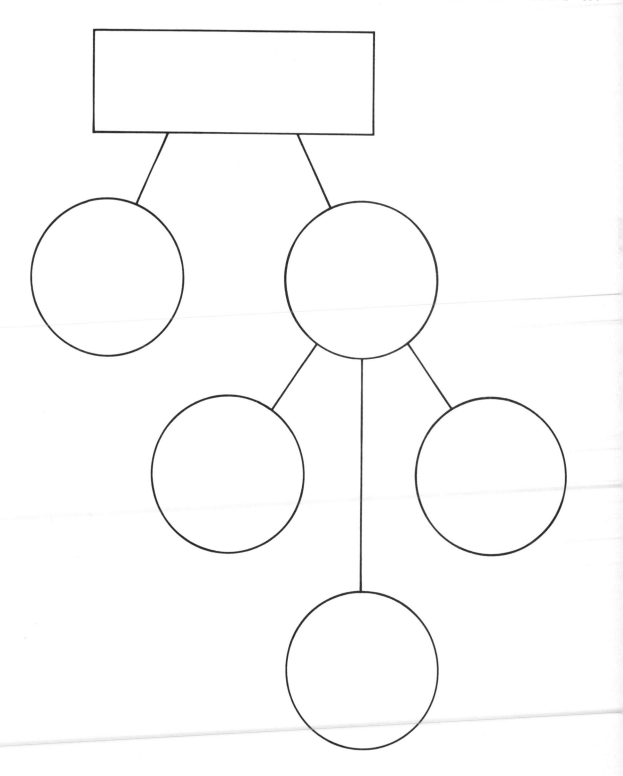

Selection 4

In some ways, there is bound to be some physical decline or slowing down during the years of middle age. A number of signs of aging can be identified. The bone structure, for one thing, stiffens and even shrinks a bit during the course of adulthood. This is the reason why some people may be shorter at their fortieth high school reunion than they were when they were students. Another sign of aging is that skin and muscles begin to lose some elasticity so that, for example, areas of the face and jaws begin to sag. Another sign is the tendency to accumulate more subcutaneous fat, especially in certain areas such as the midriff. There are more sensory defects during the adult years, too. Vision tends to be constant from adolescence to the forties or early fifties, when visual acuity may begin to show signs of decline. However, nearsighted people often are able to see better in middle age than they could as young adults. There is an increased incidence of hearing problems during mid-adulthood, especially hearing loss in the upper frequencies. Long-term exposure to high levels of noise increases the likelihood of hearing loss. Therefore, some factory workers and many city dwellers may be particularly prone to hearing problems in later years.

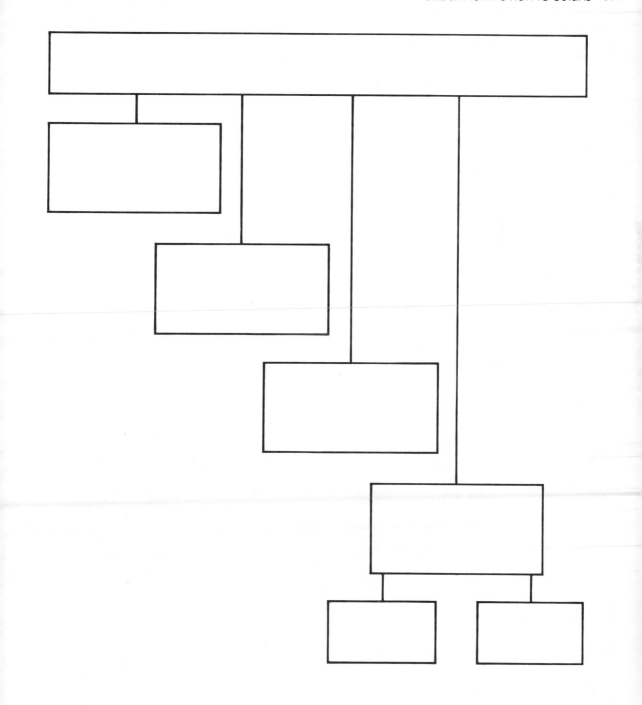

SKILL 7: KNOWING HOW TO SUMMARIZE

To understand the summarizing process, first read the following selection and summary. Then study the points about summarizing that follow.

> In another kind of coping behavior, *rationalization,* an acceptable motive is substituted for an unacceptable one. Put another way, we "make excuses"— we give a different reason from the real one for what we are doing. Rationalization is a common defense mechanism for avoiding the anxiety connected with an unacceptable motive. A student who has sacrificed studying to have a good time may blame his or her failing grades on bad teaching, unfair examinations, or too heavy a work load. A father may beat his child just because he is angry but rationalize it by saying that he is acting for the child's good.

Summary

> *Rationalization—a kind of coping behavior in which an acceptable motive is substituted for an unacceptable one.*
>
> *Ex.—father rationalizes beating child by saying it's for child's good.*

POINTS TO NOTE ABOUT SUMMARIZING

1   A *summary,* like an outline, is a reduction of a large quantity of information to the most important points. Unlike an outline, however, a summary does not use symbols such as A, 1, a, and so on, to indicate the relationships among parts of the original material. The preceding summary includes the most important points—the definition of rationalization and an example that makes clear the definition—but the other material is omitted.

2   Summarizing is helpful because it requires that you thoroughly *understand* the material you are reading. You must "get inside" the material and realize fully what is being said before you can reduce it to a few words. Work in summarizing material will help build your comprehension power. It will also markedly improve your ability to take effective classroom and textbook notes.

3   The length of a summary depends on your *purpose* in summarizing. The shortest possible summary is a title. If your purpose requires more information than that, a one-sentence summary might be enough. Longer passages and different purposes might require longer summaries. For example, in writing a report on an article or book, you might often want to have a summary that is a paragraph or more in length.

In the following practice activities you will be writing title summaries, single- and several-sentence summaries, and one-paragraph summaries. After such varied practice, you should be prepared to write whatever kind of summary you might need to.

■   *Complete the following sentences:* A summary _____ a large quantity of material to the most important points. Unless you fully

_____ the material you are reading, you will not be able to summarize it.

PRACTICE IN SUMMARIZING

Activity 1

The shortest possible summary of a selection is its title or heading. For this activity, circle the letter of the title that best summarizes each selection on the following pages. You should select the title that best answers the question "What is this about?" The title should be as specific and descriptive as possible and at the same time account for all the material in the selection.

1.   It is commonly believed that the poor are lazy people who could work if they were willing. In fact, over 60 percent of the poor consist of children under age fourteen, elderly people over age sixty-four, and people of working age who are ill or in school. Another quarter work but do not earn enough to rise above the poverty line. This leaves less than 15 percent of the poor of working age who do not work, and the vast majority of those are the mothers of young children. When it comes to work, the poor do not look as bad as their reputation, for most of them are too old, too young, too sick, or too busy caring for children to work.

What would be an accurate title for this selection?
a. Poor Children
b. Who Are the Poor?
c. The Working Poor
d. Poor Mothers

2.   Depending on weather conditions, we may or may not worry about drought in any particular year, but regardless of temporary weather conditions, our nation is using water much faster than the supply is being replenished. One-fourth of the water used in America comes from a system of aquifers—underground areas of porous soils in which water has accumulated through the ages. In some cases, such aquifers are covered by hardpan or rock, through which water penetrates only slowly, even during years of abundant rain. Consequently, although our "bank account" of water is very large, it is being overdrawn. In 1950, the nation pumped 21 trillion gallons from underground; now it pumps more than twice that much each year. In fact, each day, 21 billion more gallons are pumped out than enter the underground aquifers. One water planner notes that the rate of depletion in the Midwest differs from place to place but adds, "Some people project that as early as the year 2000, there will be parts of Nebraska with their water supplies so depleted that farming may never return."

What would be an accurate title for this selection?
a. Climate Changes
b. Our Vanishing Water Supply
c. The Coming Drought in the Midwest
d. Sources of Our Water Supply

3.　　　　Trichinosis is a disease caused by eating pork infested with the larvae (developmental stage) of a worm called the trichina. From the intestinal tract of the human body, the worm larvae enter the blood, reach the muscles, and burrow into them. Muscular pain and fever may develop about seven days after eating the pork; the fever may last for several weeks. Even after these early symptoms have subsided, however, the larvae may lie dormant in the muscles for years. In fact, some of the aches and pains of rheumatism may be caused by trichina larvae in the muscles. The government does not inspect pork for the larvae, and there is no effective treatment for the disease. Therefore, as a precaution, pork and pork products (such as sausage) should always be cooked until they are well done; thorough cooking will kill any worms that are present.

What would be an accurate title for this selection?
a.　Cooking Pork
b.　Cause and Prevention of Trichinosis
c.　Avoiding Trichinosis
d.　Worm Larvae Disease

4.　　　　Did you ever have someone's name on the tip of your tongue, and yet you were unable to recall it? When this happens again, don't try to recall it. Do something else for a few minutes, and the name may pop into your head. The name is there, since you have met this person and learned his or her name. It only has to be dug out. The initial effort to recall *primes* the mind, but it is the subconscious activities that go to work to pry up a dim memory. *Forcing* yourself to recall almost never helps because it doesn't loosen your memory; it only tightens it. Students find the *priming method* helpful on examinations. They read over the questions before trying to answer any of them. Then they answer first the ones of which they are most confident. Meanwhile, deeper mental activities in the subconscious mind are taking place; work is being done on the more difficult questions. By the time the easier questions are answered, answers to the more difficult ones will usually begin to come into consciousness. It is often just a question of *waiting* for recall to be loosened up.

What would be an accurate title for this selection?
a.　Memory Techniques
b.　How the Mind Works
c.　Success in Exams
d.　The Priming Method of Memory

Activity 2

Write an accurate heading or title for each of the paragraphs that follow. Each heading should be only a phrase—not a complete sentence. The heading should condense into several words the essential thoughts of each selection. It will be the shortest possible summary of the selection. A good way to proceed is to try to find the fewest words that will answer the question "What is this about?"

Note that you will be doing exactly the kind of summarizing that textbook authors do when they write headings and subheads for their work. The experience of "writing labels" should help you appreciate—and take advantage of—the headings given by textbook authors.

1. Heading: _____

   One good way to start a talk is to say something to wake your audience out of apathy. You could tell a funny anecdote or something shocking. For example, Henry Ward Beecher, the famous preacher, was to give a talk on the evils of blasphemy. His opening words were, "It's a damned hot day." This surely took his audience by surprise. Then, after he had gained his listeners' attention, he paused and then went on to say,"That's what I heard a man say here this afternoon!"

2. Heading: _____

   There has been a significant change in the overall profile of homeless Americans during the last decade. In the past, the homeless were primarily older white males living as alcoholics in skid row areas. However, today's homeless persons are comparatively younger—with an average age in the low thirties—and are more likely to be suffering from mental illnesses. Moreover, along with the rise in the number of homeless men, there has been a dramatic increase in the number of homeless women living on city streets.

3. Heading: _____

   Instead of letting your mind wander or preparing what you are going to say when you have a chance, you can practice and use active listening skills. *Active listening* includes repeating important details to yourself; questioning; paraphrasing; distinguishing among governing idea, main points, and detail; and, in some situations, note-taking. Active listening involves you in the process of determining meaning. Too often people think of the listening experience as a passive activity in which what they remember is largely a matter of chance. In reality, good listening is hard work that requires concentration and willingness to mull over and, at times, verbalize what is said. Good listening requires using mental energy. If you really listen to an entire fifty-minute lecture, for instance, when the lecture is over you will feel tired because you will have put as much energy into listening as the lecturer put into talking.

4. Heading: _____

On the American plains, buffalo were once so numerous that they were counted in the millions. A herd of buffalo could cover the prairie as far as the eye could see. The hoofbeats of an approaching buffalo herd could be heard several miles away. Amazingly, within only a few decades, the vast numbers of buffalo would be reduced to a mere handful by the white man. After railroads reached the plains area, bringing more and more whites, the buffalo were doomed. Special trains would carry passengers into buffalo country; passengers armed with rifles would shoot into the herd from the train windows. The "hunters" did not even collect the buffalo carcasses. Thousands of pounds of buffalo meat and hide were left to rot in the sun. Occasionally the buffalo tongue, a delicacy, would be retrieved. After the carcasses had rotted, local farmers would collect wagonloads of bones, in order to sell them as fertilizer at $5 a ton. The buffalo slaughter was so enormous that one hunter, after witnessing the destruction of a herd, wrote, "A man could have walked twenty miles on their carcasses." By the end of the nineteenth century, this wanton waste had made the buffalo practically extinct.

Activity 3

Your instructor may ask you to condense into a sentence the essential thought of each of the preceding five selections. To do this, first see if there is a sentence that expresses the main idea of the selection. In some cases, it might be all the summary you need. In other cases, you should outline before you summarize. That is, you should locate and number the series of points that back up the main idea. Then put the main idea and the main supporting points into your summary sentence.

Use separate sheets of paper for this activity.

Activity 4

Read the following article (pages 386–387) and then write a one-paragraph summary of 100 to 125 words. Here are some guidelines for summarizing an article:

a   Think about the title for a minute or so. The title often summarizes what the article is about.

b   Consider any subtitle that may appear. The subtitle, caption, or other words in large print under or next to the title often provide a quick insight into the meaning of an article.

c   Note any subheadings that appear in the article. Subheadings provide clues to the article's main points and give an immediate sense of the content of each section.

d   Make an outline of the article before beginning to write.

e   Express the author's ideas in your own words—not the words in the article itself.

f   Do not write an overly detailed summary. Remember that the purpose of a summary is to reduce the original material to its main ideas and essential supporting points.

g   Do not begin your sentences with expressions like ''the author says''; equally important, do not introduce your own opinions into the summary with comments like ''another good point made by the author.'' Instead, concentrate on presenting directly and briefly the author's main points.

WHEN KIDS COME HOME TO AN EMPTY HOUSE
EXPERTS WORRY ABOUT THE EFFECTS OF ''LATCHKEYISM''
AND SUGGEST SOME COUNTERMEASURES.

Wearing the front-door key on a chain around his neck, eleven-year-old Jeremy Cavin comes home from school each day to an empty house.

"Lonely is the word for it," says Jeremy, an only child who is not allowed to have friends over while his parents are at work.

Says Jeremy's father, Bob: "I don't like the situation. I don't think any parent does." But with no suitable after-school programs in their area of North Carolina, the Cavins feel they have no choice. For as long as both of his parents work, Jeremy will be a so-called *latchkey child.*

The label has been around since the nineteenth century, but the number of latchkey kids between the ages of seven and thirteen has burgeoned in recent years. Because of the dramatic increases in one-parent and two-paycheck families, there are now more than two million children who fend for themselves for part of every workday. And with two out of every three mothers expected to work outside the home by the end of this decade, the latchkey legion can only grow larger still.

Until recently, little was known about this phenomenon. Now research is under way, "survival" courses geared to latchkey kids are being offered, and some communities are beginning to come up with attractive alternatives.

Some Real Problems

One of the new studies reveals that some latchkey children face very real emotional problems. Dr. Thomas Long, professor of education at the Catholic University of America, and his wife, Dr. Lynette Long, assistant professor of education at Loyola University, interviewed more than fifty latchkey kids in Washington, D.C. One child who lost her key recalled crying on the front porch for hours until her mother returned from work. Another told of climbing into a chair and clutching her shoe as a possible weapon when she heard suspicious noises outside.

Latchkey children can also suffer from being bored, isolated, and confined, the Longs believe. "Where is play for these kids?" asks Thomas Long. "For years these children are denied a social life at a critical time in their development." Kids left alone at home watched up to seven hours of television a day, according to the Longs' study.

But beyond marathon TV watching, the Longs worry about the possible long-term effects of "latchkeyism": feelings of alienation leading to academic failure, violence, vandalism, and experimentation with drugs and alcohol. Thomas Long says police in his area are seeing more and more latchkey kids in trouble. But he and other experts concede that any conclusive link between latchkey children and delinquency remains hypothetical.

What Can Be Done

What can worried latchkey parents do to minimize the risks? Long suggests that parents help structure empty hours by assigning chores and suggesting a schedule to follow, and by trying to arrange for some after-school activities—scouting, dance lessons, recreation programs—to vary their kids' solo routines. From the comments of children in his study, he also believes that pets can help by providing comfort and companionship in an empty house. Above all, Long suggests that once parents return home, they should put off household duties and "make an extended effort to get into their child's world."

Another study now in progress by Dr. Hyman Rodman, director of the Family Research Center at the University of North Carolina at Greensboro, reveals how nearly twelve hundred latchkey mothers are trying to make the arrangement as *safe* as possible. The women said they worry about fires, forgotten keys, and other frightening possibilities. But most stay in close touch with their children by phone, have a neighbor to turn to in emergencies, and have rules for the kids to follow. Among the most common rules:

No one is allowed in the house, even friends, without prior special permission.

The door is not to be opened when someone knocks unless the child is told beforehand that certain persons can be let in or unless it is someone well known to the family.

Children are given specific tasks which they are expected to do while they care for themselves.

No use of the stove or other electrical appliances, except the TV, radio, or record player, is allowed.

No one who calls on the telephone is to be told by the children that they are alone.

Most latchkey mothers who have these rules told Dr. Rodman they were satisfied, if not happy, with the arrangement. Many believed that their children were learning responsibility and self-reliance.

Activity 5

Write a one-paragraph summary of an article in a weekly or monthly magazine. Identify at the start of the summary the title and author of the work. Also, include in parentheses the date of publication. For example, "In an article titled 'Surprises from Uncle Sam' (*Newsweek,* November 19, 1990), Jane Bryant Quinn states. . . ."

Then, in your own words, summarize the main point of the article and the key details used to support or develop that point.

Finally, be sure to clip or make a copy of the article and attach it to your summary.

Activity 6

Watch a television show of special interest to you. Then prepare a one-paragraph summary of the show. In your first sentence, give basic information about the show by using a format such as the following: "The November 17, 1991, broadcast of CBS's *60 Minutes* examined. . . ."

Activity 7

Write a one-paragraph summary of an important concept from one of your textbooks. Try to choose a general-interest subject such as psychology or sociology rather than a highly specialized field such as anatomy or electronics.

In your summary, first provide the necessary identifying information. For example, "In the chapter 'Intellectual Development in Adolescence' in *A Child's World* (McGraw-Hill, 1990), Papalia and Olds explain. . . ." Then present the important idea in the chapter, along with key details that support or develop that idea.

■ Review Test

Circle the letter of the title that best summarizes each selection on the following pages. Remember that the title should be as specific and descriptive as possible and at the same time account for all the material in the selection.

1.   Sheer proximity is perhaps the most decisive factor in determining who will become friends. Our friends are likely to live nearby. Although it is said that absence makes the heart grow fonder, it also causes friendships to fade. While relationships may be maintained in absentia by correspondence, they usually have to be reinforced by periodic visits, or they dissolve. Several researchers decided to investigate the effects of proximity on friendships. They chose an apartment complex made up of two-story buildings with five apartments to a floor. People moved into the project at random, so previous social attachments did not influence the results of the study. In interviewing the residents of the apartment complex, the researchers found that 44 percent said they were most friendly with their next-door neighbors, 22 percent saw the people who lived two doors away the most often socially, and only 10 percent said that their best friends lived as far away as down the hall. People were even less likely to be friendly with those who lived upstairs or downstairs from them.

What would be an accurate title for this selection?
a. Proximity
b. Factors in Determining Friendships
c. The Need for Friendships
d. Proximity as a Factor in Friendships

2.   The institutional care we give our older people is a good reflection of the overall attitude of our society toward the aged. In the past few years, nursing homes have received wide attention as boring, meaningless places where people often have little else to do but wait for the end of their lives. Senile wards in mental hospitals are even worse. One of the shocking things about nursing homes has been the unwillingness of people on the outside to show real concern for what happens in these institutions. Even people who are entrusting a parent to the care of a home rarely ask about the nurse-patient ratio, about the kind of creative facilities or physical therapy equipment available, or even about the frequency of doctors' visits. And the government has provided federal money without enforcing high standards of care. In fact, federal standards were lowered in 1974; therefore, in some sense our concern for the aged seems to be moving backward, not forward.

What would be an accurate title for this selection?
a. Institutional Care
b. The Elderly
c. A National Disgrace
d. Failure of Care for the Elderly

3. During the post–Civil War years students entered schools at all levels in ever-increasing numbers. Between 1870 and 1910, public school enrollment rose from 6.9 to 17.8 million. Most of this growth occurred in the first eight grades, but the number attending public high schools increased from 80,000 to 915,000. Private schools taught thousands more. College enrollments revealed comparable gains, rising from only 52,000 in 1870 to 355,000 forty years later. Compulsory school attendance, typically for children between eight and fourteen, was an important factor in the growing enrollments. By 1898 thirty-one states and territories had laws setting minimum attendance requirements; unfortunately, these statutes were often poorly enforced. With more children in school, expenditures for education jumped sharply. The cost of public elementary and secondary education in the United States rose from $63.4 million in 1870 to $426 million in 1910.

What would be an accurate title for this selection?
a. The Post–Civil War Years
b. Education in America after the Civil War
c. Public Schools: 1870–1910
d. The Cost of Education after the Civil War

4. Sacrifice is a rather widespread ritual. It is generally based on the hope that if an individual gives up something of value to honor a supreme being, he or she will receive a divine blessing. A common sacrificial custom within industrial societies is making a contribution to a religious institution, as in the practice of tithing (giving one-tenth of one's income to a church). Other examples of religious sacrifice include fasting on holy days (such as Yom Kippur, the Day of Atonement for Jews) and giving up worldly goods (as Christians do for Lent). Yet the most ancient form of sacrifice—still commonly found throughout the world in the 1980s—is the burial of goods with a corpse. Such artifacts as food, clothing, money, and weapons are intended to provide the soul of the deceased with whatever will be needed during an afterlife. In American society, the provision of comfortable coffins for well-dressed corpses and the regular placement of flowers near a grave are forms of sacrifice offered in a similar spirit.

What would be an accurate title for this selection?
a. Tithing
b. Religious Rituals
c. Ancient Rituals
d. Rituals of Sacrifice

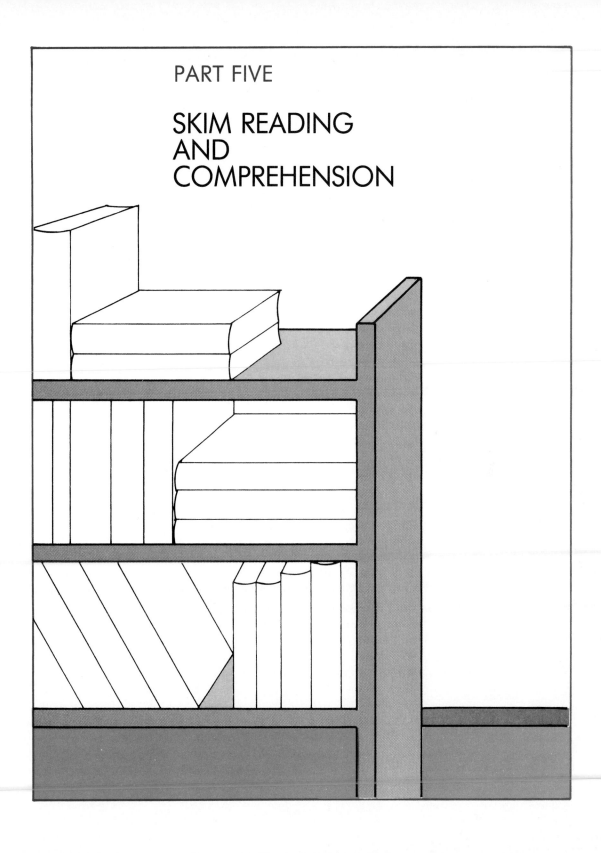

PART FIVE

SKIM READING AND COMPREHENSION

PREVIEW

Part Five shows you how to do skimming, or selective reading. You will read quickly through a series of selections, looking for and writing down what seem to be important ideas. To locate the important ideas, you will be asked to apply several of the comprehension skills that you learned in Part Four. Each article or textbook chapter that you skim-read and take notes on will be timed, and you will check your performance by answering questions on the selections afterward. Through a progress chart, you will be able to measure both your skim-reading rate and your comprehension score for each selection.

INTRODUCTION

One of the chief myths that students believe about reading is that they must read every word. Consider, though, that the average textbook contains about six hundred pages, or more than 350,000 words. If students have several textbooks and try to read every word of every assignment, they are likely to have little time left to study what they have read—let alone to attend to the essentials of their everyday lives!

Fortunately, not every word in a book must be read, nor must every detail be learned. The purpose of this part of the book is to give you practice in *skimming,* or selective reading. In skimming, you do not read every word; instead, you go quickly and selectively through a passage, looking for and marking off important ideas but skipping secondary material. You can then go back later to read more closely and take notes on important points.

Skim reading will help you when you do not need to read every word of every assignment. Skim reading will also help make you a flexible reader, which should be your final reading goal. Flexible readers, depending on their purpose in reading and the nature of the material, are able to practice several different kinds of reading: study reading (using the skills learned in Part Four), rapid reading (the concern of Part Six), and skim reading—the subject of this part of the book.

HOW TO SKIM-READ

To skim-read effectively, you must be able to apply several of the comprehension skills you learned in Part Four. You must know how to do the following things:

1 *Find definitions:* Remember that they are often signaled by special type, especially *italics*. Look also for one example that makes a definition clear to you.

2 *Locate enumerations:* And remember that it does not help to locate a numbered series of items if you do not know what *label* the series fits under. So be sure to look for a clear heading for each enumeration.

3 *Look for relationships between headings and subheadings:* Such relationships are often the key to basic enumerations. And when it seems appropriate, you will also want to *change headings into questions* and find the answers to the questions.

4 *Look for emphasis words and main ideas:* If time permits, look for points marked by emphasis words and for main ideas in what seem to be key paragraphs.

■ What is one of the chief myths about reading? _____

_____

■ What is often a real alternative to reading every word of a selection? _____

_____

■ What are three skills to practice when skim reading?

   1. _____

   2. _____

   3. _____

The four reading selections that follow will give you practice in skim reading. You will have a limited amount of time to (1) read and (2) take notes on each selection. At the end of a time period, you will be asked questions about important ideas in the selection, and you can use your notes to answer the questions. You should do well on the quizzes if you have been able to quickly pick out and write down main ideas.

The timed practice will have several benefits. It will teach you skim reading, improve your note-taking and handwriting efficiency, and help you solidify the comprehension skills you practiced in Part Four. By using the progress chart on page 410, you will be able to measure your performance as you move through the selections.

SELECTION 1

You have ten minutes to skim the following textbook selection for its main points and to take notes on those points. Be sure to time yourself or have your instructor time you as you read and take notes on the selection.

Hint: Definitions and enumerations are the keys to the important points in this selection.

THE NATURE OF POWER

Niccolo Machiavelli (1469–1527) wrote *The Prince* as a way of giving advice to Italian princes (such as Cesare Borgia) in their struggle against the pope to establish an Italian state. Machiavelli saw the power of the prince as a means for achieving the moral goal of Italian unification. In the following passage, he makes an important distinction:

> You must know, then, that there are two methods of fighting, the one by law, the other by force: the first method is that of men, the second of beasts; but as the first method is often insufficient, one must have recourse to the second. . . .
>
> Thus it is well to seem merciful, faithful, humane, sincere, religious, and also to be so; but you must have the mind so disposed that when it is needful to be otherwise you may be able to change to the opposite qualities. . . . And therefore, he must have a mind disposed to adapt itself according to the wind, and as the variations of fortune dictate, and, as I said before, not deviate from what is good if possible, but be able to do evil if constrained.

In this celebrated passage, Machiavelli is discussing power. *Power in society is the ability to control the behavior of others—against their will if necessary—by using force, authority, or influence*. As the passage indicates, there are different kinds of power. Machiavelli recognized two kinds: force and law. Contemporary sociologists, however, find it more useful to speak of three kinds of power: *force, authority, and influence*.

Force

Machiavelli is not a particularly popular person in Italian history, partly because of his favorable attitude toward the use of *force*. Force is *physical coercion or the threat of such coercion*. In Machiavelli's terms, it is the method "of beasts" rather than "of men." Yet he advised his prince to resort to it whenever other means of controlling people's behavior fail. The use of force is at odds with many of our fundamental values, such as equality, freedom, and the importance of the individual personality. Yet there are situations, as illustrated by the aggression of Hitler's Germany or that of a gunman on the loose, where such values are threatened by people willing to use force. Using force to counter force in such situations can protect those values, but it also conflicts with them at the same time.

Authority

A second type of power is *authority*, which may be defined as *legitimate power*, that is, power based on values and norms. Machiavelli contrasted the use of force with the rule of law, and the latter illustrates authority. Authority tends to be a much larger component of most existing power than is force. The socialization process teaches us to conform to a wide variety of norms that allow others—parents, teachers, friends, employers, and officials of all kinds—to direct our behavior.

Three Kinds of Authority: Max Weber enables us to gain some historical perspective on the nature of authority. At the same time, he distinguishes three kinds of authority: charismatic, traditional, and legal. *Charismatic authority is rule based on belief in the extraordinary personal qualities of the ruler.* Weber illustrates such authority by referring to "the magical sorcerer, the prophet, the leader of hunting and booty expeditions, the warrior chieftain, the so-called 'Caesarist' ruler." For example, we might think of Jesus Christ, Joan of Arc, Adolf Hitler, and Winston Churchill as exercising charismatic authority. They all had qualities of personality which deeply appealed to their followers.

Traditional authority is rule based on conformity to established modes of behavior. It is illustrated by the patriarchal domination of a family by the father or husband, by the rule of the lord over vassals and serfs, or by the rule of the master over slaves. By contrast, *legal authority is rule based on law or formal decrees and regulations.* It is exemplified by the authority of a president, a police officer, a member of Congress, a court official, the head of a government agency, a member of a school board, and a welfare investigator. With the development of industrial society has come a shift from traditional to legal authority. Charismatic authority has existed in the past and continues to exist in the present. It can be combined with the other two kinds of authority.

Influence

The third component of power is *influence,* which may be defined as *the ability to control the behavior of others beyond any authority to do so.* In certain situations, a leader may neither choose to exert force nor have any authority—legal, traditional, or charismatic—yet nevertheless may wish to assert power. He or she may be able to exert our third type of power, influence, simply on the basis of the "exchanges" which can be made. A teacher can influence students to develop interest in a subject by proving to be trustworthy as well as helpful. Such interest cannot be compelled on the basis of the teacher's authority.

The different aspects of power—force, authority, and influence—may be illustrated by Mohandas K. Gandhi's success in leading India toward independence from Great Britain. Gandhi was seen by his followers as a highly charismatic person. Further, his manner of living embodied such traditional ideals as humility, self-sacrifice, and spirituality. He refused to use force and, in its place, developed techniques of passive resistance. Among other things, he trained volunteers to march forward and allow themselves to be struck down by police clubs without defending themselves. Gandhi's leadership illustrates charismatic and traditional authority as well as influence. This was reflected in the title "mahatma" (great soul) that his followers bestowed on him.

Gandhi opposed his authority and influence against the force and legal authority of the British, and that opposition proved to be highly effective. For example, the British exercise of force, although perfectly legal in British terms, came to be seen as immoral not only by Indians but also by large segments of the British population.

The Gandhian approach to conflict influenced Martin Luther King to develop his own techniques of passive resistance in the struggle of American blacks against discrimination. For example, black boycotts of buses in Montgomery, Alabama, in 1955 (in reaction to the injustice of being forced to sit only in the backs of buses) were almost 100 percent effective. Here King, as Gandhi had done, avoided the use of force and combined charismatic and traditional authority with personal influence to undermine the legal authority of the local government.

When the ten minutes are up, try to answer the questions on page 410 by referring to your notes but *not* referring to the text.

SELECTION 2

You have ten minutes to skim the following article for its main points and to take notes on those points.

Hint: Definitions and enumerations are the keys to the important points in this article.

FATIGUE

Fatigue is one of the most common complaints brought to doctors, friends, and relatives. You'd think in this era of labor-saving devices and convenient transportation that few people would have reason to be so tired. But probably more people complain of fatigue today than in the days when hay was baled by hand and laundry was scrubbed on a washboard. Witness these typical complaints:

"It doesn't seem to matter how long I sleep—I'm more tired when I wake up than when I went to bed."

"Some of my friends come home from work and jog for several miles or swim laps. I don't know how they do it. I'm completely exhausted at the end of a day at the office."

"I thought I was weary because of the holidays, but now that they're over, I'm even worse. I can barely get through the week, and on the weekend I don't even have the strength to get dressed. I wonder if I'm anemic or something."

"I don't know what's wrong with me lately, but I've been so collapsed that I haven't made a proper meal for the family in weeks. We've been living on TV dinners and packaged mixes. I was finally forced to do a laundry because the kids ran out of underwear."

The causes of modern-day fatigue are diverse and only rarely related to excessive physical exertion. The relatively few people who do heavy labor all day long almost never complain about being tired, perhaps because they expect to be. Today, physicians report, tiredness is more likely a consequence of underexertion than of wearing yourself down with overactivity. In fact, increased physical activity is often prescribed as a *cure* for sagging energy.

Kinds of Fatigue

There are three main categories of fatigue. These are physical fatigue, pathological fatigue, and psychological fatigue.

Physical.   This is the well-known result of overworking your muscles to the point where metabolic waste products—carbon dioxide and lactic acid—accumulate in your blood and sap your strength. Your muscles can't continue to work efficiently in a bath of these chemicals. Physical fatigue is usually a pleasant tiredness, such as that which you might experience after playing a hard set of tennis, chopping wood, or climbing a mountain. The cure is simple and fast: You rest, giving your body a chance to get rid of accumulated wastes and restore muscle fuel.

Pathological.   Here fatigue is a warning sign or consequence of some underlying physical disorder, perhaps the common cold or flu or something more serious like diabetes or cancer. Usually other symptoms besides fatigue are present that suggest the true cause.

Even after an illness has passed, you're likely to feel dragged out for a week or more. Take your fatigue as a signal to go slow while your body has a chance to recover fully even if all you had was a cold. Pushing yourself to resume full activity too soon could precipitate a relapse and almost certainly will prolong your period of fatigue.

Even though illness is not a frequent cause of prolonged fatigue, it's very important that it not be overlooked. Therefore, anyone who feels drained of energy for weeks on end should have a thorough physical checkup. But even if nothing shows up as a result of the various medical tests, that doesn't mean there's nothing wrong with you.

Unfortunately too often a medical work-up ends with a battery of negative test results, the patient is dismissed, and the true cause of serious fatigue goes undetected. As Dr. John Bulette, a psychiatrist at the Medical College of Pennsylvania Hospital in Philadelphia, tells it, this is what happened to a Pennsylvania woman who had lost nearly fifty pounds and was "almost dead—so tired she could hardly lift her head up." The doctors who first examined the woman were sure she had cancer. But no matter how hard they looked, they could find no sign of malignancy or of any other disease that could account for her to be wasting away. Finally, she was brought to the college hospital, where doctors noted that she was severely depressed.

They questioned her about her life and discovered that her troubles had begun two years earlier, after her husband died. Once treated for depression, the woman quickly perked up. She gained ten pounds in just a few weeks, and then she returned home to continue her recovery with the aid of psychotherapy.

Psychological. Emotional problems and conflicts, especially depression and anxiety, are by far the most common causes of prolonged fatigue. Fatigue may represent a defense mechanism that prevents you from having to face the true cause of your depression, such as the fact that you hate your job. It is also your body's safety valve for expressing repressed emotional conflicts, such as feeling trapped in an ungratifying role or an unhappy marriage. When such feelings are not expressed openly, they often come out as physical symptoms, with fatigue as one of the most common manifestations. "Many people who are extremely fatigued don't even know they're depressed," Dr. Bulette says. "They're so busy distracting themselves or just worrying about being tired that they don't recognize their depression."

One of these situations is so common it's been given a name—tired housewife syndrome. The victims are commonly young mothers who day in and day out face the predictable tedium of caring for a home and small children, fixing meals, dealing with repair persons, and generally having no one interesting to talk to and nothing enjoyable to look forward to at the end of their boring and unrewarding day. The tired housewife may be inwardly resentful, envious of her husband's job, and guilty about her feelings. But rather than face them head-on, she becomes extremely fatigued.

Today, with nearly half the mothers of young children working outside the home, the tired housewife syndrome has taken on a new twist: that of conflicting roles and responsibilities and guilt over leaving the children, often with an overlay of genuine physical exhaustion from trying to be all things to all people.

Emotionally induced fatigue may be compounded by sleep disturbance that results from the underlying psychological conflict. A person may develop insomnia or may sleep the requisite number of hours but fitfully, tossing and turning all night, having disturbing dreams, and awakening, as one woman put it, feeling as if she "had been run over by a truck."

Understanding the underlying emotional problem is the crucial first step toward curing psychological fatigue and by itself often results in considerable lessening of the tiredness. Professional psychological help or career or marriage counseling may be needed.

What You Can Do about It

There is a great deal you can do on your own to deal with both severe prolonged fatigue and periodic washed-out feelings. Vitamins and tranquilizers are almost never the right answer, sleeping pills and alcohol are counterproductive, and caffeine is at best a temporary solution that can backfire with abuse and cause life-disrupting symptoms of anxiety. Instead, you might try:

Diet. If you eat a skimpy breakfast or none at all, you're likely to experience midmorning fatigue, the result of a drop in blood sugar, which your body and brain depend on for energy. For peak energy in the morning, be sure to eat a proper breakfast, low in sugar and fairly high in protein, which will provide a steady supply of blood sugar throughout the morning. Coffee and a doughnut are almost worse than nothing, providing a brief boost and then letting you down with a thud. . . .

The same goes for the rest of the day: Frequent snacking on sweets is a false pick-me-up that soon leaves you lower than you were to begin with. Stick to regular, satisfying, well-balanced meals that help you maintain a trim figure. Extra weight is tiring both physically and psychologically. Getting your weight down to normal can go a long way toward revitalizing you. . . .

Exercise. Contrary to what you may think, exercise enhances, rather than saps, energy. Regular conditioning exercises, such as jogging, cycling, or swimming, help you to resist fatigue by increasing your body's ability to handle more of a work load. You get tired less quickly because your capability is greater.

Exercise also has a well-recognized tranquilizing effect, which helps you work in a more relaxed fashion and be less dragged down by the tensions of your day. At the end of the day exercise can relieve accumulated tensions, give you more energy in the evening, and help you sleep more restfully. . . .

Sleep. If you know you're tired because you haven't been getting enough sleep, the solution is simple: Get to bed earlier. There's no right amount of sleep for everyone, and generally sleep requirements decline with age. Find the amount that suits you best and aim for it. Insomnia and other sleep disorders should not be treated with sleeping pills, alcohol, or tranquilizers, which can actually make the problem worse. . . .

Knowing Yourself. Try to schedule your most taxing jobs for the time of day when you're at your peak. Some are "morning people" who tire by midafternoon; others do their best work in the evening. Don't overextend yourself trying to climb the ladder of success at a record pace or to meet everyone's demands or expectations. Decide what you want to do and what you can handle comfortably and learn to say no to additional requests. Recognize your energy cycles and plan accordingly. For example, many women have a low point premenstrually, during which time extra sleep may be needed and demanding activities are particularly exhausting.

Taking Breaks. No matter how interesting or demanding your work, you'll be able to do it with more vigor if now and again you stop, stretch, and change the scenery. Instead of coffee and a sweet roll on your break, try meditation, yoga, calisthenics, or a brisk walk. Even running up and down the staircase can provide refreshment from a sedentary job. If your job is physically demanding, relax in a quiet place for a while. The do-something-different rule also applies to vacations; "getting away from it all" for a week or two or longer can be highly revitalizing, helping you to put things in perspective and enabling you to take your job more in stride upon your return.

When the ten minutes are up, try to answer the questions on page 411 by using your notes but *not* referring to the text.

SELECTION 3

You have ten minutes to skim the following textbook selection for its main points and to take notes on those points.

SCIENCE AND THE SEARCH FOR TRUTH

A pathologist after elaborate preparation places a slide under the microscope and adjusts the lens carefully. A Purari war party watch carefully as they place their canoe in the water, for unless it rocks, the raid will not be successful. A man steps from a new station wagon, cuts a forked twig, and carries it around holding it above the ground, while a well-drilling crew stands by, waiting to drill where the twig tells them water will be found. A woman in Peoria, anxious over her teenage daughter, prays to God for guidance. A physician leafs through the pages of a parasitology textbook and tries to identify the puzzling skin rash of a patient. A senator scans the latest public opinion poll and wonders how to vote on the farm bill.

Each of these persons is seeking guidance. Their problems vary, and their sources of truth are different. Where shall human beings find truth? How can they know when they have found it? In the million years, more or less, of human life on this earth, people have sought truth in many places. Where are some of them?

Some Sources of Truth

Intuition. Galen, a famous Greek physician of the second century, prepared an elaborate chart of the human body, showing exactly where it might be pierced without fatal injury. How did he know the vulnerable spots? He just *knew* them. True, he had learned a good deal of human anatomy through his observations and those of his associates, but beyond this, he relied upon his intuition to tell him which zones were fatal. *Intuition is any flash of insight (true or mistaken) whose source the receiver cannot fully identify or explain.* Hitler relied heavily upon his intuition, much to the distress of his generals. His intuition told him that France would not fight for the Rhineland, that England would not fight for Czechoslovakia, that England and France would quit when he attacked Russia. He was right on the first two insights and wrong on the last two.

Intuition is responsible for many brilliant hypotheses, which can later be tested through other methods. Perhaps intuition's greatest value is in the forming of hypotheses.

Authority.   Two thousand years ago, Galen knew more about human anatomy than any other mortal; as recently as 1800, physicians were still quoting him as an authority. Aristotle stated that a barrel of water could be added to a barrel of ashes without overflowing, and for two thousand years thereafter, a student who might suggest trying it out would be scolded for his impertinence. For many centuries, creative thought was stifled by Aristotelian authority, for since an authority is *right,* any conflicting ideas must be wrong. Authority does not discover new truths, but it can prevent new truth from being discovered or accepted.

Dangerous though authority may be, we cannot get along without it. Our accumulation of knowledge is too great for anyone to absorb, so we must rely upon specialists who have collected the reliable knowledge in a particular field. An *authority* is a necessary and useful source of knowledge—*in the field in which he is an authority.* Science recognizes no authorities on "things in general."

Authority is of several sorts. *Sacred* authority rests upon the faith that a certain tradition or document—the Bible, the Koran, the Vedas—is of supernatural origin. *Secular* authority arises not from divine revelation but from human perception. It is of two kinds: *secular scientific* authority, which rests upon empirical investigation, and *secular humanistic* authority, which rests upon the belief that certain "great men" have had remarkable insight into human behavior and the nature of the universe. The search for truth by consulting the "great books" is an example of the appeal to secular humanistic authority.

Tradition.   Of all sources of truth, tradition is one of the most reassuring. Here is the accumulated wisdom of the ages, and one who disregards it may expect denunciation as a scoundrel or a fool. If a pattern has "worked" in the past, why not keep on using it?

Tradition, however, preserves both the accumulated wisdom and the accumulated bunkum of the ages. Tradition is society's attic, crammed with all sorts of useful customs and useless relics. A great deal of "practical experience" consists in repeating the mistakes of our ancestors. One task of social science is to sort out our folklore into the true and the merely ancient.

Common Sense.   Common sense and tradition are closely interwoven, with many commonsense propositions becoming part of a people's traditional lore. If a distinction is to be drawn, it may be that traditional truths are those which have long been believed, while commonsense truths are uncritically accepted conclusions (recent or ancient) which are currently believed by one's fellows.

What often passes for common sense consists of a group's accumulation of collective guesses, hunches, and haphazard trial-and-error learnings. Many commonsense propositions are sound, earthy, useful bits of knowledge. "A soft answer turneth away wrath" and "Birds of a feather flock together" are practical observations on social life. But many commonsense conclusions are based on ignorance, prejudice, and mistaken interpretation. When medieval Europeans noticed that feverish patients were free of lice while most healthy people were lousy, they made the commonsense conclusion that lice would cure fever and therefore sprinkled lice over feverish patients. Not until the fever subsided would the lice be removed. Common sense, like tradition, preserves both folk wisdom and folk nonsense, and to sort them out one from the other is a task for science.

Science.   Only within the last two or three hundred years has the scientific method become a common way of seeking answers about the natural world. *Science* may be defined as a method of study whereby a body of organized, scientific knowledge is discovered. Science has become a source of knowledge about the *social* world even more recently; yet in the brief period since human beings began to rely upon the scientific method, they have learned more about their world than they learned in the preceding ten thousand years. The spectacular explosion of knowledge in the modern world parallels the use of the scientific method. What makes the scientific method so productive? How does it differ from other methods of seeking truth?

Characteristics of Scientific Knowledge

Verifiable Evidence.   Scientific knowledge is based on verifiable evidence. By *evidence* we mean concrete factual observations which other observers can see, weigh, measure, count, or check for accuracy. We may think the definition too obvious to mention; most of us have some awareness of the scientific method. Yet only a few centuries ago medieval scholars held long debates on how many teeth a horse had, without bothering to look into a horse's mouth to count them.

At this point we raise the troublesome methodological question, "What is a fact?" While the word looks deceptively simple, it is not easy to distinguish a fact from a widely shared illusion. Suppose we define a fact as a descriptive statement upon which all qualified observers are in agreement. By this definition, medieval ghosts were a fact, since all medieval observers agreed that ghosts were real. There is, therefore, no way to be *certain* that a fact is an accurate description and not a mistaken impression. Research would be easier if facts were dependable, unshakable certainties. Since they are not, the best we can do is to recognize that a fact is a *descriptive statement of reality which scientists, after careful examination and cross-checking, agree in believing to be accurate.*

Ethical Neutrality. Science is knowledge, and knowledge can be put to differing uses. Atomic fission can be used to power a city or to incinerate a nation. Every use of scientific knowledge involves a choice between values. Our values define what is most important to us. Science tells us that overeating and cigarette smoking will shorten our life expectancy. But can science tell us which we should choose—a longer life or a more indulgent one? Science can answer questions of fact but has no way to prove that one value is better than another.

Science, then, is ethically neutral. Science seeks knowledge, while society's values determine how this knowledge is to be used. Knowledge about group organization can be used to preserve a democracy or to establish a dictatorship.

When the ten minutes are up, try to answer the questions your instructor gives you by using your notes but *not* referring to the text.

SELECTION 4

You have ten minutes to skim the following textbook selection for its main points and to take notes on those points.

DEFENSE MECHANISMS

Maintaining a good self-concept and high self-esteem is not easy. Each day there are many events that could shatter your self-image. If you notice a new blemish or wrinkle on your face, receive a low grade, or are not invited to lunch by the group, you need to take action to protect your self-esteem. The methods you use to protect your self-esteem are called *defense mechanisms*.

Suppression and Repression

One way to protect your self-esteem is to avoid thinking about your problem. For example, you might intentionally go to a movie to avoid thinking about an argument. This defense mechanism, a deliberate attempt to avoid stressful thoughts, is labeled "suppression." Scarlett O'Hara in *Gone with the Wind* is among the more famous practitioners of suppression. Remember her line, "I'll think about it tomorrow"? Scarlett was suppressing her unpleasant thoughts. Have you ever felt lonely and intentionally kept yourself busy with chores, sports, or shopping to avoid thinking about your loneliness? If so, you were using suppression.

Suppression is useful only for minor problems. Usually you can pretend a problem does not exist for only a short period. Thoughts and worries tend to come back and may be even more stressful if they have been bottled up. Suppression requires a conscious and voluntary effort and has limited use as a defense mechanism.

Issues that are deeply wounding to self-esteem may be too painful to reach consciousness. You unconsciously put them out of your mind. Unconsciously motivated forgetting is called "repression." Everyone tends to push unpleasant thoughts out of the conscious mind. Since thoughts that are repressed are not conscious, people can become aware of them only through dreams or hypnosis.

Repression is the most basic defense mechanism. Most other defense mechanisms stem from repression. In its simplest form repression is unconscious forgetting. Suppose you forget to contribute money to a going-away gift for a close friend. Unconsciously you wish your friend were not leaving. Forgetting appointments, birthdays, weddings, and other important events can be signs of repression. Have you ever met someone who was rejecting and cruel to you? If you have difficulty recalling any persons or names, you may be repressing them! Usually thoughts and feelings that are repressed bring on other defense mechanisms.

"Normally I don't let rejection bother me, but . . ."

The rejection stamped on his forehead may also become buried in his unconscious. Time for some defense mechansims . . .

Other Defense Mechanisms

Assuming the fellow in the cartoon above is deeply worried about being rejected, he may repress the situation. As a result he could forget the name of the woman, their entire conversation, what he was drinking, and where he was that evening. Rather than admit his rejection and suffer, he could also use a number of other unconscious defense mechanisms.

Withdrawal: If the man in the cartoon has trouble talking to women in the future, it could be that he unconsciously fears rejection. *Withdrawal* usually results when people become intensely frightened or frustrated by a situation. People who fear rejection often avoid or withdraw from social situations. Sometimes the result is shyness. Often people fear rejection even when it is unlikely. Many famous and likable people have suffered from shyness.

If you have ever tried to escape from an unpleasant situation, you have used a withdrawal defense mechanism. If used cautiously, withdrawal can be a healthy defense mechanism. Often, stepping out of a situation can help you gain a better perspective. However, withdrawal can also result in quitting jobs, dropping out of school, separations, and divorces.

Fantasy: Sometimes people withdraw into a make-believe or *fantasy* world. If the rejected man in the cartoon used a fantasy defense mechanism, he might daydream about his successes with women. He could create his own dream world where he would always be accepted, admired, and loved. Used in moderation, daydreaming and fantasy can be healthy and lead to creative thinking. Everyone daydreams as a method of reducing anxiety. Fantasy can bring a healthy escape from boredom and aid mental relaxation. Reading a novel or watching a soap opera can provide fantasy escapes. However, if fantasy is used excessively, it can become an unhealthy substitute for activity.

Regression: *Regression* is withdrawal into the past. If the rejected fellow regressed in a childlike way, he would behave as a child. He might burst into tears, or pout, suck his thumb, throw things, scream, and have a tantrum. Regression requires a return to earlier ways of handling problems. It is generally used when a person is deeply upset and cannot cope in a mature manner. Young children who have been toilet-trained and taught to drink from cups often regress and forget their training when a new baby arrives in their home. The older child does not know how to win parental affection in the new situation. Consequently the child must resort to previous methods for gaining attention and love. The result is regression.

Rationalization: *Rationalization* is a distortion of the truth to maintain self-esteem. It provides an excuse or explanation for a situation that is really unacceptable. The man in the cartoon might rationalize that the woman was not really his type and that he was delighted to be rid of her so he could arrive home at a reasonable hour. He might even rationalize that he was just having an unlucky day. Failures are often rationalized as being the result of some external factor, but success is deemed the result of personal abilities.

Most people are unaware of how often they rationalize. Although rationalization is indeed a misuse of logic, it can help to reduce anxiety. Have you ever excused yourself from a poor grade by arguing that the test was unfair or that you were feeling sick when you took the test? Rationalization can also allow you to look at the bright side. If an unpleasant event has already occurred, often little or nothing can be done to change it. After losing the 1960 presidential election, Richard Nixon reportedly commented that he would have more time to devote to his family. This was clearly a rationalization but probably aided his acceptance of a painful reality.

Projection: *Projection* is based on guilt. Rather than accept personal weaknesses, unacceptable features are projected onto another person. The rejected man could project his rejection onto the lady who stamped him. He would then maintain that it was she who was rejected by everyone. Projection permits you to accuse someone else of your weaknesses. Perhaps you have heard complaints from one fraternity that members of another fraternity hated them. They could easily be projecting their own feelings onto the other group.

Or maybe you have known a flirt who complained that every male she met flirted with her. Psychologists often use projective tests to uncover problems. It is assumed that individuals will project their own feelings onto the pictures and illustrations in the test material.

Displacement: *Displacement* requires finding a target or victim for pent-up feelings. The rejected fellow at the bar might ridicule and chastise the bartender for poor drinks or slow service. The chosen victim is usually a safe person, someone who is not likely to deflate self-esteem. Spouses are often selected. As a result husbands and wives often learn to avoid controversial topics when their mate has had a bad day.

Compensation: *Compensation* allows a person to make up for inadequacies by doing well in another area. Perhaps the rejected fellow at the bar could go back to work and prove himself an outstanding accountant, attorney, or automobile salesman. Compensation allows you to deemphasize your weaknesses and play up your strengths. A child who is a poor student may try learning clever jokes to become popular. Compensation is a reasonable defense mechanism and usually leads to a healthy adjustment.

Sublimation: *Sublimation* is the most accepted defense mechanism. Unacceptable impulses are channeled into something positive, constructive, or creative. If the man left the bar and wrote a beautiful blues song about rejection and loneliness, he would be sublimating. Some of the finest poetry and folk music have emerged from oppressed groups, an example of their sublimations.

Of the many defense mechanisms, compensation and sublimation are considered the most healthy and acceptable. Since defense mechanisms are unconscious, usually people are completely unaware of them. Think about some of your own behavior. Can you identify the defense mechanisms you choose most often?

When the ten minutes are up, try to answer the questions your instructor gives you by using your notes but *not* referring to the text.

SKIM-READING PROGRESS CHART

On the following chart are skim-reading speeds for the selections in Part Five. The term WPM refers here to the number of words *processed* per minute. (You have not been able to literally *read* every word in the limited time involved.) The reading speeds assume that you have taken one-quarter of your time to read each selection and three-quarters of your time to take notes on what you have read.

Selection	WPM	Comprehension
1 The Nature of Power (1,152 words)	460	
2 Fatigue (1,957 words)	783	
3 Science and the Search for Truth (1,464 words)	525	
4 Defense Mechanisms (1,625 words)	660	

Note: Reading speed will vary depending on the nature and difficulty of the material. In the four preceding selections, the highest speed is for "Fatigue," an article by popular health writer Jane Brody taken from a newspaper. Because the three other selections, all from textbooks, contain more information to process, slightly lower skim-reading rates are suggested.

QUESTIONS ON THE SKIM-READING SELECTIONS

■ **Selection 1**

1. What are the three kinds of power?

   _____

   _____

   _____

2. What is force? _____

   _____

3. What are the three kinds of authority?

   _____

   _____

   _____

4. What is influence? _____

   _____

   Score: Number correct (_____) × 12.5 = _____%

■ **Selection 2**

1. What are the three main categories of fatigue?

   _____

   _____

   _____

2. What is pathological fatigue? _____

   _____

3. Which category of fatigue does the tired housewife syndrome belong to?

   _____

4. What are the five areas of their lives that people can change in order to fight fatigue?

   _____

   _____

   _____

   _____

   _____

Score: Number correct (_____) × 10 = _____%

■ **Selection 3**

Your instructor will refer to the Instructor's Manual to give you the questions for Selection 3.

■ **Selection 4**

Your instructor will refer to the Instructor's Manual to give you the questions for Selection 4.

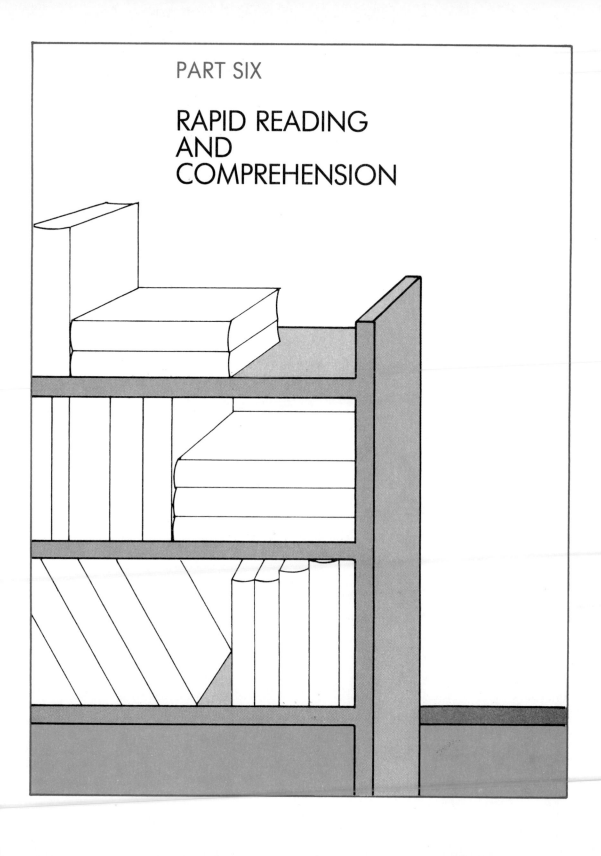

PART SIX

RAPID READING AND COMPREHENSION

PREVIEW

Part Six is concerned with developing your comprehension and increasing the number of words that your eyes take in and "read" per minute. Poor perception habits that may slow down your reading rate are explained, and an activity is provided to show you how your eyes move when they read. You then learn how a conscious effort to increase your speed is a key to overcoming careless perception habits and achieving a higher reading rate. A series of timed reading selections and sets of questions give you practice in building up your reading speed and comprehension. Through a progress chart, you will be able to compare your reading and comprehension scores as you move through the selections.

INTRODUCTION

This section will give you further practice in developing comprehension skills. At the same time, the section will help you work on increasing the number of words that your eyes take in and "read" per minute. You should remember, however, that while an increase in reading rate can be valuable, it is no cure-all for reading problems. If you feel you are reading your college assignments too slowly or ineffectively, factors other than reading speed are probably responsible. For example, perhaps you don't know where and how to look for main ideas and key supporting details in a textbook chapter. You may need to work on the reading comprehension and skim-reading skills presented in Parts Four and Five of this book. Also, you may need to learn more about such study skills as textbook previewing, marking, and note-taking, which are described in Part Three. And you may have to learn how to read more flexibly. This means that you adjust your speed and style of reading to accommodate your purpose as well as the level of difficulty of the material. In summary, there is much more to effective reading than an increase in speed alone. It is equally true, however, that rapid or speed reading can at times be a helpful skill. The activities in this part of the book will show you how to acquire that skill.

- *Complete the following sentence:* _____ reading is only one part of effective reading.

POOR PERCEPTION HABITS

If you read material of average or less than average difficulty slowly, you can probably significantly increase your present reading speed. In all likelihood, poor perception habits are slowing down your reading. Such habits include *subvocalizing* (pronouncing words silently to yourself as you read); slow and stilted *word-for-word reading;* unnecessary *regressions* (returns to words you have already read); and *visual inaccuracy* (the tendency to misread letters and words on the page). Poor concentration habits often cause this last problem.

■ How many bad perception habits are mentioned in the preceding paragraph?

_____

HOW THE EYES READ

You will understand more clearly how the eyes work during reading when you perform the following experiment. Punch a hole with a pen or pencil through the black dot that follows this paragraph. Hold the page up for another person to see and have him or her read a paragraph or two silently. As the person reads, put your eye close to the hole and watch his or her eye movements. In the space provided here, write down your observations, including a description of how the reader's eyes moved across the lines of print.

●

_____

_____

In performing this activity, you probably observed that the reader's eyes did not move smoothly across the printed lines. Instead, they moved in jerks, making stop-and-go motions across the lines of print. These stops, which you may have been able to count as you peeked through the hole, are called *fixations,* and only during such fixations do you actually read. You may remember as a child trying— and failing—to catch your eyes moving as you looked in a mirror. You never saw them move because the eyes go too quickly between fixations for any clear vision. The eye must fixate, or stop, in order to see clearly. In summary, then, the eye reads by making a number of fixations or stops as it proceeds across a line of print.

In addition to the stops, you probably also noted the sweep of the eyes, like the carriage return of a typewriter, back and down to the beginning of each new line. Possibly you also noticed an occasional backward eye movement, or regression, when the eyes skipped back to reread words or phrases a second time.

Eye reading speed can be increased, in part, by reducing the number of fixations per line. Persons who make eight stops per line are not reading as quickly as those who make four. To read faster, they should learn to take in several words at each stop rather than only one or two. And as this is done, the tendencies to subvocalize and to read one word at a time will also be minimized. In addition, speed can be increased by reducing the duration of each pause or stop, by increasing the speed of the return sweep, and by cutting down on the number of backward eye movements or regressions. Finally, with improved concentration, the eyes can be made to read with greater accuracy as well as speed.

THE KEY TO RAPID READING

Eye speed can be increased and bad perception habits overcome through practice with timed passages in which you consciously *try to read faster*. As you read for speed in the situations that follow, remember that your *mind* is probably not slowing you down, your *eyes* are. The mind is an incredible, computerlike instrument that can process words at an extraordinary rate of speed. What holds it back is the limited rate at which your eyes feed in words for it to process. Consciously force your eyes to move and work at ever higher and higher speeds. Your deliberate effort to "turn on" your speed through practice should yield surefire results.

On the following pages are six selections to use in developing your reading speed. You should read only the first selection at your normal rate of speed. You can then use this rate to measure later increases in speed. As you finish each selection, get your time from your instructor—or time yourself—and record it in the space provided. Then, without looking back at the passage, answer the comprehension questions.

Afterward, find your reading rate with the help of the table on pages 444–445. Also, check your answers with the instructor and fill in your comprehension score in the space provided. Finally, record both your reading rate and your comprehension score in the progress chart on page 443.

■ Many people have paid hundreds of dollars for speed-reading courses whose message or "secret" can be reduced to four simple words. What are the words? _____

SOME FINAL THOUGHTS ABOUT RAPID READING

You are about to practice rapid reading—making your eyes and brain work together to process words at a high rate of speed. When you finish, you will probably be a faster reader than you were when you started, as your initial and final reading rates may show. If you want to maintain and even increase your rate of speed, you must practice on a regular basis. You can, for example, work on increasing your speed by rapidly reading newspaper columns, magazine articles, or other material of average difficulty.

At the same time, be sure to keep rapid reading in perspective. It is different from slow and leisurely reading, in which your purpose is pleasure. It is different from skim reading, in which your purpose is to locate the main points in an article or chapter. It is different from the kind of slow study reading that you do to increase your understanding of a difficult selection. It is but one of the many skills of an effective reader, and it is useful at certain times for certain reading purposes.

SELECTION 1

Remember to read this first selection at your present comfortable rate of speed. You can then use the difference in speeds between this selection and the ones that follow to measure any advances in your reading rate.

FROM
THE AUTOBIOGRAPHY OF MALCOLM X
MALCOLM X AND ALEX HALEY

Words to Watch

> *riffling* (line 12): flipping through
>
> *succeeding* (line 28): following
>
> *inevitable* (line 34): bound to happen

It was because of my letters [which Malcolm X wrote to people outside while he was in jail] that I happened to stumble upon starting to acquire some kind of a homemade education.

I became increasingly frustrated at not being able to express what I wanted to convey in letters that I wrote. . . . And every book I picked up had few sentences which didn't contain anywhere from one to nearly all the words that might as well have been in Chinese. When I skipped those words, of course, I really ended up with little idea of what the book said. . . .

I saw that the best thing I could do was get hold of a dictionary—to study, to learn some words. I requested a dictionary along with some tablets and   10 pencils from the Norfolk Prison Colony school.

I spent two days just riffling uncertainly through the dictionary's pages. I'd never realized so many words existed! I didn't know *which* words I needed to learn. Finally, just to start some kind of action, I began copying.

In my slow, painstaking, ragged handwriting, I copied into my tablet   15 everything printed on that first page, down to the punctuation marks. I believe it took me a day. Then, aloud, I read back to myself everything I'd written on the tablet. Over and over, aloud, to myself, I read my own handwriting.

I woke up the next morning, thinking about those words—immensely proud to realize that not only had I written so much at one time, but I'd written words that I never knew were in the world. Moreover, with a little effort, I also could remember what many of these words meant. I reviewed the words whose meanings I didn't remember. Funny thing, from the dictionary's first page right now, that *aardvark* springs to my mind. The dictionary had a picture of it, a long-tailed, long-eared, burrowing African mammal, which lives off termites caught by sticking out its tongue as an anteater does for ants.

I was so fascinated that I went on—I copied the dictionary's next page. And the same experience came when I studied that. With every succeeding page, I also learned of people and places and events from history. Actually, the dictionary is like a miniature encyclopedia. Finally, the dictionary's A section had filled a whole tablet—and I went on into the B's. That was the way I started copying what eventually became the entire dictionary. It went a lot faster after so much practice helped me to pick up handwriting speed.

I suppose it was inevitable that as my word-base broadened, I could for the first time pick up a book and read and now begin to understand what the book was saying. Anyone who has read a great deal can imagine the new world that opened. Let me tell you something: from then until I left the prison, in every free moment I had, if I was not reading in the library, I was reading on my bunk. You couldn't have gotten me out of books with a wedge. Months passed without my even thinking about being imprisoned. In fact, up to then, I never had been so truly free in my life.

20

25

30

35

40

Time: _____   *Reading Rate (see page 444):* _____ WPM

■   **Check Your Understanding**

1. Malcolm X had trouble writing letters and reading books because
   a. he was not given free time.
   b. it was too dark in his cell.
   c. he didn't know enough words.
   d. he needed eyeglasses.
2. Malcolm compares the dictionary to
   a. the Bible.
   b. a miniature encyclopedia.
   c. a thesaurus.
   d. an almanac.

3. How much of the dictionary did Malcolm eventually copy?
    a. A's
    b. A's and B's
    c. A through P
    d. All of it

4. Malcolm's way of learning new words was to
    a. first copy them out on paper.
    b. open up the dictionary at random to a word he didn't know.
    c. study them right off the dictionary page.
    d. recite them silently to himself.

5. *True or false?* _____ One of the first words that Malcolm studied in the dictionary was *anteater*.

6. *True or false?* _____ Only when Malcolm's vocabulary increased was he able to read and understand books.

7. Malcolm says that to know and imagine the new world that books opened up for him, a person would
    a. have to read the same books he did.
    b. have to read many books.
    c. have to be in prison.
    d. have to be as ignorant as he was when he began.

8. Having books to read and knowing how to read them, Malcolm says that
    a. he became truly free even though in prison.
    b. he was still bored and restless occasionally.
    c. he felt like an educated man.
    d   he gained the admiration of his fellow prisoners.

Number Wrong: _____   *Score:* _____

0 wrong = 100%	2 wrong = 75%	4 wrong = 50%	6 wrong = 25%
1 wrong = 88%	3 wrong = 63%	5 wrong = 38%	7 wrong = 13%

SELECTION 2

Your purposes here are to understand the selection and, in addition, *to try to increase your reading speed significantly*.

Do not be alarmed if, over the next several passages, your comprehension drops. This often happens when you try not only to understand but to read quickly as well. Your comprehension should "catch up with" your reading rate as you continue to practice.

THE FINE ART OF COMPLAINING
SCOTT REGO

Words to Watch

slink (line 14): sneak
disembodied (line 33): without a body
full-blown (line 48): completely developed

You waited forty-five minutes for your dinner, and when it came it was cold—and not what you ordered in the first place. You asked for a seat in the nonsmoking section, and the flight attendant put you between two chain-smokers. Your new car broke down the first month, and the dealer wouldn't honor the warranty.   5

Do these examples of life's annoyances sound familiar to you? They probably do— because things just like them happen to all of us. And when they do, most of us just sit there and take it. We eat cold meals we didn't want. We cough on secondhand smoke. We pay for repairs that were supposed to be free.   10

What we don't often do is complain effectively. We talk about standing up for our rights, but when the opportunity comes, we don't. Perhaps we make one awkward attempt at protest—"Uh, excuse me, but I don't think I ordered squid and onions. . . ." Then we give up and suffer in silence. Or slink quietly away. We're afraid to "make a scene."   15

The truth is, though, that complaining often works. As the old proverb says, "The squeaky wheel gets the grease." Complain about a problem and it may be solved for you. If you don't complain, nothing will be done. But complaining is an art form. In order to do it successfully, you have to know two things: how to complain, and whom to complain to.   20

How to Complain

The way to complain is to act businesslike and important. If your complaint is immediate—you got the wrong order at a restaurant or the wrong seat at a theater—make a polite but firm request to see the manager or supervisor. When the manager comes, ask his or her name, and then state your problem and what you expect to have done about it. Be polite; shouting or acting rude   25
will get you nowhere. But also be firm. Don't say, "I, uh, was sort of expecting . . . ." Say, "I expected . . . ."

Act important. This doesn't mean to puff up your chest and say, "Do you know who I am?" What it means is that people are often treated the way they expect to be treated. If you act like someone who expects a fair request to be   30
granted, chances are it will be granted.

The worst way to complain is over the telephone. You are speaking to a disembodied voice, so you can't tell how the person on the line is reacting. It is easy for that person to give you "the runaround." Complaining in person or by letter is generally more effective.   35

If your complaint does not require a this-moment response, it often helps to complain by letter. If you have an appliance that doesn't work, for example, send a letter to the store that sold it, the company who made it, or both. Be businesslike and stick to the point—don't spend a paragraph on how your Uncle Joe tried to fix the problem and couldn't. Here's an outline for an   40
effective letter of complaint, including a "P.S.":

Paragraph 1: Explain what the problem is. Include any facts that back up your story.

Paragraph 2: Tell how you trust the company and are confident that your reader will fix the problem. (This is to "soften up" the reader a little bit.)

Paragraph 3: Carefully explain what you want done (repair, replacement, refund, etc.).

P.S. (Readers always notice a "P.S.") State when you expect the problem to be solved and what you'll do if it isn't.

Notice that the P.S. says what you'll do if your problem isn't solved. In other words, you make a (polite) threat. Your threat ought to be believable. A threat that you'll burn down the store if your purchase payment isn't refunded is not believable. (And if it were believed, it could get you thrown in jail.) A   45
threat to report the store to the Better Business Bureau, on the other hand, is believable.

One common threat is "I'll sue!" A full-blown lawsuit, with lawyers, is more trouble than most problems are worth. But most areas have a small-claims court where suits involving relatively modest amounts of money are 50 heard. These courts don't use complex legal language or procedures, and you don't need a lawyer to use them. A store or company will often settle with you (if you have a fair claim) rather than go to small-claims court.

Whom to Complain To

One of the greatest frustrations in complaining is talking to a clerk or receptionist who can't solve your problem and whose only purpose seems to 55 be to drive you crazy. Getting mad doesn't help, for the person you're mad at probably had nothing to do with your actual problem.

When complaining in person, ask for the manager or supervisor. When complaining by letter, get the name of the store manager or company president. (A librarian can help you find this information.) If you are complaining over 60 the phone, ask for the customer-relations department. If there is none, then ask for the manager or appropriate supervisor. Or talk to the head telephone operator, who will probably know who is responsible for solving problems.

Be persistent. One complaint may not get results. In that case, it may work to simply keep on complaining. This will "wear down" resistance on the other 65 side. If you have a problem with a store, call the store two or three times every day. Chances are someone there will get tired of you and take care of your complaint in order to be rid of you. *The squeaky wheel gets the grease.*

Time: _____   *Reading Rate (see page 444):* _____ *WPM*

■ **Check Your Understanding**

1. Which sentence best expresses the main idea of the selection?
   a. Life is full of annoyances.
   b. Most people don't like to complain.
   c. It is usually most effective to complain in person or by letter.
   d. Complaining succeeds if you know how to complain and whom to complain to.
2. The best way to complain is to
   a. act rudely.
   b. be polite but firm.
   c. be loud and angry.
   d. hire a lawyer.

3. To get results, complainers should
   a. act as if they expect their problem to be fixed.
   b. complain only over the phone.
   c. never threaten.
   d. write long letters.

4. Successful complainers
   a. prefer complaining over the phone.
   b. make violent results.
   c. complain to receptionists.
   d. are persistent.

5. *True or false?* _____ According to the author, companies would often rather settle with a complaining customer than go to small-claims court.

6. The author implies that when you write a complaint letter, you should
   a. have a lawyer sign it.
   b. provide a list of witnesses.
   c. use professional stationery.
   d. use a little flattery.

7. We can conclude that small claims courts
   a. are useless.
   b. are expensive.
   c. are used by ordinary citizens.
   d. forbid the use of lawyers.

8. From the selection, we can conclude that
   a. it's our duty to complain.
   b. the author is a lawyer.
   c. complaining takes effort.
   d. receptionists can solve complainers' problems.

Number Wrong: _____   *Score:* _____

0 wrong = 100%	2 wrong = 75%	4 wrong = 50%	6 wrong = 25%
1 wrong = 88%	3 wrong = 63%	5 wrong = 38%	7 wrong = 13%

SELECTION 3

Once again, you should make a deliberate effort to read at a rapid rate of speed. You must *will* your eyes to move faster, and you must *will* your brain to process rapidly the incoming facts, ideas, and details.

If you are not already doing so, sit up straight, put your feet flat on the floor, and hold the book at a comfortable angle. Consciously force your eyes to move at a higher rate of speed. Make the decision that you are going to read faster, and do it!

LEARNING TO KEEP YOUR COOL DURING TESTS
MARGARET JERRARD

Words to Watch

secreted (line 6): formed and released

peripheral sight (line 9): the ability to see beyond the edges of the line of direct sight

optimum (line 29): most favorable

keyed up (line 31): excited or tense

interspersing (line 38): doing at varying intervals

intuitive (line 51): done without reasoning

Have you ever felt so panicky during an examination that you couldn't even put down the answers you *knew*? If so, you were suffering from what is known as test anxiety.

According to psychologist Ralph Trimble, test anxiety is a very real problem for many people. When you're worried over your performance on an exam,   5 your heart beats faster, your pulse speeds up, hormones are secreted. These reactions trigger others: You may sweat more than normal or suffer from a stomachache or headache. Your field of vision narrows and becomes tunnel-like, leaving you with very little peripheral sight. Before you know it, you're having difficulty focusing.   10

"What I hear students say over and over again," says Dr. Trimble, who is involved with the Psychological and Counseling Center at the University of Illinois, "is, 'My mind went blank.' "

For a number of years, Dr. Trimble helped many students learn how to function better during exams and to bring up their grades. Some of these students were interested in sharing what they learned and, with Trimble's help, began holding workshops on overcoming test anxiety. For many students, just being in a workshop with other sufferers was a relief. They realized they weren't freaks, that they were not the only ones who had done poorly on tests because of tension. The workshops were so successful that they are still given. 20

In the workshops, students are taught that anxiety is normal. You just have to prevent it from getting the best of you. The first step is to learn to relax. If before or during an examination you start to panic, stretch as hard as you can, tensing the muscles in your arms and legs; then suddenly relax all of them. This will help relieve tension. 25

But keep in mind that you don't want to be *too* relaxed. Being completely relaxed is no better than being too tense. "If you are so calm you don't *care* how you do on an examination, you won't do well," Trimble says. "There is an optimum level of concern when you perform at your best. Some stress helps. There are people who can't take even slight stress. They have to learn 30 that in a challenging situation, being keyed up is good and will help them to do better. But if they label it anxiety and say, 'It's going to hit me again,' that will push them over the edge."

As a student you must also realize that if you leave too much studying until a day or two before the examination, you can't do the impossible and learn it 35 all. Instead, concentrate on what you *can* do and try to think what questions are likely to be asked and what you can do in the time left for studying.

When you sit down to study, set a moderate pace and vary it by interspersing reading, writing notes, and going over any papers you have already written for the course, as well as the textbooks and notes you took in class. Review 40 what you know. Take breaks and go to sleep in plenty of time to get a good night's rest before the exam. You should also eat a moderate breakfast or lunch, avoiding drinks with caffeine and steering clear of fellow students who get tense. Panic is contagious.

Get to the exam room a few minutes early so that you will have a chance 45 to familiarize yourself with the surroundings and get out your supplies. When the examination is handed out, read the directions twice and underline the significant instructions, making sure you understand them. Ask the teacher or proctor to explain if you don't. First answer the easiest questions, then go back to the more difficult. If you are stumped on a multiple-choice question, first 50 eliminate the impossible answers, then make as good an intuitive guess as possible and go on to the next.

On essay questions, instead of plunging right in, take a few minutes to organize your thoughts, make a brief outline, and then start off with a summary sentence. Keep working steadily, and even when time starts to run out, don't 55 speed up.

After the examination is over, don't torture yourself by thinking over all the mistakes you made, and don't start studying immediately for another exam. Instead, give yourself an hour or two of free time.

Among the students who are working now as volunteer leaders in the   60
workshops are a number who started out panicky and unable to function on exams. They learned how to deal with test anxiety and are now teaching others. It's almost as easy as ABC.

Time: _____   *Reading Rate (see page 444):* _____ *WPM*

■ Check Your Understanding

1. Which would be a good alternative title for this selection?
   a. How to Overcome Test Anxiety
   b. The Physical Side of Anxiety
   c. How to Get Better Grades
   d. Why Students Are Concerned about Grades
2. Which sentence best expresses the main idea of the selection?
   a. Most students suffer from test anxiety.
   b. Test anxiety can be controlled.
   c. Being relaxed is essential to doing well on exams.
   d. All students should attend stress-management workshops.
3. If you start to panic during a test, you should
   a. leave the room briefly.
   b. drink a cup of coffee.
   c. stretch and then relax your arms and legs.
   d. skip the essay questions.
4. The first thing to do when you receive the exam is to
   a. answer the questions you are sure of.
   b. underline the important instructions.
   c. make an outline of what you know.
   d. begin timing yourself.
5. *True or false?* _____ Anxiety can cause a well-prepared student to perform poorly on a test.
6. From the selection we can conclude that
   a. textbooks make better study guides than do class notes.
   b. anxiety is learned behavior that can be unlearned.
   c. students who do poorly in tests may need glasses.
   d. good students are completely calm before tests.

7. Which of the following tips is *not* mentioned in the article?
    a. Do easy questions first.
    b. Organize your thoughts before starting to write an essay answer.
    c. Ask the instructor to explain unclear directions.
    d. Budget your time for each part of the test.
8. The author implies that
    a. you should get to the exam room at the last minute in order to avoid panicky students.
    b. you should never guess on an exam.
    c. caffeine can increase anxiety.
    d. if you have kept up with the work, there's no need to study for the test.

Number Wrong: ——   *Score:* ——

0 wrong = 100%	2 wrong = 75%	4 wrong = 50%	6 wrong = 25%
1 wrong = 88%	3 wrong = 63%	5 wrong = 38%	7 wrong = 13%

SELECTION 4

With this selection, you may want to try the following technique. As you read, lightly underline each line of print with your index finger. Do not rest your hand on the page, and do not point to individual words with your finger. Hold your hand slightly above the page and use your finger as a pacer, moving it a little more quickly than your eyes can comfortably follow. Try to glide your finger smoothly across each line of print, and to make your eyes follow just as smoothly. If the technique helps you attend closely and read rapidly, use it in other selections as well.

AN ELECTRONIC FOG HAS SETTLED OVER AMERICA
PETE HAMILL

Words to Watch

erratic (line 14): irregular

baffled (line 16): puzzled

pondered (line 17): considered carefully

distracted (line 22): had (his) attention drawn away

disconsolate (line 79): cheerless

The year his son turned fourteen, Maguire noticed that the boy was getting dumber. This was a kid who had learned to talk at fourteen months, could read when he was four, was an A student for his first six years in school. The boy was bright, active, and imaginative. And then, slowly, the boy's brain began to deteriorate.   5

"He started to slur words," Maguire told me. "He couldn't finish sentences. He usually didn't hear me when I talked to him and couldn't answer me clearly when he did. In school, the A's became B's, and the B's became C's. I thought maybe it was something physical, and I had a doctor check him out. He was perfectly normal. Then the C's started to become D's. Finally, he started failing   10 everything. Worse, the two younger kids were repeating the pattern. From bright to dumb in a few short years."

Maguire was then an account executive in a major advertising agency; his hours were erratic, and the pace of his business life was often frantic. But when he would get home at night and talk to his wife about the kids, she would shake her head in a baffled way and explain that she was doing her best. Hustling from the office of one account to another, Maguire pondered the creeping stupidity of his children. Then he took an afternoon off from work and visited his oldest boy's school. 15

"They told me he just wasn't doing much work," Maguire said. "He owed them four book reports. He never said a word in social studies. His mind wandered, he was distracted, he asked to leave the room a lot. But the teacher told me he wasn't much different from all the other kids. In some ways, he was better. He at least did some work. Most of them, she told me, didn't do any work at all." 25

Maguire asked the teacher if she had any theories about why the kids behaved this way.

"Of course," she said. "Television."

Television? Maguire was staggered. He made his living off television. Often, he would sit with the kids in the TV room and point out the commercials 30 he had helped to create. Television had paid for his house in the suburbs, for his two cars, his clothes, his food, the pictures on the walls. It even paid for the kids' schools.

"What do you mean, television?" he said.

"Television rots minds," the teacher said flatly. "But most of us figure 35 there's nothing to be done about it anymore."

At work the next day, Maguire told his secretary to do some special research for him. Within a week, he had some scary numbers on his desk. The Scholastic Aptitude Tests (SATs) showed that the reading scores of all American high school students had fallen in every year since 1950, the year of 40 television's great national triumph. The mathematics scores were even worse. The average American kid spent four to six hours a day watching television and by age sixteen had witnessed eleven thousand homicides on the tube.

"I came home that night, and the kids were watching television with my wife," he said. "I looked at them, glued to the set. They nodded hello to me. 45 And suddenly I got scared. I imagined these four people, their brains rotted out, suddenly adding me to the evening's homicide count because I wanted them to talk to me. I went to the bedroom, and for the first time since college, I took down *Moby Dick* and started to read."

In the following week, Maguire accumulated more and more ideas about 50 the impact of television on the lives of Americans. All classes and colors had been affected intellectually; reading requires the decoding of symbols, the transforming of a word like *cat* into a cat that lives in the imagination. Television shows the cat. No active thought is required. Television even supplies a laugh track and music to trigger the emotions the imagination will 55 not create or release.

"I read somewhere that the worst danger to kids who become TV addicts is that while they are watching TV, they're not doing anything else," Maguire said. "They're not down in the school yard playing ball, or falling in love, or getting in fights, or learning to compromise. They're alone, with a box that   60
doesn't hear them if they want to talk back. They don't have to think, because everything is done for them. They don't have to question, because what's the point if you can't challenge the guy on the set?"

Television had also changed politics; Maguire's kids had political opinions based on the way candidates looked and how they projected themselves   65
theatrically. Politics, which should be based on the structure of analysis and thought, had become dominated by the structures of drama, that is to say, by conflict.

"I knew Reagan would win in a landslide," Maguire said. "As an actor, he fit right into the mass culture formed by thirty years of television."   70

Maguire tried to do something. He called a family conference after dinner one night, explained his discoveries, and suggested a voluntary limiting of television watching or its complete elimination for three months.

"I said we could start a reading program together," he told me. "All read the same book and discuss it at night. I told them we'd come closer together,   75
that I'd even change my job so I could be home more and not work on television commercials anymore."

After ten minutes, the kids began to squirm and yawn, as if expecting a commercial. Maguire's wife dazed out, her disconsolate face an unblinking mask. He gave up. Now, when he goes home, Maguire says hello, eats dinner,   80
and retreats to his bedroom. He is reading his way through Balzac.

Beyond the bedroom door, bathed in the cold light of the television set, are the real people of his life. Their dumbness grows, filling up the room, moving out into the quiet suburban town, joining the great gray fog that has enveloped America.   85

Time: _____   Reading Rate (see page 444): _____ WPM

■ **Check Your Understanding**

1. Which would be a good alternative title for this selection?
   a. Why Students Dislike School
   b. Maguire's Story
   c. The Dangers of Television
   d. How to Cut Down on TV Watching

2. Which sentence best expresses the main idea of the selection?
   a. Maguire's family has become dumber from watching TV.
   b. Children must watch less TV if they want to do well in school.
   c. Neglecting one's family life can lead to serious problems.
   d. By deadening thought, television has turned us into zombies.

3. *True or false?* _____ The average American child spends four to six hours a day watching television.

4. Television is most dangerous to children because it makes them
   a. bored.
   b. passive.
   c. violent.
   d. depressed.

5. Maguire believes that many politicians are elected on the basis of their
   a. experience.
   b. images.
   c. wealth.
   d. conservative beliefs.

6. *True or false?* _____ The teacher interviewed by Maguire appeared resigned to the influence of TV on her students.

7. The author implies that
   a. Maguire's children would have been better students if Maguire had been home more.
   b. the Maguires' problem could be found in most of the households in America.
   c. President Reagan's acting abilities made him a better leader.
   d. educational television does not rot the mind.

8. The "great gray fog" symbolizes
   a. a decline in moral standards.
   b. political corruption.
   c. growing passivity and weakening intellectual skills.
   d. the use of television as a political tool and mind-control instrument.

Number Wrong: _____   *Score:* _____

| 0 wrong = 100% | 2 wrong = 75% | 4 wrong = 50% | 6 wrong = 25% |
| 1 wrong = 88% | 3 wrong = 63% | 5 wrong = 38% | 7 wrong = 13% |

SELECTION 5

Remember that it is your *deliberate effort to read faster*, along with extensive practice, that will make you a speed reader. Keep this crucial fact in mind as you read this selection.

CIPHER IN THE SNOW
JEAN MIZER TODHUNTER

Words to Watch

cipher (title): a person of little importance
bleakly (line 44): gloomily
meager (line 47): insufficient
annotations (line 57): notes
resilience (line 63): the ability to recover full strength and spirits
peaked (line 68): thin and sickly

On most snowy mornings on my way to the high school where I teach, I drive behind the school bus. I was trailing the bus on one biting cold February morning when it veered and stopped short at the town hotel. It had no business doing this, and I was annoyed as I had to bring my car to an unexpected stop. A boy lurched out of the bus, reeled, stumbled, and collapsed on the snowbank   5 at the curb. The bus driver and I reached him at the same moment. His thin, hollow face was white even against the snow.

"He's dead," the driver whispered.

It didn't register for a minute. I glanced quickly at the scared young faces staring down at us from the school bus. "A doctor! Quick! I'll phone from   10 the hotel. . . ."

"No use. I tell you he's dead." The driver looked down at the boy's still form. "He never even said he felt bad," he muttered, "just tapped me on the shoulder and said, real quiet, 'I'm sorry. I have to get off at the hotel.' That's all. Polite and apologizing like."   15

At school the giggling, shuffling morning noise quieted as the news went down the halls. I passed a huddle of girls. "Who was it? Who dropped dead on the way to school?" I heard one of them half whisper.

434

"Don't know his name; some kid from Milford Corners," was the reply.

It was like that in the faculty room and the principal's office. "I'd appreciate 20
your going out to tell the parents," the principal told me. "They haven't a
phone, and anyway, somebody from school should go there in person. I'll
cover your classes."

"Why me?" I asked. "Wouldn't it be better if you did it?"

"I didn't know the boy," the principal admitted levelly. "And in last year's 25
sophomore personalities column I noted that you were listed as his favorite
teacher."

I drove through the snow and cold down the bad canyon road to the Evans
place and thought about the boy, Cliff Evans. His favorite teacher! Why, he
hasn't spoken two words to me in two years! I could see him in my mind's eye 30
all right, sitting back there in the last seat in my afternoon literature class. He
came in the room by himself and left by himself. "Cliff Evans," I muttered to
myself, "a boy who never talked." I thought a minute. "A boy who never
smiled. I never saw him smile once."

The big ranch kitchen was clean and warm. I blurted out my news 35
somehow. Mrs. Evans reached blindly for a chair. "He never said anything
about bein' ailing."

His stepfather snorted. "He ain't said nothin' about anything since I moved
in here."

Mrs. Evans got up, pushed a pan to the back of the stove, and began to 40
untie her apron. "Now hold on," her husband snapped. "I got to have
breakfast before I go to town. Nothin' we can do now anyway. If Cliff hadn't
been so dumb, he'd have told us he didn't feel good."

After school I sat in the office and stared bleakly at the records spread out
before me. I was to close the boy's file and write his obituary for the school 45
paper. The almost bare sheets mocked the effort. "Cliff Evans, white, never
legally adopted by stepfather, five half brothers and sisters." These meager
strands of information and the list of D grades were about all the records had
to offer.

Cliff Evans had silently come in the school door in the mornings and gone 50
out of the school door in the evenings, and that was all. He had never belonged
to a club. He had never played on a team. He had never held an office. As
far as I could tell, he had never done one happy, noisy kid thing. He had never
been anybody at all.

How do you go about making a boy into a zero? The grade school records 55
showed me much of the answer. The first and second grade teachers'
annotations read "sweet, shy child"; "timid but eager." Then the third grade
note had opened the attack. Some teacher had written in a good, firm hand,
"Cliff won't talk. Uncooperative. Slow learner." The other academic sheet
had followed with "dull"; "slow-witted"; "low IQ." They became correct. The 60
boy's IQ score in the ninth grade was listed at 83. But his IQ in the third grade
had been 106. The score didn't go under 100 until the seventh grade. Even
timid, sweet children have resilience. It takes time to break them.

I stomped to the typewriter and wrote a savage report pointing out what education had done to Cliff Evans. I slapped a copy on the principal's desk and another in the sad, dog-eared file; slammed the file; and crashed the office door shut as I left for home. But I didn't feel much better. A little boy kept walking after me, a boy with a peaked face, a skinny body in faded jeans, and big eyes that had searched for a long time and then had become veiled.

I could guess how many times he'd been chosen last to be on a team, how many whispered child conversations had excluded him. I could see the faces and hear the voices that said over and over, "You're dumb. You're dumb. You're just a nothing, Cliff Evans."

A child is a believing creature. Cliff undoubtedly believed them. Suddenly it seemed clear to me: When finally there was nothing left at all for Cliff Evans, he collapsed on a snowbank and went away. The doctor might list "heart failure" as the cause of death, but that wouldn't change my mind.

We couldn't find ten students in the school who had known Cliff well enough to attend the funeral as his friends. So the student body officers and a committee from the junior class went as a group to the church, looking politely sad. I attended the service with them and sat through it with a lump of cold lead in my chest and a big resolve growing in me.

I've never forgotten Cliff Evans or that resolve. He has been my challenge year after year, class after class. Each September, I look up and down the rows carefully at the unfamiliar faces. I look for veiled eyes or bodies scrouged into a seat in an alien world. "Look, kids," I say silently, "I may not do anything else for you this year, but not one of you is going out of here a nobody. I'll work or fight to the bitter end doing battle with society and the school board, but I won't have one of you leaving here thinking yourself into a zero."

Most of the time—not always, but most of the time—I've succeeded.

Time: _____   *Reading Rate (see page 444):* _____ WPM

■ Check Your Understanding

1. The writer was surprised that Cliff Evans
   a. had no friends.
   b. regarded her as his favorite teacher.
   c. was always so quiet.
   d. never spoke more than he did.

2. As a result of what she learned about Cliff Evans, the writer resolved to
   a. write an article about him.
   b. resign her job.
   c. protect other children from a similar fate.
   d. register a protest with the school board.

3. *True or false?* _____ Cliff Evans's IQ remained the same through his years at school.

4. *True or false?* _____ Cliff was both legally and personally rejected by his stepfather.

5. The writer believes that Cliff died because
   a. of heart failure.
   b. he was ignored and rejected at home.
   c. he believed he was a nothing.
   d. of rejection by his teachers.

6. *True or false?* _____ The writer believes that because previous teachers labeled Cliff as a slow learner, he eventually became one.

7. *True or false?* _____ Cliff Evans's funeral was attended by the ten students who knew him best at school.

8. The writer's tone is one of
   a. detachment.
   b. puzzlement.
   c. resignation.
   d. anger.

Number Wrong: _____   *Score:* _____

0 wrong = 100%	2 wrong = 75%	4 wrong = 50%	6 wrong = 25%
1 wrong = 88%	3 wrong = 63%	5 wrong = 38%	7 wrong = 13%

SELECTION 6

This is the last selection you will read. Try to make your speed here your fastest. Think of yourself as a runner ready to jump from the starting line at the shot of the gun. Make up your mind to go through the selection at the highest speed of which you are capable without losing comprehension.

DARE MIGHTY THINGS
ART WILLIAMS

Words to Watch

> *ignoble* (line 1): dishonorable
>
> *strenuous* (line 2): requiring great effort or energy
>
> *contenders* (line 43): fighters
>
> *perseverance* (line 62): persistence
>
> *adversity* (line 62, line 82): trouble
>
> *faltered* (line 100): weakened

"I wish to preach, not the doctrine of ignoble ease, but the doctrine of the strenuous life," said Theodore Roosevelt in an 1899 speech before the Hamilton Club in Chicago. I would like to add to Roosevelt's doctrine of the strenuous life the equally important doctrine of the winning attitude.

You're not born with it. It's not for sale. You can't go to college and get   5
a degree in it. But a winning attitude may be the single most important ingredient in your personal and career success.

Over the years, I've come to believe that attitude is often the determining factor in success or failure. It's an intangible thing—you can't see it or touch it. But you can see the effects of attitude, both positive and negative, in the   10
results it creates in people's lives.

Everyone has the opportunity to win in life, but most people won't win. Most people will get tired and give up, because they're not willing to pay the price. They have the ability, but they lack the most important determining factor in success—the will to win. The will to win is simply a part of attitude. If you   15
have that one quality, you can do almost everything else wrong and still come out a winner.

When I first started as a salesman, I made a lot of mistakes. I would come home every night and say, "Art, how could you do something that stupid? How could you mess things up like that?" Then I'd go out the next day and make   20
another mistake, and I'd come home the next night saying the same thing. I made a million dumb mistakes, but something kept me going.

And looking back, I'm convinced that the only thing that kept me from giving up, and kept me holding on until I started to do things right, was the will to win. I learned the importance of a winning attitude from my father, a head   25
coach in Cairo, Georgia. That thin thread of determination turned out to be a lifeline that has helped me across all the tough spots in my life.

The sports arena is one of the best places in the world to learn about attitude. We've all seen the underdog football or baseball team that lacked seasoned talent, was racked by injuries and bad luck and branded as losers   30
rise above all the odds and beat teams three times as talented.

Once in my coaching career, I inherited a weak little football team of underweight, inexperienced kids, who had such a history of losing that they didn't even want to dress out at practice. I knew that I couldn't make them physically perfect and professional in one season. No coach could have. The   35
only thing I could do was to make them see themselves as winners.

We practiced as if there were no tomorrow, and we worked harder than any other team. But, most important, every day I told these kids they were winners. I let them know from day one that I expected them to have a winning season. I stressed not only physical toughness but mental toughness.   40

At first, they must have thought I was crazy. But, you know, slowly they began to believe it. Little by little, they began to look at themselves as contenders. When they won their first game, they were sold on themselves, and after that there was no stopping them. They had developed a winning attitude. They hadn't become different people overnight. They still weren't in   45
a class with other teams in the area. But they saw themselves as winners, and that perception changed everything.

That perception is the key to achievement. Writers and researchers who have spent years studying successful people conclude that success is made of three parts: one part talent, one part "breaks" (or being at the right place at   50
the right time), and one part "will to win." A common denominator among successful people is their ability to perceive themselves as winners, even at their lowest moments. Why is this so important? Because it's a fact of life that everyone lives up to his own expectations of himself. Winners have in common a "burning desire" to succeed, and that quality provided the motivation that   55
was needed to make that team's goals a reality.

I firmly believe that life will give you whatever you will accept. If you accept being average and ordinary, life will make you average and ordinary. If you accept being poor (either financially or in spirit), life will make you poor; and if you accept being unhappy, life will deliver that, too.   60

You must expect to win. "Will to win" in action means an attitude of perseverance, even in the face of every adversity, and a determination to succeed, even when the odds are stacked against you. The greatest definition of a winner I've ever seen goes like this: "Most people can stay motivated for two or three months. A few people can stay motivated for two or three years. 65 But a winner will stay motivated for as long as it takes to win."

In business, I encounter people almost every day who have dozens of good reasons that they don't succeed. They usually go something like this: "People like me don't get a chance in today's world." "The odds are stacked against me." "Someone from my background can't compete with people who are born 70 with a silver spoon in their mouths." "I don't have a college education." "I'm held back by my responsibilities."

Excuses don't count. Everyone has the ability to begin where he is right now to turn his life around, to start becoming somebody special. The decision to do it is the starting point. The feeling that you can do it—a winning attitude— 75 will make it work for you.

Someone once said, "Tough times don't last—tough people do." Life gets tough for all of us at one time or another. The many devastating things that can happen—business failure, personal unhappiness, family tragedy—all have the potential to destroy the heart of a person. But tough people can turn these 80 times into determination to move ahead. They can make the most miserable circumstances a challenge to survive and defeat adversity. Nobody ever said it was easy. It's not. But the results of becoming that kind of person will have an effect on every aspect of your life.

Sounds good, you say, but how do I develop this attitude? 85

My theory is this: If you want to be "a winner," you've got to become a dreamer again. Most people in America have stopped dreaming. They grow up with everyone telling them how special they are. They are really "turned on" about life and about becoming somebody that they'll be proud of. Then they're thrown out into the big, real world, and these once motivated, enthusiastic 90 people go into a shell. They begin to develop an attitude that "Life has passed me by. Life has dealt me a bad hand."

To develop a winning attitude you must relearn how to dream. You must become excited, confident, and enthusiastic about your life just one more time.

I can think of a particular instance of someone who succeeded in turning 95 a battered outlook on life into a winning attitude. Cindy joined our company as a part-time employee and made good progress; eventually her husband began to work with her in the business. Then misfortune hit. Her daughter contracted a serious disease. Their house caught fire. Several of her associates quit suddenly, and her business faltered. Both cars were about to be repos- 100 sessed. The money completely ran out, and things got progressively worse.

The situation came to a head when, suddenly, her husband's mother became ill. On the day she will always view as the worst of her life, she took her husband to his mother's, returned to her house (which was also in the process of being repossessed), and realized there was nothing in the home to 105 eat and no money.

For Cindy, that day was the turning point of her life. It was the day she decided to take control of her life—and to win.

When her husband returned, they counseled together. He took an outside job, and she threw herself back into the business. With no money and thousands 110 of dollars worth of debts, they began again. And inch by inch, day by day, one debt at a time, they crawled back.

What brought Cindy back? A winning attitude. A determination not to be defeated, a decision never to make excuses. She found the ability to dream of being a winner, even when every standard of society said she was the worst 115 kind of loser. She became motivated, and she stayed motivated for as long as it took to win.

When people in our company come to me and want advice on how to succeed, I don't waste time with business tips. My best advice is to tell them to look inside themselves and pull out the ability to dream big. I tell them to 120 grab on to that person who is deep down in there somewhere—the one who always knows, "I can win." And I know that if they can do that, the rest of it will surely follow.

It's worth thinking about. I've seen it work too many times to attribute it to luck. Think about it, and consider it for your own life. Reach inside and 125 find that dream you've been hanging on to—the one about becoming somebody special, doing something great with your life. And use that dream to build your own winning attitude. If you believe in it, *really* believe in it, you'll have the security of knowing that nothing can defeat you. And that's real security, the kind that only true winners have.   130

The little football team did have a winning season. Today, Cindy is a top executive with a flourishing business. In both cases, the ability to develop a winning attitude made all the difference. The tough times didn't last and the people involved are still going strong. Tough people always do. That's why they call them "winners."   135

Time: _____   *Reading Rate (see page 444):* _____ WPM

■ **Check Your Understanding**

1. Which of the following would be a good alternative title for this selection?
   a. How to Improve Your Attitude
   b. An Underdog Team
   c. How to Cope with Tough Times
   d. The Importance of a Winning Attitude

2. Which sentence best expresses the main idea of the selection?
   a. A winning attitude is the key to success.
   b. Cindy overcame incredible personal problems.
   c. Losers often make excuses for not succeeding.
   d. Success is partly talent and partly lucky breaks.

3. Which of the following is *not* one of the three parts that, in the author's view, make up success?
   a. Breaks
   b. Talent
   c. Will to win
   d. Money to get started

4. In order to develop a winning attitude, one must
   a. become a dreamer.
   b. try to become wealthy.
   c. make excuses for one's failures.
   d. expect life to deliver unhappiness.

5. According to the author, one of the best settings for learning about attitude is
   a. sports.
   b. an assertiveness training course.
   c. school.
   d. self-help books.

6. From the selection we can conclude that
   a. the author once had a losing attitude.
   b. you can never help someone else to become a winner.
   c. the author feels sorry for ''born losers.''
   d. you can help a friend develop a winning attitude.

7. *True or false?* _____ The author implies that a positive attitude is enough to overcome any adversity in life.

8. The author implies that
   a. some people can never develop a winning attitude.
   b. all winners become well off financially.
   c. most losers eventually become winners.
   d. it is possible for a winner to become a loser.

Number Wrong: _____   *Score:* _____

0 wrong = 100%	2 wrong = 75%	4 wrong = 50%	6 wrong = 25%
1 wrong = 88%	3 wrong = 63%	5 wrong = 38%	7 wrong = 13%

RAPID READING PROGRESS CHART

Reading Selection	Speed (WPM)	Comprehension (%)
1 Malcolm X		
2 Complaining		
3 Tests		
4 TV Fog		
5 Cipher		
6 Dare Mighty Things		

Initial Reading Rate ("Malcolm X")

Speed _____ WPM; comprehension _____ %

Final Reading Rate ("Dare")

Speed _____ WPM; comprehension _____ %

READING RATE TABLE

You can use the following table to find the number of words you read per minute in each of the six selections in Part Six and in the mastery test on page 499. Suppose, for example, that you read selection 5 in three minutes and thirty seconds (3:30). To locate your WPM, go across the 3:30 column until you come to column 5. The place where the two columns meet gives your WPM—in this case, 304.

Enter your WPM and your comprehension score for a selection into the progress chart on the preceding page.

Time	1 Malcolm X	2 Complaining	3 Tests	4 TV Fog	5 Cipher	6 Dare	Mastery Test
1:00	510	906	800	1050	1065	1560	770
1:10	437	777	689	905	912	1345	660
1:20	382	680	602	789	798	1173	578
1:30	340	604	533	700	710	1040	513
1:40	306	544	482	633	639	934	462
1:50	278	494	437	574	580	852	420
2:00	255	453	400	525	532	780	385
2:10	235	418	370	486	491	722	355
2:20	218	388	343	451	456	670	330
2:30	204	362	320	420	426	624	308
2:40	191	340	301	395	399	584	288
2:50	180	320	283	371	375	551	271

(Continued)

Time	1 Malcolm X	2 Complaining	3 Tests	4 TV Fog	5 Cipher	6 Dare	Mastery Test
3:00	170	302	267	350	355	520	256
3:10	161	286	253	332	336	494	243
3:20	152	272	240	315	319	468	231
3:30	145	259	229	300	304	445	220
3:40	139	247	219	287	290	425	210
3:50	133	236	209	274	277	407	200
4:00	127	227	200	263	266	390	192
4:10	122	217	192	252	225	375	184
4:20	117	209	185	242	245	360	177
4:30	113	201	178	233	236	346	171
4:40	109	194	172	225	228	334	165
4:50	105	187	166	217	220	322	159
5:00	102	181	160	210	213	312	154
5:10	98	175	155	203	206	302	149
5:20	95	170	150	197	199	292	144
5:30	92	165	145	191	193	283	140
5:40		160	141	186	187	275	135
5:50		155	137	180	182	267	132
6:00		151	133	175	177	260	128
6:10		147	130	170	172	253	124
6:20		143	126	166	168	246	121

(Continued)

Time	1 Malcolm X	2 Complaining	3 Tests	4 TV Fog	5 Cipher	6 Dare	Mastery Test
6:30		140	123	162	163	240	118
6:40		136	120	158	159	233	115
6:50		133	117	154	155	228	112
7:00		130	114	150	152	222	110
7:10		126	112	147	148	217	107
7:20		124	109	143	145	212	105
7:30		121	107	140	142	208	102
7:40		118	104	137	138	203	100
7:50		116	102	134	135	199	98
8:00		113		131	133	195	
8:10		111		127	130	191	
8:20		109		126	127	187	
8:30		107		124	125	183	
8:40		105		121	122	180	
8:50		103		119	120	177	
9:00		101		117	118	173	
9:10		99		115	116	170	
9:20				113	114	167	
9:30					112	164	111
9:40					110	161	109
9:50					108	158	107
10:00					106	156	105

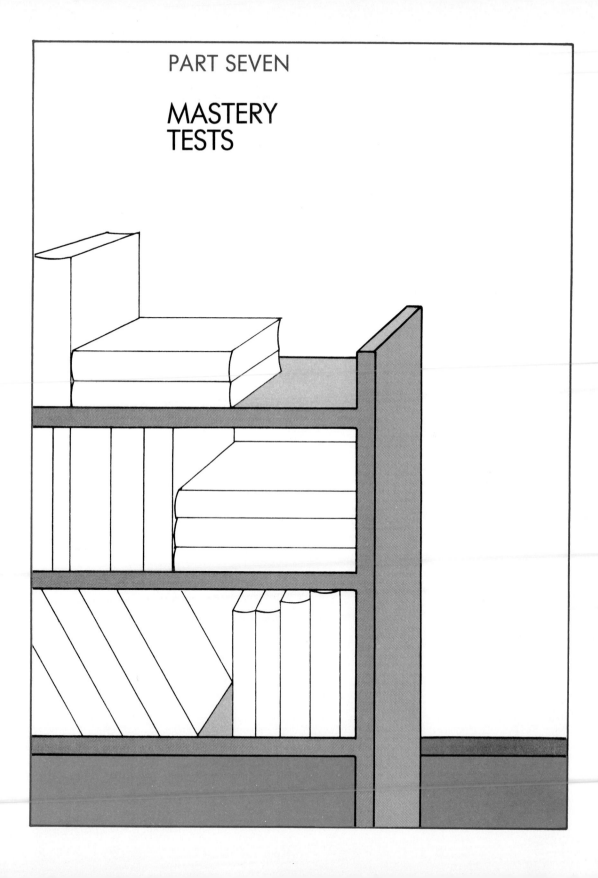

PART SEVEN

MASTERY TESTS

PREVIEW

Part Seven consists of a series of mastery tests for many of the skills in the book. Such tests can be used as homework assignments, supplementary activities, in-class quizzes at the end of a section, or review tests at any point during the semester. As much as possible, the tests are designed so that they can be scored objectively, using the special box at the bottom of each test page.

NOTE TO INSTRUCTORS

Another complete set of mastery tests for use with *Reading and Study Skills* is included in the Instructor's Manual.

MOTIVATIONAL SKILLS

■ Mastery Test

Answer the following questions.

1. An inner commitment to doing the work college demands
   a. is impossible when your life is confusing and difficult.
   b. is the most important factor in doing well in school.
   c. will help solve your personal and family problems.
   d. guarantees that you will get A and B grades.

2. To achieve a long-term career goal, a person must first set and work toward

   a continuing series of _____ goals.

3. *True or false?* _____ One way you can begin to set a career goal is by visiting the college counseling center.

4. Career-oriented courses should be
   a. the only courses you take.
   b. geared toward an area with promising employment opportunities.
   c. entertaining, not boring.
   d. studied in specialized, vocational-type schools.

5. *True or false?* _____ Because the author spent most of his first college years in the student game room, he had to drop his mathematics and chemistry courses.

6. According to Jean Coleman's recommendation, a student with a forty-hour-a-week job should take
   a. four courses.
   b. no courses.
   c. two courses.
   d. one course.

7. *True or false?* _____ According to Jean Coleman, younger students are more prone to dropping out of school than are older students.

8. Jean Coleman sees two kinds of students each semester: ones with a childish

   attitude toward school and ones with a _____ attitude.

9. Withdrawing from college
   a. never helps.
   b. shows a weak character.
   c. is sometimes the best response.
   d. will solve your personal problems.

10. Which of the following is *not* one of the avoidance tactics described in the section about students' attitudes?
   a. "I'll do it later."
   b. "I'm too disorganized."
   c. "I can't do it."
   d. "I'm bored with the subject."

Score: Number correct (_____) × 10 = _____%

TAKING CLASSROOM NOTES

■ Mastery Test

Some of the questions that follow are true-false or multiple-choice questions, and some require you to write short answers.

1. To guard against forgetting, it is essential to _____ the material that you hear in class.
2. What symbol should you use in the margin of your notes to mark examples that you have written down? _____
3. To get a head start on understanding a topic, you should read in advance in your _____ a topic to be presented in class.
4. Which of the following methods might an instructor use to signal the importance of an idea?
   a. repetition of a point
   b. emphasis signals
   c. tone of voice
   d. enumerations
   e. all of the above
5. Often the most important single step you can take to perform well in a course is to
   a. sit where the instructor can see you and listen carefully.
   b. write down definitions and examples.
   c. be there and take effective notes.
   d. not stop taking notes during discussion periods or at the end of a class.
6. *True or false?* _____ Some teachers present important ideas during discussion periods rather than in a formal lecture.
7. Circle the two methods that are effective ways of studying your classroom notes:
   a. Put them on a tape recorder and listen to the recorder after class.
   b. Pick out key recall words on each page and write them in the margin.
   c. Make up brief study notes on each page of notes.
   d. Rewrite the notes as neatly as possible.
8. Take notes in outline form as far as possible by starting main points at the margin and by _____ secondary points.

9. *True or false?* _____ Taking too few rather than too many notes in class is one reason students have trouble doing well in their courses.

10. How would you abbreviate the term *self-actualization* during a fast-moving psychology lecture? _____

Score: Number correct (_____) × 10 = _____%

TIME CONTROL AND CONCENTRATION

■ Mastery Test

Some of the questions that follow are true-false or multiple-choice questions, and some require you to write short answers.

1. What dates should you mark off on a large monthly calendar?

   _____

2. What are the three principal steps that you should take to gain control of your time?
   a. Watch your health.
   b. Use a daily or weekly "to do" list.
   c. Try to study each class day.
   d. Use a large monthly calendar.
   e. Keep your schedule flexible.
   f. Make up a weekly study schedule.

3. *True or false?* _____ During a study session, you should try to ignore lapses of concentration.

4. You can probably study most effectively in a
   a. very tense position.
   b. slighty tense position.
   c. completely relaxed position.

5. Studying may be more effective in time blocks of
   a. 15 minutes.
   b. 30 minutes.
   c. 60 minutes.
   d. 120 minutes.

6. The value of regular study hours is that
   a. you will make studying a habit.
   b. you will stay up-to-date on courses.
   c. you will learn more effectively by spacing your study sessions.
   d. all of the above will happen.

7. Where should you place your monthly calendar and weekly study schedule?

   _____

8. When you make up a "to do" list, you should
   a. schedule one-hour blocks of study time.
   b. mark down exam deadlines.
   c. decide on priorities.
   d. hang it on your wall.

9. *True or false?* _____ As a general rule, you should not reward yourself after a period of effective study time.

10. One benefit of setting specific study goals at the start of a study session is that
   a. you work on one subject during an entire study session.
   b. you keep track of your lapses of concentration.
   c. you avoid working on difficult subjects.
   d. your task is broken down into manageable units.

Score: Number correct (_____) × 10 = _____%

TEXTBOOK STUDY I

■ Mastery Test

Some of the questions that follow are true-false or multiple-choice questions, and some require you to write short answers.

1. Circle the one thing you do *not* do when previewing a selection.
   a. Study the title.
   b. Read over the first and last paragraphs.
   c. Write down important ideas.
   d. Look for relationships between headings and subheadings.

2. *True or false?* _____ Many students mark off too much material when reading a textbook.

3. *True or false?* _____ Your first reading of a chapter should proceed slowly, and you should stop as often as necessary to reread material until you are sure you understand it all.

4. *Choose the best answer:* Examples should be
   a. underlined.
   b. circled.
   c. labeled *ex* in the margin.
   d. underlined and labeled *ex* in the margin.

5. You should set off definitions in the text by _____ them.

6. Use _____ to mark off each point in an enumeration (list of items).

7. *True or false?* _____ Every note that you write down should have a symbol in front of it, such as A, B, 1, 2, a, b, or the like.

8. To study a textbook chapter, first you *preview* the chapter. Then you _____ it through once, marking off what appear to be important ideas.

9. As the third step in studying a chapter, you reread, decide on the important ideas, and _____ study notes. Finally, you recite the material to yourself, over and over, until you have learned it.

10. Leave space in the margin of your notes so that you can write key _____ to help you study the notes.

Score: Number correct (_____) × 10 = _____%

TEXTBOOK STUDY II

■ Mastery Test

Complete the four-step study process that follows this selection from a sociology textbook.

STATUSES

A *status* is a position an individual occupies in a social structure. In a sense, a status is a social address. It tells people where the individual "fits" in society—as a mother, college professor, senior citizen, or prison inmate. Knowing a person's status—knowing that you are going to meet a judge or a janitor, a ten-year-old or a fifty-year-old—tells you something about how that person will behave toward you and how you are expected to behave toward him or her. Misjudging status is a frequent cause of embarrassment—as when a woman invites a man she assumes is a bachelor to an intimate dinner and discovers he is married.

Social statuses can be divided into two groups. Some social statuses are *achieved*, or attained through personal effort. For example, individuals achieve the status of senator or sanitation-man, concert pianist or soccer coach, wife or divorcee, through their own choices and behavior. The statuses of convict, junkie, and high school dropout are also achieved. Other social statuses are *ascribed*, or assigned to the individual at birth or at different stages in the life cycle. For instance, men and women, blacks and whites, occupy different statuses in American society because of "what they are," not because of anything they do. Age is another ascribed status. Children occupy one position in society, adults another, elderly people still another. Individuals at each level are expected to act their age. It is important to note that while individuals have considerable control over achieved statuses, they have little or no control over ascribed statuses. The Prince of Wales, for example, was born to his position; he is a prince whether he likes it or not; there is almost nothing he can do to change his "social address."

Step 1: Preview.   Take about fifteen seconds to preview the above passage. The title tells you that the passage is about _____. How many terms are set off in italics in the passage? _____

Step 2: Read and Mark. Read the passage straight through. As you do, underline the definitions you find. Mark with an *Ex* in the margin an example that makes each definition clear for you. Also, number the items in the basic enumeration in the passage.

Step 3: Write.   Complete the following study notes on "Statuses":

Status—_____

_____

Two kinds of _____

1. _____

   Ex.—_____

2. _____

   Ex.—_____

Individuals can control achieved statuses but not ascribed ones. E.g., Prince of Wales has ascribed status from birth.

Step 4: Recite.   Jot down in the spaces below the recall words that could help you recite the material to yourself.

_____   _____

Score: Number correct (_____) × 10 = _____%

TEXTBOOK STUDY III

■ Mastery Test

Complete the four-step study process that follows this selection from a psychology textbook.

REASONS FOR FORGETTING

Forgetting can be embarrassing, inconvenient, and unpleasant. The kind of forgetting of greatest concern to psychologists is of items or events that have been stored in long-term memory and that have become difficult to retrieve. Several explanations have been given to describe why this type of retrieval problem occurs.

Repression

One possible explanation for being unable to retrieve memories is *repression*. Repression is unconsciously motivated forgetting; it is an unconscious blocking of things that are frightening or threatening. Traumatic events and anxiety-provoking people and situations can be painful if they are retrieved from long-term memory. Everyone has encountered some form of repression. Any time you refuse to talk or think about an unpleasant happening, you are experiencing a type of repression. According to Freud, it is a way of protecting yourself from remembering things that are distressing.

Suppression

Have you ever wanted to forget something? Perhaps you did something embarrassing or foolish and wanted to suppress the memory. *Suppression* is a conscious effort to avoid thinking about an event. Since you are aware of the event, suppression is different from repression.

Amnesia

Amnesia is a disorder that displays the most extreme form of repression. It is a loss of memory or a memory gap that includes forgetting personal information that would normally be recalled. Because of the dramatic effect, amnesia patients have been used as the subjects of novels, films, and soap operas. While amnesia victims forget almost all basic information, they do retain basic memories. They remember how to add, subtract, read, write, dress, and cook.

Like repression, amnesia is a limited explanation of why forgetting occurs. It is not nearly as common as the media suggest and can account for only a tiny percentage of forgetting.

Interference

Interference is the most popular explanation for why forgetting occurs. You forget because other information interferes with your memory. According to the interference description of forgetting, there are two types of obstructions to remembering: proactive interference and retroactive interference.

Proactive interference. Proactive means "acting forward." *Proactive interference* refers to instances when previous memories block the recall of more recent learnings. Suppose you meet a new psychology instructor named Professor Kassel, who reminds you of your old girlfriend, Flora Belle. You may have difficulty remembering the professor's correct name and want to call her Flora Belle. In proactive interference, earlier learning interferes with new learning.

Retroactive interference. Retroactive means "acting backward." *Retroactive interference* refers to instances where recent learning blocks the recall of previous memories. If the next time you meet your old girlfriend Flora Belle, you have difficulty remembering her name and have an urge to call her "Professor," retroactive inhibition will be contributing to your forgetting.

Step 1: Preview. Take about thirty seconds to preview the above passage. The title tells you that the passage is about the reasons for forgetting. How many subheads are there in the passage? _____ How many terms are set off in italics in the passage? _____

Step 2: Read and Mark. Read the passage straight through. As you do, underline the definitions you find. Mark with an *Ex* in the margin any example that helps make a definition clear. Also, number the items in the two enumerations in the passage.

Step 3: Write. Complete the following study notes on "Reasons for Forgetting":

Reasons for forgetting:

1. Repression—_____

    _____

2. Suppression—_____

    _____

3. Amnesia—_____

    _____

4. Interference—Forget because other information interferes with your learning.
   a. Proactive interference—_____

   _____

       Ex—Want to call new Professor Kassel by name of your old girlfriend Flora Belle.

   b. Retroactive interference—_____

   _____

       Ex.—_____

Step 4: Recite. To remember the four reasons for forgetting, create a *catchword:* a word made up of the first letters in the four reasons for forgetting. Write your catchword here:

_____

To remember the two kinds of interference, create a *catchphrase:* a two-word sentence in which the first word begins with P (for *proactive*) and the second word begins with R (for *retroactive*). Write your catchphrase here:

_____

Score: Number correct (_____) × 10 = _____%

BUILDING A POWERFUL MEMORY

■ **Mastery Test**

Some of the questions that follow are true-false or multiple-choice questions, and some require you to write short answers.

1. The first step in effective remembering is to _____ the material to be learned.

2. The best way to avoid passive studying is to
   a. study right before bed.
   b. test yourself on the material to be learned.
   c. copy several times the material to be learned.
   d. review material in the morning.

3. *True or false?* _____ Material is best studied in a single long session rather than spaced out over several sessions.

4. Overlearning is
   a. unnecessary memorization.
   b. going over a lesson you already know.
   c. incompatible with learning.
   d. a way to "push out" old ideas so that you can learn new ones.

5. If you reduce ideas to key words and memorize the key words, they will often serve as _____ that will help you pull the ideas into memory.

6. What aid to memory is illustrated by the fact that someone will always remember the name of a person who owes him or her money?
   a. Spacing memory work
   b. Intending to learn
   c. Using key words as hooks
   d. Overlearning

7. To gain the good overall understanding you need to learn material effectively, you should
   a. attend class lectures regularly.
   b. read textbook assignments.
   c. take classroom and textbook notes.
   d. do all of the above.

8. One memory aid is to include as a study period the time just before _____.

9. Write a catchword that will help you remember the first letters of the following kinds of defense mechanisms: *projection, repression, identification.*

_____

10. Write a catchphrase that will help you remember the following kinds of taxes: *self-employment, income, sales, property.* _____

_____

Score: Number correct (_____) × 10 = _____%

TAKING OBJECTIVE EXAMS

■ Mastery Test

All the questions that follow have been taken from actual college tests. Answer the questions by using the specific hints for multiple-choice and true-false questions that are listed below. Also, in the space provided, give the letter of the hint used to determine the correct answer.

Test-Taking Hints

a   The longest multiple-choice answer is often correct.

b   A multiple-choice answer in the middle, especially one with the most words, is often correct.

c   Answers with qualifiers, such as *generally, probably, most, almost, often, may, some,* and *sometimes,* are usually correct.

d   Answers with absolute words, such as *all, always, everyone, everybody, never, no one, nobody, none,* and *only,* are usually incorrect.

Hint _____   1. *True or false?* _____ IQ tests are always reliable measures of intelligence.

Hint _____   2. *True or false?* _____ After June 1944, the Allies had almost completely eliminated the German submarine threat in the Atlantic.

Hint _____   3. A good justification for establishing a new business would be
   a.   a strong personal desire to run a business.
   b.   a shrinking market.
   c.   successful businesses nearby.
   d.   an expanding market combined with the presence of inefficient firms.

Hint _____   4. Diabetics lack
   a.   vitamins.
   b.   insulin, an enzyme needed to use sugar properly.
   c.   amino acids.
   d.   epinephrine.

Hint _____   5. *True or false?* _____ Generally, single-story buildings are preferred for most types of factory operations.

Hint _____   6. During World War II, black Americans
   a.   achieved social equality.
   b.   lived mostly in the South.
   c.   found more job opportunities open and benefited from the movement for equality fostered by the war.
   d.   served in fully integrated service units.

Hint _____ 7. *True or false?* _____ The only function of the hypothalamus is to activate the sympathetic nervous system.

Hint _____ 8. Affective explanations are statements intertwined with
   a. altruistic behavior.
   b. love and intimacy.
   c. emotions, values, or expectations regarding self-control.
   d. antisocial behavior.

Hint _____ 9. *True or false?* _____ There are no gaps between scientific ideals and the realities of any actual research project.

Hint _____ 10. In an attempt to deal with unemployment, President Hoover
   a. established the NRA.
   b. began a welfare program.
   c. created unemployment insurance.
   d. established the Reconstruction Finance Corporation to make loans to business.

Score: Number correct (_____) × 10 = _____%

TAKING ESSAY EXAMS

■ **Mastery Test**

Spend a half hour getting ready to write a one-paragraph essay on the subject ''Describe eight points to remember when planning a weekly study schedule.'' The eight points are presented on pages 73–75.

Study Hint: First summarize each of the eight points in the spaces below. Then study the points by following the advice given in step 2 on pages 221–222.

Important Points about a Weekly Study Schedule:

1. _____

   _____

2. _____

   _____

3. _____

   _____

4. _____

   _____

5. _____

   _____

6. _____

   _____

7. _____

   _____

8. _____

   _____

When the half hour is up, write your essay answer on the other side of this sheet.

_____

_____

_____

_____

_____

_____

_____

_____

_____

_____

_____

_____

_____

_____

_____

_____

_____

_____

_____

_____

_____

_____

_____

_____

_____

_____

_____

_____

_____

_____

_____

_____

Score: Number correct (_____) $\times$ 12.5 = _____%

TAKING OBJECTIVE AND ESSAY EXAMS

■ Mastery Test

You have five kinds of questions to answer on this quiz: following directions, matching, sentence completion, true-false, and multiple-choice.

Following Directions: Print your full name, last name first, under the line at the right-hand side below. Write your full name, first name last, on the line at the left-hand side below.

1. _____   2. _____

Matching: Enter the appropriate letter in the space provided next to each definition.

3. Show similarities between two things. _____

4. Explain by giving examples. _____

5. Give the formal meaning of a term. _____

6. Words that tell you exactly what to do. _____

7. Give a series of points and number them 1, 2, 3, etc. _____

8. Give a condensed account of the main points. _____

a. Define
b. Contrast
c. Direction words
d. List
e. Compare
f. Illustrate
g. Summarize

Fill-Ins: Write the word or words needed to complete each of the following sentences.

9. You should _____ consistently in order to avoid last-minute cram situations that may cause exam panic.

10. On either an objective or an essay exam, you will build up confidence and momentum if you do the easier questions _____.

11. Because essay exam time is limited, instructors can give you only a few questions to answer. They will reasonably focus on questions dealing with the _____ areas of the subject.

12. Before starting an objective or essay test, you should _____ your time.

True or False: Write the word *true* or *false* to the left of the following statements.

_____ 13. Often the main reason that students choke, or block, on exams is that they are not well prepared.

_____ 14. When studying for an essay test, prepare a good outline answer for each question and memorize the outlines.

_____ 15. If you have to cram, you should try to study everything in your class notes and textbook.

_____ 16. You should spend the night before an exam organizing your notes.

Multiple-Choice: Circle the letter of the answer that best completes each of the following statements.

17. One step that is *not* necessarily recommended in preparing for and taking an essay exam is to
    a. list ten or so probable questions.
    b. prepare an outline answer for each question.
    c. concentrate on details in your class and text notes.
    d. understand direction words.

18. When taking an objective test, remember that
    a. absolute statements are always false.
    b. absolute statements are often false.
    c. absolute statements are never false.
    d. only a and c above are true.

19. When taking an essay exam, you should
    a. outline your answers before you begin to write.
    b. be direct when you write.
    c. use signal words to guide your reader through the answer.
    d. do all of the above.
    e. do none of the above.

20. In preparing for an objective or essay exam, pay attention to
    a. key terms and their definitions.
    b. major lists of items.
    c. points emphasized in class or in the text.
    d. all of the above.

Score: Number correct (_____) × 5 = _____%

USING THE LIBRARY

■ Mastery Test

1. Books placed on reserve by instructors are often shelved near the
   a. stacks.
   b. main desk.
   c. periodical area.
   d. reference section.

2. A card catalog usually indexes books according to
   a. author.
   b. title.
   c. subject.
   d. all of the above.

3. To locate a book in the stacks, you need to know its _____.

4. Periodicals are
   a. books.
   b. card files.
   c. magazines.
   d. all of the above.

5. *True or false?* _____ To find out whether a library has the specific issue of the magazine you want, you should check the file of periodical holdings.

6. *True or false?* _____ If you were looking up books about Ralph Nader, you would look under *R* in the *Authors* section of the card catalog.

Below is an entry from the *Readers' Guide to Periodical Literature*. Answer the questions about the entry that follow it.

Diabetes
A slow, savage killer. J.M. Nash
il *Time* 136:52–59 N '90

7. What is the title of the article? _____

8. What is the name of the magazine? _____

9. On what pages of the magazine does the article appear? _____

10. In what month and year did the article appear in the magazine? _____

Score: Number correct (_____) × 10 = _____%

UNDERSTANDING WORD PARTS

■ **Mastery Test**

Complete the italicized word in each sentence by adding the correct word part. Use the meaning of the word part and the sentence context to determine the correct answer in each case.

> *port*—carry *psych*—mind *trans*—across *mis*—badly *in*—not
> *tract*—draw *tact*—touch *inter*—between *post*—after *dis*—apart

1. The (. . . *ition*) _____ from prison to life on the "outside" can cause psychological problems.

2. To show his (. . . *content*) _____ with the restaurant meal, Fred dumped his dinner on the floor.

3. When two burly customers started to fight, the skinny bartender was afraid to (. . . *vene*) _____.

4. The (*re . . . able*) _____ ballpoint pen leaked red ink all over the inside of my purse.

5. A blind person's (. . . *ile*) _____ sense is highly developed; the fingertips transmit a wealth of information.

6. Mark, enrolled in five difficult courses, felt he had been (. . . *guided*) _____ by his college counselor.

7. In a (. . . *script*) _____ to his will, the crazy old man left a million dollars to the Internal Revenue Service.

8. The (. . . *er*) _____ was told to bring a mop and a pail to the lobby; a bottle of orange juice had smashed on the floor.

9. (. . . *iatrists*) _____ must qualify as medical doctors before specializing in studies of the mind.

10. The (. . . *edible*) _____ pancakes oozed a sticky white batter as they lay on the plate.

> *Score:*   Number correct (_____) × 10 = _____%

USING THE DICTIONARY

■ Mastery Test

Refer to the following excerpt from the paperback *American Heritage Dictionary* to answer the questions that follow.

---

e•merge (ĭ-mûrj′) *v.* **e•merged, e•merg•ing.** **1.** To rise up or come forth into view; appear. **2.** To come into existence. **3.** To become known or evident. [Lat. *emergere.*] —**e•mer′gence** *n.* —**e•mer′gent** *adj.*

e•mer•gen•cy (ĭ-mûr′jən-sē) *n., pl.* **-ies.** An unexpected situation or occurrence that demands immediate attention.

e•mer•i•tus (ĭ-měr′ĭ-təs) *adj.* Retired but retaining an honorary title: *a professor emeritus.* [Lat., p.p. of *emereri,* to earn by service.]

em•er•y (ĕm′ə-rē, ĕm′rē) *n.* A fine-grained impure corundum used for grinding and polishing. [< Gk *smuris.*]

e•met•ic (ĭ-mĕt′ĭk) *adj.* Causing vomiting. [< Gk. *emein,* to vomit.] —**e•met′ic,** *n.*

—**emia** *suff.* Blood: *leukemia.* [< Gk. *haima,* blood.]

em•i•grate (ĕm′ĭ-grāt′) *v.* **-grat•ed, -grat•ing.** To leave one country or region to settle in another. [Lat. *emigrare.*] —**em′i•grant** *n.* —**em′i•gra′tion** *n.*

é•mi•gré (ĕm′ĭ-grā′) *n.* An emigrant, esp. a refugee from a revolution. [Fr.]

em•i•nence (ĕm′ə-nəns) *n.* **1.** a position of great distinction or superiority. **2.** A rise or elevation of ground; hill.

em•i•nent (ĕm′ə-nənt) *adj.* **1.** Outstanding, as in reputation; distinguished. **2.** Towering above others; projecting. [< Lat. *eminēre,* to stand out.] —**em′i•nent•ly** *adv.*

em•phat•ic (ĕm-făt′ĭk) *adj.* Expressed or performed with emphasis. [< Gk. *emphatikos.*] —**em•phat′i•cal•ly** *adv.*

em•phy•se•ma (ĕm′fĭ-sē′mə) *n.* A disease in which the air sacs of the lungs lose their elasticity, resulting in an often severe loss of breathing ability. [< Gk. *emphusēma.*]

em•pire (ĕm′pīr′) *n.* **1.** A political unit, usu. larger than a kingdom and often comprising a number of territories or nations, ruled by a single central authority. **2.** Imperial dominion, power, or authority. [<Lat. *imperium.*]

em•pir•i•cal (ĕm-pîr′ĭ-kəl) *adj.* Also **em•pir•ic** (-pîr′ik). **1.** Based on observation or experiment. **2.** Relying on practical experience rather than theory. [<Gk. *empeirikos,* experienced.] —**em•pir′i•cal•ly** *adv.*

em•pir•i•cism (ĕm-pîr′ĭ-sīz′əm) *n.* **1.** The view that experience, esp. of the senses, is the only source of knowledge. **2.** The employment of empirical methods, as in science.— **em•pir′i•cist** *n.*

em•place•ment (ĕm-plās′mənt) *n.* **1.** A prepared position for guns within a fortification. **2.** Placement. [Fr.]

em•ploy (ĕm-ploi′) *v.* **1.** To engage or use the services of. **2.** To put to service; use. **3.** To devote or apply (one's time or energies) to an activity. —*n.* Employment. [< Lat. *implicare,* to involve.] —**em•ploy′a•ble** *adj.*

em•ploy•ee (ĕm-ploi′ē, ĕm′ploi-ē′) *n.* Also **em•ploy•e.** One who works for another.

ă pat ā pay â care ä father ĕ pet   ē be ĭ pit ī tie î pier ŏ pot ō toe ô paw, for oi noise ōō took ōō boot ou out th thin *th* this ŭ cut û urge yoo abuse zh vision ə about, item, edible, gallop, circus

---

1. How many syllables are in the word *emphatic?* _____

2. Where is the primary accent in the word *emphysema?* _____

3. Where is the primary accent in the word *empiricism?* _____

4. What word in the pronunciation key tells you how to pronounce the *i* in *emeritus?* _____

5. What word in the pronunciation key tells you how to pronounce the *oi* sound in *employ?* _____

6. In the word *eminence,* the first *e* is pronounced like the *e* in
   a. heat.
   b. pet.
   c. trace.
   d. item.

7. In the word *empirical,* the *a* is pronounced like
   a. long *a.*
   b. short *a.*
   c. schwa.
   d. short *e.*

8. *True or false?* _____ The word *emery* may be pronounced two ways.

9. In the sentence ''Picasso's *eminence* in the art world is a result of talent and hard work,'' which meaning of *eminence* applies?
   a. Meaning 1
   b. Meaning 2

10. In the sentence ''The teacher said, 'Martin, please *employ* your pen for taking class notes, not for letters to classmates,' '' which meaning of *employ* applies?
    a. Verb meaning 1
    b. Verb meaning 2
    c. Verb meaning 3
    d. The noun meaning

Score: Number correct (_____) × 10 = _____%

WORD PRONUNCIATION

■ Mastery Test

Using the rules in the box, divide the following words into syllables. And for each word, write the number of the rule or rules that apply. Note the example that is provided.

```
1. Divide between two consonants.
2. Divide before a single consonant.
```

Example
enigma   _____e-nig-ma_____   _2_   _1_

Part A: General-Interest Words

	Syllable Division	Rule Numbers
1. culprit	_____	_____
2. rampant	_____	_____
3. harbinger	_____	____ ____
4. martinet	_____	____ ____
5. subterfuge	_____	____ ____
6. conjecture	_____	____ ____
7. importune	_____	____ ____
8. abrogate	_____	____ ____
9. masticate	_____	____ ____
10. cognizant	_____	____ ____

Part B: Specialized Words

	Syllable Division	*Rule Numbers*
11. visceral	_____	_____ _____
12. aversive	_____	_____ _____
13. glucose	_____	_____
14. antigen	_____	_____ _____
15. atropine	_____	_____ _____
16. carcinoma	_____	_____ _____ _____
17. charisma	_____	_____ _____
18. malignancy	_____	_____ _____ _____
19. compensation	_____	_____ _____ _____
20. elucidative	_____	_____ _____ _____

Score: Number correct (_____) × 5 = _____%

SPELLING IMPROVEMENT

■ Mastery Test

Use the four spelling rules you reviewed earlier in the book to spell the following words.

1. refer	+ ed	=	_____
2. lively	+ hood	=	_____
3. shr_____k		=	_____
4. win	+ ing	=	_____
5. city	+ es	=	_____
6. involve	+ ment	=	_____
7. drive	+ ing	=	_____
8. safe	+ ty	=	_____
9. pity	+ ful	=	_____
10. n_____ce		=	_____
11. fantasy	+ es	=	_____
12. rebel	+ ion	=	_____
13. arrange	+ ment	=	_____
14. lucky	+ ly	=	_____
15. write	+ ing	=	_____
16. conc_____ted		=	_____
17. state	+ hood	=	_____
18. marry	+ ed	=	_____
19. admit	+ ance	=	_____
20. achieve	+ able	=	_____

Score: Number correct (_____) × 5 = _____%

VOCABULARY DEVELOPMENT

■ Mastery Test

Read each of the following sentences carefully. Then decide which of the four choices provided comes closest in meaning to the word in italic type. Circle the letter of your choice.

1. Because of the *brusque* manner of the waitress, I decided to leave no tip.
   a. Slow
   b. Courteous
   c. Rude
   d. Passive

2. We kept our plans *tentative,* so we could quickly change them in case there were new developments.
   a. Fixed
   b. Indefinite
   c. Superficial
   d. Honest

3. I could not tolerate an *austere* apartment like the one she lives in; I need plants, pictures, and plenty of furnishings.
   a. Bare
   b. Lavish
   c. Expensive
   d. Small

4. She is a *tenacious* person; even though she failed her first biology tests, she kept studying and eventually passed the course.
   a. Humorous
   b. Stingy
   c. Softhearted
   d. Persistent

5. Among the many *paradoxes* in the Bible are that the meek shall inherit the earth and the first shall be last.
   a. Famous passages
   b. Verses
   c. Apparent contradictions
   d. Prayers

6. His clothes are neat and tasteful, but his hair, *incongruously,* is unkempt and oily.
   a. Boldly
   b. Inconsistently
   c. Apologetically
   d. Consistently

7. My English paper had many good details but lacked *coherence;* the teacher said I had a lot to learn about how to structure my ideas.
   a. Unity
   b. Support
   c. Sentence skills
   d. Organization

8. I used to be a three-letter athlete in school; now I enjoy sports in a *vicarious* way by watching them on television.
   a. Curious
   b. Dangerous
   c. Substitute
   d. Inexpensive

9. My progress in school was *impeded* by poor study habits and a poor attitude.
   a. Aided
   b. Increased
   c. Hindered
   d. Reinforced

10. The counselor listened in a *perfunctory* way as she doodled on her note pad; I felt she wasn't really interested in my problem.
   a. Indifferent
   b. Responsive
   c. Intense
   d. Apologetic

Score: Number correct (_____) × 10 = _____%

DEFINITIONS AND EXAMPLES

■ Mastery Test

In the spaces provided, write the number of the sentence in each selection that contains a definition. Then write the number of the *first* sentence that provides an example of the definition.

1.   ¹Admittedly a good deal of our social interaction is motivated by self-interest. ²You may offer to run an errand for a professor because you hope that he or she will take that help into account when awarding grades. ³Or you may offer to take care of the neighbors' dog while they are away on vacation because you want them to take care of your cat when you go on vacation. ⁴But if behavior that benefits others is *not* linked to personal gain, it is called altruistic behavior. ⁵For example, many people go to considerable trouble to help a sick neighbor, take in a family left homeless by fire, or serve as hospital aides. ⁶Charitable contributions are often directed at strangers and made anonymously.

Definition: _____   Example: _____

2.   ¹Generally, nurses work directly with patients. ²However, in some instances, they function as *patients' advocates;* that is, they work indirectly on behalf of the patient or intercedes for the patient. ³For example, the nurse who lobbies in the legislature in support of programs of benefit to the consumer of health services functions as a patient advocate. ⁴A few other examples are the nurse who seeks the services of other health practitioners on behalf of a patient; the nurse who intercedes for patients by helping them obtain services from various community health agencies; and the nurse who intercedes for the patients by interpreting their needs to family. ⁵Nurses become patient advocates also as they plan total health care while serving as a member of the health team.

Definition: _____   Example: _____

3.   [1]Price lining is based on the fact that most retailers have more than one product to price, and a number of substitute products or brands within each product category. [2]For instance, a women's clothing store may offer a variety of wool scarves. [3]But consumers will not respond to a series of minor price differences, such as scarves at $6.50, $6.60, $6.70, $6.90, $7.00, and so on. [4]Instead, buyers prefer a *few* prices that seem to differentiate the product into "lines" based on some attribute such as quality or prestige. [5]For instance, there may be scarves priced at $5, $8, $10, and $16. [6]These prices clearly indicate that there are scarves for the economy-minded at $5, medium-quality scarves at $8 and $10, and top-of-the-line scarves at $16. [7]Price lining means, then, that a limited number of prices are established for the products or brands within a product class.

Definition: _____   Example: _____

4.   [1]When teachers feel that a certain child will do well in school, that child probably will do well. [2]The *self-fulfilling prophecy*, by which people act as they are expected to, has been documented in many different situations. [3]In the "Oak School experiment," some teachers in this California school were told at the beginning of the term that some of their pupils had shown unusual potential for intellectual growth. [4]Actually, the children had been chosen at random. [5]Yet several months later many of them—especially first- and second-graders—showed unusual gains in IQ. [6]And the teachers seemed to like the "bloomers" better. [7]Their teachers do not appear to have spent more time with them than with the other children or to have treated them differently in any obvious ways. [8]Subtler influences may have been at work, possibly in the teachers' tone of voice, facial expression, touch, and posture.

Definition: _____   Example: _____

5.   [1]Resocialization differs from other types of adult socialization in that it points to a rapid and drastic change, usually one that is forced on the individual to some degree. [2]Military service involves resocialization, since it is a deliberate attempt to remold a person's life and personality in certain respects. [3]The recruit is stripped of previous status and gains a new status only by meeting the demands of the military. [4]A more extreme example is that of religious conversion, in which the person may feel completely reoriented—a sense of rebirth into a new personality or of having been "born again." [5]Both the recruit and the convert experience a change from an old life-style to a new one that is willingly accepted and not seen as abandoning old loyalties.

Definition: _____   Example: _____

Score: Number correct (_____) × 10 = _____%

ENUMERATIONS

■ Mastery Test

Locate and number the enumerations in the selections that follow. Then, in the space beneath each selection, summarize briefly the points in the enumeration. Note that headings have already been provided for you.

1.   Credit cards can be divided into three basic groups. One type, the easiest to obtain, is the retail credit card. These are the cards issued by department stores, boutiques, and gasoline companies. Interest is charged on unpaid balances, but the minimum payment required per month may vary; department stores usually require the highest monthly payments. Another type of credit card is the bank card, such as MasterCard or Visa. Overall, these credit corporations issue more cards than anyone else, but a card must be obtained from a local bank. Like retail cards, bank cards require a minimum monthly payment and charge about 18 percent interest annually on the balance. Some also charge an annual membership fee. These cards may be used in a wide variety of places for items from food to clothes to college tuition payments. A third type of card is that offered by American Express, Carte Blanche, and Diners' Club. Unlike the other types, these companies expect payment in full every month. They also charge a yearly membership fee to card owners. Such cards are usually the most difficult to obtain, since these companies look for more affluent customers capable of meeting all monthly charges.

Types of Credit Cards

(1)   _____

(2)   _____

(3)   _____

2.   As you might guess, pollutants do their greatest damage to the organs of the breathing system. There are several kinds of damage that can occur. The tubes and passages of the breathing system are lined with hairlike structures called cilia. The cilia are constantly moving back and forth; they function like a broom that sweeps out foreign material inhaled from the air. Some pollutants can slow down these cilia—or stop them altogether. This leaves the lungs with one of their protective devices out of order.

      Besides the cilia, the air passages and tubes are also lined with a sticky fluid called mucus, which traps particles that have been inhaled. Mucus production greatly increases when certain pollutants are inhaled. This is a defensive response by the body. Normally, the cilia would sweep out the mucus and much of the foreign matter. But when they do not function, the mucus builds up and narrows the tubes and air passages. Coughing results, and breathing is more difficult.

Pollutants can also cause muscle spasms in the tubes of the lungs. During the spasms, the muscle contracts and gets thicker. This narrows the passageway in the tubes and makes breathing more difficult. Along with the muscle spasms, the membranes inside the tubes may swell. This results in more narrowing of the tubes and more difficulty in breathing.

Ways That Pollutants Damage the Breathing System

(1) _____

(2) _____

(3) _____

3.   Experts agree that Indians have the sad distinction of being the most depressed of America's racial and ethnic groups. The harsh facts about Indian life are undeniable. For one thing, no minority group in this country is as poor as the 380,000 or so Indians who live on reservations. The average family income for Indians is said to be about $1,500, but the average on-reservation income is much lower. The Bureau of Indian Affairs estimates that 71 percent of reservation Indians live in inadequate housing. The infant mortality rate is two to three times that of the rest of the population. Records compiled by the University of Colorado School of Medicine indicated a rate of 88.2 deaths per 1,000 live births among the Utes in 1960. Finally, the life expectancy of a reservation Indian is forty-six years, considerably less than that of both whites and blacks.

Harsh Facts about Indian Life

(1) _____

(2) _____

(3) _____

(4) _____

Score: Number correct (_____) × 10 = _____%

HEADINGS AND SUBHEADINGS

■ **Mastery Test**

Part 1: Answer the questions below about the selection that follows.

Questions: What is meant by *burnout?* What are the results of burnout?

"BURNOUT" IN THE PROFESSIONS

While professional-level jobs provide prestige, a relatively high income, and other benefits, they are far from perfect. Boredom and alienation are associated with certain types of professional work. Poverty-program lawyers, physicians, prison personnel, social workers, clinical psychologists, psychiatric nurses, and other professionals who work extensively with human problems often feel unable to cope continually with distress. Eventually, they may see themselves as "burned out." Behavioral scientists have found that many handled "burned-out" feelings by distancing themselves from clients and treating suffering people in detached, dehumanizing ways. As emotions grew increasingly negative, these workers experienced severe tension-related problems, including alcoholism.

Answers: _____

_____

_____

Part 2: Using words such as *what, why, who, which, in what ways,* and *how,* write two meaningful questions for each of the textbook heads that follow.

1. Emotional Problems in Childhood   a. _____

   b. _____

2. Reconstruction in the South   a. _____

   b. _____

3. Infectious Diseases   a. _____

   b. _____

4. Our Business System:
   Its Expansion and Regulation   a. _____

   b. _____

Part 3:   Scrambled together in the list that follows are three textbook headings and three subheadings for each of the headings. Write the headings in the lettered blanks (A, B, C) and write the appropriate subheadings in the numbered blanks (1, 2, 3). Two items have already been inserted for you.

Paranoia

The Siege of
   Petersburg

Cardiac Muscle

The Battle of
   Gettysburg

The Muscular
   System

Schizophrenia

Behavior Disorders

Smooth Muscle

Sherman's March

Major Events of
   the Civil War

Skeletal Muscle

Psychosis

A. _____

   1. _____

   2. _____

   3. *Smooth Muscle* _____

B. _____

   1. _____

   2. _____

   3. _____

C. _____

   1. _____

   2. _____

   3. *Psychosis* _____

Score: Number correct of possible twenty (_____) × 5 = _____%

SIGNAL WORDS

■ Mastery Test

In the spaces provided, write the major signal words used in the following selections. The number and kind of signal words that you should look for are shown at the start of each selection.

Selection 1: Two contrast signals; one cause-and-effect signal; one addition signal.

> The elderly age segment is a growing market that presents many opportunities for marketers. Demand will continue to rise for health care and services, books, nursing homes, travel, retirement housing, and many leisure-time activities. But people in this age group do not like to be stereotyped, and marketers must be sensitive in communicating with them. Several years ago, the H. J. Heinz Company test-marketed a line of "Senior Foods"—lamb, beef, and chicken dishes in eight-ounce containers. The products were dropped six months later; the reason was that older people did not like to see their age reflected in the product's name. On the other hand, the marketing focus of Gerber Products Company does not inhibit older consumers from purchasing and consuming (for dietary reasons) an estimated 6 percent of its baby food. Also, a study conducted by Dannon Yogurt found that 25 percent of the company's sales were made to people over age fifty-five. Clearly, the elderly have unique needs that marketers must try to satisfy.

1. _____

2. _____

3. _____

4. _____

Selection 2:   One emphasis signal; one cause-and-effect signal; two addition signals; two contrast signals.

Speed-reading courses often claim that an increase in speed will mean an automatic increase in comprehension. But this claim is simply not true. With difficult material, understanding is likely to fall as rate rises. Speed-reading courses may increase the number of words your eyes take in and "read" per minute. In addition, comprehension may improve while you take such a course. The cause for this, however, is that you tend to concentrate more as you read faster. The best way to reading speed *and* comprehension is to develop reading comprehension skills. Speed will come as you learn how to identify main ideas and go quickly over lesser points and supporting details. Also, speed will come as you learn how to vary your reading rate according to the nature of the material and your purpose in reading.

5. _____

6. _____

7. _____

8. _____

9. _____

10. _____

Score: Number correct (_____) × 10 = _____%

MAIN IDEA

■ Mastery Test

Locate and underline the main-idea sentence in each selection that follows. Then, in the spaces provided in the margin, put the number of each sentence you underlined.

_____ 1. ¹Violence surrounds us—not only in real life but in our entertainment. ²Films emphasize it—as those who saw _The Godfather_ and its sequels know. ³In fact, violence is big at the box office. ⁴A drive-in favorite was _The Texas Chainsaw Massacre,_ which graphically portrayed a series of murders perpetrated by unemployed cattle butchers. ⁵Indeed, the realism with which film violence is staged is ever increasing. ⁶Improved techniques allow close-ups of realistically bruised and mutilated bodies. ⁷Television, in both its news reports and its entertainment, provides a steady diet of violence. ⁸Riots, uprisings, wars, terrorists' raids—all are a part of our daily lives in the evening news. ⁹Even children's toys can encourage aggression.

_____ 2. ¹One of childhood's saddest figures is the child who is chosen last for every team, hangs around the fringes of every group, walks home alone after school, is not invited to any of the birthday parties, and sobs in despair, "Nobody wants to play with me." ²There are many reasons why this child and other children can be unpopular. ³Sometimes such children are withdrawn or rebellious. ⁴They are often the youngsters who walk around with a "chip on the shoulder," showing unprovoked aggression and hostility. ⁵Or they may act silly and babyish, "showing off" in immature ways. ⁶Or they may be anxious and uncertain, exuding such a pathetic lack of confidence that they repel other children, who don't find them any fun to be with. ⁷Extremely fat or unattractive children, children who behave in any way that seems strange to the others, and retarded or slow-learning youngsters are also outcasts.

_____ 3. ¹Companies are constantly changing the packaging that covers their products. ²At times, however, the changes backfire and reduce rather than increase customer satisfaction with the product in question. ³One of the most successful packages has been the Camel cigarette pack, which shows a camel, two pyramids, and three palm trees. ⁴An executive at R. J. Reynolds some years ago decided that the package would be more striking if the pyramids and trees were removed. ⁵The surgery was performed, but the public howled. ⁶Camel sales fell off instantly, and, not surprisingly, Reynolds quickly returned the camel's props.

_____ 4. ¹Colonial farmers in America grew all their own food, with the exception of certain imported luxury items, such as coffee, tea, and sugar. ²Farm animals such as sheep, pigs, and cows provided milk and meat. ³Clothing was made from plant and animal sources. ⁴The flax plant's fibers were dyed with berry juices, spun into thread, woven into cloth, and sewn into shirts and dresses. ⁵Sheep provided wool for heavier clothing, and the hides of pigs and cows were tanned into leather. ⁶Leather could be cut and crafted into shoes, boots, gloves, shirts, and leggings; leather was also needed for harnesses, bridles, whips, and reins. ⁷The abundant forests of a young America were filled with timber for houses and fuel. ⁸Colonists chopped down trees and corded wood in order to cook and to heat their homes. ⁹Only a few necessary items, such as glass and iron, were bought by the farmers. ¹⁰Luxuries such as books, china, and lace were purchased when it was possible; they were by no means considered essential items. ¹¹This self-sufficiency, or ability to provide for themselves, was a characteristic of many early American settlers.

_____ 5. ¹A bottle of cologne on a department store counter catches your eye. ²It is beautifully packaged in a handsome bottle and shiny box. ³You check the price tag, which reads "$17.50," and walk away wondering how two ounces of cologne can be so expensive. ⁴After all, cologne is made from only a few pennies' worth of alcohol and essential oils mixed with a good amount of water. ⁵How can a department store charge so much for it? ⁶The price on the cologne box reflects not only the cost of the raw materials but a variety of additional costs. ⁷The department store is paying the salary of the salesperson behind the counter and the cost of the space needed to store the cologne inventory. ⁸The department store also provides services such as charge accounts; the cost of each piece of merchandise is raised accordingly. ⁹The manufacturer of the cologne may have spent more on its fancy bottle and box than on the fragrance itself. ¹⁰The packaging caught your eye, which the manufacturer wanted, but you are going to pay for it. ¹¹You'll also pay for the advertising done by the nationally known cosmetics company and the cost of the transportation used to ship the cologne to the store. ¹²And if the cologne was made in and shipped from France, the price goes up even more!

Score: Number correct (_____) × 20 = _____%

OUTLINING

■ Mastery Test

Read the selection below and then complete the outline that follows.

Stress is a factor in all our lives. Learning to deal with stress in a positive, intelligent way is essential to good health. One way to combat stress is to work it off in physical activities. Anything from jogging around the neighborhood to a workout on the dance floor can relieve stress and, surprisingly, give you more energy to cope with life. Stress can also be controlled by changing your mental attitude. Learn to accept things; fighting against the unavoidable or the inevitable is useless. Learn to take one thing at a time. Rather than trying to do everything at once, deal with more important problems first, and leave the rest to another day. Learn to take your mind off yourself. Since stress is self-centered, doing something for others helps reduce it. Finally, talking about stress is important. When events in your life seem overwhelming, talk about your troubles. This can be done informally, by opening up to your family. You can also set aside special time to confide in friends. When your emotional life is severely shaken, however, formal help may be needed. Seek out a psychologist who has been recommended to you by a reliable source. Alternatively, find a professional counselor who will assess your difficulties and help you deal with them.

A. _____

B. _____

    1. _____

    2. _____

    3. _____

C. _____

    1. _____

        (a) _____

        (b) _____

    2. _____

        (a) _____

        (b) _____

Read the selection below and then complete the diagram that follows.

Credit cards have both advantages and disadvantages, depending on how the credit card holder chooses to use them. One of the benefits of credit cards, for example, is that they can be used to obtain interest-free loans for up to two months. By purchasing goods just after the close of one billing cycle, taking advantage of the grace period of twenty-five days or so for payment, and then paying the bill in full, you have borrowed the amount of your purchase with no interest fee. Another advantage of credit cards is that they are convenient. You can buy anywhere without the hassle of carrying large amounts of money or trying to use a personal check. Credit cards, however, do have disadvantages. Occasionally, billing mix-ups occur, and customers may be overcharged or charged for items they never purchased. The major problem presented by credit cards, though, is the fact that they tempt some consumers to overspend. Such people find it easy to charge items they would probably not purchase for cash; when the bills arrive, they have trouble making the payment. Or they find themselves trapped in a cycle of making minimum payments and thereby paying high finance charges on a never-shrinking balance.

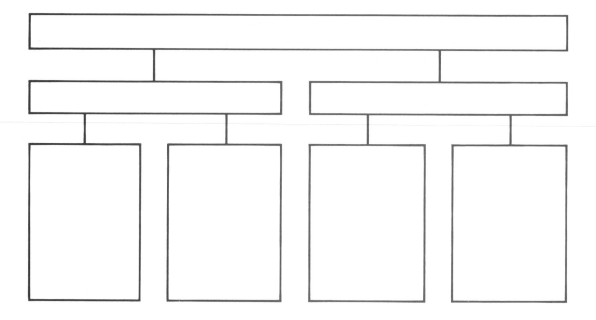

Score: Number correct (_____) × 5 = _____%

SUMMARIZING

■ Mastery Test

Circle the letter of the title that best summarizes each selection. Remember that the title should be as specific and descriptive as possible and at the same time account for all the material in the selection.

1.   Suppose a friend of yours has the habit of wearing absolutely atrocious clothes. You decide to go on a campaign to help reform his taste. How do you go about it? Your friend has just one outfit in which he looks great—but which he rarely wears. Every time he wears a shirt the same color as the one you like, you compliment him, and perhaps you also mention the shirt you're trying to "promote." After *that* shirt appears more frequently for a while, you "reinforce" only it—not the less attractive ones of the same color. At the same time, you try to suggest that your favorite shirt looks so good on him that he really should get more like it. And when he does, you compliment him on the new outfits. Gradually, you are "shaping his behavior," though you might not call it that.

Which would be an accurate title for this selection?
a. Helping a Friend
b. Shaping Behavior through Reinforcement
c. A Change in Dress
d. Clothing Psychology

2.   Between 1862 and 1871, New York City politics was controlled by a political machine called Tammany Hall, led by William Marcy Tweed. "Boss" Tweed and his henchmen bilked the city out of millions of dollars. They usually sold contracts for city work to corrupt companies. These companies would overcharge the city government for the job and "kick back" a fee to the political machine. Once, one of Tweed's friends billed the city for $179,729.60 for three tables and forty chairs. Of course, the Tweed Ring received a good share of that money. Gradually, the press began to take notice. Especially damaging to Tweed were the political cartoons by Thomas Nast. Nast drew cartoons showing Tweed and his men as vultures preying on the body of New York. Tweed's Ring eventually collapsed, and Tweed died in jail while awaiting trial.

Which would be an accurate title for this selection?
a. Boss Tweed and Tammany Hall
b. Political Corruption
c. Thomas Nast and Boss Tweed
d. The Collapse of Tammany Hall

3. The Leboyer method of childbirth seeks to protect a newborn's delicate senses from the shock of bright lights, harsh sounds, and rough handling. After the baby's head has begun to emerge, lights are dimmed and the delivery room is quieted. The baby is not held by the ankles and slapped to encourage the first breath; Leboyer states that since the fetus's spinal column has never been in a straight position, this kind of handling is a severe shock to the infant. Instead, the baby, with the umbilical cord still attached, is gently placed on the mother's abdomen until breathing begins naturally. At this point, the baby is rinsed in a tepid bath, rather than weighed on a cold scale. Babies born this way are usually relaxed and smiling, not tense and screaming. Some studies of Leboyer and standard-delivery babies have shown that Leboyer children are slightly more physically advanced and quicker to learn. Parents of Leboyer children, in general, saw the birth as a positive, exhilarating experience.

Which would be an accurate title for this selection?
a. Types of Delivery Rooms
b. A Baby's First Moments
c. The Leboyer Method
d. Protecting the Senses

4. We are all familiar with a slogan spoken by a stern bear in a forest ranger hat: "Only you can prevent forest fires!" For many years, an extensive advertising campaign has been conducted, using symbols like Smokey the Bear and Woodsy Owl, to warn the public about the dangers of forest fires. We are told that forest fires are ugly, destructive, and dangerous. They are actually beneficial to the forest ecology, clearing out underbrush and debris on the forest floor. The fire consumes this unnecessary material, and the larger, more resistant trees are spared. Without regular, small forest fires, the dry tender of brush and fallen limbs on the forest floor builds to a high level. Then, if a fire starts, it will be intense enough to destroy every tree, large and small. Forest fires also eliminate undesirable species of trees that take root in the forest from wind-borne seeds. Some special forests are actually dependent on fire to exist. In New Jersey's Pine Barrens, seeds are liberated from tightly closed pine cones by the intense heat of a fire. The cones pop open as the fire passes, and a new generation of trees begins.

Which would be an accurate title for this selection?
a. Advertising Campaigns and Forest Fires
b. Forest Ecology
c. Dangers of Forest Fires
d. Benefits of Forest Fires

Score: Number correct (_____) × 25 = _____%

SKIM READING

■ Mastery Test

Take five minutes to skim-read the following selection and to take notes on it. Then see if you can answer the questions that follow by referring to your notes but *not* referring back to the text.

THE HOSPICE PROGRAM

Objectives of the Hospice Program

The hospice program is a fairly new method of caring for the dying. While there is no solid definition of *hospice*, it is generally considered a program with two objectives. The first objective is to keep patients free from pain on a continuous basis. The second objective is to provide the dying with a homelike atmosphere in which to spend their final days.

How Hospices Reach Their Goals

Hospices reach their goals through one of several approaches. Some hospices work on an outpatient basis and thus have no physical facility from which to work. Outpatient hospices depend on team efforts of professionals from several institutions. An outpatient team could consist of a member of the clergy, social workers, nurses, doctors, and psychologists. A second approach some hospices have adopted is to work on an inpatient basis, using a building that is set up to have a homelike atmosphere. These buildings include some sort of sleeping quarters, eating facilities, and lounges or some other recreational area. In these inpatient facilities, the patients decide when to eat, sleep, and relax. Still other hospices use a combination of inpatient and outpatient services. Services are provided in the home when possible and in the hospice facility when necessary.

How Hospices Differ from Other Health Care Facilities

Even if a hospice operates only on an inpatient basis, it still differs from hospitals and nursing homes. Hospices differ from other health care facilities in four major ways. First, there is a lack of scheduling and structure in hospices. For one thing, there are no time schedules (with the exception of medication schedules) forced on hospice patients. This means open-ended visiting hours, mealtimes, bedtimes, etc. Patients can adjust more easily to their condition if they are allowed to live by their own life patterns in the "no-schedule" atmosphere. Lack of structure means something else too: no diet or activity restrictions. If a patient wants to have a favorite dessert at every meal or if a visitor brings a patient a special snack, the patient is allowed to have the food. If patients desire to try a strenuous activity one day and the activity tires them out so much that they must spend the next day in bed, so be it. The patient's schedule is what he or she wants it to be.

Another aspect of hospices that differs from other care facilities is that the facility personnel concentrate solely on the patient and don't become involved in side activities such as research and teaching. Patients' psychological needs, for example, are a main concern to hospice personnel. If a patient needs to talk over his or her feelings with someone in the middle of the night, personnel are there to listen. Personnel have time to be with patients because they have no other duties to distract or detain them.

View of pain control is another aspect of hospice care that sets it apart from care in hospitals and other facilities. In traditional health care institutions, patients may be expected to bear pain until it is unbearable. In hospices, patients are given medication as often as necessary to keep pain from surfacing at all.

Finally, unlike the philosophy of most health care facilities, the hospice theme includes the patient's family in the care cycle. Family needs are mainly psychological. Hospices provide the family members with counseling to help them accept the eventual death of their relative. Once the family member has died, hospices also provide the family with bereavement follow-up services.

Questions about the Selection

What are the two objectives of the hospice program?

1. _____

2. _____

What are three ways that hospices reach their goals?

3. _____

4. _____

5. _____

What are three ways that hospices differ from other health care facilities?

6. _____

7. _____

8. _____

Score: Number correct (_____) × 12.5 = _____%

RAPID READING PASSAGE

■ Mastery Test

Read this selection as rapidly as you can without sacrificing comprehension. Then record your time in the space provided and answer the comprehension questions that follow.

THE JAPANESE DETENTION CAMPS

John is a junior college English teacher. When he was three years old, the United States government sent him, and his family, to a detention camp. Howard, a newspaper publisher, spent eight months imprisoned with his wife and children in a one-room tarpaper shack. He had committed no crime; his imprisonment was legal. Jeanne, an author, was sent to a prison camp when she was seven. She spent three years there and now says: "All I knew was that we were in camp, behind barbed wire. Everything had fallen apart. No more Christmas, Thanksgiving."

John, Howard, and Jeanne had all been in America; neither they nor their families had committed, been tried for, or been convicted of a crime. They were imprisoned in "internment camps" simply because their parents or grandparents (or even great-grandparents) had come to America from Japan. They had Japanese faces.

In December 1941, the Japanese attacked Pearl Harbor and destroyed America's Pacific fleet. The rallying cry in America was "Remember Pearl Harbor!" and the country was plunged into a wave of anti-Japanese sentiment. On February 19, 1942, President Franklin Roosevelt signed Executive Order 9066. It allowed the military to move Japanese American civilians to ten relocation camps, stretching from California to Arkansas. Most Japanese Americans live on the West Coast, and the government acted on fears that they would become saboteurs and spies for Japan.

Eventually, almost 110,000 civilians, over two-thirds of whom were American citizens, were forced to move. Laws were passed penalizing those who disobeyed military orders. Indeed, the Supreme Court ruled that the confinement of these people, based only on race, was legal; the Court also upheld rulings on curfews and travel restrictions for Japanese Americans.

Many of those who were interned left families, prosperous businesses, farms, and personal possessions behind. The resettlement was swift; money was lost in the shuffle or confiscated by the government. One California bank, in 1942, estimated the loss by Japanese Americans at $400 million. Japanese American homes were searched without warrants, and workers were fired for no reason.

The Japanese, of course, were not America's only enemies in World War II; we also fought Germans and Italians. However, none of these immigrants or their children received the treatment that the Japanese did. They were not interned or taken to "safe" locations. Strong racial prejudice against the Japanese seemed to be at work. Earl Warren (later to become Chief Justice of the United States Supreme Court) was then attorney general of California. Even Warren, who became known as a strong fighter for civil liberties, appeared to show racial bias. In 1942, he said: "We believe that when we are dealing with the Caucasian race we have methods that will test the loyalty of them . . . but when we deal with the Japanese we are in an entirely different field and we cannot form any opinion that we believe to be sound."

During the war, second-generation Japanese Americans (called Nisei) were eventually allowed to join the army; they made up a special unit, the 442d Regimental Combat Team, that fought in the European theater, especially the Italian campaign. Many of these men came out of internment camps to fight for the country they loved, the country that had so wronged them. The Nisei won more decorations than any regiment in history and suffered an extremely high casualty rate. Senator Daniel Inouye, who served on the Watergate investigation committee, is a Nisei who lost an arm in the war.

When the war ended, the Japanese Americans were released. They went back to their homes and attempted to pick up the pieces of their lives. The Evacuation Claims Act of 1948 was to compensate them for their economic losses, but it only returned $38 million to the internees—less than 10 percent of the estimated losses.

How do Japanese Americans feel about this treatment now? One, an army sergeant, says:

I was born in [a camp] in 1944. Living quarters were small, and they never had enough blankets. . . . The guns around the camp were always pointed into the camp, not outward. . . . My folks say they want to forget this ever happened. They lost a lot of relatives who went to Europe with the 442d Combat Team.

Some Japanese Americans feel that a financial repayment is called for. Others feel that money is no longer important, but justice is. Since their rights were violated, since they were denied the privileges of citizens, they want an apology. One woman says: "It is the gesture, the recognition, the honor that is restored. It is the symbolic gesture of the government standing up and saying it was wrong." Since no other immigrant group has ever been singled out for such harsh and unfair treatment, this seems to be the least our government could do.

Time: _____

Check Your Understanding

1. *True or false?* _____ Japanese Americans were not allowed to fight in World War II.

2. On February 19, 1942, President Franklin Roosevelt signed Executive Order 9066, which
   a. imposed curfews.
   b. imposed travel restrictions.
   c. allowed the military to move Japanese Americans.
   d. confiscated the property of Japanese Americans.

3. Two-thirds of the interned Japanese Americans were
   a. American citizens.
   b. farm owners.
   c. from the West Coast.
   d. homeowners.

4. Economic losses of Japanese Americans were estimated at
   a. $20 million.
   b. $40 million.
   c. $200 million.
   d. $400 million.

5. The word *Nisei* means
   a. second-generation Japanese Americans.
   b. a Japanese American combat regiment.
   c. a Japanese American senator.
   d. an internment camp.

6. The Evacuation Claims Act of 1948
   a. fully restored all financial losses.
   b. partially restored financial losses.
   c. declared that Japanese Americans should be interned.
   d. was signed by President Roosevelt.

7. The main idea in the selection is that
   a. Japanese Americans are bitter about their treatment.
   b. the government's action against the Japanese was unfair and unjust.
   c. Germans and Italians should have received the same treatment as the Japanese did.
   d. Americans were hysterical during the war.

8. The government feared the Japanese Americans would
   a. hide their money.
   b. defect to Japan.
   c. join the armed services.
   d. spy for Japan.

9. The 442d Regimental Combat Team
   a. fought in the Pacific theater.
   b. won more decorations than any other regiment.
   c. had a low casualty rate.
   d. fought the internment policy.
10. The writer suggests that Japanese Americans
    a. were reasonably compensated for their losses.
    b. wish to forget the detention camps.
    c. deserve an official apology.
    d. lacked patriotism during the war.

Score: Number correct (_____) × 10 = _____%

PART EIGHT

ADDITIONAL
LEARNING SKILLS

PREVIEW

Part Eight takes up some extra learning skills that will help you get more out of your studies. ''Reading Graphs and Tables'' explains how to understand the technical illustrations and tabular material that often appear in textbooks. In ''Studying Mathematics and Science'' you'll find tips that will help you deal more effectively with math and science courses. A related chapter is ''Reading Literature and Making Inferences,'' which provides some guidelines that will better equip you to read literary works. Next, ''Reading for Pleasure: A List of Interesting Books'' offers short descriptions of a number of widely admired books that will give you reading practice and may provide you with some of the most pleasurable and illuminating experiences of your life. ''Understanding Connections between Reading and Writing'' explains why writing is an important part of a textbook on reading and study skills, and also gives you an opportunity to practice your writing skills. Finally, ''Writing a Research Paper'' presents a series of basic steps to follow in preparing a paper involving research.

READING GRAPHS AND TABLES

INTRODUCTION

Sometimes, being a skillful reader means more than just the ability to read words. It can also mean being able to read the visual information presented in graphs and tables. As a student, you will probably encounter a number of graphs and tables in your textbooks. Such visual material can help you understand important ideas and details as you read. Knowing graphics will probably also help in your career work as well, for occupations in our computerized age increasingly rely on graphics to convey information.

Graphs and tables present information by using lines, images, or numbers as well as words. They often compare quantities or show how things change over a period of time. Reading a graph or table involves four steps:

- *Step 1: Read the title and any subtitles.* This important first step gives you a concise summary of all the information in the graph or table.

- *Step 2: Read any information at the top, at the bottom, and along the sides.* Such information may include an explanatory key to the material presented. It may also include a series of years, percentages, or figures.

- *Step 3: Ask yourself the purpose of the graph or table.* Usually, the title can be turned into a question beginning with *What, How much* or *many,* or *How*. The purpose of the graph or table is to answer that question.

- *Step 4: Read the graph or table.* As you read, keep in mind the purpose of the material.

Using these four steps, let us analyze the sample graph and table that follow.

SAMPLE GRAPH

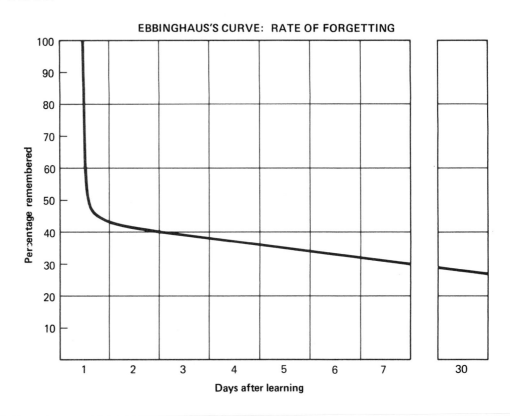

EBBINGHAUS'S CURVE: RATE OF FORGETTING

Step 1: The title of the graph is "Ebbinghaus's Curve: Rate of Forgetting." Therefore, the information in the graph will show the rate at which people forget material.

Step 2: On one side of the graph is a series of numbers, ranging from 10 to 100 and labeled "Percentage (of material) remembered." Along the bottom of the graph is a series of numbers labeled "Days after learning." The numbers are in sequence from 1 to 7; then there is a gap on the graph followed by the number 30. The curved line on the graph will show what percentage of material is remembered on day 1, day 2, and so on—up to day 30.

Step 3: We can turn the title of the graph into the question "What is the rate at which people forget material?" The purpose of the graph is to answer that question. The graph will show us what percentage of material people remembered as days passed.

Step 4: Read the graph and try to answer the following questions. Put your answers in the spaces provided.

1. What was the percentage of material remembered *by the end of* day 1?
   _____

2. What percentage of material did people remember on day 3? _____
3. On what day did the percentage of material remembered drop to approximately

   30 percent? _____

4. *True or false?* _____ The percentage of material remembered dropped drastically between day 7 and day 30.

On day 1, the percentage of material remembered dropped from 100 percent to approximately 50 percent; therefore, people remembered only 50 percent of the material by the end of the day. On day 3, people remembered approximately 40 percent of the material they had learned. (By moving *up* the graph on the line labeled "Day 3" to the heavy black graph line and then moving *across* the graph to the left-hand column, you will arrive at "40": the percentage remembered.) On day 7, the percentage of material remembered dropped to approximately 30 percent. (By locating "30" in the left-hand column, moving across the graph to the point where the heavy line appears, and then moving down to the series of numbers on the base of the graph, you arrive at day 7.) The percentage of material did not drop drastically between days 7 and 30.

SAMPLE TABLE

SOUND LEVELS AND HUMAN RESPONSES

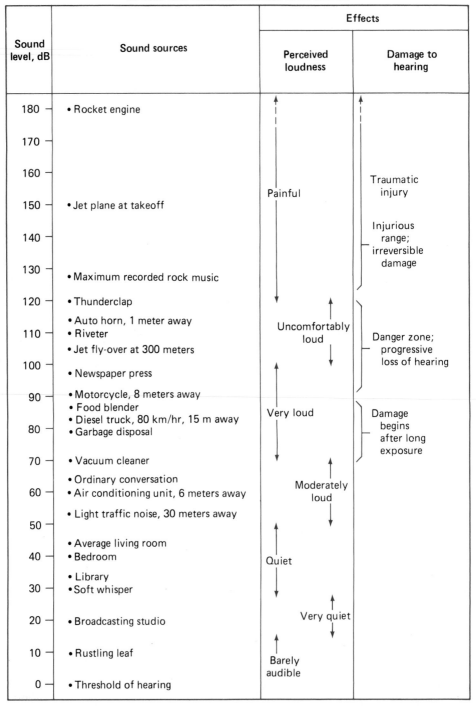

Sound level, dB	Sound sources	Effects	
		Perceived loudness	Damage to hearing
180	• Rocket engine	Painful	Traumatic injury
170			
160			
150	• Jet plane at takeoff		Injurious range; irreversible damage
140			
130	• Maximum recorded rock music		
120	• Thunderclap		Danger zone; progressive loss of hearing
110	• Auto horn, 1 meter away • Riveter • Jet fly-over at 300 meters	Uncomfortably loud	
100	• Newspaper press		
90	• Motorcycle, 8 meters away • Food blender	Very loud	Damage begins after long exposure
80	• Diesel truck, 80 km/hr, 15 m away • Garbage disposal		
70	• Vacuum cleaner		
60	• Ordinary conversation • Air conditioning unit, 6 meters away	Moderately loud	
50	• Light traffic noise, 30 meters away		
40	• Average living room • Bedroom	Quiet	
30	• Library • Soft whisper		
20	• Broadcasting studio	Very quiet	
10	• Rustling leaf		
0	• Threshold of hearing	Barely audible	

Follow the four reading steps listed on pages 506–507, and then try to answer the following questions about the sample table. Put your answers in the spaces provided.

1. What is the title of the table?

    _____

2. What is the decibel (dB) level of a vacuum cleaner? _____
3. List two sounds that are described as "Uncomfortably loud":

    _____

    _____

4. List one item that can lead to hearing damage after long exposure:

    _____

Since the title of the table is "Sound Levels and Human Responses," the table will answer the question "What are the human responses to various levels of sound?" By reading the information along the top and side of the table, we can locate the answers to the next three questions. We can locate "vacuum cleaner" by looking down the column labeled "Sound sources." In the column to the left, we find the decibel (dB) level of a vacuum cleaner: 70 dB. Looking below the column head "Perceived loudness," we find "Uncomfortably loud." The arrow shows that several items on the column to the left fit this description: thunderclap, auto horn that is one meter away, riveter, and jet fly-over at three hundred meters. Looking down the column labeled "Damage to Hearing," we find the heading "Damage begins after long exposure." Listed to the left of it are the items "food blender," "diesel truck," "garbage disposal," and "vacuum cleaner."

PRACTICE IN READING GRAPHS AND TABLES

Activity 1

1. Follow the four reading steps listed on pages 506–507, and then try to answer the questions about the following graph.

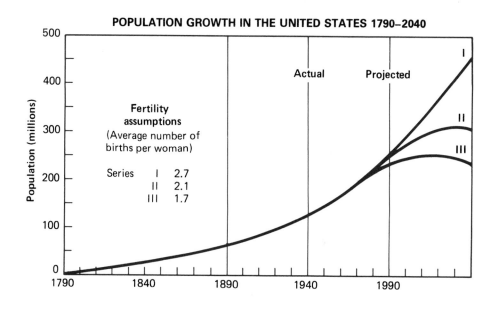

POPULATION GROWTH IN THE UNITED STATES 1790–2040

a. What is the purpose of this graph? _____

_____

b. What (approximately) was the population of the United States in 1940?

_____

c. What (approximately) was the population of the United States in 1990?

_____

d. If we assume that each woman gives birth to 2.7 children between now and 2040, what will the U.S. population be (approximately) in 2040?

_____

e. What will the U.S. population be in 2040 if the projected Series III actually occurs? _____

2. Follow the four reading steps listed on pages 506–507, and then try to answer the questions about the following table.

WHAT IT COSTS TO RUN YOUR APPLIANCES

Appliance	Avg. Hrs. Per Yr.	Avg. Kwh Per Yr.	Avg. Cost Per Yr.
Blender	2.4	0.7	$ .05
Coffee maker/percolator	750	138	9.11
Coffee maker/drip	695	146	9.64
Electric frypan	135	100.4	6.63
Food processor	2.5	0.9	.06
Hand-held hair dryer	33.3	33.3	2.20
Heating pad	104	3.4	.22
Iron	104	59.5	3.93
Hand-held mixer	12.5	1.3	.09
Electric shaver	30	0.5	.03
Toaster oven:			
toasting	25	37.5	2.47
oven	140	54.6	3.60
Slow cooker	693	138.6	9.15
Refrig./freezer (17.5 cu. ft., frost-free)	6,100	1,126	74.31
TV (solid state, color)	1,500	300	19.80
Vacuum cleaner	73	46	3.03
Portable heater	133	176	11.61
Washing machine (without cost of hot water)	198	103	6.80
Sewing machine	147	11	.73
Phonograph with radio	1,000	109	7.19
Radio	1,211	86	5.68
Electric range/oven	58	700	46.20
Range/oven, self-cleaning	61	730	48.18
Clothes dryer	204	993	65.53
Microwave oven	88	132	8.71

a. What is the title of the table? _____

b. What is the average number of hours per year that people use a washing machine? _____

c. Of all the appliances listed, which is the most expensive to run for a year? _____

d. How much energy per year (the average kwh, or kilowatt hours) does a color TV use? _____

e. What is the average cost per year of running a portable heater?

_____

Activity 2

1. Follow the four reading steps listed on pages 506–507, and then try to answer the questions about the following graph.

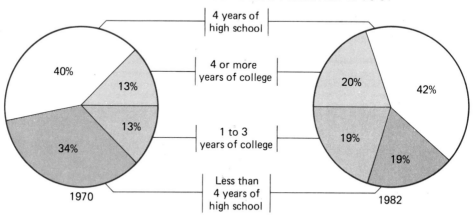

PERCENT DISTRIBUTION OF LABOR FORCE AGE 18 TO 64

a. What is the purpose of the graph? _____

_____

b. In 1970, what percentage of the labor force had attended one to three years of college? _____ In 1982, what was the percentage? _____

c. In 1970, what percentage of the labor force had attended four or more years of college? _____ In 1982, what was the percentage? _____

d. In 1970, the proportion of workers with a college background was 26 percent; in 1982, what was the percentage? _____

e. Which educational group changed the most (*either* by increasing or decreasing) between 1970 and 1982? _____

2. Follow the four reading steps listed on pages 506–507, and then try to answer the questions about the following table.

CHANGING CHARACTER OF AMERICAN HOUSEHOLDS: 1970–1980

	1970		1980		Percentage change in proportion
	Number	Percentage	Number	Percentage	
All households	63,401,000	100.0%	79,108,000	100.0%	
Family households	*51,456,000*	*81.2%*	*58,426,000*	*73.9%*	− 9.0%
Married couples	44,728,000	70.6%	48,180,000	60.9%	− 13.7%
Women heads only	5,500,000	8.7%	8,540,000	10.8%	+ 24.1%
Men heads only	1,228,000	1.9%	1,706,000	2.2%	+ 15.3%
Nonfamily households	*11,945,000*	*18.8%*	*20,682,000*	*26.1%*	+ 38.8%
Single person	10,851,000	17.1%	17,816,000	22.5%	+ 31.6%
Two people	877,000	1.4%	2,316,000	2.9%	+107.1%
Three or more	217,000	0.3%	550,000	0.7%	+133.3%

a. What is the purpose of the table? _____

_____

b. In 1970, what percentage of households were headed by women?

_____

c. Did the number of households headed by women increase or decrease between 1970 and 1980, and by how much? _____

d. How many nonfamily households of three or more people were there in 1980? _____

e. What kind of household experienced the largest decrease in numbers between 1970 and 1980? _____

Activity 3

The following questions are based on tables and graphs in "The Family," the sample textbook chapter on pages 141–185. The table or graph you need to look at in order to answer each question is indicated in parentheses after each question, along with the page number.

1. What percentage of adult American children talk to their parents once a week or more? _____ (Table 12-1, page 151)

2. What percentage of adult American children give their parents financial help? _____ (Table 12-1, page 151)

3. What percentage of Americans were married couples with children in 1970? _____ In 1988? _____ (Figure 12-1, page 152)

4. What percentage of women were living alone in 1988? _____ What percentage of men? _____ (Figure 12-1, page 152)

5. What percentage of Americans over 25 have never married? _____ (Figure 12-2, page 153)

6. Which are a larger percentage of the American singles population over 25, men or women? _____ (Figure 12-2, page 153)

7. What ages were the men and women covered in Table 12-2? _____ (page 166)

8. How many hours per week did the average male subject of Table 12-2 spend on cooking meals in 1985? _____ How many hours did women spend? _____ (page 166)

9. Judging by Figure 12-3, who are more likely to miss a work day because of family obligations, working men or women? _____ (page 168)

10. What percentage of working fathers refused a job change because it would mean less family time? _____ (Figure 12-3, page 168)

STUDYING MATHEMATICS AND SCIENCE

For many people, mathematics and science courses are terrifying. There are several very understandable reasons for this feeling. Many of us, first of all, come to class weak in the basics we need to know to handle such courses. A college mathematics or biology teacher, for example, may expect students to know how to handle fractions, decimals, proportions, and simple algebra. Some of the students, in contrast, have forgotten (or never learned) these skills. Without this kind of foundation, the work in the class starts out on a difficult level indeed.

Another reason students dread these courses is that there is no way to pass them without doing a great deal of hard work. Mathematics and science courses *demand* excellent attendance, complete notes, extensive homework, and intensive study sessions. Students looking for courses they can just "slide by" in are naturally wary of mathematics and science. But other students—ones who need chemistry or calculus, for example, to become medical technicians, nurses, or computer programmers—are willing to work hard; the problem is that they don't know how to deal with such courses. Their note-taking and study skills just don't seem adequate for mathematics and science.

Doing well in mathematics and science courses *is* possible. But you must be aware of the adjustments you should make when you switch to mathematics and science from your less technical subjects. The pointers that follow will help you gain control over these subjects.

- *In mathematics and science, knowledge is cumulative.* The learning that you do in mathematics and science courses is cumulative—each fact or formula you learn must rest on a basic structure of all you have learned before. You have to begin with the essentials and build your knowledge in a methodical, complete way. For this reason, *absences from class or weaknesses that are never corrected can be academically fatal.* You will not understand a simple algebra equation, for example, if you are not sure what a ''variable'' is. It is essential to stay current in such courses and to attack your weak points early. If you don't understand something, ask your teacher for help or visit the tutoring center. Every day you wait makes it more likely that you will do poorly in the course.

- *In mathematics and science, great emphasis is placed on specialized vocabulary, rules, and formulas.* Mathematics and science deal in precision. Everything has a specific name, and every problem can be solved with specific rules and formulas. In a way, this quality makes such courses easier because there is little fuzziness involved and few individual interpretations required. If you know the vocabulary and have the rules down pat, you should do well.

    An important study technique for mathematics and science is the use of flashcards. These are three- by five-inch index cards that help you memorize and test yourself on terms and formulas. On one side of the card, write the term, rule, or formula you need to know (for instance, ''photosynthesis,'' ''Bohr's energy law,'' or ''formula for weight density''). On the other side, write the information that you must memorize. Flashcards enable you to study the material conveniently and to discover quickly what you know and what exactly you are unsure of.

- *In mathematics and science, special emphasis is placed on homework.* In many mathematics and science classes, you will be given numerical problems to solve outside class. Often, these problems will not be checked by the instructor; their purpose is to give you practice in the kinds of material you will find on tests. Many students do a hurried job on—or skip completely— any work that is not graded. If you are not conscientious about this homework, however, you will be panicky before tests and unprepared for what is on them. If you want to pass your mathematics and science classes, you *must* take the responsibility for much of the necessary learning yourself by doing the problems and asking questions in class about problems that puzzle you.

- *Taking clear notes in class is crucial.* In your class notes for mathematics and science, you will often be copying problems, diagrams, formulas, and definitions from the blackboard. In addition, you will be trying to follow your instructor's train of thought as he or she explains how a problem is solved or how a process works. Such classes obviously demand intense concentration. As you copy material from the board, be sure to include in your notes any information the instructor gives that can help you see the *connections between steps or the relationship of one fact to another.* For example, if a teacher is explaining and diagraming human blood circulation patterns, you should copy the diagram; you should also be sure you have definitions (''alveoli,'' ''aorta'') and any important connecting information (''blood moves from artery to capillaries'').

  As soon as possible after a mathematics or science class, you should clarify and expand your notes while the material is still fresh in your mind.

- *Mathematics and science require patient, slow reading.* The information in mathematics and science tests is often densely packed; texts are filled with special terms that are often unfamiliar; blocks of text are interspersed with numerical formulas, problems to solve, charts, diagrams, and drawings. Such textbooks cannot be read quickly; for this reason, you have to keep up with the assigned reading. It is impossible to read and understand fifty pages— even ten pages—the night before a test.

  The good news about mathematics and science textbooks is that they are usually organized very clearly. They also have glossaries of terms and concise reviews at the ends of chapters. When you are reading mathematics and science books, proceed slowly. Do not skip over any unfamiliar terms; check the index or the glossary in the back of the book for the definition. With mathematics textbooks, spend time going over each sample problem. After you have gone over the sample, you might want to write out the problem on a piece of paper and then see if you remember how to solve it. With science textbooks, be sure to study the visual material that accompanies the written explanations. Study each chart or diagram until you understand it. Being able to visualize such material can be crucial when you are asked to reproduce it or write an essay on it during an exam.

You can succeed in mathematics and science classes if you are organized, persistent, and willing to work. When passing these courses is necessary to achieve your goals, the effort must be made.

READING LITERATURE AND MAKING INFERENCES

The comprehension skills you've learned in this book apply to everything you read. But to get the most out of literature, you also need to be aware of several important elements that shape fiction. And you need to know how to make inferences. Following, then, are a few guidelines to help you understand fiction more fully.

KEY ELEMENTS IN LITERATURE

Important elements in a work of literature are theme, plot, setting, characters, conflict, climax, narrator, and figures of speech:

- Look for the *theme,* or the overall idea, that the author is advancing. This is the very general idea that is behind the author's entire effort and unifies the work. For example, the theme in much of Katherine Anne Porter's writing is that separateness and misunderstanding are fundamental facts of the human condition.

- Make sure you understand the *plot*—the series of events that take place within the work. For instance, the plot of Philip Roth's short story "Goodbye, Columbus" is that boy meets girl, they fall in love, and then—because of different values—they fall out of love.

- Observe the *setting,* that is, the time and place of the plot. The setting of *The Adventures of Huckleberry Finn,* by Mark Twain, for instance, is nineteenth-century America.

- Examine the *characters*—the people in the story. Each character will have his or her own unique qualities, behaviors, needs, and values.

- Be alert for the main *conflict* of a story. The conflict is the main struggle of the plot. It may be within a character, between two or more characters, or between one or more characters and some force in the environment. For example the conflict in *Moby-Dick* is between the hunter Captain Ahab and the animal he hunts—a white whale (the Moby-Dick of the title).

- Watch for the *climax,* the final main turning point of a story. The main conflict of a story is usually solved or explained in a final way at this point in the plot. For example, the climax of Shirley Jackson's story ''The Lottery'' comes when a woman's neighbors surround her and stone her to death.

- Be aware of the *speaker,* or *narrator,* who tells the story and the *tone* of that speaker. Both strongly influence the character of a work. The speaker is not the author but the fictional voice the author uses to narrate the story. In Mark Twain's *Huckleberry Finn,* for instance, the speaker is the title character, not the author. The tone is the style or manner of a piece. It reflects the speaker's attitude and is strongly related to the author's attitude and purpose as well.

- Note *figures of speech,* expressions in which words are used to mean something other than they usually do. These expressions are often comparisons which make a special point. Examples of figures of speech are ''I wandered lonely as a cloud'' (William Wordsworth), ''my love is like a red, red rose'' (Robert Burns), and ''the slings and arrows of outrageous fortune'' (William Shakespeare).

MAKING INFERENCES IN LITERATURE

To get the most out of reading literature, it is very important to make *inferences.* In other words, you must ''read between the lines'' and come to conclusions on the basis of the given information. While writers of factual material often directly *state* what they mean, writers of fiction often *show* what they mean. It is then up to the reader to infer the point of what the writer has said. For instance, a nonfiction author might write, ''Harriet was angry at George.'' But the novelist might write, ''Harriet's eyes narrowed when George spoke to her. She cut him off in mid-sentence with the words, 'I don't have time to argue with you.' '' The author has *shown* us the anger with specific details rather than simply stating its existence abstractly. The reader must observe the details about Harriet and George and infer that she is angry.

Nowhere is inference more important than in reading poetry. Poetry, by its nature, implies much of its meaning. Implications are often made through figures of speech. For practice, read the poem on the next page; note that definitions of the more difficult words are provided at the beginning. Then do the activity that follows.

WHEN I WAS ONE-AND-TWENTY
A. E. HOUSMAN (1859–1936)

Words to Watch

crowns, pounds, guineas: forms of English money
fancy: desire
in vain: with little consequence
rue: sorrow, or regret

When I was one-and-twenty
I heard a wise man say,
"Give crowns and pounds and guineas
But not your heart away;
Give pearls away and rubies
But keep your fancy free."
But I was one-and-twenty,
No use to talk to me.

When I was one-and-twenty
I heard him say again,
"The heart out of the bosom
Was never given in vain;
'Tis paid with sighs a-plenty
And sold for endless rue."
And I am two-and-twenty,
And oh, 'tis true, 'tis true.

A. E. Housman (1859–1936)

Activity 1

Answer each question by circling the inference most solidly based on "When I Was One-and-Twenty." Then read the explanations.

1. To "give . . . your heart away" is a figure of speech meaning
   a. to fall in love.
   b. to be dishonest.
   c. to become ill.
2. To "keep your fancy free" is a figure of speech meaning
   a. don't charge others for your company.
   b. don't be rich.
   c. don't desire only one person.

3. The wise man's advice was:
   a. It's best to be poor.
   b. It's less costly to give riches away than to fall in love.
   c. An expensive romance is never harmful.
4. When the speaker says, "But I was one-and-twenty/No use to talk to me," the meaning is that he or she
   a. welcomed the wise man's advice.
   b. misunderstood the wise man's advice.
   c. ignored the wise man's advice.
5. The speaker accepted the wise man's advice when
   a. the speaker was twenty-one.
   b. the speaker first fell in love.
   c. the speaker, at the age of twenty-two, had a disappointing romance.

Following is an explanation of each item:

1. "To give . . . your heart away" is a fairly common figure of speech, and so you probably knew right away that it means to fall in love. The answer to this item is *a*.
2. Since *fancy* means "desire," "keep your fancy free" must mean to keep your desire free—of attachments. Thus the answer to this question is *c*—"don't desire only one person."
3. "Crowns and pounds and guineas," "pearls," and "rubies" all represent riches. Thus the wise man's advice was *b*—"It's less costly to give riches away than to fall in love."
4. Since it was "no use" for the wise man to talk to the speaker when he or she was twenty-one, we can infer that at that age, the speaker ignored the wise man's advice. Thus the answer to this question is *c*.
5. At first, the speaker didn't accept the wise man's advice, so we must infer that something happened between the ages of twenty-one and twenty-two to make him or her think differently. From the emotional end of the poem— "And oh, 'tis true, 'tis true"—we can infer that the speaker had an unhappy romance. The answer to this item is thus *c*.

Activity 2

On the following pages is the beginning of Philip Roth's story "Goodbye, Columbus." Your inference skills will be helpful in understanding the speaker, the characters, figures of speech, and the bit of plot and setting included here. After reading this excerpt, go on to the questions that follow it, which test your ability to make inferences.

FROM "GOODBYE, COLUMBUS"
PHILIP ROTH

The first time I saw Brenda she asked me to hold her glasses. Then she stepped out to the edge of the diving board and looked foggily into the pool; it could have been drained, myopic Brenda would never have known it. She dove beautifully, and a moment later she was swimming back to the side of the pool, her head of short-clipped auburn hair held up, straight ahead of her, as though it were a rose on a long stem. She glided to the edge and then was beside me. "Thank you," she said, her eyes watery though not from the water. She extended a hand for her glasses but did not put them on until she turned and headed away. I watched her move off. Her hands suddenly appeared behind her. She caught the bottom of her suit between thumb and index finger and flicked what flesh had been showing back where it belonged. My blood jumped.

That night, before dinner, I called her.

"Who are you calling?" my Aunt Gladys asked.

"Some girl I met today."

"Doris introduced you?"

"Doris wouldn't introduce me to the guy who drains the pool, Aunt Gladys."

"Don't criticize all the time. A cousin's a cousin. How did you meet her?"

"I didn't really meet her. I saw her."

"Who is she?"

"Her last name is Patimkin."

"Patimkin I don't know," Aunt Gladys said, as if she knew anybody who belonged to the Green Lane Country Club. "You're going to call her you don't know her?"

"Yes," I explained. "I'll introduce myself."

"Casanova," she said, and went back to preparing my uncle's dinner. None of us ate together: my Aunt Gladys ate at five o'clock, my cousin Susan at five-thirty, me at six, and my uncle at six-thirty. There is nothing to explain this beyond the fact that my aunt is crazy.

"Where's the suburban phone book?" I asked after pulling out all the books tucked under the telephone table.

"What?"

"The suburban phone book. I want to call Short Hills."

"That skinny book? What, I gotta clutter my house with that, I never use it?"

"Where is it?"

"Under the dresser where the leg came off."

"For God's sake," I said.

"Call information better. You'll go yanking around there, you'll mess up my drawers. Don't bother me, you see your uncle'll be home soon. I haven't even fed *you* yet."

"Aunt Gladys, suppose tonight we all eat together. It's hot, it'll be easier for you."

"Sure, I should serve four different meals at once. You eat pot roast, Susan with the cottage cheese, Max has steak. Friday night is his steak night, I wouldn't deny him. And I'm having a little cold chicken. I should jump up and down twenty different times? What am I, a workhorse?"

"Why don't we all have steak, or cold chicken—"

"Twenty years I'm running a house. Go call your girl friend."

Now answer each question by circling the inference most solidly based on the excerpt from "Goodbye, Columbus."

1. The narrator of the story is
   a. Aunt Gladys.
   b. Aunt Gladys's nephew.
   c. Philip Roth.

2. The setting of the story is
   a. colonial America.
   b. nineteenth-century America.
   c. twentieth-century America.

3. The figure of speech comparing Brenda's hair to "a rose on a long stem" reflects
   a. the narrator's concern with flowers.
   b. the narrator's admiration of Brenda.
   c. Brenda's occupation.

4. We know that Brenda is
   a. a good swimmer.
   b. a lifeguard.
   c. both of the above.

5. *True or false?* _____ Aunt Gladys's nephew probably wants to call Brenda to ask her out on a date.

6. Aunt Gladys's ideas
   a. about dating are old-fashioned.
   b. make perfect sense to her nephew.
   c. both of the above.

7. Brenda lives
   a. in the city.
   b. in the suburbs.
   c. at the country club.

8. We can assume that Doris
   a. is related to the narrator.
   b. is disliked by the narrator.
   c. both of the above.

9. We can assume that Aunt Gladys
   a. belongs to the Green Lane Country Club.
   b. has never met Brenda Patimkin.
   c. both of the above.

10. We can assume that the members of Aunt Gladys's family
    a. dislike each other.
    b. have different tastes in foods.
    c. have different working hours and so cannot eat together.

READING
FOR PLEASURE:
A LIST OF
INTERESTING BOOKS

On the following pages are short descriptions of some books that might interest you. Some are popular books of the last few years; some are among the most widely read "classics"—books that have survived for generations because they deal with basic human experiences that all people can understand and share.

AUTOBIOGRAPHIES AND OTHER NONFICTION

Maya Angelou, *I Know Why the Caged Bird Sings*
The author writes with love, humor, and honesty about growing up black and female.

Alicia Appleman-Jurman, *Alicia: My Story*
Alicia was a Jewish girl living with her family in Poland when the Germans invaded in 1941. Her utterly compelling and heartbreaking story shows some of the best and worst of which human beings are capable.

Lauren Bacall, *Lauren Bacall by Myself*
A Hollywood star tells how she broke into movies, married tough guy Humphrey Bogart, and picked up the pieces of her life when he died of cancer.

Russell Baker, *Growing Up*
Russell Baker's mother, a giant presence in his life, insisted that he make something of himself. In his autobiography, the prize-winning journalist shows that he did, with an engrossing account of his own family and growing up.

Dee Brown, *Bury My Heart at Wounded Knee*
The harsh treatment that Native Americans have suffered at the hands of a white culture is vividly detailed in this history.

Lynn Caine, *Widow*
Few people are prepared for the loss of a loved one. Caine tells how devastating it can be to be left alone.

Truman Capote, *In Cold Blood*
A frightening story about the murder of a family that is also an investigation into what made their killers tick.

Richard P. Feynman, *Surely You're Joking, Mr. Feynman!*
The apt subtitle of this book by a Nobel prize–winning scientist is ''Adventures of a Curious Character.'' Feynman has a boundless curiosity, enthusiasm, and love of life. In no way a ''stuffy scientist,'' he, like his book, is utterly delightful.

Anne Frank, *The Diary of a Young Girl*
To escape the Nazi death camps, Anne Frank and her family hid for years in an attic. Her journal tells a story of love, fear, and courage.

Viktor Frankl, *Man's Search for Meaning*
How do people go on when they have been stripped of everything, including human dignity? The author describes his time in a concentration camp and what he learned there about survival.

Bob Greene, *Be True to Your School*
Bob Greene is a celebrated, popular, nationally-syndicated newspaper columnist. This book, based on a diary he kept when he was a teenager, will take you back to some of the happiness, hurt, and struggle to grow up that you experienced in high school.

Dick Gregory, *Nigger*
Dick Gregory, social activist, writes about the experience of being black in a racist society.

John Howard Griffin, *Black Like Me*
A white man chemically darkens his skin and travels through the South of the 1960s to experience racial prejudice and injustice firsthand.

James Herriot, *All Creatures Great and Small*
Warm and funny stories about the experiences of an English veterinarian.

Helen Keller, *The Story of My Life*
How Miss Keller, a blind and deaf girl who lived in isolation and frustration, discovered a path to learning and knowledge.

M. E. Kerr, *Me Me Me Me Me*
A charming, easy-to-read account of a young woman's growing up. The
    author provides a series of warm and witty stories that will be enjoyed
    by people of all ages.

Herbert Kohl, *Thirty-Six Children*
An idealistic and caring young teacher describes some of the challenges he
    faced in trying to help his students survive and learn in the hard world
    of an inner-city school.

Jerry Kramer, *Distant Replay*
Whether you're a sports fan or not, you will be captivated by this portrait of
    stars of the Green Bay Packers football team, coached by Vince Lombardi,
    that won the first two Super Bowls. You learn just what happens to each
    of them in the twenty years after their great football victories.

Malcolm X and Alex Haley, *The Autobiography of Malcolm X*
Malcolm X, the controversial black leader who was assassinated by one of
    his followers, writes about the experiences that drove him to a leadership
    role in the Black Muslims.

Mark Mathabane, *Kaffir Boy*
A powerful description of what it's like to be black and live in a South
    African ghetto and experience apartheid first-hand.

Mark Owens and Delia Owens, *Cry of the Kalahari*
A husband and wife give up the comforts of academic life, sell everything
    they own, and go to Africa to study wildlife there and to try to save
    some animals from destruction. They describe their adventures with
    hyenas, lions, and a more dangerous species of predator—human beings.

Gilda Radner, *It's Always Something*
Before her death, the beloved comedienne from *Saturday Night Live* wrote
    about the trials and fortunes of her life—and described how everything
    changed when she learned she had ovarian cancer.

Andy Rooney, *Not That You Asked . . .*
Well-known for his commentaries on *60 Minutes,* Andy Rooney has also
    expressed his views in this book and several other books of short essays.
    Rooney has a lot of everyday things to complain about and poke fun at,
    and he does so in an admirable writing style that is clear, simple, and to
    the point.

Piri Thomas, *Down These Mean Streets*
Life in a Puerto Rican ghetto is shown vividly and with understanding by
    one who experienced it.

James Thurber, *My Life and Hard Times*
James Thurber may be the funniest writer of all time; he writes about the absurd, the fantastic, and the eccentric with enough skill to make readers laugh out loud.

Joseph A. Wapner, *A View from the Bench*
The star of a popular TV show, *The People's Court,* Judge Wapner offers a series of real-life legal tales. At the same time, he shares insights into human nature based on his many years as a municipal and superior court judge.

FICTION

Richard Adams, *Watership Down*
A wonderfully entertaining adventure story about rabbits who act a great deal like people. The plot may sound unlikely, but it will keep you on the edge of your seat.

Willa Cather, *My Antonia*
No other American writer has written so beautifully and honestly about the experiences of the immigrants who settled the vast prairies of the Midwest.

James Dickey, *Deliverance*
A group of men go rafting down a wild Georgia river and encounter beauty, violence, and self-knowledge.

Ken Follett, *Eye of the Needle*
A thriller about a Nazi spy—''The Needle''—and the woman who is the only person who can stop him.

William Golding, *Lord of the Flies*
Can a group of children, none older than twelve, survive by themselves on a tropical island in the midst of World War III? In this modern classic, Golding shows us that the real danger is not the war outside but ''the beast'' within all of us.

Joseph Heller, *Catch-22*
The craziness of our culture—specifically, of war and the military—is precisely captured in this landmark novel.

Frank Herbert, *Dune*
In this science-fiction classic, Paul Atreides fights to regain his lost kingdom on a strange desert planet filled with warring factions, giant sandworms, and a magical spice.

Daniel Keyes, *Flowers for Algernon*
A scientific experiment turns a retarded man into a genius. But the results
are a mixture of joy and heartbreak.

Stephen King, *The Shining*
A haunted hotel, a little boy with ESP, and a deranged father—they're all
together in a horror tale of isolation and insanity.

John Knowles, *A Separate Peace*
Two schoolboys enjoy a close friendship until one grows jealous of the
other's many talents—and tragedy results.

Dean Koontz, *Watchers*
An incredibly suspenseful story about two dogs that undergo lab experiments.
One dog becomes a monster programmed to kill, and seeks to track down
the couple that knows its secret.

Harper Lee, *To Kill a Mockingbird*
A controversial trial involving a black man accused of raping a white woman
is the centerpiece of this story about childhood, bigotry, and justice.

Bernard Malamud, *The Natural*
An aging player makes a comeback that stuns the baseball world.

Margaret Mitchell, *Gone with the Wind*
The unforgettable characters and places in this book—Scarlett O'Hara, Rhett
Butler, Tara—have become part of our culture.

George Orwell, *1984*
The well-known expression "Big Brother Is Watching You" comes from
this frightening novel of a time when individuals have no control over
their lives.

Robert Peck, *A Day No Pigs Would Die*
A boy raises a pig that is intelligent and affectionate. Will the boy follow
orders and send the animal off to be slaughtered?

Philip Roth, *Goodbye, Columbus*
The title story in this collection is about a poor boy, a rich girl, and their ill-
fated love affair.

J. D. Salinger, *The Catcher in the Rye*
The frustrations and turmoil of being an adolescent have never been captured
so well as in this book. The main character, Holden Caulfield, is honest,
funny, affectionate, obnoxious, and tormented—all at the same time.

J. R. R. Tolkien, *The Lord of the Rings*
Enter an amazing world of little creatures known as *Hobbits*; you, like thousands of other readers, may never want to leave.

Edith Wharton, *Ethan Frome*
An engrossing story about a love triangle involving a middle-aged farmer, his shrewish wife, and the pretty young cousin who comes to live with them.

CLASSICS

George Eliot, *Middlemarch*
A long book that is likely to be one of the peak reading experiences of your life. Eliot writes with extraordinary insight and compassion about the problems that all human beings face in seeing themselves clearly and in coping with the difficulties of their lives.

Nathaniel Hawthorne, *The Scarlet Letter*
A compelling story, set in the days of the Puritans, about a young woman, her illegitimate baby, and the scarlet label she wears as her punishment.

Herman Melville, *Moby-Dick*
Two of the most famous characters in fiction—mad Captain Ahab and Moby-Dick, the white whale—battle it out as hunter and hunted.

Mark Twain, *The Adventures of Huckleberry Finn*
A rich book filled with wit, understanding, moral insight, and very human characters—definitely *not* for children only. Many people argue that this, or *Moby-Dick,* is the greatest American novel.

UNDERSTANDING CONNECTIONS BETWEEN READING AND WRITING

Have you wondered why writing assignments are included in a book called *Reading and Study Skills?* Perhaps you felt that you were capable of becoming a good reader and skilled student without having the additional burden of producing written assignments placed on you. Reading and writing, however, are so closely interconnected that it is virtually impossible to be competent at one without being competent at the other. The two abilities work together in several ways:

- *Reading and writing are interrelated language skills.* Through reading, you learn, almost subconsciously, how good writers put sentences together and organize ideas. In addition, you acquire new vocabulary words. Through writing, you begin to use what you have learned by reading. You also gain intensive practice in being logical, a skill that is essential to understanding more difficult reading material.

- *Both reading and writing are processes.* You become a better reader, or a more skillful writer, by treating each task as a process. You preview, read, and reread. Or, you prewrite, write, and rewrite. With each step, your skills become sharper and the end product—your understanding of what you have read or the paper you have written—becomes finer.

- *Both reading and writing are vital for communication.* Competence in reading and writing are essential survival skills if you wish to make your voice heard and your ideas known. Shutting yourself off from either one can damage your life in two ways. First, your verbal abilities suffer because you have few language models or chances to extend your word skills. Second, your message—whatever it may be, either in your personal life or on the job—is lost because you cannot get it across to other people.

531

Reading and writing, then, are so closely linked that practicing one helps the other—and neglecting one damages the other. This is why writing assignments have a role in this book, and why writing should be an important priority in your life as a student.

■ Writing Assignments

Here is a list of the assignments already presented.

- Write a paper about one of the questions that follow "Your Attitude: The Heart of the Matter" (page 19).
- Write a paper about one of the questions that follow "Learning Survival Strategies" (page 35).
- Write a paper about some aspect of concentration skills (page 85).
- Write a report on a book (page 297).
- Write a summary (pages 385–388).

Following are a number of other assignments, based on chapters or reading selections in the book. Before attempting any of these assignments, be sure to read the section that describes the four steps in good writing on pages 64–66. These steps are:

1 Make a point of some kind.
2 Support the point.
3 Organize the support.
4 Write clear sentences.

In particular, be sure you follow the advice about being specific. Vivid, concrete details will help make your paper lively and convincing.

Note: Each paper that you write should be at least one page in length.

1. Write a paper in which you respond in detail to the study situation on page 39. Apply what you have learned in the chapter to explain all the steps that Howard should take to become an effective note-taker.
2. Write a paper in which you respond in detail to the time control situation on page 67. Apply what you have learned in the chapter to explain all the steps that Cheryl should take to control her time effectively.

3. Write a paper in which you respond in detail to the textbook study situation on page 86. Apply what you have learned in the chapter to explain all the steps that Gary should take to study effectively through textbook previewing, marking, and note-taking.

4. Write a paper in which you respond in detail to the textbook study situation on page 191. Apply what you have learned in the chapter to explain all the steps that Steve should take to improve his memory.

5. Write a paper in which you respond in detail to the study situation on page 205. Apply what you have learned in the chapter to explain all the steps that Rita should take to improve her performance on objective exams.

6. Write a paper in which you respond in detail to the class assignment situation on page 230. Apply what you have learned in the chapter to explain all the steps that Pete should take to do a good job on his library assignments.

7. Read the selection about propaganda on pages 63–64. Then write a paper about an ad you have seen recently that uses several of the propaganda techniques discussed in the selection. Show specifically—by mentioning the name of the product and describing the language, slogans, characters, and settings in the ad—how the ad uses particular propaganda methods.

8. Review the section on effective writing on pages 64–66. An example given in the section to illustrate a "point" is "Proms should be banned." Write your own paper that presents a variation on this idea. Your point should be, "_____ should be banned for several reasons." The topic you choose could be one of the following or some other: smoking, grades, ads for alcoholic beverages on television, commercials aimed at children, hitchhiking, loud radios.

9. Read the section on concentration skills on pages 79–83. Then write a paper based on the idea that many students—from the youngest to the oldest—find it difficult to pay attention in school. Why might this be true? What aspects of school make it hard to pay attention? (Is it the setting? The teachers? The subject matter? The pressures? The boredom?) Write a paper on the steps a teacher could take to make it easier for students to pay attention. Make your steps practical ones that a concerned teacher at a specific level (primary school, high school, college) could take.

10. Read the selection about television on pages 430–432. Then write a paper about your own feelings toward television. Are you concerned about how much TV you and your family watch or about how TV is deadening communication within the family? Or do you have positive feelings about the role TV plays in your life? Write a paper explaining why you are *or* are not worried about the place of TV in your household. Back up your reasons with specific details about the hours spent watching TV, the kinds of shows on TV, or any other information that supports your reasons.

11. Read the selection on drug users on page 323. Then write a paper on the reasons you or the people you know use drugs. Keep in mind that drugs include caffeine, alcohol, and nicotine, as well as the "harder" substances. Therefore, most of us could probably be called drug users. Are the reasons why you or the people you know use drugs similar to or different from the ones on the list in the selection? In your paper, be sure to describe specifically the reasons certain drugs are used.

12. Cliff Evans (pages 434–436) was dehumanized by the school system. No one thought of him as a person with real problems who needed help. Do you know anyone who is a victim of dehumanization? Are you a victim? Write a paper about a person or a group of persons who are ignored by society. Describe how this person or group is treated by various organizations— schools, police, federal agencies, and so on. As you are planning your paper, you might consider the kinds of people who are often victims of dehumanization in our society: welfare recipients, minorities, women, non-English speakers, the mentally ill, the retarded, the elderly, the homeless.

WRITING A
RESEARCH PAPER

The process of writing a research paper can be divided into six steps. We'll look at each of those steps and then consider a sample paper.

STEPS IN WRITING A RESEARCH PAPER

Step 1: Select Your Topic

Select a topic that you can readily research. First of all, go to the *Subjects section* of your library book file, as described on page 233, and see whether there are at least three books on your general topic. For example, if you initially choose over-the-counter drugs as your topic, see if you can find at least three books on this topic. Also, make sure that the books are available on the library shelves.

Next, go to the *Magazine Index* or *Readers' Guide,* as described on page 237, to see if you find five or more articles on your subject.

If both books and articles are at hand, pursue your topic. Otherwise, you may have to choose another topic. You cannot write a paper on a topic for which research materials are not readily available.

Step 2: Limit Your Topic

Read about your topic, limit it, and make the purpose of your paper clear. A research paper should develop a *limited* topic. It should be narrow and deep rather than broad and shallow. Therefore, as you read through books and articles on your general topic, look for ways to limit it.

For instance, in reading through materials on the general topic of over-the-counter drugs, you might decide to limit your topic to the reasons why such drugs are so popular. Or, after reading about adoption, you might decide to limit your paper to the problems that single people have in adopting a child. The broad subject of death could be reduced to unfair pricing practices in funeral homes; divorce might be limited to its most damaging effects on the children of divorced parents.

Do not expect to limit your topic and make your purpose clear all at once. You may have to do quite a bit of reading as you work out the limited purpose of your paper. Note that many research papers have one of two general purposes. Your purpose might be to make and defend a point of some kind. For example, your purpose in a paper might be to provide evidence that gambling should be legalized. Or, depending on your course and instructor, your purpose might simply be to present information about a particular subject. For example, you might be asked to do a paper that describes the latest scientific findings about what happens when we dream.

Step 3: Take Notes on Your Topic

Take notes as you continue to read about your topic. Take notes on whatever seems relevant to or significant for your limited topic. Write your notes on sheets of loose-leaf paper. Your notes can be in the form of *direct quotations* or *summaries in your own words,* or a *combination* of the two.

Here is a copy of notes that one student took while doing a paper on over-the-counter drugs:

Advertising to doctors by the drug industry

"The industry spends roughly $2,500 per physician on advertising every year." Most of what doctors know comes from the biased salespersons of drug companies. It is common for companies to provide doctors with information that underplays the dangers of their drugs and exaggerates their effectiveness.

Goode, 99.

Keep the following points in mind when taking notes:

- Write on one side of a sheet only, so that it will be easy to refer to your notes as you are writing your paper.
- Put only one kind of information, from one source, on any one sheet. For example, the sample above has information on only one idea from one source (a book by Erich Goode).
- Identify the source and page number under your notes.
- Put quotation marks around all material which you take word for word from any source.
- Include at the top of the sheet a heading that summarizes the content of the notes. This heading will help you organize the different kinds of information that you gather on your topic.

Be sure to document information and ideas that you take from other sources. If you do not do this, you will be stealing (the formal term is *plagiarizing*—using someone else's work as your own work). It can usually be assumed that a good deal of the material in research writing will need to be documented.

Step 4: Plan Your Paper

Plan the paper, making clear your point and your support for the point. As you take notes, think constantly about the specific content and organization of your paper. Begin making decisions about the exact information your will present and the arrangement of that information. Prepare a basic outline of your paper that shows both its point and the areas of support for the point.

Point: _____

Support: (1) _____

     (2) _____

     (3) _____

See if you can divide your support into at least three different areas.

Step 5: Keep a Record of Your Sources

Keep a written record of all your sources. On a sheet of paper, record the information below about each source:

For Books	*For Magazines*
Author	Author
Title	Title of article
Place of publication	Title of magazine
Publisher	Volume number (if available)
Date of publication	Pages
Call number	Date

You will need this information later, because you are expected to place at the end of your paper a list of all the sources you consulted.

Step 6: Write Your Paper

After you have finished your reading and note-taking, you should be ready to proceed with the writing of your paper. Make a final outline and use it as a guide to write the first draft of your paper. Your paper should have five basic parts:

- A *title page,* which should give the title of the paper, your name, and the date. Center all of these on the sheet, as shown in the sample on the facing page.

- An *opening page,* which should include an introductory paragraph that (1) attracts the reader's interest, (2) states the point of the paper, and (3) gives the plan of development that the paper will follow. The sample (page 540) shows the first page of a paper, with some explanatory labels. Note that to cite a source within your paper, you should provide in parentheses both the author's name and the relevant page number. Do not give the name of a book or article. That will appear in the list of sources at the end of the paper.

- The *body* of the paper, which will develop all the areas of support for your point.

- A *concluding paragraph,* which may consist of a summary, or a final thought, or both. Note that your final thought might be in the form of a recommendation.

- A *final page,* with an alphabetical list of "Works Cited," which should include all the sources you have used. See the sample (page 541).

This is the title page of a sample research paper.

The title should be centered and in capitals.

Your name should be placed two spaces under by.

AMERICA'S DEPENDENCY ON
OVER-THE-COUNTER DRUGS

by

Linda Coleman

Near the bottom put the course title and date; you may also include the course section number and the instructor's name.

Sociology 101

November 28, 1991

*Leave about three inches of blank space
between the top of the first page and the title
of the paper. The text of the pages that
follow should begin about one inch from the top.*

AMERICA'S DEPENDENCY ON OVER-THE-COUNTER DRUGS

(Three spaces)

*Double
spacing
between
lines of the
text.*

Walk into any supermarket, pharmacy, or discount
department store in America, and you will find shelf after shelf
devoted to drugs. Taking over-the-counter (OTC) medication is a
way of life for most Americans. There's a nonprescription drug
available for every ailment, from headaches to hemorrhoids.
Fatigue, stess, anxiety, depression, insomnia, and overweight can be
banished by little colored pills, soothing ointments, and magical

*1½-inch
margin
at left*

liquids. Americans want to believe that "for whatever ails or
bothers you, there is a chemical solution on the counter" (Hughes
and Brewin 255). There are several reasons why Americans are so
dependent on over-the-counter drugs. They are heavily advertised
by the drug industry and readily available to consumers; also, they

*About one-
inch margin
at right*

appeal to our desire for quick, simple solutions to our problems.

The sale of OTC medication means big business. One reason
why such drugs are so popular, and sales are so high, is
advertising. Advertisers send us positive messages about
nonprescription drugs: they are safe, they are reliable, they are
convenient, and practically everyone uses them. Faced with a heavy
barrage of slick promotion, consumers stock their pockets, purses,
and medicine chests with all types of drugs.

*Page numbering starts with the first page of the text.
Page 1 is numbered at the bottom. Leave about
a one-inch margin at the bottom of the page.*

The heading should be in capitals and centered. Three spaces should follow before the first entry.

10

WORKS CITED

Goode, Erich. <u>Drugs in American Society</u>. New York: McGraw-Hill, 1989.

Hughes, Richard, and Robert Brewin. <u>The Tranquilizing of America: Pill Popping and the American Way of Life</u>. New York: Harcourt Brace Jovanovich, 1979.

"Is Bayer Better?" <u>Consumer Reports</u> July 1982: 347–349.

Leber, Max. <u>The Corner Drugstore</u>. New York: Warner Books, 1983.

"Rich Profits from New Lines." <u>Business Week</u> January 11, 1982: 70–74.

Sanberg, Paul R. <u>Over-the-Counter Drugs: Harmless or Hazardous</u>? New York: Chelsea House Publishers, 1986.

Stuller, Jay. "Bad Medicine? (Misuse of over-the-counter and prescription medication)." <u>The American Legion Magazine</u> April 1990: 34–38.

ACKNOWLEDGMENTS

Adapted and reprinted by permission from *The American Heritage Dictionary*, paperback edition. Copyright © 1983 by Houghton Mifflin Company. Excerpts on pages 267, 269, 275, and 475.

From *The Autobiography of Malcolm X*. Copyright © 1964 by Alex Haley and Betty Shabazz. Reprinted by permission of Random House, Inc. Selection 1 on page 419.

Michael S. Bassis, Richard J. Gelles, and Ann Levine, from *Sociology: An Introduction*, 4th ed. Copyright © 1991 by Random House, Inc. Selection on page 141.

Selection in its entirety: From M. S. Bassis and R. J. Gelles, *Sociology: An Introduction*, 4th edition, Chapter 12. © 1991. Used with permission of McGraw-Hill Publishing Company.

Figure 12-3: Data from "What Working Parents Say about Child Care," February 16, 1987, *Fortune*. © 1987 Time Inc. All rights reserved.

Figure 12-4: From Sharon J. Price and Patrick C. McHenry, *Divorce*, Copyright © 1988 by Sage Publications, Inc. Reprinted by permission of Sage Publications, Inc.

Figures 12-5 and 12-6: From *Newsweek Special Edition: The 21st Century Family*, 1988, © 1988 Newsweek, Inc. All rights reserved. Reprinted by permission.

Table 12-1: From *The Gallup Report*, no. 286, July 1989. Used by permission of The Gallup Organization.

Table 12-2: Reprinted with permission; © American Demographics, December 1988. Used by permission of Prof. John P. Robinson.

Photos: Page 141, David Grossman; 145, Kent Reno/Jerobaum; 150, Omni-Photo Communications; 154, Alan Carey, The Image Works; 156, Hazel Hankin; 162, Ellis Herwig/The Picture Cube; 182, Michael Weisbrot/Stock, Boston.

Linda L. Davidoff, from *Introduction to Psychology*. Copyright © 1976 by McGraw-Hill, Inc. Selection on page 487.

Harold S. Diehl et al., from *Health and Safety*, 4th ed. Copyright © 1975 by McGraw-Hill, Inc. Selection 3 on page 383.

Gayle Edwards and John Langan, adapted from "Preview, Read, Write, Recite" in *Ten Steps to Improving College Reading Skills*, 2d ed. Copyright © 1989 by Townsend Press. Material on the PRWR study system on pages 86–96.

Arlene Eisenberg and Howard Eisenberg, from *Alive and Well*. Copyright © 1979 by McGraw-Hill, Inc. Selection 3 on page 323; Selection 3 on page 325; Selection 1 on page 327; Selection 2 on page 370.

Diane E. Papalia and Sally Wendkos Olds, from *A Child's World,* 2d ed. Copyright © 1979 by McGraw-Hill. Selection 2 on page 359; Selection 4 on page 484; Selection 2 on page 491.

Bernard Phillips, from *Sociology.* Copyright © 1979 by McGraw-Hill, Inc. Selection on page 395; Selection 5 on page 484.

Rod Plotnik, from *Introduction to Psychology,* 2d ed. Copyright © 1989 by Random House, Inc. Reprinted by permission. Selection on page 116.

Virginia Nichols Quinn, from *Applying Psychology,* 2d ed. Copyright 1984 by McGraw-Hill Book Company. Reprinted by permission. Selection 4 on page 406.

David J. Rachman, Michael H. Mescon, Courtland L. Bovee, and John V. Thill, from *Business Today,* 6th ed. Copyright © 1990 by McGraw-Hill. Reprinted by permission. Selection on page 106.

Scott Rego, "The Fine Art of Complaining." Reprinted by permission of the author and Townsend Press.

Philip Roth, from *Goodbye, Columbus.* Copyright © 1959 by Philip Roth. Reprinted by permission of Houghton Mifflin Company. Selection on page 522.

Richard T. Schaefer, from *Sociology,* 2d ed. Copyright © 1986 by McGraw-Hill, Inc. Selection 4 on page 315; Selection 2 on page 384; Selection 4 on page 390.

Charles D. Schewe and Reuben M. Smith, from *Marketing.* Copyright © 1980 by McGraw-Hill, Inc. Reprinted by permission. Selection on page 126; Selection 3 on page 484; Selection 3 on page 491.

William L. Smallwood, from *Life Science,* 2d ed. Copyright © 1978 by McGraw-Hill, Inc. Selection on page 376; Selection 2 on page 485.

Jean Mizer Todhunter, "Cipher in the Snow." *Today's Education,* March-April 1975. Reprinted by permission. Selection 5 on page 434.

Rudolph E. Verderber, from *Communicate!* 6th ed. Copyright © 1990 by Wadsworth, Inc. Reprinted by permission of the publisher. Selection on page 116.

Bernard A. Weisberger, from *The Impact of Our Past,* 2d ed. Copyright © 1976 by McGraw-Hill, Inc. Selection 4 on page 385; Selection 2 on page 495.

Art Williams, "Dare Mighty Things," from *The Saturday Evening Post,* October 1983. Reprinted by permission. Selection 6 on page 438.

George A. Williams et al., from *Physical Science.* Copyright © 1979 by McGraw-Hill, Inc. Selection 2 on page 318; Selection 1 on page 358.

Drew H. Wolfe, from *Introduction to College Chemistry,* 2d ed. Copyright © 1988 by McGraw-Hill. Reprinted by permission. Selection on page 128.

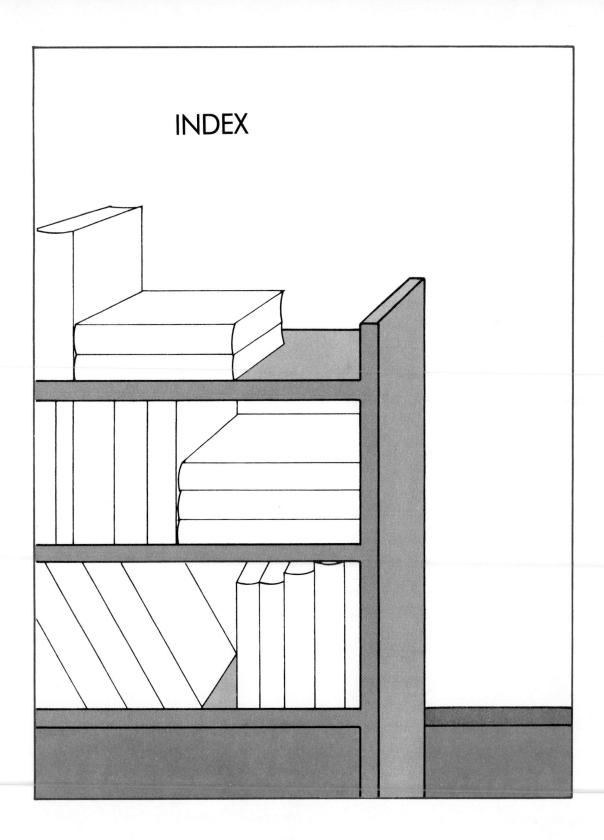

INDEX

INDEX